COLLECTED PROSE

CHARLES OLSON

Edited by Donald Allen and Benjamin Friedlander

With an Introduction by Robert Creeley

UNIVERSITY OF CALIFORNIA PRESS

Berkeley   Los Angeles   London

University of California Press
Berkeley and Los Angeles, California

University of California Press, Ltd.
London, England

© 1997 by The Regents of the University of California

Library of Congress Cataloging-in-Publication Data

Olson, Charles, 1910–1970.
    [Prose works. Selections]
    Collected prose / Charles Olson ; edited by Donald Allen and Benjamin Friedlander, with an introduction by Robert Creeley.
        p.   cm.
    Includes bibliographical references and index.
    ISBN 0–520-20319-4 (alk. paper). — ISBN 0-520-20873-0 (pbk. : alk. paper)
        I. Allen, Donald Merriam, 1912–   . II. Friedlander, Benjamin, 1959–   . III. Title.
    PS3529.L655A6   1997   97-5390
    814'.54—dc21   CIP

Printed in the United States of America
9 8 7 6 5 4 3 2 1

The paper used in this publication meets the minimum requirements of American National Standards for Information Sciences—Permanence of Paper for Printed Library Materials, ANSI Z39.48–1984.

Contents

Editors' Preface

The collection you hold in your hands contains the contents of four earlier books, *Call Me Ishmael* (1947), *Human Universe and Other Essays* (1965), *Additional Prose* (1974), and *The Post Office* (1975). Supplementing these are nine further studies: "Dostoevsky and *The Possessed*" (1940), "GrandPa, GoodBye" (1948), "Introduction to *The Sutter-Marshall Lease*" (1948), "D. H. Lawrence and the High Temptation of the Mind" (1950), "Footnote to HU (lost in the shuffle)" (1952), "Cy Twombly" (1952), "*Paterson,* Book V" (1959), "Place; & Names" (1962), and "'you can't use words . . .'" (1965). From Olson's voluminous archive of unpublished writings—enough to fill several volumes equal in length to this one—only a handful of pieces was chosen, and only pieces Olson himself prepared for publication. These are "Mr. Meyer" and "The Post Office" (from *The Post Office*), "GrandPa, GoodBye," "D. H. Lawrence and the High Temptation of the Mind," and "Cy Twombly." From *Human Universe* one piece was dropped, "Apollonius of Tyana," a long performance text more profitably read beside Olson's other works for stage. A smattering of uncollected publications from before 1945 was also excluded.

Except for adding Olson's dedication to LeRoi Jones in *Proprioception,* we have followed the texts established by Olson himself and by the various editors (especially George Butterick) who subsequently oversaw printing. (A handful of inadvertent errors was also corrected, silently.)

The notes identify quotations and offer clues to themes and procedures. Where Olson points, we shine a light; where light no longer penetrates, we let the opacity of the gesture stand. Our goal throughout has been to lead the reader more deeply into Olson's writings, into a work that Amiri Baraka calls "the proprioceptive probe"—a practice of language and act in which meaning is prized as "the continuity of Human material life, as actual history, actual matter in motion." To this end, the essays are arranged in sections that emphasize the *movement* of Olson's writings across a range of possibilities, human, material, historical.

A few of the notes are adapted from earlier annotations by George Butterick. These are identified parenthetically with GB, followed by a reference to the text and page number where the annotation originally appeared.

Our thanks are owed to many people, especially Amiri Baraka, Michael Basinski, Charles Bernstein, Carla Billitteri, Don Byrd, Cass Clarke, Marcus Coelen, Horace Coleman, Robert Creeley, Alan Gilbert, Loss Glazier, Albert Glover, Robert Glück, Oliver Heyer, Andrew Hoyem, Yunte Huang, Gerrit Lansing, Nick Lawrence, Jill Robbins, Stephen Rodefer, and Fred Wah. Thanks are also owed the Thomas J. Dodd Research Center, University of Connecticut Libraries, Storrs; the Mandeville Department of Special Collections, University of California, San Diego; the George Arents Research Library for Special Collections, Syracuse University; and the Poetry / Rare Book Collection, University Libraries, State University of New York at Buffalo. In particular, we acknowledge the assistance of Richard C. Fyffe (Storrs), Bradley D. Westbrook (San Diego), Kathleen Manwaring (Syracuse), and Robert J. Bertholf (Buffalo).

Introduction

BY ROBERT CREELEY

I have no apology to make for the friendship with Charles Olson that, veritably, changed my life. I was twenty-four as I remember, looking for material wherewith to produce with college friend Jacob Leed yet another "little magazine" of the period to be called the *Lititz Review.* We never managed to print it, but many of the associations and works thus solicited went into Cid Corman's *Origin,* the great collective finally for us all. It was Cid's friend Vincent Ferrini who put me in touch with Charles Olson. It wasn't until some other friend asked if he were the same Olson who had written the book on Melville, *Call Me Ishmael,* that I had any idea he was not—as I was—another fledgling writer, for the most part unpublished and unknown. When I found the book and read it, I was astounded—and to some degree depressed. How could I possibly find company with someone so singularly, generously brilliant, so evidently accomplished? I couldn't be simply his sidekick or straight man. Nor his disciple ever. We had to be equals, which is really what Olson here says to all who read him—and what we share as a sense of person from a place, New England. Like the *Pequod*'s crew, we are fact of a democracy which does not think itself as such but so functions. We believe in knowing, *gnosis,* we take our various worlds as a primary. We read the literal books of our lives.

Given such a life as his was, what's here collected, as Benjamin Friedlander writes on a postcard while working on Olson's papers at the library where they are kept, is only the tip of the iceberg.

> Two days rooting through CO's carbon papers makes me feel at once ghoulish (as if it were the tissue of his skin I were peeling back to see in—"God's flesh," the "eternal," as he in one spot accuses all of us—including himself—of wanting to chew) at the same time more excited than ever, as if the unread Olson were the necessary 3/4 submerged berg making possible the 1/4 ice floe, I a diver feeling along the murky depths the crevice that tore the hull of many a sea-worthy ship.

He continues, "Well stupid Romance of the reader (me) . . . " And yet it is here that any of us has to begin, at this insistent edge of *outside* and *inside,* this place which Olson's most initiating source, Herman Melville, puts in a way uncannily like Friedlander's:

> . . . Hard Berg (methought), so cold, so vast,
> With mortal damps self-overcast;
> Exhaling still thy dankish breath—
> Adrift dissolving, bound for death;
> Though lumpish thou, a lumbering one—
> A lumbering lubbard loitering slow,
> Impingers rue thee and go down,
> Sounding thy precipice below,
> Nor stir the slimey slug that sprawls
> Along thy dead indifference of walls.
>
> "The Berg," *John Marr and Other Sailors,* 1888

Such a depth is present in all that Olson writes. His study of Herman Melville's work becomes its complement in the brilliant casts of premise and particulars, its rhetorical confidence, and, uniquely, its exceptional ability to compact and identify the fact of our common humanity in, as Olson called his own era, "a late time." Again and again he comes "back to the geography of it," that human "landscape," which must be given "out . . . of this low eyeview, size." He is manifest of an *inside* that of necessity bears itself, discovers its own measure, maps a world "not discovera" unless initial in fact.

Mapping in all its senses and applications is a primary act both for Olson and for those to whom he pays attention. One recognizes quickly that it is not simply a romantic enterprise he is drawn to, but the need to know by means of determined *process,* to have been there, as Herodotus got there literally, to make a record of the fact of having witnessed one's self, or heard, or felt, or seen, something uniquely specific to the fact one hoped to make particular. I think the literary disposition is here most distorting of Olson's ways of proceeding, in that it has the habit of categories in no sense useful to him, reads story as fiction, or thinks of facts as generally distributable. Anyone so persuaded is apart, in mind, put it, from that which he or she has presumed to use as center.

So, for example, Olson fought fiercely against the widening of a street in his home town of Gloucester, Massachusetts. He knew that "habits and haunts" were never merely conveniences, something to be got by purchase or intent. Such incremental "world" was all that could and did remain of so much of "history," a submerged ledge of previous uses offering the only way back or forward. If one moved the road, then one changed unwittingly the consequence of those who had traveled it. Their "mapping" was overwritten, their particular means destroyed. Simply there is no way in which such change can be accommodated and not erase the previous condition, whether it be a "leisure" occupying shores previously committed to fishing or just a common, unintentional dismissal—as in "THE GULF OF MAINE," which Olson ends with this wry comment:

> . . . their knees
> were smashed
> on small rocks
> as their poor pinnace likewise poorly lay
>
> chawn mostly but some parts of her bruised sides
> now resting on the sands where we shall
> dig them up and set them upright as posts
> at just the signal place for tourists
> to come by and not give one idea
>
> why such odd culls
> stand along a fishing
> shore
> though not used much at the present time
> and mostly well-dressed persons
> frequent it

"THE GULF OF MAINE," *The Maximus Poems,* 1983

Olson's emphatic dislike of that which can so empty the effective authority of its source is very evident throughout his work, whether it be the contempt he feels for those "learned monsters whom people are led to think 'know'" in the second part of "Human Universe" or else the more specific qualifying he does in his comments on Cyrus Gordon and "the scholar" in "Homer and Bible." His attack is a constant throughout the early *Maximus Poems* and in others as "Letter for Melville 1951," wherein all the accumulated anger prompted by such misappropriation finds a voice. Inevitably he feels also a bitterness at seeing his own work either plagiarized or else made trivial. Such perverse professionalism is a condition he attacks all his life, and in every possible context. One may remember that he chooses to leave his employment with the Democratic Party after Roosevelt's death, because the "merchandise men" he will have to accept as defining company frustrate entirely any prospect of the art, and the vision of its possibilities, he takes as his own. So, as Tom Clark's *Charles Olson: The Allegory of a Poet's Life* notes, "Over the next three days he began work in earnest, producing several thousand words upon which he would eventually build Part One of *Call Me Ishmael*."

That text appropriately begins this collection. Immediately the apparent givens of our habitual world shift of necessity. "Put war away with time, come into space," he writes in a poem May 1946 ("La Preface"). There is no place made secure by a justifying history, nor any refuge from which to look out, objectively, upon the world's event. That curious, collapsing *sidedness,* that proposal one could be divided from what, in fact, a physical life made whole, fails altogether in Olson's thinking. Most clearly put in an introduction to *Additional Prose* by his fellow poet and friend Robert Duncan (though not published with Olson's text), "We have nowhere else to be than here, in this first history, in which vast extensions of meaning, trance, and fantasy, alchemistries of language, take over."

> He [Olson] goes "back," back home, to come into the depths of the Immediate, going over the documents and old maps, the texts of the sciences and the historical diggings, as data of what our species is, read in the light and dark of a Divine Intention. He wants to establish us, to re-establish us in the Ideal, to redeem all idealism from the commitments that claim prior authority there. "Otherwise the present will lose what America is the inheritor of: a secularization which not only loses nothing of the divine but by seeing process in reality redeems all idealism from theocracy or mobocracy, whether it is rational or superstitious, whether it is democratic or socialism."
>
> "As an Introduction: Charles Olson's *Additional Prose*"

Much of the literary questioning of Olson's work is based upon the presumption that literature is attendant to what one otherwise thinks of as actual. It is the familiar sense of "holding a mirror up to life," making of literature a reflective act which has as its most decisive effect a seemingly accurate description or judgment of that which it so addresses. "To tell what subsequently I saw and what heard," in William Carlos Williams's phrase, would be its most significant disposition, the act of testament, of bearing witness to an otherwise unac-knowledged world.

But that very word ("world") in its own history makes emphatic that a world is never other than a human life, that it is, quite literally, the *vir eld,* that length of time we are given to live and what we know by means of it. Hence philoso-phy, aesthetics, the sciences, all the accumulating judgments and categorizings, together, constitute what we've made humanly of the experience of living. Nothing more, nothing less. But it all stays curiously separate in mind from that which it so engages, that "world which is raging and yet apart," as D. H. Lawrence said. This assumption of an objectivity is what Olson qualifies as the "universe of discourse," the sense that there is a world and then there is the discussion of that world—and that, curiously, these two constitute distinctly specific authorities, however complementary.

But as Robert Duncan also writes in his exceptionally useful relation of Ol-son's work, "Our generation has had the duty to carry in our work the content of an excluded knowledge, to work at a 'bridgework' between the repressed content and the Consciousness that is Self."

> Charles Olson must work at ground work as an educator against a massive and
> repressive construct in which all the sciences of Man outside of the post-Christian
> rationalizing science of "EUROPE" have been declared to be out-of-bounds. Blast-
> ing at indoctrination, Olson blasts with a thunderous indoctrination. He insists
> that it must be dogmatic. A Roman Catholic in origin, he transforms the meaning
> of Catholicity to mean just that—*katha holos,* having to do with the whole of
> Mankind, to be the idea of Man in the whole of Man.

Bizarre that we can so live in the imagination of our "world" and yet so bit-terly contest any sense that it is not the actual one, or perhaps more aptly, the right one. I wonder that my own generation, having come of age in the cata-clysmic "image" of order which was World War II, finds such difficulty in con-sidering any alternative, in recognizing that it indeed might be otherwise, that the possible devastation of all worlds might be the mind awry and not simply a fact of nature. Or if it is such a fact, if our convulsion and self-immolation are "organic," then how do we think ourselves to be, and for what conceivable reason? Have all such questions been answered? Or do they even continue to matter.

Charles Olson is a great poet for many reasons. Because he was fact of his own insistence, "Come into the world." Because he read across the endless divisions of "subject," of a thinking that determined its authority by an ability to isolate and categorize. Because he did not stay put in a "lyricism—one wants it clear by now that the lyric is the ripple that precedes the Klassical reaching the shore." He abhorred epicene poets, those who stay comfortable within a given authority, no matter its character. He shared deeply with John Winthrop a sense that men and women can care about the kind of world they live in.

There is finally no reason to be impartial here at all. One is fighting for one's life and always was. I miss so much the ranging, particularizing, intensely conjecturing mind he had. Sans mind, no direction—just a rudderless drift. You had to be *minded,* he said. I think of my small town West Acton and his mill-town Worcester, and the ocean out there beyond either one of us with its incessant, shifting "place." As he said to Elaine Feinstein, "Orientate me." I loved that word—locate me, put me in the picture, draw me a map. What is poetry ever but such making, the *imago mundi,* the home we have? There are few collections of anything as powerfully engaged as are his sorties here, his impeccable propositions, his insistent engagement with what one *can* know, given attention and the heart to keep it particular.

His talk was the same. You hear it here in the pace, the "walking," the unremitting curiosity without which, as Pound emphasized, there can be no literature at all. In answer to a standard questionnaire, Charles Olson called himself "archaeologist of morning," a time still possible, still initial, still to be found. He wrote also that he had sacrificed everything, all the imagined blessings of a life, in order to achieve concentration. Here it is as if all had returned, to be again that immeasurable intensity, to think of the world and to enter it.

Call Me Ishmael

For Caresse Crosby

and for Ezra Pound

who first gave this book its walking papers

O fahter, fahter

gone amoong

O eeys that loke

Loke, fahter:

your sone!

Contents

FIRST FACT as prologue

FIRST FACT

Herman Melville was born in New York August 1, 1819, and on the 12th of
that month the *Essex,* a well-found whaler of 238 tons, sailed from Nantucket
with George Pollard, Jr. as captain, Owen Chase and Matthew Joy mates, 6 of
her complement of 20 men Negroes, bound for the Pacific Ocean, victualled
and provided for two years and a half.

A year and three months later, on November 20, 1820, just south of the
equator in longitude 119 West, this ship, on a calm day, with the sun at ease,
was struck head on twice by a bull whale, a spermaceti about 85 feet long, and
with her bows stove in, filled and sank.

Her twenty men set out in three open whaleboats for the coast of South
America 2000 miles away. They had bread (200 lb. a boat), water (65 gal-
lons), and some Galapagos turtles. Although they were at the time no great
distance from Tahiti, they were ignorant of the temper of the natives and
feared cannibalism.

Their first extreme sufferings commenced a week later when they made the
mistake of eating, in order to make their supply last, some bread which had got
soaked by the sea's wash. To alleviate the thirst which followed, they killed a
turtle for its blood. The sight revolted the stomachs of the men.

In the first weeks of December their lips began to crack and swell, and a
glutinous saliva collected in the mouth, intolerable to the taste.

Their bodies commenced to waste away, and possessed so little strength
they had to assist each other in performing some of the body's weakest functions.
Barnacles collected on the boats' bottoms, and they tore them off for food. A
few flying fish struck their sails, fell into the boats, and were swallowed raw.

After a month of the open sea they were gladdened by the sight of a small
island which they took to be Ducie but was Elizabeth Isle. Currents and storm
had taken them a thousand miles off their course.

They found water on the island after a futile search for it from rocks which they picked at, where moisture was, with their hatchets. It was discovered in a small spring in the sand at the extreme verge of ebbtide. They could gather it only at low water. The rest of the time the sea flowed over the spring to the depth of six feet.

Twenty men could not survive on the island and, to give themselves the chance to reach the mainland before the supplies they had from the ship should be gone, seventeen of them put back to sea December 27th.

The three who stayed, Thomas Chapple of Plymouth, England, and William Wright and Seth Weeks of Barnstable, Mass., took shelter in caves among the rocks. In one they found eight human skeletons, side by side as though they had lain down and died together.

The only food the three had was a sort of blackbird which they caught when at roost in trees and whose blood they sucked. With the meat of the bird, and a few eggs, they chewed a plant tasting like peppergrass which they found in the crevices of the rocks. They survived.

The three boats, with the seventeen men divided among them, moved under the sun across ocean together until the 12th of January when, during the night, the one under the command of Owen Chase, First Mate, became separated from the other two.

Already one of the seventeen had died, Matthew Joy, Second Mate. He had been buried January 10th. When Charles Shorter, Negro, out of the same boat as Joy, died on January 23rd, his body was shared among the men of that boat and the Captain's, and eaten. Two days more and Lawson Thomas, Negro, died and was eaten. Again two days and Isaac Shepherd, Negro, died and was eaten. The bodies were roasted to dryness by means of fires kindled on the ballast sand at the bottom of the boats.

Two days later, the 29th, during the night, the boat which had been Matthew Joy's got separated from the Captain's and was never heard of again. When she disappeared three men still lived, William Bond, Negro, Obed Hendricks, and Joseph West.

In the Captain's boat now alone on the sea, four men kept on. The fifth, Samuel Reed, Negro, had been eaten for strength at his death the day before. Within three days these four men, calculating the miles they had to go, decided to draw two lots, one to choose who should die that the others might live, and one to choose who should kill him. The youngest, Owen Coffin, serving on his first voyage as a cabin boy to learn his family's trade, lost. It became the duty of Charles Ramsdale, also of Nantucket, to shoot him. He did, and he, the Captain and Brazilla Ray, Nantucket, ate him.

That was February 1, 1821. On February 11th, Ray died of himself, and was eaten. On February 23rd, the Captain and Ramsdale were picked up by the Nantucket whaleship *Dauphin,* Captain Zimri Coffin.

The men in the third boat, under the command of Owen Chase, the first mate, held out the longest. They had become separated from the other two boats before hunger and thirst had driven any of the *Essex's* men to extremity. Owen Chase's crew had buried their first death, Richard Peterson, Negro, on January 20th.

It was not until February 8th, when Isaac Cole died in convulsions, that Owen Chase was forced, some two weeks later than in the other boats, to propose to his two men, Benjamin Lawrence and Thomas Nickerson, that they should eat of their own flesh. It happened to them this once, in this way: they separated the limbs from the body, and cut all the flesh from the bones, after which they opened the body, took out the heart, closed the body again, sewed it up as well as they could, and committed it to the sea.

They drank of the heart and ate it. They ate a few pieces of the flesh and hung the rest, cut in thin strips, to dry in the sun. They made a fire, as the Captain had, and roasted some to serve them the next day.

The next morning they found that the flesh in the sun had spoiled, had turned green. They made another fire to cook it to prevent its being wholly lost. For five days they lived on it, not using of their remnant of bread.

They recruited their strength on the flesh, eating it in small pieces with salt water. By the 14th they were able to make a few attempts at guiding the boat with an oar.

On the 15th the flesh was all consumed and they had left the last of their bread, two sea biscuits. Their limbs had swelled during the last two days and now began to pain them excessively. They judged they still had 300 miles to go.

On the 17th the settling of a cloud led Chase to think that land was near. Notwithstanding, the next morning, Nickerson, 17 years of age, after having bailed the boat, lay down, drew a piece of canvas up over him, and said that he then wished to die immediately. On the 19th, at 7 in the morning, Lawrence saw a sail at seven miles, and the three of them were taken up by the brig *Indian* of London, Captain William Crozier.

It is not known what happened in later years to the three men who survived the island. But the four Nantucket men who, with the Captain, survived the sea, all became captains themselves. They died old, Nickerson at 77, Ramsdale, who was 19 on the *Essex,* at 75, Chase who was 24, at 73, Lawrence who was 30, at 80, and Pollard, the captain, who had been 31 at the time, lived until 1870, age 81.

The Captain, on his return to Nantucket, took charge of the ship *Two Brothers,* another whaler, and five months from home struck a reef to the westward of the Sandwich Islands. The ship was a total loss, and Pollard never went to sea again. At the time of the second wreck he said: "Now I am utterly ruined. No owner will ever trust me with a whaler again, for all will say I am an unlucky man." He ended his life as the night watch of Nantucket town, protecting the houses and people in the dark.

Owen Chase was always fortunate. In 1832 the *Charles Carrol* was built for him on Brant Point, Nantucket, and he filled her twice, each time with 2600 barrels of sperm oil. In his last years he took to hiding food in the attic of his house.

PART ONE
Call me Ishmael

————————————

Call me Ishmael

I take SPACE to be the central fact to man born in America, from Folsom cave to now. I spell it large because it comes large here. Large, and without mercy.

It is geography at bottom, a hell of wide land from the beginning. That made the first American story (Parkman's): exploration.

Something else than a stretch of earth—seas on both sides, no barriers to contain as restless a thing as Western man was becoming in Columbus' day. That made Melville's story (part of it).

PLUS a harshness we still perpetuate, a sun like a tomahawk, small earthquakes but big tornadoes and hurrikans, a river north and south in the middle of the land running out the blood.

The fulcrum of America is the Plains, half sea half land, a high sun as metal and obdurate as the iron horizon, and a man's job to square the circle.

Some men ride on such space, others have to fasten themselves like a tent stake to survive. As I see it Poe dug in and Melville mounted. They are the alternatives.

Americans still fancy themselves such democrats. But their triumphs are of the machine. It is the only master of space the average person ever knows, ox-wheel to piston, muscle to jet. It gives trajectory.

To Melville it was not the will to be free but the will to overwhelm nature that lies at the bottom of us as individuals and a people. Ahab is no democrat. Moby-Dick, antagonist, is only king of natural force, resource.

I am interested in a Melville who decided sometime in 1850 to write a book about the whaling industry and what happened to a man in command of one of the most successful machines Americans had perfected up to that time—the whaleship.

This captain, Ahab by name, knew space. He rode it across seven seas. He was an able skipper, what the fishing people I was raised with call a highliner. Big catches: he brought back holds barrel full of the oil of the sperm, the light of American and European communities up to the middle of the 19th century.

This Ahab had gone wild. The object of his attention was something unconscionably big and white. He had become a specialist: he had all space concentrated into the form of a whale called Moby-Dick. And he assailed it as Columbus an ocean, LaSalle a continent, the Donner Party their winter Pass.

I am interested in a Melville who was long-eyed enough to understand the Pacific as part of our geography, another West, prefigured in the Plains, antithetical.

The beginning of man was salt sea, and the perpetual reverberation of that great ancient fact, constantly renewed in the unfolding of life in every human individual, is the important single fact about Melville. Pelagic.

He had the tradition in him, deep, in his brain, his words, the salt beat of his blood. He had the sea of himself in a vigorous, stricken way, as Poe the street. It enabled him to draw up from Shakespeare. It made Noah, and Moses, contemporary to him. History was ritual and repetition when Melville's imagination was at its own proper beat.

It was an older sense than the European man's, more to do with magic than culture. Magic which, in contrast to worship, is all black. For magic has one purpose: compel men or non-human forces to do one's will. Like Ahab, American, one aim: lordship over nature.

I am willing to ride Melville's image of man, whale and ocean to find in him prophecies, lessons he himself would not have spelled out. A hundred years gives us an advantage. For Melville was as much larger than himself as Ahab's hate. He was a plunger. He knew how to take a chance.

The man made a mess of things. He got all balled up with Christ. He made a white marriage. He had one son die of tuberculosis, the other shoot himself. He only rode his own space once—*Moby-Dick*. He had to be wild or he was nothing in particular. He had to go fast, like an American, or he was all torpor. Half horse half alligator.

Melville took an awful licking. He was bound to. He was an original, ab-original. A beginner. It happens that way to the dreaming men it takes to dis-cover America: Columbus and LaSalle won, and then lost her to the compe-tent. Daniel Boone loved her earth. Harrod tells the story of coming upon Boone one day far to the west in Kentucky of where Harrod thought any white man had ever been. He heard sound he couldn't place, crept forward to a boul-der and there in a blue grass clearing was Boone alone singing to himself. Boone died west of the Mississippi, in his own country criminal—"wanted," a bankrupt of spirit and land.

Beginner—and interested in beginnings. Melville had a way of reaching back through time until he got history pushed back so far he turned time into space. He was like a migrant backtrailing to Asia, some Inca trying to find a lost home.

We are the last "first" people. We forget that. We act big, misuse our land, ourselves. We lose our own primary.

Melville went back, to discover us, to come forward. He got as far as *Moby-Dick*.

Ortega y Gasset puts it that the man of antiquity, before he did anything, took a step like the bullfighter who leaps back in order to deliver the mortal thrust.

Whitman appears, because of his notation of the features of American life and his conscious identification of himself with the people, to be the more poet. But Melville had the will. He was homeless in his land, his society, his self.

Logic and classification had led civilization toward man, away from space. Melville went to space to probe and find man. Early men did the same: poetry, language and the care of myth, as Fenollosa says, grew up together. Among the Egyptians Horus was the god of writing and the god of the moon, one fig-ure for both, a WHITE MONKEY.

In place of Zeus, Odysseus, Olympus we have had Caesar, Faust, the City. The shift was from man as a group to individual man. Now, in spite of the corruption of myth by fascism, the swing is out and back. Melville is one who began it.

He had a pull to the origin of things, the first day, the first man, the un-known sea, Betelgeuse, the buried continent. From passive places his imagina-tion sprang a harpoon.

He sought prime. He had the coldness we have, but he warmed himself by first fires after Flood. It gave him the power to find the lost past of America, the unfound present, and make a myth, *Moby-Dick,* for a people of Ishmaels.

The thing got away from him. It does, from us. We make AHAB, the WHITE WHALE, and lose them. We let John Henry go, Negro, worker, hammering man:

> He lied down his hammer an' he died.

Whitman we have called our greatest voice because he gave us hope. Melville is the truer man. He lived intensely his people's wrong, their guilt. But he remembered the first dream. The *White Whale* is more accurate than *Leaves of Grass.* Because it is America, all of her space, the malice, the root.

What lies under

Melville prepared the way for *Moby-Dick* by ridiculing, in 1850, the idea that the literary genius in America would be, like Shakespeare, "a writer of dramas." This was his proposition:

> great geniuses are parts of the times, they themselves are the times, and possess a corresponding colouring.

Melville raised his times up when he got them into *Moby-Dick* and they held firm in his schema:

E.g. his *crew,* a "people," Clootz and Tom Paine's people, all races and colors functioning together, a forecastle reality of Americans not yet a dream accomplished by the society;

e.g. his *job on the whaling industry,* a problem in the resolution of forces solved with all forces taken account of: (1) OWNERS Bildad and Peleg (Aunt Charity interested party); (2) Ahab, hard MASTER; (3) the MEN, and TECHNOLOGY, killer boat, tryworks and underdeck storage of yield permitting four-year voyage.

We forget the part the chase of the whale played in American economy. It started from a shortage of fats and oils. The Indian had no cattle, the colonist not enough. It was the same with pigs and goats. Red and white alike had to use substitutes. It accounts for the heavy slaughter of the passenger pigeon and the curlew, plentiful birds; and the slaughter of the buffalo.

. The Indians appear to have taken shore whales from an early time. The Makahs around Cape Flattery knew tricks only the present day Norwegian whalers have applied. They blew up seal skins to slow the run of a wounded whale like a sea anchor and to float the dead whale when heavier than water.

The American Indian continued to be a skilled part of the industry down to its end, a miserably paid tool. Melville had reason to name his ship *Pequod* and to make the Gayhead Tashteego one of his three harpooneers.

COMBUSTION. All whales yield oil. Most of the oil is a true fat, a glyceride of the fatty acids. Unlike the Indians the settlers did not find it edible. They boiled the blubber down for tallow. In addition to this fat, commonly called whale oil, the sperm whale and the bottlenose yield a solid wax called spermaceti and a liquid wax called sperm oil. The spermaceti wax is contained in the cavity of the head (vide chp. "Cistern and Buckets," *Moby-Dick*), and in the bones.

Economic historians, lubbers, fail to heft the industry in American economic life up to the Civil War. (In 1859 petroleum was discovered in Pennsylvania. Kerosene, petroleum, and paraffin began rapidly to replace whale oil, sperm oil, and spermaceti wax as illuminating oil, lubricants and raw materials for candles.)

Whaling expanded at a time when agriculture not industry was the base of labor and when foreign not domestic commerce was the base of trade. A few facts:

by 1833, 70,000 persons and $70,000,000 were tied up in whaling and such associated crafts as shipbuilding, sail-lofts, smiths to make toggle irons, the thieving outfitters, their agents and the whores of ports like New Bedford;

by 1844 (peak years roughly 1840–1860) the figure is up to $120,000,000, whaling competes successfully in attracting capital to itself with such opening industries as textiles and shoes, and the export of whale products—one-fourth of the catch—is third to meat products and lumber.

A NECESSARY DISSOCIATION: the notion that the China trade and clipper ships made and made up the maritime America which went down as did agrarian America before land and finance speculation, hard metal industry.

The China trade was, economically, distribution, appeared after England closed the West Indies to our rum merchants following the Revolution. It was the way the smugglers, themselves the answer to England's pre-Revolutionary restrictions, went straight.

Whaling was production, as old as the colonies and, in capital and function, forerunner to a later America, with more relation to Socony than to clippers and the China trade.

As early as 1688 there is a record at Boston of a New York brig petitioning Governor Andross for permission to set out "upon a fishing design about the Bohames Islands, And Cap florida, for sperma Coeti whales and Racks."

This was new to whaling, BRAND NEW, American. A FIRST. All the way back to French and Spanish Basques of the Middle Ages it had been cold water whales, the black, right or Greenland whales of northern waters, which had been hunted. But the Yankees had discovered that the Sperm whale had the finest oil and brought the biggest price.

They went after it. And it led them into all the oceans. And gave whaling its leading role in making the Pacific the American lake the navy now, after a lapse of 100 years, has been about the business of certifying.

A FACT: whale logbooks are today furnishing sea lawyers first claims to islands—the flag & all that;

for whaler as pioneer, cf. chp. "The Advocate," *Moby-Dick.*

You will also discover in that chapter Melville's figures on the value of the industry. Compare to mine above. Thus:

we whalemen of America now outnumber all the rest of the banded whalemen in the world; sail a navy of upward of seven hundred vessels; manned by eighteen thousand men; yearly consuming 4,000,000 dollars; the ships worth, at the time of sailing, $20,000,000; and every year reporting into our harbours a well-reaped harvest of $7,000,000.

About this outnumbering: of 900 whaling vessels of all nations in 1846, 735 were American.

All this is by way of CORRECTION. I don't intend to dish up cold pork. There are histories of whaling if you are interested. BUT no study weighs the industry in the scale of the total society. What you get is this: many of the earliest industrial fortunes were built on the "blessing" of the whale fishery!

TWO INTERPOLATIONS. Melville did not know Number 1. Maybe somewhere he does point out Number 2. For he was wide. Add to his knowledge of whaling:

merchant marine	(read *Redburn*)
the Navy	(ditto *White-Jacket*)
assorted carriers of the	
Pacific	(*Omoo, Mardi,* etc.)
and the Spanish	(by all means read "Benito Cereno" and "The Encantadas," the finest things outside *Moby-Dick*)

Interpolation 1

1762: the colonies still very English, so much so they have little to do with one another, face and act toward London.

Rhode Island: makers of spermaceti candles meet and make covenant to raise the price of wax candles—and keep it raised, it goes without saying. The first American TRUST.

Name: The United Company of Spermaceti Chandlers.

Importance: "shows how colonial boundaries were being eliminated in the minds of the moneyed groups as contrasted with the as yet extremely provincial outlook and provincial patriotism of the smaller people of town and country."

I'm putting a stress Melville didn't on whaling as *industry*. Cutting out the glory: a book *Moby-Dick* turns out to be its glory. We still are soft about our industries, wonder-eyed. What's important is the energy they are a clue to, the drive in the people. The things made are OK, too, some of them. But the captains of industry ain't worth the powder etc. Take the Revolution so long as we're on the subject: whose revolution was it but the "moneyed groups'"; Breed's Hill two weeks after Lexington and it was all over for the "smaller people" until Jefferson gave them another chance.

Don't think whaling was any different from any other American industry. The first men in it, the leaders, explorers, were WORKERS. The money and the glory came later, on top with the exploiters. And the force went down, stayed where it always does, at the underpaid bottom. Where the worker is after the leader is gone.

Whaling started, like so many American industries, as a collective, communal affair. See any history of Sag Harbor or Nantucket. And as late as 1850 there were still skippers to remember the days when they knew the fathers of every man in their crew. But it was already a sweated industry by the time Melville was a hand on a lay (1841–43).

THE TRICK—then as now:

reduce labor costs lower than worker's efficiency—during the 1840's and '50's it cost the owners 15¢ to 30¢ a day to feed each crew member

combine inefficient workers and such costs by maintaining lowest wages and miserable working conditions—vide TYPEE, early chps., and *Omoo*, same.

THE RESULT: by the 1840's the crews were the bottom dogs of all nations and all races. Of the 18,000 men (Melville above) *one-half* ranked as green hands and more than *two-thirds* deserted every voyage.

There were so many Pacific natives like Queequeg, the second colored harpooneer, that a section of Nantucket came to be known as New Guinea.

There were so many Portuguese from the Islands that a section of New Bedford was called Fayal.

The third of Melville's harpooneers was the imperial African Negro Ahasuerus Daggoo.

For bottom dogs made pretty SEE the balletic chapter called "Midnight, Forecastle," in *Moby-Dick*.

I insert here a document of our history left out of the published works of Herman Melville. It was written at the same time as *Moby-Dick* and is headed:

"What became of the ship's company of the whaleship 'Acushnet,' according to Hubbard who came home in her (more than a four years' voyage) and who visited me at Pittsfield in 1850."

Captain Pease—retired & lives ashore at the Vineyard
Raymond 1st Mate—had a fight with the Captain & went ashore at Payta
Hall 2nd Mate came home & went to California
3rd Mate, Portuguese, went ashore at Payta
Boatsteerer Brown, Portuguese, either ran away or killed at Ropo one of the
   Marquesas
Smith went ashore at Santa coast of Peru, afterwards committed suicide at
   Mobile

Barney boatsteerer came home
Carpenter went ashore at Mowee half dead with disreputable disease

The Crew:
Tom Johnson, black, went ashore at Mowee half dead (ditto) & died at the
    hospital
Reed—mulatto—came home
Blacksmith—ran away at St. Francisco
Backus—little black—Do
Bill Green—after various attempts at running away, came home in the end
The Irishman ran away at Salango, coast of Columbia
Wright went ashore half dead at the Marquesas
John Adams & Jo Portuguese came home
The old cook came home
Haynes ran away aboard of a Sydney ship
Little Jack—came home
Grant—young fellow—went ashore half dead, spitting blood, at Oahu
Murray went ashore, shunning fight, at Rio Janeiro
The Cooper—came home

   Melville himself is a case in point. He deserted the *Acushnet,* his first whaleship, at the Marquesas. He was one of eleven mutineers aboard his second, a
Sydney ship the *Lucy Ann,* at Tahiti. Nothing is known of his conduct on the
third, except that he turned up after it, ashore, at Honolulu.

   So if you want to know why Melville nailed us in *Moby-Dick,* consider whaling. Consider whaling as FRONTIER, and INDUSTRY. A product wanted, men
got it: big business. The Pacific as sweatshop. Man, led, against the biggest
damndest creature nature uncorks. The whaleship as factory, the whaleboat
the precision instrument. The 1840's: the New West in the saddle and Melville
No. 20 of a rough and bastard crew. Are they the essentials?

   BIG? Melville may never have seen the biggest of whales, the blue, the principal kill of the present day. He reaches his full size, 100 feet, at 11 years, lives
20 to 25 years, and weighs 150 tons—or four times the estimated weight of

the biggest prehistoric monster and equal to the weight of 37 elephants or 150 fat oxen.

There are two classes of whale: the baleen and the toothed whale. The blue is a baleen. Melville was satisfied with the biggest of the toothed whales, the sperm.

Whales have lungs. To breathe they come to the surface about every half hour. It is this fact that makes them vulnerable to attack by the only important enemy they have—the whaleman.

Melville didn't put it all on the surface of *Moby-Dick*. You'll find the frontier all right, and Andrew Jackson regarded as heavyweight champion (READ end of first "Knights and Squires" chapter for finest rhetoric of democracy). And the technic of an industry analyzed, scrupulously described. But no economics. Jefferson and John Adams observed that in their young days very few men had thought about "government," there were very few writers on "government." Yes, the year *Moby-Dick* was being finished Marx was writing letters to the N.Y. *Daily Tribune.* But Melville . . . . . .

SOME NECESSARY ECOLOGY. With his baleen the blue whale strains out of the water and eats KRILL. Krill is a shrimplike fish which itself feeds on floating green diatoms. These algae develop in summer in the neighborhood of drift ice.

color: krill spawn at the border of arctic and antarctic ice. The offspring
drift with the currents toward the equator. They are in such abundance they turn the waters pink.

The sperm whale feeds on cuttlefish, particularly on the GIANT SQUID which grows to a 33-foot spread of tentacles and an arm length of 21 feet. Compare *Moby-Dick,* LIX, SQUID. The squid lives on big prawn and small fish, and to catch him the whale dives into depths of several hundred fathom. The struggle leaves sores and marks of the armed suckers on the whale's skin around the mouth.

. . . . . . what counts, Melville had, the *experience,* what lies under. And his own *force* to resolve the forces.

Interpolation No. 2

Quote. The American whaling era—in contrast to the Basque, French, Dutch
and English—

developed independently

concentrated on different species of whale

covered all seas including the Arctic

yielded on a larger scale than in any other country or group of countries
before.

Unquote.

Usufruct

1841
Jan.–June

"When I was on board the ship Acushnet of Fairhaven, on the passage to the Pacific cruising-grounds, among other matters of forecastle conversations at times was the story of the Essex. It was then that I first became acquainted with her history and her truly astounding fate.

"But what then served to specialize my interest at the time was the circumstance that the Second mate of our ship, Mr. Hall, an Englishman & Londoner by birth, had for two three-years voyages sailed with Owen Chace (then in command of the whaleship "Charles Carroll" of Nantucket). This Hall always spoke of Chace with much interest & sincere regard—but he did not seem to know anything more about him or the Essex affair than any body else.

December

"Somewhere about the latter part of A.D. 1841, in this same ship the Acushnet, we spoke the "Charles Carroll" of Nantucket, & Owen Chace was the captain, & so it came to pass that I saw him. He was a large, powerful well-made man; rather tall; to all appearances something past forty-five or so; with a handsome face for a Yankee, & expressive of great uprightness & calm unostentatious courage. His whole appearance impressed me pleasurably. He was the most prepossessing-looking whalehunter I think I ever saw.

"Being a mere foremast-hand I had no opportunity of conversing with Owen (tho' he was on board our ship for two hours at a time) nor have I ever seen him since.

29

"But I should have before mentioned, that before seeing
Chace's ship, we spoke another Nantucket craft & *gammed*
with her. In the forecastle I made the acquaintance of a fine
lad of sixteen or thereabouts, a son of Owen Chace! I ques-
tioned him concerning his father's adventure; and when I left
his ship to return again the next morning (for the two vessels
were to sail in company for a few days) he went to his chest &
handed me a complete copy (same edition as this one) of the
Narrative. This was the first printed account of it I had ever
seen, & the only copy of Chace's Narrative (regular & authentic)
except the present one.

"The reading of this wondrous story upon the landless sea, &
close to the very latitude of the shipwreck had a surprising effect upon me."

November

All the above—under the heading *"What I Know of Owen Chace, &c"*—is
written in Melville's own copy of

NARRATIVE OF THE MOST EXTRAORDINARY AND
DISTRESSING SHIPWRECK OF THE WHALE-SHIP ESSEX,
OF NANTUCKET; WHICH WAS ATTACKED AND FINALLY
DESTROYED BY A LARGE SPERMACETI-WHALE, IN THE
PACIFIC OCEAN. By OWEN CHASE, of NANTUCKET, First
Mate of Said Vessel. LONDON, 1821.

1851

The comments by Melville appear to have been written in the
spring of 1851. Melville at that time was already a year out on
the writing of *Moby-Dick* and was approaching the end, preparing to close with the destruction by the White Whale of the
ship *Pequod,* the three-day catastrophe which parallels what
happened to the *Essex.*
The front fly-leaf carries this inscription in Melville's hand:
Herman Melville from Judge Shaw, April, 1851. The Chief

Justice, his father-in-law, had acquired the copy for Melville a month earlier from Thomas Macy at Nantucket.*

"*General Evidence*

"This thing of the Essex is found (stupidly altered) in many compilations of nautical adventure made within the last 15 or 20 years.

"The Englishman Bennett in his exact work (*Whaling Voyage Round the Globe*) quotes the thing as an acknowledged fact.

"Besides seamen, some landsmen (Judge Shaw & others) acquainted with Nantucket, have evinced to me their unquestioning faith in the thing; having seen Captain Pollard himself, & being conversant with his situation in Nantucket since the disaster.

"*Authorship of the Book*

"There seems no reason to suppose that Owen himself wrote the narrative. It bears obvious tokens of having been written for him; but at the same time, its whole air plainly evinces that it was carefully & conscientiously written to Owen's dictation of the facts.—It is almost as good as tho' Owen wrote it himself.

"*Another Narrative of the Adventure*

"I have been told that Pollard, the Captain, wrote, or caused to be wrote under his own name, his version of the story. I have seen extracts purporting to be from some such work. But I have never seen the work itself.—I should imagine Owen Chace to have been the fittest person to narrate the thing."

---

*I publish these notes for the first time through the courtesy of the present owner of the volume, Mr. Perc Brown.

I have raised questions about the *Essex,* as well as on the *Acushnet* and the *Globe,* with friends Tripp of New Bedford and Stackpole of Nantucket, and they have been most kind. As were Dr. and Mrs. Will Gardner when I was last on the Island.

In Melville's copy the last pages of the Narrative are missing. So he adds in his notes—under the title "*Sequel*"—a summary of what happened to the "poor fellows" in the Captain's boat and what he had learned of the fate of the three men left on Elizabeth Isle. He records how Pollard fetched his next command up on unknown rocks off the Sandwich Islands, disclosing that "I got this from Hall, Second Mate of the Acushnet." Melville goes on:

> "Pollard, it seems, now took the hint, & after reaching home from the second shipwreck, moved to abide ashore. He has ever since lived in Nantucket. Hall told me that he became a butcher there. I believe he is still living."

At this point he makes a general comment:

> "All the sufferings of these miserable men of the Essex might, in all human probability, have been avoided had they, immediately after leaving the wreck, steered straight for Tahiti, from which they were not very distant at the time and *to* which there was a fair trade wind. But they dreaded cannibals & strange to tell knew not that for more than 20 years the English missions had been resident in Tahiti, & that in the same year of the shipwreck—1820—it was entirely safe for the ships to touch at Tahiti. But they chose to stem a head wind & make a passage of some thousand miles (an unavoidably roundabout one, too) in order to gain a civilized harbour on the coast of South America."

He continues with remarks "*Further Concerning Owen Chace*":

> "The miserable pertinaciousness of misfortune which pursued Pollard, the Captain, in his second disaster & entire shipwreck, did likewise hunt poor Owen, tho' somewhat more dilatory in overtaking him, the second time.
>
> "For, while I was in the Acushnet we heard from some whaleship that we spoke, that the captain of the "Charles Carroll"— that is Owen Chace—had recently received letters from home, informing him of the certain infidelity of his wife, the mother

of several children, one of them being the lad of sixteen, whom I alluded to as giving me a copy of his father's narrative to read. We also heard that this receipt of this news had told most heavily upon Chace, & that he was a prey to the deepest gloom."

There is a last note, without a heading. It reads:

probably
July, 1852

"Since writing the foregoing I—sometime about 1850–3—saw Capt. Pollard on the island of Nantucket, and exchanged some words with him. To the islanders he was a nobody—to me, the most impressive man, tho' wholly unassuming, even humble, that I ever encountered."

And added, in pencil, along the margin of his earlier remarks concerning Pollard, this:

"a night-watchman"

PART TWO
Shakespeare

"Which is the best of Shakespeare's plays?
I mean in what mood and with what ac-
companiment do you like the sea best?"

Keats, *Letter to Jane Reynolds*

Sept. 14, 1817

Shakespeare, or the discovery of *Moby-Dick*

Moby-Dick was two books written between February, 1850 and August, 1851.
The first book did not contain Ahab.

It may not, except incidentally, have contained Moby-Dick.

On the 7th of August, 1850, the editor Evert Duyckinck reported to his brother:

> Melville has a new book mostly done, a romantic, fanciful & most
> literal & most enjoyable presentment of the Whale Fishery—some-
> thing quite new.

It is not surprising that Melville turned to whaling in February, 1850, on his return from a trip to England to sell his previous book, *White-Jacket*. It was the last of the materials his sea experience offered him.

He had used his adventures among the South Sea islands in *Typee* (1846) and *Omoo* (1847). He had gone further in the vast archipelago of *Mardi,* written in 1847 and 1848, to map the outlines of his vision of life. The books of 1849, *Redburn* and *White-Jacket,* he had based on his experiences aboard a merchant ship and a man-of-war. The whaling voyage in the *Acushnet* was left.

There is no evidence that Melville had decided on the subject before he started to write in February. On the contrary. Melville's reading is a gauge of him, at all points of his life. He was a skald, and knew how to appropriate the work of others. He read to write. Highborn stealth, Edward Dahlberg calls originality, the act of a cutpurse Autolycus who makes his thefts as invisible as possible. Melville's books batten on other men's books. Yet he bought no books on whaling among the many volumes purchased in England on his trip and soon after his return Putnam's the publishers were picking up in London for him such things as Thomas Beale's *The Natural History of the Sperm Whale*.

He went at it as he had his last two books, "two jobs," as he called *Redburn* and *White-Jacket* in a letter to his father-in-law, "which I have done for money—being forced to it, as other men are to sawing wood." He had a family to support.

By May it was half done. So he told Richard Henry Dana in a letter on the 1st, the only other information of the first Moby-Dick which has survived. The book was giving Melville trouble. Referring to it as "the 'whaling voyage,'" he writes:

> It will be a strange sort of a book, I fear; blubber is blubber you know; tho you may get oil out of it, the poetry runs as hard as sap from a frozen maple tree;—& to cook the thing up, one must needs throw in a little fancy, which from the nature of the thing, must be ungainly as the gambols of the whales themselves. Yet I mean to give the truth of the thing, spite of this.

That's the record of Moby-Dick No. 1, as it stands. There is nothing on why, in the summer of 1850, Melville changed his conception of the work and, on something "mostly done" on August 7th, spent another full year until, in August, 1851, he had created what we know as *Moby-Dick or, The Whale*.

"Dollars damn me." Melville had the bitter thing of men of originality, the struggle between money and me. It was on him, hard, in the spring of 1850. He says as much in the Dana letter: "I write these books of mine almost entirely for 'lucre'—by the job, as a wood-sawyer saws wood," repeating on Moby-Dick what he had said about *Redburn* and *White-Jacket*.

He knew the cost if he let his imagination loose. He had taken his head once, with *Mardi*. In this new work on whaling he felt obliged, as he had, after *Mardi,* with *Redburn* and *White-Jacket,* "to refrain from writing the kind of book I would wish to."

He would give the truth of the thing, spite of this, yes. His head was lifted to Dana as it was to his father-in-law seven months earlier. He did his work clean. *Exs: Redburn* and *White-Jacket.* "In writing these two books I have not repressed myself much—so far as *they* are concerned; but have spoken pretty much as I feel."

There was only one thing in the spring of 1850 which he did not feel he could afford to do: "So far as I am individually concerned, & independent of my pocket, it is my earnest desire to write those sort of books which are said to 'fail.'"

In the end, in *Moby-Dick,* he did. Within three months he took his head again. Why?

Through May he continued to try to do a quick book for the market: "all my books are botches." Into June he fought his materials: "blubber is blubber." Then something happened. What, Melville tells:

> I somehow cling to the strange fancy, that, in all men hiddenly reside certain won-drous, occult properties—as in some plants and minerals—which by some happy but very rare accident (as bronze was discovered by the melting of the iron and brass at the burning of Corinth) may chance to be called forth here on earth.

When? Melville is his own tell-tale: he wrote these words in July, 1850. They occur in an article he did for Duyckinck's magazine. He gave it the title HAWTHORNE AND HIS MOSSES, WRITTEN BY A VIRGINIAN SPENDING A JULY IN VERMONT.

The subject is Hawthorne, Shakespeare and Herman Melville. It is a docu-ment of Melville's rights and perceptions, his declaration of the freedom of a man to fail. Within a matter of days after it was written (July 18 ff.), Melville had abandoned the account of the Whale Fishery and gambled it and himself with Ahab and the White Whale.

The *Mosses* piece is a deep and lovely thing. The spirit is asweep, as in the book to come. The confusion of May is gone. Melville is charged again. *Moby-Dick* is already shadowed in the excitement over genius, and America as a sub-ject for genius. You can feel Ahab in the making, Ahab of "the globular brain and ponderous heart," so much does Melville concern himself with the distinc-tion between the head and the heart in Hawthorne and Shakespeare. You can see the prose stepping off.

The germinous seeds Hawthorne has dropped in Melville's July soil begin to grow: Bulkington, the secret member of the crew in *Moby-Dick,* is here, hid-den, in what Melville quotes as Hawthorne's self-portrait—the "seeker," rough-hewn and brawny, of large, warm heart and powerful intellect.

Above all, in the ferment, Shakespeare, the cause. The passages on him—

the manner in which he is introduced, the detail with which he is used, the intensity—tell the story of what had happened. Melville had read him again. His copy of THE PLAYS survives. He had bought it in Boston in February, 1849. He described it then to Duyckinck:

> It is an edition in glorious great type, every letter whereof is a soldier, & the top of every 't' like a musket barrel.
> I am mad to think how minute a cause has prevented me hitherto from reading Shakespeare. But until now any copy that was come-atable to me happened to be a vile small print unendurable to my eyes which are tender as young sperms. But chancing to fall in with this glorious edition, I now exult over it, page after page.

The set exists, seven volumes, with passages marked, and comments in Melville's hand. The significant thing is the rough notes for the composition of *Moby-Dick* on the fly-leaf of the last volume. These notes involve Ahab, Pip, Bulkington, Ishmael, and are the key to Melville's intention with these characters. They thus relate not to what we know of the Moby-Dick that Melville had been working on up to July but to *Moby-Dick* as he came to conceive it at this time.

Joined to the passages on Shakespeare in the *Mosses* piece, the notes in the Shakespeare set verify what *Moby-Dick* proves: Melville and Shakespeare had made a Corinth and out of the burning came *Moby-Dick,* bronze.

A note of thanks

The Melville people are rare people, and this is the right place to tell:

of Eleanor Melville Metcalf and Henry K. Metcalf, with whom the Shakespeare was only a beginning, for they have made all Melville's things mine, indeed have made me a member of their family;

of Raymond Weaver and Henry A. Murray, Jr., the other true biographer, who have been my generous friends;

and of those early criers of Melville, Carl Van Doren and Van Wyck Brooks, who have spoken up for me.

For the original use of the Shakespeare set and Melville's notes in it I wish also to thank another granddaughter, Mrs. Frances Osborne.

American Shiloh

Shakespeare emerged from the first rush of Melville's reading a Messiah: as he put it in the *Mosses* piece in 1850, a "Shiloh"; as he put it to Duyckinck in 1849, "full of sermons-on-the-mount, and gentle, aye, almost as Jesus." Melville had a way of ascribing divinity to truth-tellers, Solomon, Shakespeare, Hawthorne, or Jesus.

He next limited Shakespeare. He advanced a criticism in his second letter to Duyckinck in 1849 which is central to all his later published passages on the poet. It keeps him this side of idolatry. It arises from what Melville takes to be an "American" advantage:

> I would to God Shakespeare had lived later, & promenaded in Broadway. Not that I might have had the pleasure of leaving my card for him at the Astor, or made merry with him over a bowl of the fine Duyckinck punch; but that the muzzle which all men wore on their souls in the Elizabethan day, might not have intercepted Shakespeare's free articulations, for I hold it a verity, that even Shakespeare was not a frank man to the uttermost. And, indeed, who in this intolerant universe is, or can be? But the Declaration of Independence makes a difference.

In the *Mosses* piece, a year and a half later, he gives it tone:

> In Shakespeare's tomb lies infinitely more than Shakespeare ever wrote. And if I magnify Shakespeare, it is not so much for what he did do as for what he did not do, or refrained from doing.
>
> For in this world of lies, Truth is forced to fly like a scared white doe in the woodlands; and only by cunning glimpses will she reveal herself, as in Shakespeare and other masters of the great Art of Telling the Truth,—even though it be covertly and by snatches.

In his copy of the PLAYS, when Shakespeare muzzles truth-speakers, Melville is quick to mark the line or incident. In *Antony and Cleopatra* he puts a check beside Enobarbus' blunt answer to Antony's correction of his speech: "That truth should be silent I had almost forgot."

In *Lear* he underscores the Fool's answer to Lear's angry threat of the whip: "Truth's a dog must to kennel; he must be whipp'd out, when Lady the brach may stand by th' fire and stink." The very language of Melville in the *Mosses* thing is heard from the Fool's mouth.

As an artist Melville chafed at representation. His work up to *Moby-Dick* was a progress toward the concrete and after *Moby-Dick* a breaking away. He had to fight himself to give truth dramatic location. Shakespeare's dramatic significance was not lost upon him, but he would have been, as he says, "more content with the still, rich utterance of a great intellect in repose." Melville's demand uncovers a flaw in himself.

Fortunately—for *Moby-Dick*—the big truth was not sermons-on-the-mount. Melville found these in *Measure for Measure.* It is, rather

> those deep far-away things in him; those occasional flashings-forth of the intuitive Truth in him; those short, quick probings at the very axis of reality;—these are the things that make Shakespeare, Shakespeare.

Such reality is in the mouths of the "dark" characters, Hamlet, Timon, Lear and Iago, where the drama Melville could learn from, lay. For blackness fixed and fascinated Melville. Through such dark men Shakespeare

> craftily says, or sometimes insinuates the things which we feel to be so terrifically true, that it were all but madness for any good man, in his own proper character, to utter or even hint of them!

It is this side of Shakespeare that Melville fastens on. Madness, villainy and evil are called up out of the plays as though Melville's pencil were a wand of black magic. To use Swinburne's comment on *Lear,* it is not the light of revelation but the darkness of it that Melville finds most profound in Shakespeare. He was to write in *Moby-Dick:*

> Though in many of its aspects the visible world seems formed in love, the invisible spheres were formed in fright.

Man, to man

Shakespeare reflects Melville's disillusion in the treacherous world. In *The Tempest,* when Miranda cries out "O brave new world!", Melville encircles Prospero's answer "'Tis new to thee," and writes this note at the bottom of the page:

> Consider the character of the persons concerning whom Miranda says this—then Prospero's quiet words in comment—how terrible! In *Timon* itself there is nothing like it.

Shakespeare frequently expresses disillusion through friendship and its falling off. The theme has many variations. Melville misses none of them. Caesar and Antony on the fickleness of the people to their rulers, in *Antony and Cleopatra.* Achilles and Ulysses on the people's faithlessness to their heroes, in *Troilus and Cressida.* Henry V and Richard II on treachery within the councils of the state. Melville pulls it out of the tragedies: in *Lear,* when the Fool sings how fathers who bear bags draw forth love and those who wear rags lose love; and in *Hamlet,* the lines of the Player King:

> For who not needs, shall never lack a friend
> And who in want a hollow friend doth try,
> Directly seasons him his enemy.

To betray a friend was to make—for Melville as for Richard—a second fall of cursed man. Shakespeare gives the theme its great counterpoint in *Timon.* In that play the whole issue of idealism is objectified through friendship. When his friends fail him Timon's love turns to hate. His world—and with it the play—wrenches into halves as the earth with one lunge tore off from a sun.

Melville took a more personal possession of the tragedy of Timon than of any of the other dark men. In *Lear* he found ingratitude, but what gave *Timon* its special intensity was that Timon was undone by friends, not daughters.

Melville makes little out of the love of man and woman. It is the friendship of men which is love. That is why Hawthorne was so important to him, to whom he wrote his best letters and to whom he dedicated *Moby-Dick*. That is why he never forgot Jack Chase, the handsome sailor he worked under in the Pacific, to whom he dedicated his last book, *Billy Budd.*

Melville had the Greek sense of men's love. Or the Roman's, as Shakespeare gives it in *Coriolanus*. In that play the only place Melville heavily marks is the long passage in which Coriolanus and Aufidius meet and embrace. They are captains, with the soldier's sense of comrade. Melville's is the seaman's, of a shipmate. Aufidius speaks the same passionate images of friendship Melville uses to convey the depth of feeling between Ishmael and Queequeg in *Moby-Dick*. Ishmael and Queequeg are as "married" as Aufidius feels toward Coroiolanus:

> that I see thee here
> Thou noble thing, more dances my rapt heart
> Than when I first my wedded mistress saw
> Bestride my threshold.

Like Timon Melville found only disappointment. He lost Jack Chase, and Hawthorne, shyest grape, hid from him. In a poem of his later years Melville wrote:

> To have known him, to have loved him
>   After loneness long
> And then to be estranged in life
>   And neither in the wrong
> Ease me, a little ease, my song!

Timon is mocked with glory, as his faithful Steward says, lives, as Melville notes, but in a dream of friendship. Melville uses the blasted hero as a symbol throughout his books, sometimes in Plutarch's convention as a misanthrope, often as another Ishmael of solitude, most significantly—in *Pierre*—as disillusion itself, man undone by goodness. It is the subject of *Pierre* and the lesson of *The Confidence-Man*.

Melville's feeling for the play is summarized by a line he underscores in it, the Stranger's observation on the hypocrisy of Timon's friends:

> Why, this is the world's soul.

Lear and *Moby-Dick**

It was *Lear* that had the deep creative impact. In *Moby-Dick* the use is pervasive. That its use is also the most implicit of any play serves merely to enforce a law of the imagination, for what has stirred Melville's own most is heaved out, like Cordelia's heart, with most tardiness.

In the Hawthorne-Mosses article it is to Lear's speeches that Melville points to prove Shakespeare's insinuations of "the things we feel to be so terrifically true:"

> Tormented into desperation, Lear, the frantic king, tears off the mask, and speaks the same madness of vital truth.

His copy of the play is marked more heavily than any of the others but *Antony and Cleopatra.* Of the characters the Fool and Edmund receive the attention. I have said Melville found his own words in the Fool's mouth when the Fool cries, "Truth's a dog must to kennel." He found them in such other speeches of that boy, as

> Nay, an thou canst not smile as the wind sits, thou'lt catch cold shortly.

For Melville sees the Fool as the Shakespeare he would have liked more of, not one who refrained from hinting what he knew.

Melville is terrified by Edmund who took his fierce quality in the lusty stealth of nature and who, in his evil, leagued with that world whose thick rotundity Lear would strike flat. The sources of this man's evil, and his qualities, attract the writer who is likewise drawn to Goneril, to Iago—and who himself creates a Jackson in *Redburn* and a Claggart in *Billy Budd.*

---

*Under this title an earlier version of this material appeared in the magazine *Twice-A-Year.*

It is the positive qualities in the depraved: Edmund's courage, and his power of attracting love. When Edmund outfaces Albany's challenge, denies he is a traitor, and insists he will firmly prove his truth and honor, Melville writes this footnote:

The infernal nature has a valor often denied to innocence.

When Edmund is dying he fails to revoke his order for the death of Lear and Cordelia, only looks upon the bodies of Goneril and Regan and consoles himself: "Yet Edmund was belov'd!" This Melville heavily checks. It is a twisting ambiguity like one of his own—Evil beloved.

Melville is dumb with horror at the close, blood-stop double meaning of Shakespeare's language in the scene of the blinding of Gloucester. His comment is an exclamation: "Terrific!" When Regan calls Gloucester "Ingrateful fox!" Melville writes:

Here's a touch Shakespearean—*Regan* talks of *ingratitude!*

First causes were Melville's peculiar preoccupation. He concentrates on an Edmund, a Regan—and the world of *Lear,* which is almost generated by such creatures, lies directly behind the creation of an Ahab, a Fedallah and the White, lovely, monstrous Whale.

Melville found answers in the darkness of *Lear.* Not in the weak goodness of an Albany who thinks to exclude evil from good by a remark as neat and corrective as Eliphaz in the Book of Job:

Wisdom and goodness to the vile seem vile;
Filths savor but themselves.

The ambiguities do not resolve themselves by such "right-mindedness." Albany is a Starbuck.

Melville turned rather to men who suffered as Job suffered—to Lear and Edgar and Gloucester. Judged by his markings upon the scene in which Edgar discovers, with a hot burst in his heart, his father's blindness, Melville perceived what suggests itself as a symbol so inherent to the play as to leave one amazed it has not been more often observed—that to lose the eye and capacity to see, to lose the physical organ, "vile jelly," is to gain spiritual sight.

The crucifixion in *Lear* is not of the limbs on a crossbeam, but of the eyes put out, the eyes of pride too sharp for feeling. Lear himself in the storm scene senses it, but Gloucester blind speaks it: "I stumbled when I saw."

Lear's words:

Poor naked wretches, wheresoe'er you are,
That bide the pelting of this pitiless storm,
How shall your houseless heads and unfed sides,
Your loop'd and window'd raggedness, defend you
From seasons such as these? O, I have ta'en
Too little care of this! Take physic, pomp;
Expose thyself to feel what wretches feel,
That thou mayst shake the superflux to them
And show the heavens more just.

Gloucester's words come later, Act IV, Sc. 1. It is the purgatorial dispensation of the whole play. Gloucester, who aches to have his son Edgar back—

Might I but live to *see thee in my touch,*
I'ld say I had eyes again!

—has his wish and does not know it. He does not know, because he cannot see, that Edgar is already there beside him in the disguise of Tom o' Bedlam. Gloucester takes him for the poor, mad beggar he says he is. He seconds Lear thus:

Here, take this purse, thou whom the heavens' plagues
Have humbled to all strokes. That I am wretched
Makes thee the happier. Heavens, deal so still!
Let the superfluous and lust-dieted man,
That slaves your ordinance, that will not see
Because he does not feel, feel your pow'r quickly;
So distribution should undo excess,
And each man have enough.

The underscore is Melville's.

What moves Melville is the stricken goodness of a Lear, a Gloucester, an Edgar, who in suffering feel and thus probe more closely to the truth. Melville is to put Ahab through this humbling.

• • •

Shakespeare drew *Lear* out of what Melville called "the infinite obscure of his background." It was most kin to Melville. He uses it as an immediate obscure around his own world of *Moby-Dick*. And he leaves Ishmael at the end to tell the tale of Ahab's tragedy as Kent remained to speak these last words of Lear:

> Vex not his ghost. O, let him pass! He hates him
> That would upon the rack of this tough world
> Stretch him out longer.

A *Moby-Dick* manuscript

It is beautifully right to find what I take to be rough notes for *Moby-Dick* in the Shakespeare set itself. They are written in Melville's hand, in pencil, upon the last fly-leaf of the last volume, the one containing *Lear, Othello* and *Hamlet*. I transcribe them as they stand:

> Ego non baptizo te in nomine Patris et
> Filii et Spiritus Sancti—sed in nomine
> Diaboli. —madness is undefinable—
> It & right reason extremes of one,
> —not the (black art) Goetic but Theurgic magic—
> seeks converse with the Intelligence, Power, the
> Angel.

The Latin is a longer form of what Melville told Hawthorne to be the secret motto of *Moby-Dick*. In the novel Ahab howls it as an inverted benediction upon the harpoon he has tempered in savage blood:

> Ego non baptizo te in nomine patris, sed in nomine diaboli.
> I do not baptize thee in the name of the father, but in the name of the devil.

The change in the wording from the notes to the novel is of extreme significance. It is not for economy of phrase. The removal of Christ and the Holy Ghost—Filii et Spiritus Sancti—is a mechanical act mirroring the imaginative. Of necessity, from Ahab's world, both Christ and the Holy Ghost are absent. Ahab moves and has his being in a world to which They and what They import are inimical: remember, Ahab fought a deadly scrimmage with a Spaniard before the altar at Santa, and spat into the silver calabash. The conflict in Ahab's world is abrupt, more that between Satan and Jehovah, of the old dispensation

51

than the new. It is the outward symbol of the inner truth that the name of Christ is uttered but once in the book and then it is torn from Starbuck, the only possible man to use it, at a moment of anguish, the night before the fatal third day of the chase.

Ahab is Conjur Man. He invokes his own evil world. He himself uses black magic to achieve his vengeful ends. With the very words "in nomine diaboli" he believes he utters a Spell and performs a Rite of such magic.

The Ahab-world is closer to *Macbeth* than to *Lear.* In it the supernatural is accepted. Fedallah appears as freely as the Weird Sisters. Before Ahab's first entrance he has reached that identification with evil to which Macbeth out of fear evolves within the play itself. The agents of evil give both Ahab and Macbeth a false security through the same device, the unfulfillable prophecy. Ahab's tense and nervous speech is like Macbeth's, rather than Lear's. Both Macbeth and Ahab share a common hell of wicked, sleep-bursting dreams. They both endure the torture of isolation from humanity. The correspondence of these two evil worlds is precise. In either the divine has little place. Melville intended certain exclusions, and Christ and the Holy Ghost were two of them. Ahab, alas, could not even baptize in the name of the Father. He could only do it in the name of the Devil.

That is the Ahab-world, and it is wicked. Melville meant exactly what he wrote to Hawthorne when the book was consummated:

I have written a wicked book, and feel as spotless as the lamb.

Melville's "wicked book" is the drama of Ahab, his hot hate for the White Whale, and his vengeful pursuit of it from the moment the ship plunges like fate into the Atlantic. It is that action, not the complete novel *Moby-Dick.* The *Moby-Dick* universe contains more, something different. Perhaps the difference is the reason why Melville felt "spotless as the lamb." The rough notes in the Shakespeare embrace it.

"Madness is undefinable." Two plays from which the thought could have sprung are in the volume in which it is written down: *Lear* and *Hamlet.* Of the modes of madness in *Lear*—the King's, the Fool's—which is definable? But we need not rest on supposition as to what Melville drew of madness from *Hamlet,* or from *Lear: Moby-Dick* includes both Ahab and Pip. Melville forces his analysis of Ahab's mania to incredible distances, only himself to admit that

"Ahab's larger, darker, deeper part remains unhinted." Pip's is a more fathomable idiocy: "his shipmates called him mad." Melville challenges the description, refuses to leave Pip's madness dark and unhinted, declares: "So man's insanity is heaven's sense."

The emphasis in this declaration is the key to resolve apparent difficulties in the last sentence of the notes in the Shakespeare volume:

> It & right reason extremes of one,—not the (black art) Goetic but Theurgic magic—seeks converse with the Intelligence, Power, the Angel.

I take "it" to refer to the "madness" of the previous sentence. "Right reason," less familiar to the 20th century, meant more to the last, for in the Kant-Coleridge terminology "right reason" described the highest range of the intelligence and stood in contrast to "understanding." Melville had used the phrase in *Mardi*. What he did with it there discloses what meaning it had for him when he used it in these cryptic notes for the composition of *Moby-Dick*. *Mardi*:

> Right reason, and Alma (Christ), are the same; else Alma, not reason, would we reject. The Master's great command is Love; and here do all things wise, and all things good, unite. Love is all in all. The more we love, the more we know; and so reversed.

Now, returning to the notes, if the phrase "not the (black art) Goetic but Theurgic magic" is recognized as parenthetical, the sentence has some clarity: "madness" and its apparent opposite "right reason" are the two extremes of one way or attempt or urge to reach "the Intelligence, Power, the Angel" or, quite simply, God.

The adjectives of the parenthesis bear this reading out. "Goetic" might seem to derive from Goethe and thus *Faust,* but its source is the Greek "goetos," meaning variously trickster, juggler and, as here, magician. (Plato called literature "Goeteia.") Wherever Melville picked up the word he means it, as he says, for the "black art." "Theurgic," in sharp contrast, is an accurate term for a kind of occult art of the Neoplatonists in which, through self-purification and sacred rites, the aid of the divine was evoked. In thus opposing "Goetic" and "Theurgic" Melville is using a distinction as old as Chaldea between black and white magic, the one of demons, the other of saints and angels, one evil, the other benevolent. For white or "Theurgic" magic, like "madness" and "right reason," seeks God, while the "black art Goetic" invokes only the devil.

Now go to *Moby-Dick*. In the Ahab-world there is no place for "converse with the Intelligence, Power, the Angel." Ahab cannot seek it, for understood between him and Fedallah is a compact as binding as Faust's with Mephistopheles. Melville's assumption is that though both Ahab and Faust may be seekers after truth, a league with evil closes the door to truth. Ahab's art, so long as his hate survives, is black. He does not seek true converse.

"Madness," on the contrary, does, and Pip is mad, possessed of an insanity which is "heaven's sense." When the little Negro almost drowned, his soul went down to wondrous depths and there he "saw God's foot upon the treadle of the loom, and spoke it." Through that accident Pip, of all the crew, becomes "prelusive of the eternal time" and thus achieves the converse Ahab has denied himself by his blasphemy. The chapter on "The Doubloon" dramatizes the attempts on the part of the chief active characters to reach truth. In that place Starbuck, in his "mere unaided virtue," is revealed to have no abiding faith: he retreats before "Truth," fearing to lose his "righteousness." . . . Stubb's jollity and Flask's clod-like stupidity blunt the spiritual. . . . The Manxman has mere superstition, Queequeg mere curiosity. . . . Fedallah worships the doubloon evilly. . . . Ahab sees the gold coin solipsistically: "three peaks as proud as Lucifer" and all named "Ahab!" Pip alone, of all, has true prescience: he names the doubloon the "navel" of the ship—"Truth" its life.

"Right reason" is the other way to God. It is the way of man's sanity, the pure forging of his intelligence in the smithy of life. To understand what use Melville made of it in *Moby-Dick* two characters, both inactive to the plot, have to be brought forth.

Bulkington is the man who corresponds to "right reason." Melville describes him once early in the book when he enters the Spouter Inn. "Six feet in height, with noble shoulders, and a chest like a coffer-dam." In the deep shadows of his eyes "floated some reminiscences that did not seem to give him much joy." In the "Lee Shore" chapter Bulkington is explicitly excluded from the action of the book, but not before Melville has, in ambiguities, divulged his significance as symbol. Bulkington is Man who, by "deep, earnest thinking" puts out to sea, scorning the land, convinced that "in landlessness alone resides the highest truth, shoreless, indefinite as God."

The rest of the *Pequod*'s voyage Bulkington remains a "sleeping-partner" to the action. He is the secret member of the crew, below deck always, like the music under the earth in *Antony and Cleopatra,* strange. He is the crew's heart, the sign of their paternity, the human thing. And by that human thing alone can they reach their apotheosis.

There remains Ishmael. Melville framed Ahab's action, and the parts Pip, Bulkington and the rest of the crew played in the action, within a narrative told by Ishmael. Too long in criticism of the novel Ishmael has been confused with Herman Melville himself. Ishmael is fictive, imagined, as are Ahab, Pip and Bulkington, not so completely perhaps, for the very reason that he is so like his creator. But he is not his creator only: he is a chorus through whom Ahab's tragedy is seen, by whom what is black and what is white magic is made clear. Like the Catskill eagle Ishmael is able to dive down into the blackest gorges and soar out to the light again.

He is passive and detached, the observer, and thus his separate and dramatic existence is not so easily felt. But unless his choric function is recognized some of the vision of the book is lost. When he alone survived the wreck of the *Pequod,* he remained, after the shroud of the sea rolled on, to tell more than Ahab's wicked story. Ahab's self-created world, in essence privative, a thing of blasphemies and black magic, has its offset. Ahab has to dominate over a world where the humanities may also flower and man (the crew) by Pip's or Bulkington's way reach God. By this use of Ishmael Melville achieved a struggle and a catharsis which he intended, to feel "spotless as the lamb."

Ishmael has that cleansing ubiquity of the chorus in all drama, back to the Greeks. It is interesting that, in the same place where the notes for *Moby-Dick* are written in his Shakespeare, Melville jots down: "Eschylus Tragedies." Ishmael alone hears Father Mapple's sermon out. He alone saw Bulkington, and understood him. It was Ishmael who learned the secrets of Ahab's blasphemies from the prophet of the fog, Elijah. He recognized Pip's God-sight, and moaned for him. He cries forth the glory of the crew's humanity. Ishmael tells *their* story and *their* tragedy as well as Ahab's, and thus creates the *Moby-Dick* universe in which the Ahab-world is, by the necessity of life—or the Declaration of Independence—*included.*

Ahab and his fool

Life has its way, even with Ahab. Melville had drawn upon another myth besides Shakespeare's to create his dark Ahab, that of both Marlowe and Goethe: the Faust legend. But he alters it. After the revolutions of the 18th–19th century the archetype Faust has never been the same. In Melville's alteration the workings of Lear and the Fool can also be discerned.

The change comes in the relation of Ahab to Pip. Ahab does not die in the tempestuous agony of Faustus pointing to Christ's blood and crying for His mercy. He dies with an acceptance of his damnation. Before his final battle with the White Whale Ahab has resigned himself to his fate.

His solipsism is most violent and his hate most engendered the night of "The Candles" when he raises the burning harpoon over his crew. It is a night of storm. The setting is *Lear*-like. Ahab, unlike Lear, does not in this night of storm discover his love for his fellow wretches. On the contrary, this night Ahab uncovers his whole hate. He commits the greater blasphemy than defiance of sun and lightning. He turns the harpoon, forged and baptized for the inhuman Whale alone, upon his own human companions, the crew, and brandishes his hate over them. The morning after the storm Ahab is most subtly dedicated to his malignant purpose when he gives the lightning-twisted binnacle a new needle. Melville marks this pitch of his ego:

In his fiery eyes of scorn and triumph, you then saw Ahab in all his fatal pride.

In a very few hours the change in Ahab sets in and Pip—the shadow of Pip—is the agent of the change. Like a reminder of Ahab's soul he calls to Ahab and Ahab, advancing to help, cries to the sailor who has seized Pip: "Hands off that holiness!" It is a crucial act: for the first time Ahab has offered to help another human being. And at that very moment Ahab speaks Lear's phrases:

> Thou touchest my inmost centre, boy; thou art tied to me by cords woven of my heart-strings. Come, let's down.

Though Ahab continues to curse the gods for their "inhumanities," his tone, from this moment, is richer, quieter, less angry and strident. He even questions his former blasphemies, for a bottomed sadness grows in him as Pip lives in the cabin with him. There occurs a return of something Peleg had insisted that Ahab possessed on the day Ishmael signed for the fatal voyage. Peleg then refuted Ishmael's fears of his captain's wicked name—that dogs had licked his blood. He revealed that Ahab had a wife and child, and concluded:

> hold ye then there can be any utter, hopeless harm in Ahab? No, no, my lad; stricken, blasted, if he be, Ahab has his humanities!

These humanities had been set aside in Ahab's hate for the White Whale. One incident: Ahab never thought, as he paced the deck at night in fever of anger, how his whalebone stump rapping the boards waked his crew and officers. The aroused Stubb confronts Ahab. Ahab orders him like a dog to kennel. For Stubb cannot, like Pip, affect Ahab. When it is over Stubb's only impulse is to go down on his knees and pray for the hot old man who he feels has so horribly amputated himself from human feelings.

Pip continues to be, mysteriously, the agent of this bloom once it has started. Says Ahab: "I do suck most wondrous philosophies from thee!" He even goes so far as to ask God to bless Pip and save him. BUT before he asks that, he threatens to murder Pip, Pip so weakens his revengeful purpose.

Though Pip recedes in the last chapters, the suppleness he has brought out of old Ahab continues to grow. Pip is left in the hold as though Ahab would down his soul once more, but above decks Ahab is no longer the proud Lucifer. He asks God to bless the captain of the *Rachel,* the last ship they meet before closing with Moby-Dick, the vessel which later picks Ishmael up after the tragedy. The difference in his speech is commented on: "a voice that prolongingly moulded every word." And it is noticed that when, toward the last days, Ahab prepares a basket lookout for himself to be hoisted up the mast to sight Moby-

Dick, he trusts his "life-line" to Starbuck's hands. This running sap of his humanities gives out its last shoots in "The Symphony" chapter: observe that Ahab asks God to destroy what has been from the first his boast—"God! God! God! stave my brain!" He has turned to Starbuck and talked about his wife and child! And though this apple, his last, and cindered, drops to the soil, his revenge is now less pursued than resigned to. His thoughts are beyond the whale, upon easeful death.

In the three days' chase he is a tense, mastered, almost grim man. He sets himself outside humanity still, but he is no longer arrogant, only lonely: "Cold, cold . . ." After the close of the second day, when Fedallah cannot be found, he withers. His last vindictive shout is to rally his angers which have been hurled and lost like Fedallah and the harpoon of lightning and blood. He turns to Fate, the handspike in his windlass: "The whole act's immutably decreed." That night he does not face the whale as was his custom. He turns his "heliotrope glance" back to the east, waiting the sun of the fatal third day like death. It is Macbeth in his soliloquy of tomorrow, before Macduff will meet and match him. On the third day the unbodied winds engage his attention for the first time in the voyage. Even after the White Whale is sighted Ahab lingers, looks over the sea, considers his ship, says goodbye to his masthead. He admits to Starbuck he foreknows his death: the prophecies are fulfilled. In his last speech he moans only that his ship perishes without him:

Oh, lonely death on lonely life! Oh, now I feel my topmost greatness lies in my topmost grief.

He rushes to the White Whale with his old curse dead on his lips.

The last words spoken to him from the ship had been Pip's: "O master, my master, come back!"

What Pip wrought in Ahab throws over the end of *Moby-Dick* a veil of grief, relaxes the tensions of its hate, and permits a sympathy for the stricken man that Ahab's insistent diabolism up to the storm would not have evoked. The end of this fire-forked tragedy is enriched by a pity in the very jaws of terror.

The lovely association of Ahab and Pip is like the relations of Lear to both the Fool and Edgar. What the King learns of their suffering through companionship with them in storm helps him to shed his pride. His hedging and self-deluding authority gone, Lear sees wisdom in their profound unreason. He becomes capable of learning from his Fool just as Captain Ahab does from his cabin-boy.

In *Lear* Shakespeare has taken the conventional "crazy-witty" and brought him to an integral place in much more than the plot. He is at center to the poetic and dramatic conception of the play. Melville grasped the development.

Someone may object that Pip is mad, not foolish. In Shakespeare the gradations subtly work into one another. In *Moby-Dick* Pip is both the jester and the idiot. Before he is frightened out of his wits he and his tambourine are cap and bells to the crew. His soliloquy upon their midnight revelry has the sharp, bitter wisdom of the Elizabethan fool. And his talk after his "drowning" is parallel not only to the Fool and Edgar but to Lear himself.

A remark in *Moby-Dick* throws a sharp light over what has just been said and over what remains to be said. Melville comments on Pip:

all thy strange mummeries not unmeaningly blended with the black tragedy of the melancholy ship, and mocked it.

For Pip by his madness had seen God.

Shakespeare, concluded

Melville was no naïve democrat. He recognized the persistence of the "great man" and faced, in 1850, what we have faced in the 20th century. At the time of the rise of the common man Melville wrote a tragedy out of the rise, and the fall, of uncommon Ahab.

In the old days of the Mediterranean and Europe it was the flaw of a king which brought tragedy to men. A calamity was that which "unwar strook the regnes that been proude." When fate was feudal, and a great man fell, his human property, the people, paid.

A whaleship reminded Melville of two things: (1) democracy had not rid itself of overlords; (2) the common man, however free, leans on a leader, the leader, however dedicated, leans on a straw. He pitched his tragedy right there. America, 1850 was his GIVEN:

"a poor old whale-hunter" the great man;
fate, the chase of the Sperm whale, plot (economics is the administration of scarce resources);
the crew the commons, the Captain over them;

EQUALS:

tragedy.

For a consideration of dominance in man, read by all means the chapter in *Moby-Dick* called "The Specksynder," concerning emperors and kings, the forms and usages of the sea:

Through these forms that certain sultanism of Ahab's brain became incarnate in an irresistible dictatorship.

For be a man's intellectual superiority what it will, it can never assume the practical, available supremacy over other men, without the aid of some sort of external arts and entrenchments, always, in themselves, more or less paltry and base.

Nor will the tragic dramatist who would depict mortal indomitableness in its fullest sweep and direct swing, ever forget a hint, incidentally so important in his art, as the one now alluded to.

Much, much more.

Melville saw his creative problem clearly:

He had a prose world, a NEW.
But it was "tragedie," old.
Shakespeare gave him a bag of tricks.

The Q.E.D.: *Moby-Dick*.

The shape of *Moby-Dick,* like the meaning of its action, has roots deep in THE PLAYS. Melville studied Shakespeare's craft. For example, *characterization.* In at least three places Melville analyzes *Hamlet.* There are two in *Pierre.* One enlarges upon the only note he writes in his copy of the play: "the great Montaignism of Hamlet." The third and most interesting passage is in *The Confidence-Man.* There Melville makes a distinction between the making of "odd" and the creation of "original" characters in literature. Of the latter he allows only three: Milton's Satan, Quixote, and Hamlet. The original character is

like a revolving Drummond light, raying away from itself all round it—everything is lit by it, everything starts up to it (mark how it is with Hamlet).

Melville likens the effect to "that which in Genesis attends upon the beginning of things." In the creation of Ahab Melville made the best use of that lesson he knew how.

Structure, likewise. *Moby-Dick* has a rise and fall like the movement of an Elizabethan tragedy. The first twenty-two chapters, in which Ishmael as chorus narrates the preparations for the voyage, are precedent to the action and prepare for it. Chapter XXIII is an interlude, "The Lee Shore"; Bulkington, because he is "right reason," is excluded from the tragedy. With the next chapter the book's drama begins. The first act ends in the "Quarter-Deck" chapter, the first precipitation of action, which brings together for the first time Ahab, the crew, and the purpose of the voyage—the chase of the White Whale. All the descriptions of the characters, all the forebodings, all the hints are brought to their first manifestation.

Another interlude follows: Ishmael expands upon "Moby-Dick" and "The Whiteness of the Whale."

Merely to summarize what follows, the book then moves up to the meeting with the *Jeroboam* and her mad prophet Gabriel (chp. LXXI) and, after that, in a third swell, into the visit of Ahab to the *Samuel Enderby* to see her captain who had lost his arm as Ahab his leg to Moby-Dick (chp. C). The pitch of the action is the storm scene, "The Candles." From that point on Ahab comes to repose, fifth act, in his fate.

In this final movement Moby-Dick appears, for the first time. It is a mistake to think of the Whale as antagonist in the usual dramatic sense. (In democracy the antagonisms are wide.) The demonisms are dispersed, and Moby-Dick but the more assailable mass of them. In fact the actual physical whale finally present in *Moby-Dick* is more comparable to death's function in Elizabethan tragedy: when the white thing is encountered first, he is in no flurry, but quietly gliding through the sea, "a mighty mildness of repose in swiftness."

Obviously *Moby-Dick* is a novel and not a play. It contains creations impossible to any stage—a ship the *Pequod,* whales, Leviathan, the vast sea. In the making of most of his books Melville used similar things. In *Moby-Dick* he integrated them as he never had before nor was to again.

The whaling matter is stowed away as he did not manage the ethnology of *Typee* nor was to, the parables of *The Confidence-Man.* While the book is getting under way—that is, in the first forty-eight chapters—Melville allows only four "scientific" chapters on whaling to appear. Likewise as the book sweeps to its tragic close in the last thirty chapters, Melville rules out all such exposition. The body of the book supports the bulk of the matter on the Sperm whale—"scientific or poetic." Melville carefully controls these chapters, skillfully breaking them up: the eight different vessels the *Pequod* meets as she moves across the oceans slip in and cut between the considerations of cetology. Actually and deliberately the whaling chapters brake the advance of the plot. Van Wyck Brooks called them "ballast."

Stage directions appear throughout. *Soliloquies,* too. There is a significant use of the special Elizabethan soliloquy to the skull in Ahab's mutterings to the Sperm whale's head in "The Sphinx" (chp. LXX). One of the subtlest *supernatural effects,* the "low laugh from the hold" in the "Quarter-Deck" scene, echoes Shakespeare's use of the Ghost below ground in *Hamlet.*

Properties are used for precise theater effect. Ahab smashes his quadrant as Richard his mirror. Of them the Doubloon is the most important. Once Ahab has nailed the coin to the mast it becomes FOCUS. The imagery, the thought, the characters, the events precedent and to come, are centered on it. It is there, midstage, Volpone, gold.

Of the soliloquies Ahab's show the presence of *Elizabethan speech* most. The cadences and acclivities of Melville's prose change. Melville characterized Ahab's language as "nervous, lofty." In the soliloquies it is jagged like that of a Shakespeare hero whose speech like his heart often cracks in the agony of the fourth and fifth acts.

The long ease and sea swell of Ishmael's narrative prose contrasts this short, rent language of Ahab. The opposition of cadence is part of the counterpoint of the book. It adumbrates the part the two characters play, Ishmael the passive, Ahab the active. More than that, it arises from and returns, contrapunto, to the whole concept of the book revealed by the notes in Melville's copy of Shakespeare—the choric Ishmael can, like the Catskill eagle, find the light, but Ahab, whose only magic is Goetic, remains dark. The contrast in prose repeats the theme of calm and tempest which runs through the novel. Without exception action rises out of calm, whether it is the first chase of a whale, the appearance of the Spirit Spout, the storm, or the final chase of Moby-Dick precipitously following upon "The Symphony."

As the strongest literary force Shakespeare caused Melville to approach tragedy in terms of the drama. As the strongest social force America caused him to approach tragedy in terms of democracy.

It was not difficult for Melville to reconcile the two. Because of his perception of America: Ahab.

It has to do with size, and how you value it. You can approach BIG America and spread yourself like a pancake, sing her stretch as Whitman did, be puffed up as we are over PRODUCTION. It's easy. THE AMERICAN WAY. Soft. Turns out paper cups, lies flat on the brush. N.G.

Or recognize that our power is simply QUANTITY. Without considering purpose. Easy too. That is, so long as we continue to be INGENIOUS about machines, and have the resources.

Or you can take an attitude, the creative vantage. See her as OBJECT in MOTION, something to be shaped, for use. It involves a first act of physics. You can observe POTENTIAL and VELOCITY separately, have to, to measure THE THING. You get approximate results. They are usable enough if you include the Uncertainty Principle, Heisenberg's law that you learn the speed at the cost of exact knowledge of the energy and the energy at the loss of exact knowledge of the speed.

Melville did his job. He calculated, and cast Ahab. BIG, first of all. ENERGY, next. PURPOSE: lordship over nature. SPEED: of the brain. DIRECTION: vengeance. COST: the people, the Crew.

Ahab is the FACT, the Crew the IDEA. The Crew is where what America stands for got into *Moby-Dick*. They're what we imagine democracy to be. They're Melville's addition to tragedy as he took it from Shakespeare. He had to do more with the people than offstage shouts in a *Julius Caesar*. This was the difference a Declaration of Independence made. In his copy of the play Melville writes the note

TAMMANY HALL

in heavy strokes beside Casca's description of the Roman rabble before Caesar:

> If the tag-rag people did not clap him and hiss him, according as he pleas'd and displeas'd them, as they use to do the players in the theatre, I am no true man.

Melville thought he had more searoom to tell the truth. He was writing in a country where an Andrew Jackson could, as he put it, be "hurled higher than a throne." A political system called "democracy" had led men to think they were "free" of aristocracy. The fact of the matter is Melville couldn't help but give the "people" a larger part because in the life around him they played a larger part. He put it this way:

> This august dignity I treat of, is not the dignity of kings and robes, but that abounding dignity which has no robed investiture.

> Thou shalt see it shining in the arm that wields a pick and drives a spike; that democratic dignity which, on all hands, radiates without end from God; Himself! The great God absolute! The center and circumference of all democracy! His omnipresence, our divine equality!

> If, then, to meanest mariners, and renegades and castaways, I shall hereafter ascribe high qualities, though dark; weave round them tragic graces; if even the most mournful, perchance the most abased, among them all, shall at times lift himself to the exalted mounts; if I shall touch that workman's arm with some ethereal light; if I shall spread a rainbow over his disastrous set of sun; then against all mortal critics bear me out in it, thou just Spirit of Equality, which hast spread one royal mantle of humanity over all my kind!

Remember Bulkington.

To MAGNIFY is the mark of *Moby-Dick*. As with workers, castaways, so with the scope and space of the sea, the prose, the Whale, the Ship and, OVER ALL, the Captain. It is the technical act compelled by the American fact. Cubits of tragic stature. Put it this way. Three forces operated to bring about the dimensions of *Moby-Dick:* Melville, a man of MYTH, antemosaic; an experience of SPACE, its power and price, America; and ancient magnitudes of TRAGEDY, Shakespeare.

It is necessary now to consider *Antony and Cleopatra,* the play Melville pencilled most heavily. Rome was the World, and Shakespeare gives his people and the action imperial size. His hero and heroine love as Venus and Mars, as planets might.

> His legs bestrid the ocean; his rear'd arm
> Crested the world.

So Cleopatra dreamed of Antony. Melville marked her words. He marked Antony's joyful greeting to Cleopatra after he has beaten Caesar back to his camp:

> O thou day o' th' world!

And Cleopatra's cry of grief when Antony dies:

> The crown o' th' earth doth melt.

Antony and Cleopatra is an East. It is built as Pyramids were built. There is space here, and objects big enough to contest space. These are men and women who live life large. The problems are the same but they work themselves out on a stage as wide as ocean.

When Enobarbus comments on Antony's flight from Actium in pursuit of Cleopatra, we are precisely within the problems of *Moby-Dick:*

> To be furious
> Is to be frighted out of fear, and in that mood
> The dove will peck the estridge. I see still
> A diminution in our captain's brain
> Restores his heart. When valour preys on reason
> It eats the sword it fights with.

In exactly what way Ahab, furious and without fear, retained the instrument of his reason as a lance to fight the White Whale is a central concern of Melville's in *Moby-Dick*. In his Captain there was a diminution in his heart.

From whaling, which America had made distinctly a part of her industrial empire, he took this "poor old whale-hunter," as he called him, this man of "Nantucket grimness and shagginess." Out of such stuff he had to make his tragic hero, his original. He faced his difficulties. He knew he was denied "the outward majestical trappings and housings" that Shakespeare had for his Antony, his Lear and his Macbeth. Melville wrote:

> Oh, Ahab! what shall be grand in thee, must needs be plucked at from the skies, and dived for in the deep, and featured in the unbodied air!

He made him "a khan of the plank, and a king of the sea, and a great lord of leviathans." For the American has the Roman feeling about the world. It is his, to dispose of. He strides it, with possession of it. His property. Has he not conquered it with his machines? He bends its resources to his will. The pax of legions? the Americanization of the world. Who else is lord?

Melville isolates Ahab in "a Grand-Lama-like exclusiveness." He is captain of the *Pequod* because of "that certain sultanism of his brain." He is proud and morbid, willful, vengeful. He wears a "hollow crown," not Richard's. It is the Iron Crown of Lombardy which Napoleon wore. Its jagged edge, formed from a nail of the Crucifixion, galls him. He worships fire and swears to strike the sun.

OVER ALL, hate—huge and fixed upon the imperceptible. Not man but all the hidden forces that terrorize man is assailed by the American Timon. That HATE, extra-human, involves his Crew, and Moby-Dick drags them to their death as well as Ahab to his, a collapse of a hero through solipsism which brings down a world.

At the end of the book, in the heart of the White Whale's destruction, the Crew and Pip and Bulkington and Ahab lie down together.

> All scatt'red in the bottom of the sea.

FACT # 2 is dromenon

FACT # 2

On the night of January 26, 1824, as the Nantucket whaleship the *Globe*
cruised in the Pacific Ocean off Fannings Island, latitude 3 49′ North, longitude
158 29′ West, one of the vessel's two harpooneers, called boatsteerers,
Samuel B. Comstock, aged 21, the son of a Quaker schoolmaster of Nantucket
and a descendent on his mother's side of the Mitchells, a family as organic to
the life of the island as the Coffins, Starbucks, Gardners and Macys, went
down into the cabin shortly after 12 o'clock and, with a short axe, split the
Captain's head in two as he slept, killed the Chief Mate the same way, confronted the two remaining officers with the cry, "I am the bloody man, I have
the bloody hand and I will have revenge," shot the Third Mate with a musket
and left the Second Mate dying from the wounds he gave him with a boarding
knife, a two-edge instrument four feet long, three inches wide, used in whaling
to cut the blubber from the body of a whale.

PART THREE
Moses

The book of the law of the blood

In *Moby-Dick* the sea, its creature, and man are all savage. The Whale is "athirst for human blood." Ahab has "that that's bloody on his mind." The sea will "forever and forever, to the crack of doom, insult and murder man."

It is cannibalism. Even Ishmael, the orphan who survives the destruction, cries out: "I myself am a savage, owing no allegiance but to the King of Cannibals; and ready at any moment to rebel against him."

It is the facts, to a first people.

(Nothing is without efficient cause)

1. Melville wanted a god. Space was the First, before time, earth, man. Melville sought it: "Polar eternities" behind "Saturn's gray chaos." Christ, a Holy Ghost, Jehovah never satisfied him. When he knew peace it was with a god of Prime. His dream was Daniel's: the Ancient of Days, garment white as snow, hair like the pure wool. Space was the paradise Melville was exile of.

When he made his whale he made his god. Ishmael once comes on the bones of a Sperm whale pitched up on land. They are massive, and he is struck with horror at the "antemosaic unsourced existence of the unspeakable terrors of the whale."

When Moby-Dick is first seen he swims a snow-hill on the sea. To Ishmael he is the white bull Jupiter swimming to Crete with ravished Europa on his horns: a prime, lovely, malignant, white.

2. Melville was agonized over paternity. He suffered as a son. He had lost the source. He demanded to know the father.

Kronos, in order to become god, armed himself with a sickle and castrated his father Uranus. Saturn used a pruning knife. Kronos and Saturn in turn were overthrown by their sons banded together in a brother horde. The new gods of Jupiter were, in their turn, attacked by other sons. These sons—they were the "Giants"—lost. They are described as more akin to men.

Enceladus was among them. He is a constant image in Melville. Melville saw his likeness in defeated and exiled heroes, not in successful sons who, by their triumph, become the fathers.

3. The fable of *Moby-Dick* is vengeance. On a previous voyage Ahab and the White Whale had met and fought. The whale had suddenly swept "his sickle-shaped lower jaw beneath him" and reaped away Ahab's leg—"as a mower a blade of grass in the field."

(Osiris, Egyptian hero and god, was mangled by his son and enemy Seth in the shape of a boar, rent into fourteen pieces and scattered on the Nile, where fish ate his phallus.)

Ahab then had one purpose: "an audacious, immitigable, and supernatural revenge." For Ahab "piled upon the whale's white hump the sum of all the general rage and hate felt by his whole race from Adam down."

4. It is necessary to understand this rage and hate. Melville is not Jonathan Edwards. His answer to the angry god is an Ahab, a man of elements not of sins:

> Talk not to me of blasphemy, man; I'd strike the sun if it insulted me.

Melville's ethic is mythic. Shame with him was precedent to any Eden, was of Prime: the concord of Space, "sweet milk" to Melville as universal peace was to Shakespeare's Malcolm, was curdled and made sour by man, and blood.

It was not acts but Act, Original Act, that gave man guilt. Man's "imperial theme" is the fruit of First Murder.

Crime is large and imponderable when a man's experience of violence is mutiny, on wide sea. To kill a Captain!

Conscience is not the caliper to measure it:

> (remember the story of the ship the *Town-Ho* in *Moby-Dick?* who can pass judgment on Steelkilt when it is the White Whale who executes justice on the First Mate, Radney?)

immediately that Macbeth murders the King he strides hugely forward into the mystery. He steps from Scotland into the spheres to be damned:

Thou seest the heavens, as troubled with man's act
Threaten his bloody stage.

Space and time were not abstraction but the body of Melville's experience, and he cast the struggle in their dimension. The White Whale became the biggest single creature a man has been pitted against and Ahab's rage and hate is scaled like Satan's, the largest enemy of the Father man has imagined.

5.   Ahab's birth was dark, uncanonical. Starbuck took him for "more demon than man." To Stubb he was "old man of oceans." Ishmael saw him "gnawed within and scorched without." Ahab felt himself to be "deadly faint, bowed and humped as though I were Adam."

Ahab had known an earlier terror than the sea. He had woe on him. He was branded with a "slender rod-like mark, lividly whitish" the length of him. The prophet Elijah told Ishmael that Ahab lay in a trance like dead for three days and nights off Cape Horn. At another time he looked like a man cut away from a stake.

The night of "The Candles," when lightning turns his masts to tapers, Ahab seizes the conductor chains of his ship. He does it, he says, to match his blood with fire. He cries up into the night:

Oh, thou clear spirit, of thy fire thou madest me,
and like a true child of fire, I breathe it back to thee.

(There is a myth that Prometheus did more than steal fire from the sun and bring it down to man: it is said that Prometheus fathered man.)

6.   In *Moby-Dick,* when Ishmael has said all he can say about Ahab, he admits that the larger, darker, deeper part of the man is obscure. He suggests the same holds true for any man and insists it is necessary to go down to a place far beneath a man's upper earth in order to uncover the unknown part.

There, he says, a man will find that his root of grandeur, his whole awful essence sits in bearded state

an antique buried beneath antiquities and throned on torsos.

Ishmael makes this comment:

So, with a broken throne, the great gods mock that captive king.

He answers his own question who the king is:

it is your own grim sire, who died beget ye, exiled sons.

Then, for a climax, offers this enigma:

from him only will the old State-secret come.

The Melville who wrote *Moby-Dick* had a firm hold on that secret. He was a strong and sure-footed son as a result. He was not weakened by any new testament world. He had reached back to where he belonged. He could face up to Moses: he knew the great deed and misdeed of primitive time. It was in himself.

This once he had his answer—how man acquires the lost dimension of space. There is a way to disclose paternity, declare yourself the rival of earth, air, fire and water.

Now he counted his birthdays as the Hebrews did: a son's years gathered not from the son's birth but from the father's death. Another Moses Melville wrote in *Moby-Dick* the Book of the Law of the Blood.

PART FOUR
Christ

for Edward Dahlberg, my other genius of the Cross and the Windmills. If the Fool is in this book, you nurtured him.

Melville read *Don Quixote* as you have. He did it at a most important time, when he was turning for succor, as I imagine you have turned, to the Mediterranean world, and Christ. He acquired his copy in September, 1855.

Two of the passages he marked belong to your experience as to his. I want you particularly to have them:

Sancho Panza alone believed all that his master said to be true, knowing who he was, and having been acquainted with him from his birth.

The other is Don Antonio's cry against all the Simon Carrascos of life who gloat when they have unseated a poor Knight:

Oh! sir, God forgive you the injury you have done the whole world, in endeavoring to restore to his senses the most diverting madman in it.

Christile

In 1841 Melville had gone to the Pacific. In 1856 he went to the Holyland. It is in such contrast that the work of his last forty years, from *Moby-Dick* in 1851 to his death in New York in 1891, stands to the Pacific experience and the books which issued from it: *Typee, Omoo, Mardi, White-Jacket,* and *Moby-Dick.*

The trip of 1856 is an unnatural twin to the better known earlier voyage. He made it at a critical time in his career and it tells, as story, what is the truth, as I see it, of his loss of power.*

When he set out in October of that year he had reasons of health for doing so. The writing of *Moby-Dick* had hurt him. He was 31. The immediate labor on *Pierre* aggravated his condition. It went so far his family in 1853 called in doctors, among them Oliver Wendell Holmes, Pittsfield neighbor, to judge his sanity.

As early as 1851 Melville had figured it would help if he got away. A relative who came to call in December shortly after the publication of *Moby-Dick* reported her conversation with Melville to Duyckinck in New York:

> I laughed at him somewhat and told him that the recluse life he was leading made
> his city friends think that he was slightly insane—he replied that long ago he
> came to the same conclusion himself but if he left home to look after Hungary
> the cause in hunger would suffer.

---

* The principal acts of the last forty years are: *Pierre,* a novel of New York, written 1851–2 (1852); "Bartleby the Scrivener," "The Encantadas" and "Benito Cereno," three important short prose pieces, two of them throw-backs to the Pacific; first published in Putnam's Monthly Magazine, 1853, '54, '55, collected in *The Piazza Tales* (1856); *The Confidence-Man,* a novel called a "masquerade," apparently written from 1854 to 1856 (1857); the Holyland journey, October 1856–May 1857; verse from 1859 on, including the two-volume narrative in four parts *Clarel, A Poem and Pilgrimage in the Holyland* (1876); and the return to prose, *Billy Budd, Foretopman,* a short novel, written 1888–91, found in mss. 1919.

By 1856 and the writing of *The Confidence-Man,* wild and whirling words, the whole persistent multitude of Melvilles and Shaws felt that something had to be done, that there had to be some disposition, once and for all, of this man whom some tolerated and others feared, and of whom most were ashamed and all seemed weary. The money for the trip came from his father-in-law, Justice Shaw. This time Melville did not go away on his own; he was—though guardedly—sent away.

In England, to book passage on a Mediterranean steamer, he visited Hawthorne. Hawthorne describes him as "looking much as he used to do (a little paler, and perhaps a little sadder), a rough outside coat, and with his characteristic gravity and reserve of manner." The two men spent a day by the sea near Southport, sheltering themselves from the wind in a hollow among the sandhills. They had what Melville calls in his journal simply "good talk." Hawthorne, in his, says more:

> Melville, as he always does, began to reason of Providence and futurity, and of everything that lies beyond human ken, and informed me that he had "pretty much made up his mind to be annihilated"; but still he does not seem to rest in that anticipation, and, I think, will never rest until he gets hold of a definite belief.
>
> It is strange how he persists—and has persisted ever since I knew him, and probably long before—in wandering to and fro over these deserts, as dismal and monotonous as the sandhills amid which we were sitting. He can neither believe, nor be comfortable in his unbelief; and he is too honest and courageous not to try to do one or the other.
>
> If he were a religious man, he would be one of the most truly religious and reverential; he has a very high and noble nature and is better worth immortality than most of us.

Hawthorne saw Melville again the day before he sailed: "He said that he already felt better than in America; but observed that he did not anticipate much pleasure in his rambles, for the spirit of adventure is gone out of him. He certainly is much overshadowed since I saw him last; but I hope he will brighten as he goes onward."

Seven years earlier, before *Moby-Dick,* Melville had almost made the same trip. 1849, at sea, bound for England to sell *White-Jacket:*

> This afternoon Dr Taylor and I sketched a plan for going down the Danube from Vienna to Constantinople; thence to Athens on the steamer; to Beyroot and Jerusalem—Alexandria and the Pyramids. . . .

> I am full (just now) of this glorious Eastern jaunt. Think of it: Jerusalem and the
> Pyramids!—Constantinople, the Aegean and also Athens!

Age 37 now, Melville goes to the Mediterranean world to refresh himself.
He offers himself, as he says, a "passive subject" to a more immediate past
than at 21 he had found in primitive Polynesia.

He does not bring back a *Typee*. The *Journal Up the Straits* is an uncreated
thing. It is the record of Melville's rediscovery of the East and then, his loss of it.
The story can be told now that Raymond Weaver has, after much labor, made
the text available. It lies under the *Journal*'s illegible surface.

The sun and the darker races stirred up feelings Melville had for twelve years
beaten back, even as he worked. In spite of his writing he had become wedded
to a white guilt. The pressures had originated from his environment America
and tightened inwards. The stifling forces had a traitorous agent to help them:
the ethical and Northern Melville.

There seems no doubt he brought back from the South Seas a number of
shames, social shames to add to earlier ones reaching back to his father's sins
and failures. Melville's behavior in the years 1851–56 was ill. He remained periodically violent to his wife, and strange with his mother. There was shock in
him. *Pierre* is documentation enough. Add *The Confidence-Man*. In each Christ
is of the subject and the matter.

In the *Journal Up the Straits* the story of Melville's return starts after Cape
Finisterre is passed, off Cape Vincent. The entry for that day is a dumb show
of what is to follow. The contraries of the man who now turns to the East for
some resolution of them lie in these natural sentences, as outward as gestures:

Sunday, Nov. 23, 1856	Sunday 23d. Passed within a third of a mile of Cape St. Vincent. Light house & monastery on bold cliff. Cross. Cave underneath light house. The whole Atlantic breaks here. Lovely afternoon. Great procession of ships bound for Crimea must have been descried from this point.

Melville had started a ghost. What he sees on the cliff is, quick, his, life: HEIGHT
and CAVE, with the CROSS between. And his books are made up of these things:
light house, monastery, Cross, cave, the Atlantic, an afternoon, the Crimea:
truth, celibacy, Christ, the great dark, space of ocean, the senses, man's past.

•   •   •

First act, the Mediterranean. It is reiteration, it might have been rite. Melville makes this entry his first day on it: "Pacific." A Noah, Melville had dominated and survived his Flood. *Moby-Dick,* ark, is behind him, and so are the waters of his Flood, the Atlantic and the Pacific. He returns to smaller waters, the Mediterranean. "In landlessness alone resides the highest truth, shoreless, indefinite as God," Melville had written, to characterize Bulkington, in the "Lee Shore" chapter of *Moby-Dick.*

The Mediterranean is a close sea, is in the middle of the land, is the old center of earth. On its shores Noah's children, Shem, Ham and Japheth, and their sons, have worked out life since flood. Melville had the alternative Noah had when the waters shrank: to be a husbandman. There was much for him to do—as much had been done—from Genesis on, before Christ. Melville had room in an old testament world, ample space and time to reify. There was a Covenant for him to share, the everlasting one between God and every living creature of all flesh that is upon the earth. The pity of it, in 1856, is this: the only place Melville manages to see the token of covenant, the rainbow, is over the waters of the Dead Sea.

He missed his own truth. The Atlantic, the Pacific and the Mediterranean formed a trinity more natural to him, as poète d'espace, than that other Trinity, that desert he chose to wander to and fro in, his last forty years. "Ego non baptizo te in nomine Patris et Filii et Spiritus Sancti—sed in nomine Diaboli."

Constantinople gave Melville back to sensation. He had shown a marked interest in the women of two harems aboard ship on the passage in. He likens the city to a woman: "The fog lifted from about the skirts of the city. . . . It was a coy disclosure, a kind of coquetting . . . like her Sultanas she was thus seen veiled in her 'ash-mack.'" It is an unusual image for Melville to use. There is not only an absence of palpable woman in his works, there is rarely a sense of what accompanies her, clothes, charm, pleasure. Fayaway, of *Typee,* perhaps, as a memory, a dream. There are the two pairs, Lucy and Isabel of *Pierre* and their prototypes, Yillah and Hautia of *Mardi.* And there is only one other, the best of them, the Chola Widow of "The Encantadas," who takes body from the tale of her suffering.

The two pairs are unfelt and unfleshed. Hautia is a Pacific island "Queen" whom Melville, in trying to turn into a Salem witch, handles as gingerly as Cotton Mather did poor Margaret Rule. She is unburnt, unconfessed, her "zone unbound," "brazen" and inviting, "I the vortex that draws all in," absurd. Isabel too. She is Melville's chromo Cenci, sorceress and "sister" to Pierre, their common spell a lampish incest. Lucy, meant to be as Yillah a contrast, is a "betrothed" who sketches and sews, a chalkish lady, a lace of "earthly frailty" who can give Pierre nothing but a text: "heaven hath called me to a wonderful office toward thee"!

That Melville did, on this trip, at Constantinople and elsewhere, find some spontaneity toward woman suggests a change in the contours of his psyche profound enough to free forces in him long checked. He ranges the polyglot city wildly, writes about it extravagantly. He mixes in the crowds of the suburbs of Galata and Pera. He mounts the bridges to watch them moving below. When he leans over the First Bridge his body is alive as it has not been since he swung with Jack Chase in maintops above the Pacific. The difference: he is brooding over a city of a million and a half human human beings, not so many square miles of empty ocean:

> To the Bazaar. A wilderness of traffic. Furniture, arms, silks, confectionery, shoes, sandles—everything. (Cairo). Crowded overhead with stone arches, with side openings.
>
> Immense crowds. Georgians, Armenians, Greeks, Jews, & Turks are the merchants. Magnificent embroidered silks & gilt sabres & caparisons for horses.
>
> You loose yourself & are bewildered & confounded with the labyrinth, the din, the barbaric confusion of the whole.
>
> The Propontis, the Bosphorus, the Golden Horn, the domes, the minarets, the bridges, the men of war, the cypresses. Indescribable.

What is common to all passages is the attention to the human and natural, the concrete, what has been husbanded. Architecture buds and leafs. He finds the source of the mosque dome in the tents of the nomadic tribes, the form of the minaret in the cypress tree. Asia and Europe confronting each other at the Bosphorus are two women in "a contest of beauty." The color of Asia is "like those Asiatic lions one sees in menageries—lazy & torpid."

Turn your attention now to stone. To stone as it is. As it is built with. As it is rubble.

Turn first to standing stone, to Egypt. The *Journal* comes to climax before the Pyramids.

Whether it is the appropriation of space involved or the implied defiance of time or the enceladic assault on the heavens, MASONRY is especially associated with MYTH in man. The tale of the Great Tower is as ultimate a legend as the Flood, Eden, Adam.

Whatever the explanation of the great pyramid at Cholula or the source of Plato's description of the watchtowers of Atlantis, they, like the Pyramids, partake of this need of man to persist in monument as well as in myth. The temple of the sun at Babel was named E-sagila, meaning, the House of the Lifting of the Head.

THE PYRAMIDS loom, a long slope of crags and precipices, the tablerock overhanging, adhering solely by mortar, twisted at angles like broken cliffs. Masonry—and is it man's? The lines of stone do not seem like courses of masonry, but like strata of rocks. Slanting up the sweeping flanks people move like mules on the Andes. They ascend guided by Arabs in flowing white mantles, conducted as by angels. These are the steps Jacob lay at.

I shudder at the idea of the ancient Egyptians. It was in these pyramids that the idea of Jehovah was born. A terrible mixture of the cunning and the awful. Moses was learned in all the lore of the Egyptians.

No wall, no roof. In other buildings, however vast, the eye is gradually inured to the sense of magnitude, by passing from part to part. But here there is no stay or stage. It is all or nothing. It is not the sense of height or breadth or length or depth that is stirred. It is the sense of immensity that is stirred.

The theory that they were built as a defense against the desert is absurd. They might have been created with the Creation.

As with the ocean, you learn as much of its vastness by the first five minutes' glance as you would in a month, so with the pyramid.

Its simplicity confounds you. Finding it vain to take in the sea's vastness man has taken to sounding it and weighing its density; so with the pyramid, he measures the base and computes the size of individual stones. It refuses to be studied or adequately comprehended. It still looms in my imagination, dim and indefinite.

The tearing away of the casing, though it removed enough stone to build a walled-town, has not one whit subtracted from the apparent magnitude. It has had just the contrary effect. When the pyramid presented a smooth plane, it must have lost as much in impressiveness as the ocean does when unfurrowed. A dead calm of masonry. But now the ridges majestically diversify.

It has been said in panegyric of some extraordinary works of man, that they affect the imagination like the works of Nature. But the pyramid affects one in neither way exactly. Man seems to have had as little to do with it as Nature.

It was that supernatural creature, the priest. They must needs have been terrible inventors, those Egyptian wise men. And one seems to see that, as out of the crude forms of the natural earth they could evoke by art the transcendent mass and symmetry and awe of the pyramid, so out of the rude elements of the insignificant thoughts that are in all men, they could rear the transcendent conception of a God.

But for no holy purpose was the pyramid founded.

Nor *Moby-Dick* written. But see how Melville turned, turned to stone as it is rubble, to Judea:

> Stones of Judea. We read a good deal about stones in Scriptures. Monuments & memorials are set up of stones; men are stoned to death; the figurative seed falls in stony places; and no wonder . . . Judea is one accumulation of stones.

It is LAST ACT. When Melville went from the Pyramids to Jerusalem he lost all he had gained. The power so to describe the Pyramids leaves him, as did the power to do *Moby-Dick,* prey to Christ. He had observed in Egypt that the Sphinx has its "back to desert & face to verdure." Melville reversed his Sphinx. He thought he faced verdure in Christ. It turned out to be desert.

Barrenness of Judea

> Whitish mildew pervading whole tracts of landscape—bleached—leprosy—encrustation of curses . . . bones of rocks, —crunched, knawed, & mumbled—mere refuse & rubbish of creation. . . .

> No moss as in other ruins—no grace of decay—no ivy— the unleavened nakedness of desolation—whitish ashes—lime-kilns—You see the anatomy—compares with ordinary regions as skeleton with living & rosy man.

Two weeks in the Holyland sealed Melville in a bitterness of disillusion from which he never recovered, out of which, fifteen years later, he wrote *Clarel,* that rosary of doubt, a two-volume *Poem and Pilgrimage in the Holyland* and, thirty-odd years later, *Billy Budd,* that most Christian tale of a ship, and mutiny. The stones, the rubble in the pool of Bethesda, Sodom's "bitumen & ashes," the Dead Sea with the foam on its beach "like slaver of mad dog," and the Holy Sepulcher "a sickening cheat" led Melville to one final question:

> Is the desolation of the land the result of the fatal embrace of the Deity?

Melville became Christ's victim, and it was death, and lack of love, that let him be it. "Poor soul, the centre of my sinful earth," Shakespeare wrote. Melville became unsure of the center. It had been strong, a backward and downward in him like Ahab's, like a pyramid's:

The old mummy lies buried in cloth on cloth; it takes time to unwrap this Egyptian king.

With the coming of despair he called it a bulb of nothing. In the middle of the writing of *Moby-Dick* he wrote to Hawthorne:

But I feel that I am now come to the inmost leaf of the bulb, and that shortly the flower must fall to the mould.

In *Pierre*—it was between these two books that the change came—he wrote:

By vast pains we mine into the pyramid; by horrible gropings we come to the central room; with joy we espy the sarcophagus; but we lift the lid—and no body is there!—appallingly vacant as vast is the soul of man!

He denied himself in Christianity. It is space, and its feeding on man, that is the essence of his vision, bred in him here in America, and it is time which is at the heart of Christianity. What the Pacific had confirmed for him he allowed Christ to undo. It was on the promise of a future life that Melville caught.

Death bothered him. That bare-headed life under the grass, his own, worried him, in Dickinson's words, like a wasp. He looked for solace to the Resurrection. He got nothing. For the loss of mortality he got nothing in return. The dimensions of life as he had felt them merely dwindled. Objects lost their gravity as they bulk in space.

All he has left in 1856 is the shell of his own faith: he tells Hawthorne he has "pretty much made up his mind to be annihilated." The charge Melville levels at Christ in *Clarel* is the lie in the promise of life beyond death:

Behold him—yea—behold the Man
Who warranted if not began
The dream that drags out its repulse.

He mocks Christ with His own cry to the Father, why hast Thou forsaken me:

Upbraider! we upbraid again.

The sense of life and death that Melville forfeited is one the experience of space gives. The vision of it is *Moby-Dick,* and its savage myth. In *Pierre* it is reduced, as Melville was, to statement. There are two passages which speak out, fatty as the prose is. They may say why Christ hampered him. One is a celebration of Enceladus for his war with the other Giants to reclaim his birthright from the father. That was battle for mortality as Melville understood it best, and on which his imagination fed. The other passage celebrates annihilation freed from the doubt Christ brought:

Of old Greek times, before man's brain went into doting bondage, and bleached and beaten in Baconian fulling-mills, his four limbs lost their barbaric tan and beauty; when the round world was fresh, and rosy, and spicy, as a new-plucked apple; —all's wilted now!—in those bold times, the great dead were not, turkey-like, dished in trenchers, and set down all garnished in the ground, to glut the damned Cyclop like a cannibal; but nobly envious life cheated the glutton worm, and gloriously burned the corpse; so that the spirit up-pointed, and visibly forked to heaven!

Somewhere Yeats uses the phrase "sighing after Jerusalem in the regions of the grave." Christ's slide of future life deflected Melville's sight of past. Melville had made his act of faith in *Mardi:* "My memory is a life beyond birth." His natural sense of time was in its relation to space. It was not diverted as Christ's was, away from object, to the individual, and the passage of the personal soul. To Melville the intimate and the concrete of the present, as for example he felt it at Constantinople, enabled a man to loose himself into space and time and, in their dimensions, to feel and comprehend such an object as the Pyramids, to create, in like dimensions, an Ahab and a White Whale. Time was not a line drawn straight ahead toward future, a logic of good and evil. Time returned on itself. It had density, as space had, and events were objects accumulated within it, around which men could move as they moved in space. The acts of men as a group stood, put down in time, as a pyramid was, to be reexamined, reenacted. He wrote in *Mardi:*

Do you believe that you lived three thousand years ago? No. But for me, I was at the subsiding of the Deluge, and helped swab the ground, and build the first house.

With the Israelites, I fainted in the wilderness; was in court when Solomon outdid all the judges before him.

I, it was, who suppressed the lost work of Manteo, on the Egyptian theology, as containing mysteries not to be revealed to posterity, and things at war with the canonical scriptures.

Melville was.

I have called *Moby-Dick* a book of the Old Dispensation. Christ's dispensation was as strange to Melville as it would have been to the First Adam.

Hawthorne was right, Melville could not rest without a belief, he had to have a god. In *Moby-Dick* he had one. I called him the Ancient of Days. The job was a giant's, to make a new god. To do it, it was necessary for Melville, because Christianity surrounded him as it surrounds us, to be as Anti-Christ as Ahab was. When he denied Ahab, he lost the Ancient. And Christianity closed in. But he had done his job.

Christ as god contracted his vision. The person of Jesus was another matter. Melville never did come to tolerate the god, and the religion. He merely surrendered to it. The result was creatively a stifling of the myth power in him. The work from *Moby-Dick* on is proof. Melville was the antithesis of Dante. When he permitted himself to try to put his imagination to work in a world of Christian values, as he first did in *Pierre,* it is disaster. *Pierre* is a Christ syllogism: "I hate the world." *The Confidence-Man, Clarel,* and *Billy Budd* are sorites which follow from it.

Melville paid with his flesh too. What he was left with, when he had lost his myth to Christ, was the image of Jesus the person, and he spent forty years trying to turn Him into someone he could love. But those Melville turned to for love, turned away: his mother first, his sister Augusta to her Bible, Hawthorne to his notebook to write: "Herman Melville's linen is none too clean." By the time Melville wrote *Pierre* sex had become to him "the idiot crowned with straw." In the year of his death he published these lines:

> What Cosmic jest or Anarch blunder
> The human integral clove asunder
> And shied the fractions through life's gate? *

After *Moby-Dick* Melville had only Jesus left as the image of what he calls in *Clarel* his "fonder dream of love in man toward man."

After Ahab his men decline. They are either abstraction, Pierre, or epicene, Billy Budd. Bartleby is an exception—he is parsed into being like the Carpenter in *Moby-Dick*. Benito Cereno is another exception.† The rest are portraits of Jesus: "soft, hermaphroditical Christs." They seek to come together with one another, to close "like halves of apple sweet":

> "After confidings that should wed
> Our souls in one:—Ah, call me *brother!*"
> So feminine his passionate mood
> Which, long as hungering unfed,
> All else rejected or withstood.

The character of Vine in *Clarel* is a denominator. He has "no trace of passion's soil," is shy and languid, has resisted some "demon" of desire in his "Adam's secret frame"—and shows "disuse of voice." Ahab's Pacific has shrunk to Sodom lake.

---

* They are from a poem based on an incident of the 1856 trip. It is called "After the Pleasure Party" and is addressed to "Amor Threatening."

There is another curious reflection of woman. It is the only comment Melville made in his copy of *Don Quixote,* which he read, it will be remembered, in 1855–56. It refers to this passage of Cervantes:

> I have already often said it, and now repeat it,
> that a knight-errant without a mistress is like
> a tree without leaves, a building without cement,
> a shadow without a body that causes it.

The note in Melville's hand reads:

> or as Confucius said 'a dog without a master,'
> or, to drop both Cervantes & Confucius parables
> —a god-like mind without a God.

† Both belong, along with the Chola Widow, to that short return, after *Pierre,* to his source of power the Pacific, and the last throw it gave him, from 1853 to 1855. It was the last, to those of us who find the admiration for *Billy Budd* largely a technical one. Men do lose out.

The men are also physically flawed, and in mean ways, as if it were Melville's personal revenge on flesh, not the ways of gods and whales who mangled and branded Ahab because he dared to match them in huge contest of elemental force. In *Clarel,* Vine's double, Celio, is a hump-back, a creature of "crook and lump." In *The Confidence-Man* a Negro beggar crawls along the deck of the Mississippi steamboat a cripple, Pip befouled. And the end of them all, Billy or "Baby" Budd, the Latter-day Ishmael, has a stutter. The stutter is the plot. Unable to speak Billy strikes out with his fist and kills his accuser, Claggart, the Master-At-Arms.

It all finally has to do with the throat, SPEECH. Jesus unstrung him. The creator of *Moby-Dick* comes to value the secretive and silent, what lack of love had made his flesh. The American Elizabethan ends by agreeing with a Maurice de Guérin:

> There is more power and beauty in the well-kept secret of one's self and one's thoughts than in the display of a whole heaven that one may have inside one.

Melville's comment, 1869:

> This is the finest verbal statement of a truth which everyone who thinks in these days must have felt.

In *The Confidence-Man,* when Melville used Christ himself directly as a character, he clothed him in white doe-skin—and made him a MUTE.

THE EPILOGUE of the '56 *Journal.* Off Cyprus, on his way from the Holyland to Greece, Melville can no more imagine a Venus to have risen from these waters than "on Mt. Olivet that from there Christ rose."

In *Moby-Dick,* in his analysis of what is the hidden nature of the Pacific he had compared its "gentle awful stirrings" to the "fabled undulations of the Ephesian sod over the buried Evangelist St. John." Now, off Patmos, he can "no more realize that St. John had ever had revelations here."

It is the denial. He has faced about, and goes West, to suffer the balk the rest of his days on earth.

A LAST FACT

A LAST FACT

In the back pages of the second of the two notebooks which go to make the *Journal Up the Straits,* among scattered notes which can be identified as directions made by Melville to himself for (1) stories he did not later write but turned into verse, (2) for travel lectures he had to give to help support his family the three years immediately following his return, and (3) for *Clarel,* you will find one note unrelated to the others and untraceable to the *Journal* or later work, a title, a noun (or another title) and a name, as Melville set them down together, in a triangle thus:

Eclipse.

Noah after the Flood.   Cap.[tain] Pollard.
                                                     of *Nant.*[ucket]

PART FIVE
Noah

for Constance

The conclusion: Pacific man

There was a story told before Christ of a fisherman of Boeotia named Glaucus who found an herb to revive fish as they lay gasping on shore. He ate it himself and was changed into a sea thing, half fish half man. Melville told Hawthorne he dated his life from his return from the Pacific.

> *Moby-Dick*
> Chapter CXI
> "The Pacific"
> When gliding by the Bashee isles we emerged at last upon the great South Sea; were it not for other things, I could have greeted my dear Pacific with uncounted thanks, for now the long supplication of my youth was answered; that serene ocean rolled eastward from me a thousand leagues of blue.
> There is, one knows not what sweet mystery about this sea. . . . .

What the Pacific was to HM:

(1) *an experience of SPACE* most Americans are only now entering on, 100 years after Melville. Of waters, as Russia of land, the Pacific gives the sense of immensity. She is HEART SEA, twin and rival of the HEARTLAND.

The Pacific is, for an American, the Plains repeated, a 20th century Great West. Melville understood the relation of the two geographies. A Texas painter settled in Brittany and spent his life on canvases of French fishermen and the Atlantic Ocean. But the paint, the motion, the reality turned out to be the Plains. Each canvas was the Panhandle seen through a screen of sea.

Space has a stubborn way of sticking to Americans, penetrating all the way in, accompanying them. It is the exterior fact. The basic exterior act is a BRIDGE. Take them in order as they came: caravel, prairie schooner, national road, railway, plane. Now in the Pacific THE CARRIER. Trajectory. We must go over space, or we wither.

Exception: the plane. It is a *time* experience, not of space. *Speed* is its value. The vertical is still will. Flight does not turn out to be the conquest Daedalus and Da Vinci imagined it to be. We are (inevitably?), as humans, Antaean: only in touch with the land and water of the earth do we keep our WEIGHT, retain POTENTIAL. Melville kept his by way of the Pacific.

(2) *a comprehension of PAST,* his marriage of spirit to source. The Pacific turned out to be his Atlantis, the buried place. The Pacific was "father," older than America, "new-built Californian towns," older than Asia, and Abraham:

> this mysterious, divine Pacific zones the world's whole bulk about; makes all coasts one bay to it; seems the tide-beating heart of earth. Lifted by these eternal swells, you needs must own the seductive god . . .

In Homer the god of genesis was "River Ocean." The Greeks had a myth that Venus was born from the foam of a tidal wave which swept the Aegean after the genitals of Kronos, sickled off by his son, fell into the sea.

Ishmael had to go far down below Ahab's upper earth to find out Ahab's father. Melville's voyage to the Pacific at 21 was a similar quest. The Pacific carried him, much as it did the little Negro Pip, when he drowned, to "wondrous depths where strange shapes of the unwarped primal world glided to and fro before his passive eyes." In *Moby-Dick* Melville speaks of "ocean's utmost bones":

> To have one's hands among the unspeakable foundations, ribs, and very pelvis of the world; this is a fearful thing.

In another place, the chapter THE GILDER, he is describing the Pacific, and how land-like a calm of its waters can be, when he bursts out:

> Where is the foundling's father hidden? Our souls are like those orphans whose unwedded mothers die in bearing them; the secret of our paternity lies in their grave, and we must there to learn it.

In the deep, where Pip saw "God's foot on the treadle of the loom," Melville found Ahab's "grim sire," and the State-secret. Pip came to the surface mad, Melville possessed of his imagination. The Pacific gave him the right of primogeniture.

The Egyptians believed that Osiris, after he was mutilated by his son Seth, had to be buried in the Nile and carried with the mud into the Mediterranean before he could become King of Eternity, Lord of the Underworld, and, his chief attribute, Ruler of the Dead. Noah was Osiris to the Hebrews, and it can be said of him as the Egyptians said: "This is the form of him whom one may not name, Osiris of the mysteries, who springs from the returning waters." In *Mardi* Melville wrote: "Who may call to mind when he was not? To ourselves we all seem coeval with creation. King Noah fathered us all!" After Pacific flood Melville took his dead to be all the fathers and sons of man. The Pacific taught him how to repeat great RITES, of spring. The unceasing ebb and flow took him into a patrimony of Past:

> And meet it is, that over these sea-pastures, wide-rolling watery prairies and Potters' Fields of all four continents, the waves should rise and fall; for here, millions of mixed shades and shadows, drowned dreams, somnambulisms, reveries; all that we call lives and souls, lie dreaming, dreaming still; tossing like slumberers in their beds; the ever-rolling waves but made so by their restlessness.

It was in meadows of brit he found his seed.

The Pacific was also:

(3) *a confirmation of FUTURE.* We think we measure the significance of Columbus and his discoveries. We still fail to calculate the consequence of Magellan's discovery of the Pacific. 3000 years went overboard, and the gains are still unaccomplished.

First, the economic history. Up to the discoveries of the 15th century the Mediterranean remained the center of the world. The basis of commerce was the spices and fine goods of the Orient. It was a trade in luxuries, of high value and small bulk because of limited transportation. The spices varied and made palatable the coarse food of the Middle Ages. The fine goods satisfied a need for comfort, a hunger for beauty, and a desire for display. Venice, then Florence was metropolis.

Columbus operated on the theory: sail to the West and the East will be found. He made the Atlantic the central sea. The mercantilism of 1500–1800 followed. It was the substitution of the Atlantic for the Mediterranean which worked a revolution for England. She was at the center, midway between the Baltic and the Mediterranean and thrust out toward the New World.

With the Pacific opens the NEW HISTORY. Melville: "It rolls the midmost waters of the world, the Indian Ocean and the Atlantic but its arms." The movement into it during the 19th century, of which Melville was a part, makes the third great shift.

Melville felt the movement as American. He understood that America completes her West only on the coast of Asia. He was a sea frontiersman like the whalers Fanning, Delano and other outriders. He was a contemporary in the Pacific of Commodore Charles Wilkes and the U.S. Exploring Expedition, 1838–1842. Later, when Commodore Perry wanted a writer to tell the story of the opening of Japan, Hawthorne recommended Melville as the Pacific man.

I said 3000 years went overboard in the Pacific. I was going back to Homer. The evolution in the use of Ulysses as hero parallels what has happened in economic history.

Homer was an end of the myth world from which the Mediterranean began. But in Ulysses he projected the archetype of the West to follow. It was the creative act of anticipation.

Homer's world was locked tight in River Ocean which circled it, in Anaximander's map, like a serpent with tail in mouth. But in the *Odyssey* Ulysses is already pushing against the limits, seeking a way out. Homer gave his hero the central quality of the men to come: *search, the individual responsible to himself.*

We forget that by 200 B.C. the scope of Western thought had been more or less outlined. The Mediterranean world was already born: the Athenians complain about the vulgar exchanges and busy wharves of Piraeus. Even the range of action has been prospected: Plato has located Atlantis *outside* Homer's terminus, the Pillars of Hercules.

By 1400, in Dante's hands Ulysses is again prospective. He is already an Atlantic man. In the *Inferno* he speaks, a Columbus, to his crew:

"O brothers!" I said, "who through a hundred thousand dangers have reached
the West, deny not, to this the brief vigil of your senses that remains, experience
of the unpeopled world behind the sun."

He bends the crew to his purpose, forces them West. They drive through the Pillars, cross the Equator, and after five months on the Atlantic find the New Land only to be destroyed and drowned before they can touch on it.

At the end of the *Paradisio,* when from the seventh sphere the earth is so small its features are obscured as the moon's to us, Dante recognizes one spot on all its surface—that entrance to the West, the Pillars. Dante's last glance is on the threshold to that future Columbus made possible.

The third and final odyssey was Ahab's. The Atlantic crossed, the new land America known, the dream's death lay around the Horn, where West returned to East. The Pacific is the end of the UNKNOWN which Homer's and Dante's Ulysses opened men's eyes to. END of individual responsible only to himself. Ahab is full stop.

Porphyry wrote that the generation of images in the mind is from water.

The three great creations of Melville and *Moby-Dick* are Ahab, The Pacific, and the White Whale.

The son of the father of Ocean was a prophet Proteus, of the changing shape, who, to evade philistine Aristaeus worried about bees, became first a fire, then a flood, and last a wild sea beast.

(1947)

On Melville, Dostoevsky, Lawrence, and Pound

David Young, David Old

F. Barron Freeman. *Melville's Billy Budd.* Cambridge, Mass.: Harvard University Press, 1945.

Outside of Hart Crane's natural and personal interest in Herman Melville's story of the Handsome Sailor, Billy Budd (Crane used to read it, I was told, to other Billies in Brooklyn, to charm them) and outside of one image in Auden's verses on Melville ("It is evil that is helpless like a lover and has to pick a quarrel, and succeeds") only two men can be said to have added anything to the two years, his last two, that Melville spent on the tale. F. Barron Freeman has now made himself one of those two.

The other, of course, was that gentle, dedicated man Raymond Weaver, that Tobias, who went off last spring and met the Angel. It was Weaver, and Eleanor Melville Metcalf, who found the story in manuscript in 1921, as Melville left it, and it was Weaver who first transcribed it, more accurately, Freeman's new transcription now reveals, than anyone, including Freeman himself, if Freeman is to be judged by his errors of reading from the longer of the two pages of the manuscript reproduced in his book.

What Mr. Freeman has done is something vastly more important than another text of *Billy Budd, Foretopman.* By an illuminated act of scholarship he has uncovered, from the paste and pin-up of the 36,000 word manuscript, where all others have missed it, Melville's original version of the tale, a 12,000 word short story which he has now published, alongside the novel but separate from it, under the title "Baby Budd, Sailor."

To make clear why I take it that this discovery of Freeman's is of first importance I must do what he has not done (to the detriment of his book and the invalidation of most of his long and academic introduction) nor, so far as I am aware, anyone except Richard Chase and myself, and he from other needs.

That is, to consider *Billy Budd, Foretopman* as something less than the latter-day gem it has been taken for.

I have found the story as we have had it a painful book, and have felt the interest in it, Weaver's, Crane's, Auden's, to mention three I respect, to be more amorous than imaginative. Melville's was, I am sure, and if he had not been prevented from joining his natural imagination to his love (I think we can put our finger on who prevented him) he would have written a major work. For the matter of the story—Billy the Innocent, Claggart the Master-at-Arms whose longing for Billy is twin to malice, and Vere the Captain who orders Billy hung —had a density Melville nowhere else took up (three, & primal, a triad as native to his genius as Adam, Serpent, God the Father). It is because at no point, in not one single phrase or image, even where the phrase, the situation or the image quite clearly tries to go to this hebraic heart of the matter, has Melville done it that I have found the story—it was Weaver who started the fashion to call it a "novel"—painful. *Pierre* is endurable, there are perceptions in it, strokes through the mask which *Moby-Dick* does not contain. Likewise *The Confidence-Man*. *Clarel* is endurable, because it is verse, and we excuse Melville. But *Billy Budd,* can anyone who has gone a little way into the cave of this man, has felt his air, had the thread in hand, heard the animal of the maze, can anyone be moved by anything here other than the myrrh of Melville's love for Billy (we always go farthest with our flesh). I have asked myself, is it possible that others genuinely feel Melville's accent, motion, depth in these chapters which dry up in futile digressions, in these sentences which ground on commonplace? I have not been able to believe, have deeply disbelieved and, except for those who have legitimately fallen in love with love, have distrusted the book's explainers.

They have been of two classes (or is it one). There are those of dull mind who take what is obvious, Melville's intent, and prove it where he has not. I have nothing but scorn for such pietism. The others (and they are more disturbing) are those among us who nourish themselves on that favorite posing of it, Original Sin. It is a curious trait, American surely, an act of fear in men and art. It has to do with a guard and sword against passion. Such people, whenever they find Hawthorne or Melville or Eliot interesting himself in the idea, using the phrase, band together (like patriots, or aunties) and make a cause. It is very dull. They should be reminded of what the Fox said to Mr. Eliot one fine day: "It ain't Original Sin that done us in, Possum, it's o-riginal in-nate stu-pidity!"

On *Billy Budd* these characters (and they bulk among critics, of Melville and of writing today) have sucked. Not without their reason. This once this Anak of a man tried to handle evil and innocence, his primal stuff, Cain and Eden, by the book, by concept and demonstrandum. Why? He was old. It is not true he grew. I too have measured whether there is in the language a calm deliberately sought, in the idea of a resolution of his permanent quandaries: I have asked, is this a writer's tale, a master's "Tempest"? What I have found is a pitiful thing, a moving thing, which I offer as closer to the answer: matters of magnitude proper to the man proffered in the style and process of another. For if there is myrrh in *Billy Budd,* for Billy, there is frankincense, and it is for Nathaniel Hawthorne.

Billy Budd, Foretopman is the work of a man and a wraith, and though Freeman has been alert enough to emphasize the importance of Melville's direct reference to Hawthorne's "The Birthmark" in the passage on the flaw in Billy's perfection, his stutter, he has not seen what his discovery of the short story "Baby Budd" makes it possible to see, that between the original version of the tale and Melville's rewrite of it Hawthorne intervened, and stole a strength away.

Hawthorne was long dead, and longer was the physical separation between the two men. They had been neighbors in the Berkshires for a year and a half 40 years earlier when Melville was 31 and writing *Moby-Dick. Moby-Dick* is inscribed to Hawthorne.

But time is nothing where a man of Melville's passion is concerned. This is peculiarly true of *Billy Budd,* and significant of the layer of his being Melville was working from in it. For the other man whose domination over Melville's heart is here involved is even farther removed in time than Hawthorne himself. Melville had not seen or heard of Jack Chase, to whom *Billy Budd* is dedicated and who, as much as anyone else, was the prototype of Billy, since they were shipmates together when Melville was 24.

There are two levels of love operative in *Billy Budd* (which is itself Melville's poor book of the revelations of love). That of the plot is obvious, yet to Freeman's credit he has, more thoroughly than any previous commentator, exhibited the homosexuality resident to all three of the men of the tragedy. But there is this other love implicit in the book's final presentation and it can no longer go unrecognized. For Hawthorne was as joined to Melville in his own mind as Jonathan to David, and though, in its beginnings, this love was good, when it was planted in Melville young, in the end the tree that flourished from it rove the giant out of Samuel.

The story of the composition of Billy Budd turns out to be the exact contrary to the story of the composition of *Moby-Dick*. There, a first version done quick emerged, after a year of rewrite, as the book we know and can call Melville poet for. Two things happened at the moment of the change, summer 1850; Melville read Shakespeare strong, and met Hawthorne for the first time. But here, at the end of Melville's life, it now appears that the first version of another tale done in a little under four months (November 16, 1888 to March 2, 1889) instead of gaining force was, for two full years, until April 18, 1891 (Melville died in September), worked over and over as though the hand that wrote was Hawthorne's, with his essayism, his hints, the veil of his syntax, until the celerity of the short story was run out, the force of the juxtapositions interrupted, and the secret of Melville as artist, the presentation of ambiguity by the event direct, was lost in the Salem manner.

Thanks to Freeman we can now know that. His removal of the short story from the novel impresses me the more in that the very passages which have kept me from a toleration of the "novel," every one, are what Freeman lists as the "insertions" and "drastic expansions" of the last two years.

If we do not act on that knowledge and accept Melville's first intent rather than his rewrite we will do him, old, such a disservice out of piety as he did to himself out of amor; what he did not with *Moby-Dick,* when Hawthorne was alive and fresh and Shakespeare new to him, and Melville took the double charge.

Was it not Heraclitus who said that to take thought is to thicken the blood around the heart?

(1949)

The Materials and Weights
of Herman Melville

Luther S. Mansfield and Howard P. Vincent, eds. *Moby-Dick*. New York: Hendricks House, 1952; Ronald Mason. *The Spirit above the Dust.* London: John Lehmann, 1951; Lawrence Thompson. *Melville's Quarrel with God.* Princeton, N.J.: Princeton University Press, 1952.

1

I have added Mr. Ronald Mason's book to the two books I was asked to review for the *New Republic* simply because its intelligence and limpidity measures the soddenness of the scholarship of the new edition of *Moby-Dick* and the perverseness of thinking in *Melville's Quarrel with God.* But more than that: Mr. Mason's book is the triumph of the several books which have tried to throw light on Melville's work with the foot-candle of rationalism, that series of critiques which can be said to start with John Freeman's biography, to include Mr. Mumford's more troubled rationalism, and to run the list of the bead-telling books of the last years: Matthiessen's, Sedgwick's, Chase's, Arvin's, and Brooks'—perhaps Yvor Winters' and Auden's *The Enchafèd Flood*—in other words, a rosary of praise which has (with some quietness and a little decency) been the private act of these men.

I am at some pains to see the story of Melville critique and scholarship whole, and set it before you, just because there is now so much of it: his importance is so crucial that some sharpness, and an effort at a discrimination of the present state of the knowledge of it, seems to me to be called for. For example: face to face with such a monster as this new edition of *Moby-Dick,* its stomach gurgitating 250 pages of footnotes—probably in quantity the equal of the actual pages of the text itself, I toyed with the notion of using this space to try to establish Some Principles Toward a Correct Editing of *Moby-Dick,* as severe a list of such simple demands as, say, George Lyman Kittredge might have expected from anybody doing a book on Chaucer. You yourself would feel this validity of old-fashioned scholarship if you had to grapple with the pretentiousness, the ignorance, and the intolerable ill-proportion of this work of two highly placed professors.

Or, confronted by this other sort of professor, Thompson (a newer member of the Melville lobby), I was tempted to write an essay for you on *Clarel,* that thorough thing in which that most serious man Melville tried, almost with his hands gone, to expose to any American's view in 1876 the worsening of the society of the West and the struggle of himself, in the midst of it, to keep

> Faith (who from the scrawl indignant turns
> >   With blood warm oozing from her wounded trust
> Inscribes even on her shards of broken urns
> >   The sign of the cross—the spirit above the dust!

The fact which you would not believe is, that this Mr. Thompson has written a 450-page book on the subject of Melville and God—and has given only four pages to *Clarel!*

In my quandary, a friend happened to put Mr. Mason's book in my hands; and its decency, its seriousness and the deftness of its proportion (in this respect I'd guess the most considered of all the critiques—I happen also to like, myself, Geoffrey Stone's *Melville,* though his engagement, from a Catholic position, makes for an easier ordering than Mr. Mason's less positioned spiritual one) made it possible for me to feel less burdened. And I was free to try to do two other things: to bring the total Melville picture into some sort of focus, and to offer whatever insights five additional years of work of my own might bring to correct or add to the measurement of Melville I offered in *Call Me Ishmael.*

The very badness of the two American books under review does oblige a man to call attention to such exceptional biographical scholarship as Jay Leyda's in his *Melville's Log* (I have not yet read Leon Howard's biography), to Harrison Hayford's work (still, I believe, an unpublished dissertation), to Henry A. Murray's continuing application of developed psychological tools to the question of the nature of Melville's personality, to manuscript scholarship of the usableness of F. Barron Freeman's edition of *Billy Budd,* and to the scrupulous steady study of Melville's library and his reading that Merton Sealts has been engaged in for better than ten years. These are men whose work I know and can respect—can encourage any of you to turn to, who want to add such knowledges to the experience of the reading of Melville's books.

Two others I might mark: Miss Wright, whose book, *Melville's Use of the Bible,* goes a very great way to help to right perhaps the most prevalent error of contemporary Melville critique—the tendency of it to exaggerate the New Testament and Christ as against the less conscious attention Melville gave the Old Testament as a source for himself (he went, it might be useful to remind a contemporary reader, to Judeo-Christianity as Picasso has said he went to the Communist Party—to draw from it, as women go to the fountain of the town to draw water for the daily uses of their family). A man whose work on *Clarel* I only know by snatches, Walter Bezanson, once readers have the old-fashioned concentration of mind Melville had, and had the nerve to write to, will show itself to be much more the true other weight to *Moby-Dick* of Melville's involvement with Judeo-Christian values than *Billy Budd.* You can expect *Clarel,* in fact, soon to have attention, as *The Confidence-Man* is now receiving its first attention—Melville's most considered examination of the second of his three great sources, America, the experiment of these States. So just as Mr. Chase gave the latter a fair go, Mr. Mason has given *Clarel* the beginning of its due.

Which leaves me with my tribe of men—and the chance to go a little free, and come to Melville. For now I can single out Raymond Weaver, can think about Hart Crane's amorous uses of Melville's *Billy Budd* and *Moby-Dick* (evidence of Robert Creeley's important observation that Crane had literally no other device in life than poetry, and when he thought poetry had failed him, or he had failed it, he killed himself). I can continue to trouble myself about a most different using of Melville—Edward Dahlberg's, in *Do These Bones Live.* I can also ask myself why William Carlos Williams has always drawn a blank on Melville; interested in the conundrum, as I am, because of a like care to Melville's with which Williams has devoted himself, from *In the American Grain* on, to the nature of the American consciousness. Williams is like Melville, a man who registers the going-ons of all of the human beings he lives among. He sees charge in them, worth in their fires, also a fire his own burns in, as against Ezra Pound, with that selection out of, that "the light in the conversations of—the letters of—the intelligent ones," or at least the literate ones).

And I can end this whole first part of the job I wanted to do for you—give the focus its proper depth—by not letting you or myself forget what these editors of *Moby-Dick* have so outrageously neglected to mention, that the man who more and more stands up as the one man of this century to be put with Melville, Dostoevsky and Rimbaud (men who engaged themselves with modern reality in such fierceness and pity as to be of real use to any of us who want to take on the post-modern) is D. H. Lawrence. He wrote two chapters on Melville in his *Studies in Classic American Literature* which, although they are not the equal of his Whitman chapters, are worth, to men of soul, what Melville's own words are worth.

It is those words in those novels in prose and verse, from 1846 to 1891, I propose to lead you back to. And I propose to do it by what I have found the most valuable thing in all three of these new Melville books under review, a passage from Goethe's *Dichtung und Wahrheit* which Melville is known to have read at the time he was conceiving the character of Ahab and the shape of the Whale. The crazy part of it is, that it is just these two egregious editors, Vincent and Mansfield, who have brought it to light!

2

How to extricate what Melville blindly knew and did from what he merely said, kept turning his mind to, or tossed up as material for his novels and poems. How to show that under-eye into which his small ones could enlarge or (to use his own image) open under water and they bloodshot, or that sort of blindness of his which continues to make *him* valuable, not his surfaces. Make a try.

Melville's importance, greater than ever, lies in (1) his approach to physical-ity, (2) his address to character as necessary human force, and (3) his applica-tion of intelligence to all phenomena as *the* ordering agent—what Creeley and I have elsewhere called the Single Intelligence, which is a better way of naming the total intelligence, simply that it is never more than the given man's act in the presence of *his* multiples. Melville, major figure just because he did take on the multiple when no one else saw it, and did risk havoc and wreck, had his formula for the distinction: he opposed "Right Reason" to reason, dubbing reason and her tools—logic and classification—"Baconianism."

Now if by stressing point 3, I appear to come down hard on the method-ological question, it is to make very certain, here at the outset, that no one should think that any of these three fronts of Melville's attack are anything but hooked together and unhookable, that any of them is not methodology; and that he, as any of us, is not solely an instrument for use. It is one of the losses of all the critique and scholarship which I am reviewing that the totality of Mel-ville's effort is not dealt with as one. And so the very extraordinary contribution

Melville did make still stays obscured. By his impeccable and continuous inquiries into what ways ideality ("transcendentalism" was the current word for it in Melville's time) no longer fit modern reality in a form proper to its content, he drove further than any of his predecessors toward forcing totality of effort to yield some principle out of itself. Leaving this out, failing to get it, makes so much of the work on Melville (the exception is D. H. Lawrence's) merely praise, dispraise, or history; in other words what is left is either the very rationalism Melville spent his life exposing, or just the facts of him without lending those facts an animation the equal of Melville's animation.

It happened that I opened to the chapter "The Tail" when this new (Mansfield and Vincent) edition of *Moby-Dick* came to hand, and I felt the wonder all over again of Melville's knowingness of object and motion, those factors of a thing which declare what we call its physicality (and do not mean physiology). "The Tail" is as lovely an evidence as any other of Melville's ability to go *inside* a thing, and from its motion and his to show and to know, not its essence alone (this was mostly the gift of ideality—of Gautama's, Socrates', or Christ's), but its *dimension,* that part of a thing which ideality—by its Ideal, its World Forms or its Perfections—tended to diminish; that quality of any particular thing or event which comes in any one of our consciousnesses; how it comes in on us as a force peculiar to itself and to ourself in any of those instants which do hit us & of which our lives are made up. We call it size; we say: it was a big thing—a kick; he's a big person; the day was a whopper. We have more of a vocabulary for the physics of it than Melville had. We know the literal space there is inside a microcosm, the nature of the motion hidden in any mass. Yet I do not know another writer except Homer who achieves by words so much of the actual experiencing of this *dimension* as Melville does.

If I put this first—if I put Melville in the context of Homer—I do it because, until any of us takes this given physicality and moves from its essence into its kinetic, as seriously as we are all too apt to take the other end—the goal, we'll not be busy about the civilization breeding as surely now as that other one was between Homer and 500 B.C. And we'll not know what Melville had started a hundred years ago. For the metaphysic now to be known *does* lie inside function, methodology is form, Rimbaud's question is the incisive one—"what is on the other side of despair?" There is no where else to go but in and through; there is no longer any least piece of pie in the sky. With Melville's non-Euclidean penetrations of physical reality ignored or avoided, all the important gains he made in expressing the dimensions possible to man and to story are also washed out.

The push Melville made beyond characterization as he inherited it, even from Shakespeare, and beyond fiction was inevitable, given the stance he took toward object moving in space. With such a sense of totality and yet with senses crisp enough to keep him usually safe from generalization, he had to go beyond the familiar causatives of environment, psychology and event—at least event as reduced as modern event is, seen only as the eye of the needle and the camel left out.

Several of the Melville books will be at pains to show that he did not lose any of these factors in his drive beyond them, especially those which apply crudely or sometimes finely contemporary disciplines proceeding from Marx, Freud, and Neo-Christianity. I would only get into this game to keep those players from neglecting, by their own rules, such a passage as that in *The Confidence-Man* in which Melville likens character, in this case Hamlet's, to a Drummond light raying out from itself on all other things by movement from its sources on all sides; or to insist upon the importance of "The Specksynder" chapter in *Moby-Dick,* calling attention to the new evidence of Goethe's influence on that chapter. (It is to Luther Mansfield's credit that he has brought the *Dichtung und Wahrheit* passages to light.) But the fact is that the sultanism that Goethe enabled Melville to expose by way of Ahab leaves such achievements of Melville only prophetic, like his discoveries in *Pierre* which the Freudians find pioneer or those meta-psychic ones in *Moby-Dick* which Jung has acknowledged. In "The Specksynder" passage Melville even uses just such signal words of recent political and economic fact as "dictatorship" and "centralization" ("the plebian herds crouch abased before the tremendous centralization").

It is in more thorough depths of this engagement with what men are—less substantive, and more to do with the morality implicit in form—where Melville can stand examination and more serve us. In the "Ambiguities" (Ronald Mason rightly insists upon the significance of this subtitle to *Pierre*) which tested Melville, he tried to go beyond the anti-hero. In creating the anti-hero Ahab and in trying to go beyond him, Melville put himself squarely up against the hero, and thus at the heart of narrative and verse now. I throw down the proposition that Billy Budd is a Christian Hero (it is an oxymoron: a Christian can only be a saint). And it is as perverse of the Neo-Christian critics to read Melville's Christianity their way (to fail to see what *Billy Budd* cost him) as it is for Marxians and Freudians to put Melville's pains their way. For Melville grasped the archaeological man and by doing it entered the mythological present. *Moby-Dick* is the evidence. The rest of his work is the defeat which is still our own.

Melville already knew what none of the moderns today yet know by having, in the anti-hero Ahab, confronted any good or evil negatively, and the rest of his work was a huge effort to do it the other way—to achieve personage instead of characterization. He did not see man as measure of man (Ahab got him over that Renaissance stile) but as limit. Thus he had the totalness to lend any of his creations such insides that only in his work among the moderns (not in Joyce's, say) can any of us involved in the post-modern struggle find lessons proper to the dimensional rather than the essential problem of the Hero (all that I read is either the essence or the documentation, never the act).

It was one of the several vulgarities of the two editors of this new *Moby-Dick*, that they put Melville's use of Lord Nelson in *Billy Budd* in such flatness as: Nelson was "one of Melville's greatest heroes," when the text of the novel itself shows how bitterly Melville felt his failure to give Nelson (or Billy, for that matter) the proportions, sufferings and relevances he knew man as hero to be.

In fact here is that limit of Melville which might also be seen to have been Rimbaud's, that both of them, in wholly differing ways, were prevented from work beyond what they did do (what cannot be said of Dostoevsky or Lawrence except in a dull absolute way) by an exasperation that a reality equivalent to their own penetration of reality had not come into being in their time. They both had, in themselves, manumitted man from the inaccurate estimate of reality men have had to go by since the Ionians. Both had seen ideality for the discrepancy it is. There are signs that Rimbaud had been so fierce as to come to totality, the condition of the Hero. Melville couldn't; the appeal of Christ was so strong on him. But he knew. For he had got as far as Ahab in the attack against organization or false form in men, society, or nature. Christ did stay so much the image of perfection to Melville, who had gone so far back into the nature of things that he had also given men their first image, since the biblums, of Chaos or Pre-Form, the Dragon as White Whale. In any case, the debate in his nature rove Melville, and left the job he was so much the more capable to do still to be done. He was too American to have the logic Rimbaud had—to quit, and to make money.

(1952)

Equal, That Is, to the Real Itself

Milton R. Stern. *The Fine Hammered Steel of Herman Melville*. Urbana: University of Illinois Press, 1957.

Two years before Melville was born John Keats, walking home from the mummers' play at Christmas 1817, and afterwards, he'd had to listen to Coleridge again, thought to himself all that irritable reaching after fact and reason, it won't do. I don't believe in it. I do better to stay in the condition of things. No matter what it amounts to, mystery confusion doubt, it has a power, it is what I mean by *Negative Capability*.

Keats, without setting out to, had put across the century the inch of steel to wreck Hegel, if anything could. Within five years, two geometers, Bolyai and Lobatschewsky, weren't any longer satisfied with Euclid's picture of the world, and they each made a new one, independently of each other, and remarkably alike. It took thirty-one years (Melville's age when he wrote *Moby-Dick*) for the German mathematician Riemann to define the real as men since have exploited it: he distinguished two kinds of manifold, the discrete (which would be the old system, and it includes discourse, language as it had been since Socrates) and, what he took to be more true, the continuous.

Melville, not knowing any of this but in it even more as an American, down to his hips in things, was a first practicer (Rimbaud was born the year Riemann made his inaugural lecture, 1854) of the new equation, quantity as intensive.

The idea on which this book is based, naturalism, is useless to cope with Melville, either as a life lived in such a time or as an art, the first art of space to arise from the redefinition of the real, and in that respect free, for the first time since Homer, of the rigidities of the discrete. Naturalism was already outmoded by the events above, whether one takes it as an 18th or 19th century idea.

Mr. Stern, alas, takes it every way, including the unhappy thought that Melville can be put at the head of a literary use which includes Twain, Dreiser, Hemingway, and Faulkner!

It is the error on matter sitting in naturalism which gives it its appeal, that by it one can avoid the real, which is what is left out, at what cost all over the place Mr. Stern is only one of the fools of. He writes, in summary of what he takes it Melville did prove:

> that the naturalistic perception in the years of the modern could and must take from woe not only materialism but also the humanism and the deep morality of social idealism, which are the true beginnings of wisdom.

The true beginnings of nothing but the Supermarket—the exact death quantity does offer, if it is numbers, and extension, and the appetite of matter, especially in human beings.

The change the 19th century did bring about is being squandered by the 20th, in ignorance and abuse of its truth. Melville was a part of the change, and I can do nothing, in the face of this book, but try to show how, in the terms of that change. He put it altogether accurately himself, in a single sentence of a letter to Hawthorne, written when he was writing *Moby-Dick* (1851): "By visible truth we mean the apprehension of the absolute condition of present things."

All things did come in again, in the 19th century. An idea shook loose, and energy and motion became as important a structure of things as that they are plural, and, by matter, mass. It was even shown that in the infinitely small the older concepts of space ceased to be valid at all. Quantity—the measurable and numerable—was suddenly as shafted in, to any thing, as it was also, as had been obvious, the striking character of the external world, that all things do extend out. Nothing was now inert fact, all things were there for feeling, to promote it, and be felt; and man, in the midst of it, knowing well how he was folded in, as well as how suddenly and strikingly he could extend himself, spring or, without even moving, go, to far, the farthest—he was suddenly possessed or repossessed of a character of being, a thing among things, which I shall call his physicality. It made a re-entry of or to the universe. Reality was without interruption, and we are still in the business of finding out how all action, and thought, have to be refounded.

Taking it in towards writing, the discrete, for example, wasn't any longer a good enough base for discourse: classification was exposed as mere taxonomy; and logic (and the sentence as poised on it, a completed thought, instead of what it has become, an exchange of force) was as loose and inaccurate a system as the body and soul had been, divided from each other and rattling, sticks in a stiff box.

Something like this are the terms of the real and of action Melville was an early inheritor of, and he is either held this way or he is missed entirely. With one thing more: the measurement question. What did happen to measure when the rigidities dissolved? When Newton's Scholium turned out to be the fulling-mill Melville sensed it was, via Bacon, whom he called that watch-maker brain? What is measure when the universe flips and no part is discrete from another part except by the flow of creation itself, in and out, intensive where it seemed before qualitative, and the extensive exactly the widest, which we also have the powers to include? Rhythm, suddenly, which had been so long the captive of meter, no matter how good (Shakespeare, say, in our own tongue, or Chaucer), was a pumping of the real so constant art had to invent measure anew.

Watching Melville in a lifetime trying to make prose do what his body and his soul as a heap, and his mind on top of them a tangle (this is also a way of putting a man's physicality), trying to get a measure of language to move himself into a book and over to another man's experience, is a study makes more sense now, in the midst of 20th century art, painting and music as well as narrative and verse, than it could have, previously. It wasn't image, it wasn't anything he lacked. Possibly it was only any reason he might be confident he was right, taking it all so differently as he did, from those around him, at least those known to him. Or say it as my friend Landreau does, who swings, with *The Confidence-Man:* "Melville seems entitled to 'disillusion itself,' and given his personal bitter life, possibly because of that vision, in the scene, society, he had to live it in."

Who still knows what's called for, from physicality, how far it does cover and reveal? No one has yet tried to say how Melville does manage to give the flukes of the whale immediacy as such. It is easier to isolate his skill over technology than to investigate the topological both in his soul and in his writing, but it is my experience that only some such sense of form as the topological includes, able to discriminate and get in between the vague *types* of form morphology offers and the *ideal* structures of geometry proper, explains Melville's unique ability to reveal the very large (such a thing as his whale, or himself on whiteness, or Ahab's monomania) by the small.

The new world of atomism offered a metrical means as well as a topos different from the discrete. Congruence, which there, in mathematicians' hands, lifted everything forward after Lobatschewsky (via Cayley especially, another contemporary of Melville, and Felix Klein) makes much sense, as no other meter does, to account for Melville's prose. Congruence was spatial intuition to Kant, and if I am right that Melville did possess its powers, he had them by his birth, from his time of the world, locally America. As it developed in his century, congruence, which had been the measure of the space a solid fills in two of its positions, became a point-by-point mapping power of such flexibility that anything which stays the same, no matter where it goes and into whatever varying conditions (it can suffer deformation), it can be followed, and, if it is art, led, including, what is so important to prose, such physical quantities as velocity, force and field strength.

Melville's prose does things which its rhetoric would seem to contradict. He manages almost any time he wants to, for example, to endow a more general space than other writers, than anyone except Homer I find. The delivery of Tashtego from the whale's head, say. The point is also the overall "space" of *Moby-Dick*. That space, and those of which it is made up, have the properties of projective space (otherwise they should all come out more familiar, and round, because they would stay Euclidean), and I conclude that Melville could not have achieved what amounts to elliptical and hyperbolic spaces (he makes things stand out at once transparent and homogeneous) if he were not using transformations which we have not understood and which only congruence makes possible. (The lack of it, in his verse, as negativism in his life, such as Keats knew, is one of the ways of putting how far Melville *didn't* go.)

His ideas also. In spite of the vocabulary of his time, much more is to be read out of him, I suspect, than any of us have allowed. In the rest of the letter to Hawthorne from which I have quoted, he goes on to discuss the effects of the absolute of present things on self, and being, and God and his insistence there, to get God in the street, looks to me like the first rate breakthrough of man's thought which was called for at 1851: the necessary secularization of His part in the world of things. (It doesn't diminish it, that it was probably the only time in a lifetime in which Melville did manage to throw off the Semitic notion of transcendence.)

Or take him just where so much academicism has wasted its time on classic American literature, and Mr. Stern does again: the place of allegory and symbol in Melville and his contemporaries. As the Master said to me in the dream, of rhythm is image / of image is knowing / of knowing there is / a construct. It is rather quantum physics than relativity which will supply a proper evidence here, as against naturalism, of what Melville was grabbing on to when he declared it was *visible* truth he was after. For example, that light is not only a wave but a corpuscle. Or that the electron is not only a corpuscle but a wave. Melville couldn't abuse object as symbol does by depreciating it in favor of subject. Or let image lose its relational force by transferring its occurrence as allegory does. He was already aware of the complementarity of each of two pairs of how we know and present the real—image & object, and action & subject—both of which have paid off so decisively since. At this end I am thinking of such recent American painting as Pollock's, and Kline's, and some recent American narrative and verse; and at his end, his whale itself for example, what an unfolding thing it is as it sits there written 100 years off, implicit intrinsic and incident to itself.

Melville was not tempted, as Whitman was, and Emerson and Thoreau differently, to inflate the physical: take the model for the house, the house for the model, death is the open road, the soul or body is a boat, etc. Melville equally couldn't spiritualize it, as Hawthorne tried, using such sets as the mirror image, M. du Miroir, etc., and Melville himself in "The Bell Tower," but not in "The Encantadas," or "Bartleby," and how explain the way the remark "The negro" does hold off and free in *Benito Cereno?* Melville wouldn't have known it to say it this way, but he was essentially incapable of either allegory or symbol for the best of congruent reason: mirror and model are each figures it Euclidean space, and they are *not* congruent. They require a discontinuous jump.

Finally, to take the possibilities here suggested, at their fullest—the actual character and structure of the real itself. I pick up on calm, or passivity, Melville's words, and about which he knew something, having served as a boat-steerer himself, on at least his third voyage on a whaler in the Pacific. He says somewhere a harpoon can only be thrown accurately from such repose as he also likened the White Whale to, as it finally approached, a mighty mildness of repose in swiftness is his phrase. Likewise, in handling Ahab's monomania, he sets up a different sort of a possible man, one of a company which he calls the hustings of the Divine Inert.

I am able to stress the several aspects of Melville's thought on this because, note, in each case the feeling or necessity of the inert, or of passivity as a position of rest, is joined to the most instant and powerful actions Melville can invent: the whale itself's swiftness, Ahab's inordinate will, and the harpooner's ability to strike to kill from calm only. *The inertial structure of the world is a real thing which not only exerts effects upon matter but in turn suffers such effects.*

I don't know a more relevant single fact to the experience of *Moby-Dick* and its writer than this. Unless it is the prior and lesser but more characteristic Riemannian observation, that the metrical structure of the world is so intimately connected to the inertial structure that the metrical field (art is measure) will of necessity become flexible (what we are finding out these days in painting writing and music) the moment the inertial field itself is flexible.

Which it is, Einstein established, by the phenomena of gravitation, and the dependence of the field of inertia on matter. I take care to be inclusive, to enforce the point made at the start, that matter offers perils wider than man if he doesn't do what still today seems the hardest thing for him to do, outside of some art and science: to believe that things, and present ones, are the absolute conditions; but that they are so because the structures of the real are flexible, quanta do dissolve into vibrations, all does flow, and yet is there, to be made permanent, if the means are equal.

(1958)

Dostoevsky and *The Possessed*

Sun-worshippers had more sense than we. They reverenced something organic and necessary to flesh and bone. We give our faith to the State. Day by day the modern world confirms Dostoevsky's Grand Inquisitor in his estimate of man. Beyond Germany, Russia, and Italy, men take bread for freedom, "miracle, mystery, and authority" for faith, and Caesarism for the "universal state." In terror we face this world, but subtly and pathetically we ignore that alternative even our apologist, the Inquisitor, cannot—the fearful burden of individual free choice in the knowledge of good and evil. The war of our time is not Democracy against Fascism, the Church against Communism, but the authority of Man against the authority of the State. The Inquisitor is right—man finds it easier to give his authority away, first to the Church and now to the State. But he gives it away always at his own peril and to his own destruction. His body and his spirit dies. Today man is horrified by the smell of both corruptions.

Ours is the Karamazov way. As to old Karamazov, "everything is lawful." Fearfully, Dostoevsky sensed the disintegration in man and society. Seventy-five years ago he watched our world turning away from man to the State and set down, in his novels and in *The Diary of a Writer,* a contrary vision of life. By his "cursed questioning" he prophetically anticipated, asked and sought to answer the very questions we are lost in. No man ever knew man's power of dispersion and will to violence better than Dostoevsky. Infinitely aware of the breadth and depth of man's nature, he admitted the need of discipline. He did not seek it, as we have, outside man. Dostoevsky put his faith in, and made his demands on individual man.

Dostoevsky accepted Christ's ethics. Christianity is as essential to his work as Catholicism was to Dante's. It is a Christianity burned clean by one of man's

126

great minds, forged anew through the creative consciousness of an exceptional artist, and restored as a weapon to man. Dostoevsky did for the modern world what Christ did for the Roman: he gave man back his authority, and through Christ offered him the ways to exercise it. He himself only accomplished this dynamic reconception by a wrestling like Jacob's with the Angel. He wrote in one of his notebooks:

> It was not as a child that I learnt to believe in Christ and confess his faith. My Hosanna has burst forth from a huge furnace of doubt.

"The Legend of the Grand Inquisitor" is the testament of the struggle. After his, Jacob halted upon his thigh. Look into Dostoevsky's face in the Perov portrait, painted while *The Possessed* was in progress. A brand lies upon the temple, and the cheek and mouth are scorched. The mark is there, and the blessing. The delicate skin and the eyes bespeak hosanna. A woman in his magazine office saw that face one June night turn up to the tender summer sky as he urged upon her what glory and torment it was to speak to people of the worlds beyond this. His arms woo'd the sky away, his eyes lifted altars, and his voice, bursting chains, cried out: "To other worlds." Call him Israel. He included in *The Possessed* that lovely, strange, misunderstood remark of his:

> If anyone could prove that Christ is outside the truth, and if the truth really did exclude Christ, I should prefer to stay with Christ, and not with the truth.

From Dresden in 1870 while he was brooding over *The Possessed* he confessed to Maikov:

> The chief question by which, consciously or unconsciously, I have been tormented all my life, is the existence of God.

In that hunger of the spirit of the man, all his turning against liberalism and 2 plus 2 equals 4 science, all his reaching for Christ lies wrapped.

The Possessed has raised more questions than any other novel, and whatever answers have been offered only question Dostoevsky's success with his materials and with his conception. More and more attention has been given to *The Possessed* in recent years, perhaps just because Dostoevsky is dealing in it directly with things we and our States are faced with—revolution and the agents of revolution. The book was published in 1872 and thus comes in the middle of his mature career, after *Crime and Punishment* and *The Idiot,* and before *The Raw Youth* and *The Brothers Karamazov.* His contemporaries, both liberals and radicals, dismissed the treatment of social revolt in the book as anachronistic and malicious. Today it is found conservative or reactionary. Stavrogin remains as much an enigma as Dostoevsky's dialectic of revolution. And *The Possessed* will continue to be a failure and a puzzle, two books instead of one, a political pamphlet and a philosophical novel, just so long as we refuse to take seriously in our own world the ineluctable identity of personal and social evil. For it is precisely that identity Dostoevsky considered absolute, governed as he was by spirit: to him the exaction upon man in society is the same as that upon man in solitude. Out of this concept *The Possessed* was written and in it lies the secret of the novel's unity, that which binds the story of Stavrogin and the study of revolution together.

The Possessed is Dostoevsky's Sodom and Gomorrah: all is laid waste. It is a blood tragedy without redemption. Think of the violence of death with which the book culminates—all like swine are run violently down a steep place into the lake and are choked. Only Satan remains alive to walk the earth: Peter the conspirator lives. But Shatov is murdered, and so are the Cripple and her drunken Falstaff of a brother; Kirillov is a suicide, Lisa is horribly destroyed, Shatov's wife and Stavrogin's child are dead, and Stavrogin, the citizen of the canton of Uri, is hanging there behind the door. All, all drowned in a lake of blood. A most horrible tragedy, against which a feeble old man, Stephen Trofimovitch, alone raises his voice, only himself to die.

We also are as lost as Dostoevsky's people. Like them we feel we are possessed of devils. We sense a presence of evil so sharply we instantly recognize our own human fear in the hearts of the German people when we learn they never refer to Goebbels by name but always speak of him as "der kleine Teufel." We have gone so much farther than the world contemporary with Dostoevsky we do not need, as he did, the parable from Luke on the Demoniac of Gadara to create his symbol and his title. Our demoniac of Bavaria is alive and active and a palpable fact we are confronted by every midnight broadcast and every morning paper. And we sense though we cannot, perhaps dare not name other devils, men with umbrellas, men with mitres, men with guns. But what we do not know is how to exorcise our devils, how to save ourselves from the destruction Dostoevsky visits upon his possessed.

To Dostoevsky the answers lie deeper than the Hitlers and the Goebbels. In *The Possessed* he examined such devils in the person of Peter Verhovensky and his conspirators, and anticipated much knowledge we have had forced on us by the events of the years since the first world war and of the year of the present war. For example, in the person and "system" of Shigalev, Dostoevsky exposed the authoritarian necessity of all statism:

> Starting from unlimited freedom, I arrive at unlimited despotism. . . . Everything shall be reduced to a common denominator. Complete equality. . . . Absolute submission—no individuality whatsoever. All the slaves are equal in their slavery. . . . The first thing to do is to lower the level of education, science, and ability.

And Dostoevsky saw another face of the modern revolutionary state—its religious claims. The arch-conspirator Peter cries: "A new religion is coming instead of the old one." Dostoevsky profoundly perceived that it is actually man and not the state who is finally attacked. To him only a hideous leveling of man can come when revolution establishes itself "on the elements of science and reason." What he sensed and what we know is that the modern revolutionary state denies the dignity and the value of individual human personality. It only rises upon the destruction of the individual. And so Peter Verhovensky is right when he calls "shame at having any opinion of one's own" the most important element of the revolution, "the cement that binds everything together." Success comes to the revolution and such agents of revolution as a Peter Verhovensky or a Hitler when man forsakes himself.

That conclusion Dostoevsky drew. He found the disintegration of society a consequent of man's disintegration and not a cause. He pushed his attention beyond the enemies of man to man himself. To Dostoevsky the real danger does not lie in the devils outside ourselves. It is not finally the revolution or the revolutionaries whom Dostoevsky fears, but the prostration in man out of which Verhovenskys and Shigalevs, Hitlers and Stalins are spawned and by which they grow. So, in *The Possessed,* it is not the conspirators who dominate the book but their victims. Dostoevsky sets out to show why the victims, even to the pure in heart, allow themselves to be destroyed. They are victims not because of any real power in the conspirators but because of the lack of power in themselves. They are caught in a greater web than the web of revolution—the web of apathy. It is Stavrogin, of all the people in the novel, who is most sick. He is the disease. He is disintegration, our disintegration. In Stavrogin, Dostoevsky names us.

Dostoevsky imagines Stavrogin a soiled man, and makes him the center of the book so firmly the book actually turns upon him and has its being through him. He is the novel as Hamlet the play. Stavrogin is what the conspirator Peter calls him, "the sun," the source of the book's life. All the women except the bible-peddler exist only through their relations with him—his mother, his wife the cripple, Shatov's wife who bears Stavrogin's child, Shatov's sister Darya Stavrogin's mistress, and Lisa who finally gives herself to Stavrogin. And all the men of the book but Stephen Trofimovitch likewise—in the chapter called "Night," Kirillov, Shatov and Peter Verhovensky all admit he is their source. As Stavrogin passes from one to the other through that night of rain and mud all reveal themselves as his creatures, almost faces of himself, generated by him. Not so much generated perhaps, but set and fixed as though hypnotized by a snake, for once established by Stavrogin they cannot free themselves from his influence and come to suffer from his nature.

Stavrogin is complex, possibly the most compacted character Dostoevsky ever created. He is all three of the Karamazov brothers in one skin: he has all that is sensual in the lustiness of Dmitri, all the intellection of Ivan, and even some of Alyosha's tenderness of spirit—what Peter called Stavrogin's "simple-heartedness and naiveté." But he has none of each's counterpoise. Arrogant, and impotent from more than ennui, Stavrogin annuls himself. Compare him, in all his power, to the people of his own world. He never lives upon his pulse as Shatov does: Shatov's blow upon Stavrogin's face is a more significant, whole and vital gesture than all the violent career of Stavrogin himself. Shatov, Darya, Lisa love: Stavrogin cannot. Unlearned is his old teacher Stephen's lesson of the heart. Even as a destroyer Stavrogin is never as purposeful as the engine of hate, Peter. Nor can he die like Kirillov, by a sustained act of self.

Consider him when Peter, in a frenzy like Satan's, offers Stavrogin, a mock Christ, all the land and power stretching out from the Mountain. "You are my idol. Ivan the Tsarevitch. You! You!" Peter's Kiss, Peter's prostration: "Verhovensky besought, implored." But Stavrogin is both without temptation *and,* unlike Christ, without answer: "Stavrogin wondered smiling." For Stavrogin exists without self-generation, a still point in a horribly turning world.

That temptation is a parable of our time. For the world turns and Stavrogin, though he did not yield to the large temptation, did not answer it and, as a result, he becomes a silent accomplice in Peter's and the conspirators' murder of Shatov.

When dictators offer us states in return for our manhood we too wonder smiling, fail to answer, the world turns, and there's Guernica. For the world always turns and the Stavrogins do not move. Why? Because the essence of a Stavrogin is neuter. He *is* his world's sun, but a sun without a fire and heat of its own. He gives life to others but in himself there is finally no life. He cannot generate himself. And in that immobility lies a further horrible truth—all those separate lives which he dominates when they cross each other, destroy each other. Up to a point he creates, but he creates only finally to destroy. His light is black. And it is just because he does nothing that they destroy each other. They cancel out because he, in his neutrality, lends life to the evil as well as to the good. For Stavrogin is without choice, thus he is without direction and thus he and his world are destroyed. Ultimately, *The Possessed* is a horrible puppetry, the tragedy of the inert, the neuter, the ahuman:

> I know thy works, that thou art neither cold nor hot: I would thou wert cold or hot. So then because thou art lukewarm, and neither cold nor hot, I will spue thee out of my mouth.

Stavrogin knew himself so pathetically well he did finally do what he thought he ought to do—"brush myself off the earth like a nasty insect." His letter to Darya before his suicide poses the problem of himself clearly:

> I am still capable, as I always was, of desiring to do something good, and of feeling pleasure from it; at the same time I desire evil and feel pleasure from that too. But both feelings are always too petty, and are never very strong. My desires are too weak; they are not enough to guide me.

He has one power—Stavrogin can state Stavrogin:

> Even negation has not come from me. Everything has always been petty and spiritless.

His last sight is a moan:

> Indignation and shame I can never feel, therefore not despair.

He has divulged himself, but because he knows no other answer than himself, he dies, and brings all the world of *The Possessed* down.

Why can he not deliver himself over to life? Why can he not shed his inanition? Why must this sensually hot and intellectually cold man remain lukewarm? Why, no matter what extraordinary power he has and no matter what generation he gives others, must he be destructive of himself and all others? Why must Stavrogin forever remain outside both heaven and hell, upon a Dark Plain, under the starless air, one of Dante's Trimmers? Because he refuses to exercise what Dostoevsky regarded as that essential and precious human power —"the freedom of choice in the knowledge of good and evil." Dostoevsky, like the Prisoner Christ whom the Grand Inquisitor confronts, exalted such freedom "above everything else" and in Stavrogin he portrays the most abominable abdication of the right of such freedom. Choice is the first and last necessity of life. To choose is to take up the burden of life. But Stavrogin is suspended. He can take up neither the burden of faith nor the burden of the denial of faith. Kirillov, the man who denied God and killed himself to prove himself the mangod, bared Stavrogin's tragedy in these words:

> If Stavrogin has faith, he does not believe that he has faith. If he hasn't faith, he does not believe he hasn't.

Stavrogin is a Trimmer, unable, in Dante's words, to rebel from God or be faithful to him, one of the caitiffs:

> che non furon ribelli,
> nè fur fedeli a Dio, ma per sè foro.

With Dante Dostoevsky regards such a state of man's soul as the most corrupt of all. To choose the evil, as Peter Verhovensky does, is to be damned, but even that, to Dostoevsky, is dynamic: Dante likewise gave the wicked "glory" over the Trimmers. But to have, as Stavrogin did, an awareness of good and not to move towards it or even away from it exceeds every other moral aberration. He remains an abhorrent Laodicean.

And what is the state of Stavrogin's inner life, what *is* the lukewarm state? A swamp of self in which he is mired beyond escape. Again Dante is apposite: "ma per sè foro"—the Trimmers were not for God or against him, but "were for themselves." Stavrogin is for himself, caught by his self. Because Stavrogin denies what the Grand Inquisitor calls man's "fearful burden of free choice," he loses the sweet air of the spirit, is left with only the self, and the self increasingly suffocates him until finally he cannot survive. For without the wish for God Dostoevsky found man unmotivated, abominably static, ahuman and dead. Stavrogin is bound, therefore, to disappear, as Shatov told him he would, "like rotten mildew," because he cannot attain to God. Never can the great words pass Stavrogin's lips: "Lord, I believe, help thou my unbelief!" Because, in his heart, he cannot bow down before Stephen Trofimovitch's—and Dostoevsky's—Great Idea:

> The one essential condition of human existence is that man should always be able to bow down before something infinitely great. . . . The Infinite and the Eternal are as essential for man as the little planet on which he dwells.

Dostoevsky insists over and over again that man, to be whole and alive, must choose to believe in his own immortality and in God's existence. Man must pledge himself, he must love. Otherwise, forsaking his spirit, he is left with only the self, and the self, like the bones and flesh, like States, is perishable. In fact the denial of spirit leads, in Dostoevsky's mind, to a kind of self-cannibalism— the self swallows up the whole being. Such is Stavrogin's fate, and upon him Dostoevsky passes a more terrible judgment than upon any other man or woman he ever created.

The pure in heart have what Stavrogin lacks. All the women in *The Possessed* are capable of love—and because they love, it does not matter that the one they love is Stavrogin. Amongst the men there is Stephen, a Quixote, something of the buffoon, something of the saint, but always the man searching for his truth. And there is Shatov. Dostoevsky creates him a grave and beautiful man, the one man caught in the terrible vortex of the novel who hungers for God. "Externally he was rough, but inwardly he had great delicacy." His murder is the price man pays for spawning villains like Peter, self-wills like Kirillov, and neuters like Stavrogin. And the most evil of these is Stavrogin. Against the mildew of Stavrogin's self the sweetness of the pure in heart prevails not. In Stavrogin's sin are they destroyed. Him Dostoevsky damns.

Fearful judgment though it be, western man stands in danger of it today. Suddenly a human being is worth nothing. Shatovs are murdered and man acquiesces in those murders. Fatally suspended like Stavrogin, and confused by his own apathy, man permits what he abhors. Dostoevsky cannot lose his sense of individual man in the social mass, for he knows that, in the family and in the State, like sins produce like tragedies. Nor can we: the assassination of Roehm and the bombing of Warsaw are joined implacably together. To establish and sustain his spirit man must live and judge by it. We have need of a dedication like Dostoevsky's. We may despair, but as Stavrogin sensed, indignation and shame are available when despair is felt. Possessed of them we can free ourselves of our public and private devils, for both struggles have, as Dostoevsky knew, inevitably only one ground—man's individual spirit.

(1940)

D. H. Lawrence and the
High Temptation of the Mind

When I speak of the high temptation, I am thinking of Plato, Schopenhauer, say, and, among our contemporaries, Ortega. At the same time I am thinking of Homer, Euripides, and D. H. Lawrence. And I am thinking of Christ.

Suppose we start with Christ. If Satan had wanted to tempt Christ ultimately, would he not have offered him a fourth test, offered him all the understandings the mind is capable of? For it is the putting off of this cloak that is the challenge life demands of its finest creatures. And so few can put it off.

Lawrence was one. What resistance was placed in him to enable him to do it is not of so much importance as that he did it. Lawrence somehow chose the advantage of moral perceptions to those of the intellect.

For it is these two ways that, at a certain point, diverge, and if a man does not, at that point, make the kind of choice that Lawrence seems to have made (Huxley, in his introduction to the "Letters," makes much of DHL's leaving off his intellect's skills), he will go on, as Plato did, as Ortega has (to pick one among several of our better thinkers), to a kind of death.

It is, in a peculiar way, a choice of speeds—or, rather, of the most satisfying velocity man can know against something which is so at the root of time as to be not measurable by time and, thus, no velocity at all. For moral perception, in contrast to the velocity of mind, is so instantaneous as to be immeasurable in time.

It is my impression (and Ortega leads me to it as much as anyone) that the use of the intellect in its most natural sphere, that which we call philosophy, so satisfies the vanity of man that he cannot resist it unless he is prepared to undo his vanity. He is forced to run the race as a hare, the hare's leaps seem to cover the area of truth so satisfactorily.

It may well be that the resistance I speak of as imbedded in Lawrence is merely a recognition that the tortoise of feeling has to be allowed to make his race, that a man cannot stay alive as a man unless both the tortoise and the hare he is both run the course. And that the divergence of the path of the mind is only (to use an image Lawrence uses in reference to the crisis in our culture) an act of detour, by which a man picks up that slower thing he cannot, at his peril, leave behind, no matter how fast a hare he be.

The proposition, then, is this, that the act, the Laurentian act, is the answer to metaphysics, and its high temptation. What results, what the moral advantage is, is a thing both faster than the hare and slower than the tortoise, a combination both archaic and prospective, which gives man, in his preoccupation with life, the proper instrumentation for its understanding and use.

I must, finally, offer one connection of the high temptation which is difficult to state (these days especially), but which is essential. It is the evidence of the connection between sex and the structure of the mind. When Lawrence, in one of his verses, calls the search for truth "the profoundest of all sensualities" (he calls the search for justice "the next deepest sensual experience"), he is recognizing the connection I am talking about. What is fine in his statement is, of course, that he is speaking of the satisfaction *after* the temptation has been resisted. But what I am here interested in, is the effects of sensuality (granting that it is to sensuality that thought is directly tied), if the temptation is *not* resisted.

I am aware that which is cause and which is effect is of the matter, and that what may be the resistance which enables some men to put off thought as it is metaphysical is precisely the strength of the sensual in them. I think it is. I take, for example, Plato's description of the second of the two horses in the parable of *The Phaedrus,* the evil horse, to be a measure of Plato's fear of the unruliness of the sensual, not so much as it is a universal, but as it is a thing to be checked in himself. (The viciousness with which the horse is reined in, the infliction in the imagery, as against the soft, almost sentimental handling of the good horse, will stand examination.)

There is a fear, before the sensual, a suppression here and elsewhere in Plato (and it can be examined in Schopenhauer more openly) which goes beyond the denial of appetite, and is directly related to another fear so many metaphysicians show (Ortega discloses it, in his brilliant essay on Goethe, when he characterizes art, even though he is arguing that Goethe was designed to be a poet, as superficial and frivolous when "it is compared to the terrible seriousness of life"). The problem can be posed this way: a Lawrence would never find it necessary, as Plato did, to exclude Homer as a danger to the state, to paint both Hesiod and Homer, as Polygnotus did, in hell suffering like torments to Sisyphus and Tantalus. For Lawrence knew, as no metaphysician ever does, the discipline and health of form, organic form as distinguished from that false form which the arrangements of the intellect, in its false speed, offer.

It is the validity of form, and its illuminations, which call for this critique of high thought now. Art has too long been jockeyed by philosophers into a place, so far as the intellect goes, of second power. The aridities of mind have too long led the people by the nose. The hare has arrogated to himself too much the leadership in the race. It is time we tested the philosophers by the very test they are such adepts at setting aside, the one they are so quick, because they are quick, to disarm their critics of. Lawrence was not disarmed, he made bold, because he had earned the right, he had paid the price, to test them as he tested Christ. (In *The Man Who Died* he applied the test to Christ—and is, so far as I know, the only man who has.) It is the same test by which we must measure Plato, or Ortega, any of their kind. The test of the temptation is their own lives.

(1950)

The Escaped Cock

Notes on Lawrence &
the Real

The man sleeps, but I am awake. For it is the
Lord who casts out the heart of men in order
to give men a new heart

1

I take it that CONTEST is what puts drama (what they call story, plot) into the
thing, the writer's contesting with reality, to see it, to SEE;

that climax is not
what happens to the characters or things (which is, even at its finest, no more
than a rigged puppet demonstrandum) but is, instead, the issue of this contest,
the ISSUE of the man who writes—"a broken stump" said my peer, "This is
what a plot ought to be."

The issue is what causes CHANGE, the struggle inside, the contest there, *exhibited.*

At root (or stump) what *is*, is no longer THINGS but what happens BETWEEN
things, these are the terms of the reality contemporary to us—and the terms
of what we are. If form is never more than an extension of content then the
proposition reads thus: content (contest leading to issue arriving at change)
equals form.

Myself, I take it that DHL explored the problem, was, at end, so attacking:

(1) ETRUSCAN PLACES—terminus of that extraordinary contest, Lawrence
vs place, ideal place—end to the going-around-the-earth- to find it, finding it
there, Civitavecchia; and the work of the last fifty months of his life following
thereon:

(2) LADY CHATTERLEY'S LOVER: the act of simplification to get objects in
to exert *other than psychological or introspective effects,* by pulling out of the

138

cloth ONE (red, Guatemala red, Pompeian red, for that matter, Etruscan or Sumerian RED) THREAD; and that the simplest if sturdiest of all, sex, and itself, here, the physical or animal, straight, here, and (only here excusable) the word orgasm as issue intended, that is, the triumph or delight of same as Mellors is capable of its teaching.

This—the act of simplification, the same to be carefully seen as utterly different from the *elementary* (even Stein)—he also does in (3) THE ESCAPED COCK, Part I. It is not so easy to put the simplification this time except that it is a direct question, the question the Man Who Died asks himself, on his return: is anything worth more than the most precise sharpening of the instrument, a human, to the hearing of—the hearing of *all* there is *in*—the bronze clang of a cock's crow?

(Is an X-fiction worth a cock's crow?)

In other words the next step down from Lady Chatterley's L was to the dark or phallic god who is not phallic or penissimus alone but the dark as night the forever dark, the going-on of you-me-who-ever as conduit of that dark, the well-spring, whatever it is. The next step down (out of the light, into the painted tomb, back into the shell, the painted shell, goes) THE ESCAPED COCK, is THE WHOLE SENSES as simplified from (as the next step to) the FIRST SENSE, sex. (Part 2 fails miserably, apparently because, at this new stage of narrative Lawrence was not yet able to take woman down that next step towards his etruria. His "woman" here loses by goddessissing the actuality of Constance (Frieda), an actuality the Christ gains. (Always the man leads Lawrence, in?)

2

> beauty, sd the Bearded Man
> in inception, in continuation, and in end

The thing is—has got so (love, affection, friendship: the dying into, or whatever)—has already become the FACT, is now more than, is what DHL projected in EC Part 1, is viz:

> that the thing, that what happens between, is: to hear,
absolute, as it is, the SOUND, that crow ("gold," he sd, the Man) or (as another) of another his chicken fine bird he is, two ends like they say, clean straight barring Jimmy (his father, also Jimmy, the same);

and that such hear-
ing (to find the secret of it, which means, of course, to recognize it, then to
admit it, then, of all, to participate) is worth the coming back, the putting
behind one, the over-looking, a Crucifixtion.

It strikes me that where even DHL went off (Part 2) was the abandoning of
that possibility which even Somers (kangaroo) and Mellors come to admit: that
we are, all of us, now, essentially guerrillas—maquis, frontier or side-street—
EVEN in the intimate, EVEN WHERE those old essentials (love, etc.) are, where
they took root /
                it can be put this way: that it is not a question of loss or of a
lack of love (of capability) but a deep and profound difference of the way this
thing gets itself expressed, nowadays. Confronted by rot on all hands yet still
active enough to want to go ahead—to undo that rot—those who are front
dispose themselves toward the intimate just as aslant and acocked as they do
toward all those other realities, external mostly, which are moving so curiously
fast and treacherously before the nose that why? anywhere? let a twig break?

Love, as they have it, is as dead as peace, as war is. There is one requirement, only one requirement, anywhere (and what's so different about it, actually, from what the predecessors made so much of, with that word of theirs,
that word amor plus how-they-figured-it-ought-to-behave)—the clue: open,
stay OPEN, hear it, anything, really HEAR it. And you are IN.

You are all, all of you, so glib about what is human, so goddamn glib. Take a
look. Just open your eyes, as he did, the Man who died:

1: the day of my interference is done
2: compulsion, no good; the recoil kills the advance
3: nothing is so marvellous as to be done alone in the phenomenal world
   which is raging and yet apart

(1951)

This Is Yeats Speaking

This is William Butler Yeats. I want to speak to my friends in America about a thing which troubles me even now, though I have recovered leisure, and know more than I did about structure, mathematical and otherwise.

It is my friend Ezra Pound—who has made so many beautiful things. You Americans, you have him now on trial. I remember I warned him once about politics, not as you think, that we poets should stay out of it, I said simply, do not be elected to the Senate of your country. I was thinking of my own experience. I merely observed, you and I are much out of place as would be the first composers of Sea-shanties in an age of Steam.

I am not very interested in your hysteria, or his. We of Ireland have lived with treason long. It is not as dramatic as Ezra thinks, he has always been in these things as in so much American, exterior, moral. When he shouted, and now I hear you shout, I stoop down and write with my finger on the ground.

I do not know that any of us of my generation, and few of yours—I too a revolutionist—understood the contraries which are now engaged. William Blake observed that oppositions do not make true contraries.

It was our glory, Pound's and mine, I except Eliot—tradition is too organized with him, his uncertainty before chaos leads him to confuse authority with orthodoxy—to reassert the claims of authority in a world of whiggery. It is true what Pound said, we men of the mind do stand with the lovers of order. We value it, with what labor we purchase it in our work. We opposed ourselves to a leveling, rancorous, rational time.

What a man of Eliot's words would call our sin was the opposite of his. Willing as we were to oppose and go forward, we did not seek true contrary. Because of your irascible mind, Pound, and because my bones always took to comfort like a retainer's, you were ever in haste, and I sometimes, to think these men who marched and preached a new order—we of our excitable profession are attracted to sick men and buccaneers—had taken that other chaos of men's lives up in their hands, had worked to master it as we do ours, and could shape what men now need, rest, an end to this sea of question.

I understand this, at the distance I have acquired, I have Troilus' advantage, from the seventh sphere to look back on Diomed and Cressid both.

It was Pound's error to think, because he was able to examine with courage and criticize eloquently the world we have inherited—Rapallo was a place to escape the knots of passion, it was the village in the Chinese poem to which the official retired, inhabited by old men devoted to the classics—Pound thought this power, necessary to us men who had to make the language new, also gave him the sight to know the cure. It is the frenzy that follows when the mask of man is askew. The being must brag of its triumph over its own incoherence.

I examine his work in this new light and when he lay with beauty in her corner or fed cats in the street, they have their oppressors, he was a true lover of order. I would undo no single word of all he has published, quarrel as I have with him, take as I did at times his work of twenty years, the Cantos, to be a botch of tone and colour, all Hodos Chameliontos.

He was false—out of phase—when he subordinated his critical intelligence to the objects of authority in others. If the Positive Man do that, all the cruelty and narrowness of his intellect are displayed in service of preposterous purpose after purpose till there is nothing left but the fixed idea and some hysterical hatred.

It was natural he looked for an elite, and from brawlers and poets. It was his obsession to draw all things up into the pattern of art. He was ignorant of science and he will be surprised, as Goethe will not be, to find a physicist come on as Stage Manager of the tragedy.

It is a time, yours, when forces large as centuries battle and I suppose you must be more violent in your judgment than a man like me who had age tied to his tail like a can. But this I would say to you: you must take strength by embracing the criticism of your enemy. It is the beauty of demons they rush in to struggle with a cry of hate you must hear if you will answer them.

I have advanced far enough out of the prison of my generation to understand it is civil war in which you are locked.

What day you ask when date is dead
of May, when month is lost.
I can be precise though it is no answer:
this is the day of great year
the day of fear.
Man is moon.

You will know better than I how it is to be fought. I wrote to my wife one time
from Rapallo when I had listened to Pound for an afternoon damn usury, expound credit and Major Douglas, talk the totalitarian way, it was as though
I were in the presence of one of Wyndham Lewis' revolutionary simpletons.

I had never read Hegel, but my mind had been full of Blake from boyhood
up, I saw the world as a conflict, and could distinguish between a contrary and
a negation. Yet it was not easy for me to listen when one of your young men
who had come to Rapallo to see Pound came away and said to me: "He has
mingled with ferret and chameleon, vulture and kite, every anti-Semite after
his kind. He has touched abomination and is unclean."

In my first hard spring-time I had a friend I thought half a lunatic, half knave.

And I told him so, but friendship never ends;
And what if mind seem changed,
And it seemed changed with the mind,
When thought rise up unbid
On generous things that he did
And I grow half contented to be blind!

Now in your country I hear a department called Justice speak of scripts for
wireless and Ezra, as I would expect, talk back sharp. (Words cause no man fear
except in the making of them.) I pay little heed, though there is pity in me, for
I know Pound, he is a gambler and can measure consequence.

The soul is stunned in me, O writers, readers, fighters, fearers, for another
reason, that you have allowed this to happen without a trial of your own. It is
the passivity of you young men before Pound's work as a whole, not scripts
alone, you who have taken from him, Joyce, Eliot and myself the advances we
made for you. There is a court you leave silent—history present, the issue the
larger concerns of authority than a state, Heraclitus and Marx called, perhaps
some consideration of descents and metamorphoses, form and the elimination
of intellect.

We were the forerunners—Pound only the more extreme—but our time was out of phase and made us enders. Lawrence among us alone had the true mask, he lacked the critical intelligence, and was prospective. You are the antithetical men, and your time is forward, the conflict is more declared, it is for you to hold the mirror up to authority, behind our respect for which lay a disrespect for democracy as we were acquainted with it. A slogan will not suffice.

It is a simple thing I ask as I might question a beggar who stopped me for a coin. It is the use, the use you make of us.

Are you a court to accept and/or reject JEFFERSON AND/OR MUSSOLINI, indict *GUIDE TO KULCHUR* and write a better, brief me contrary ABCs, charge why 100 CANTOS betrays your country, that poem which concerns itself so much with the men who made your Revolution for you? I have said I often found there brightly painted kings, queens, knaves but have never discovered why all the suits could not be dealt out in some quite different order. What do you find, a traitor?

Dean Swift says in a meditation on a woman who paints a dying face.

> Matter as wise logicians say
> Cannot without a form subsist;
> And form, say I as well as they,
> Must fail, if matter brings no grist.

What have you to help you hold in a single thought reality and justice?

(1946)

GrandPa, GoodBye

1

Time is in his conversation more often than anything else. I said to Lowell the other night: "There is a haste in Pound, but it does not seem to be rushing to any future or away from any past." It is mere impatience, the nerves turning like a wild speed-machine (it is how he got his work done) and, more important, an intolerance of the mind's speed (fast as his goes), an intolerance even of himself. For he is not as vain as he acts. "30 yrs, 30 yrs behind the time"— you hear it from him, over and over. It is his measure (and his rod) for all work, and men. His mind bursts from the lags he sees around him.

He speaks as though he found himself like retarded when he began. Apropos Ford (F. M.), he said to me once: "From the intellectual centre, 30 yrs start of me." He elaborated on it, another time: "Ford knew, when I was still sucking at Swinburne." (He credits Ford somewhere as the one who formulated the proposition, c. 1908: verse should be at least as well written as prose.)

Now he puts all little magazines aside, or questions about someone's work, or presentation copies, with a jerk: "I can't be bothered. I've worked 40 yrs, I've done mine, and I can't be bothered trying to find out what the new candidates don't know."

"When I was a freshman . . . ," he started once.

2

If I were asked to say what I thought was the pure point of the Old Man as poet I would say the back-trail. The more familiar observation, that it is his translations on which his fame will rest, is a step off the truth. They are a part of the career he has built on remembering, but the root is a given of his own nature. The lines and passages which stand out, from the start, capture a mood of loss, and bear a beauty of loss. It is as though Pound never had illusion, was born without an ear of his own, was, instead, an extraordinary ear of an era, and did the listening for a whole time, the sharpest sort of listening, from Dante down. (I think of Bill Williams' remark: "It's the best damned ear ever born to listen to this language!") He said to me one of the first days I visited him, when he was in the penitentiary part of the hospital, what he has now come to call the Hell-Hole to distinguish it from his first detention cell at Pisa, the Gorilla Cage (where he felt he had been broken), "Among the ruins, among the ruins, the finest memory in the Orient." (He sd, "Orient.")

His conversation, as so much of the *Cantos,* is recall, stories of Picabia, Yeats (Willie), Fordie, Frobenius, Hauptmann, of intelligent men, and it is as good as you can get. I was never made so aware of what a value he puts on anecdote as recently, when I returned from seven months on the Pacific Coast, and he jibed me, to what use I had put my time. I got around to my adventure in Hollywood, and young Huston's story of Jack Warner and the Whale. It pleased Pound much, and, as he sometimes does, wagging like an old saw, he says to Dorothy, "Well, seven months, one story, not bad, not bad at all. There aren't so many good stories after all." He's a collector—what's that line he had in the *Cantos* and took out, about scrap-bag, the *Cantos* as same?

I dare say these are now commonplaces of Pound critique, but I don't think it has been sufficiently observed, if it has been observed, how much his work is a structure of mnemonics raised on a reed, nostalgia.

3

Edward Dahlberg has it, in *Do These Bones Live,* that ennui is the malaise of the life of our fathers, modern life I think he says, and in reference to Dostoevsky, and his women. Is it far-fetched, or too easy of me to take Pound's haste, and this vertu of his verse, as born of same?

It is hard for me to do otherwise, having known him. His power is a funny thing. There is no question he's got the jump—his wit, the speed of his language, the grab of it, the intimidation of his skillfully wrought career. But he has little power to compel, that is, by his person. He strikes you as brittle—and terribly American, insecure. I miss weight, and an abundance. He does not seem—and this is a crazy thing to say in the face of his beautiful verse, to appear ungrateful for it—but I say it, he does not seem to have inhabited his own experience. It is almost as though he converted too fast. The impression persists, that the only life he had lived is, in fact, the literary, and, admitting its necessity to our fathers, especially to him who had such a job of clearing to do, I take it a fault. For the verbal brilliance, delightful as it is, leaves the roots dry. One has a strong feeling, coming away from him, of a lack of the amorous, down there somewhere. (I remember that Robert Duncan, when he returned to California from his cross-country pilgrimage to Pound, spoke of this, was struck by it.) E. P. is a tennis ball.

(When I think of what I have just said, and of those early poems!)

An attempt like this is such a presumption: said Frederick of Prussia, "Every man must save himself in his own way." You might say I am offering these notes out of curiosity, on the chance that they may or may not illumine him. He can stand it. He's no easy man. He has many devices. And he's large. I'm not sure that, precisely because of the use he has put nostalgia to, and the way he has used himself, he has not made of himself the ultimate image of the end of the West. Which is something.

(I am reminded of a remark of—I don't remember which, so help me, Lao Tse or Confucius!, that a shrewd man knows others, a true man illuminates himself.)

Wait. I think I've got it. Yes, Ezra *is* a tennis ball, does bounce on, off, along, over everything. But that's the outside of him. Inside it's the same, but different, he bounces, but like light bounces. Inside he is like light is, the way light behaves. In this sense he is light, light is the way of E. P.'s knowing, light is the *numen* of him, light is his way.

And that is why he goes as he does, and why he is able to make his most beautiful poem of love later than "Cino," not so different from "Cino" either, but vastly more complete, and make the whole Canto—I am referring to XXXVI—a straight translation from Cavalcanti, the Cavalcanti itself one whole extrapolation of love in terms of light, and drawn, in its turn, straight from Grosseteste's essay on the "physics" of light.

Thus also Pound's fine penetration of Dante? (I am thinking of those images of light in—and images of Beatrice, too—in the "Paradiso," is it, or is it at the end of the "Purgatorio"? Anyway, those which Eliot has made such a poor use of.)

Maybe now I can get at this business of *amor* as of Ezra, and get at it right. It isn't a lack of the amorous, perhaps, so much as it is a completely different sense of the amorous to that which post-Christian man contains, to that which—to be most innocent about it, and properly relative—the likes of Duncan, say, or myself may feel.

(Of the likes of Bill W.? I am struck by the image of "fire" in *Paterson*. Maybe fire is the opposite principle to light, and comes to the use of those who do not go the way of light. Fire has to consume to give off its light. But light gets its knowledge—and has its intelligence and its being—by going over things without the necessity of eating the substance of things in the process of purchasing its truth. Maybe this is the difference, the different base of not just these two poets, Bill and E. P., but something more, two contrary conceptions of love. Anyway, in the present context, it serves to characterize two differing personal *via:* one achieves its clarities by way of *claritas,* the other goes about its business blind, achieves its clarities by way of what you might call *confusio.* At which point I quote Chaucer's Cock to his Dame in the middle of the night on their perch. And quit the whole subject.

> For al so siker as *In principio,*
> *Mulier est hominis confusio,*—
> Madame, the sentence of this Latyn is,
> 'Womman is mannes joye and al his blis.'

4

A long time ago (what, 25 years?) Pound took the role of Confucius, put on that mask, for good. I'm sure he would rest his claim not, as I have put it, on the past, but forward, as teacher of history to come, Culture-Bearer in the desert and shame of now. (I don't think it is possible to exaggerate the distance he goes with his notion of himself—at the end Gate of the last Canto Confucius is to be one of the two huge figures standing there, looking on.)

It is all tied up with what he calls a truism, London, 1913: are you or are you not, a serious character? Then it was Gaudier, Lewis and himself. Now it is the Major (Douglas), Lewis and himself. He sd that the other day, when we were talking about Bill Williams. Bill had just been taken to the hospital, and one of the new candidates on 2nd Avenue had had a letter from Bill repeating over and over again, "I have nothing to say, nothing to say." E. P. didn't pay this much mind. Sd he: "Bill has always been confused. He's one of the reasons I make so much of race. It's hard enough for a man to get things clear when he's of one race, but to be Bill!—french, spanish, anglo, some jew from Saragossa. . . ." And though I left Pound that day and shall not see him again, he went on to say something which is true, that what has made Bill important is that Bill has never sd one god damned thing that hasn't first circulated entirely through his head before it comes out his mouth. (Bill never faked, and that's why he has been of such use to all us young men who grew up after him. There he was in Rutherford to be gone to, and seen, a clean animal, the only one we had on the ground, right here in the States.)

5

Pound makes a lot of the head. You can tell that he thinks of it as a pod, and most of the time comes to the conclusion that very little rattles around inside most known pods. The Major, Lewis and himself. The Major, Lewis and E. P. "Lewis," says he once, "Lewis most always gets things wrong. But he gets somethin'!"

At that point his wife got the conversation off on Eliot, and Hulme, confusing 1914 with 1913. Pound did not say that Eliot was not a serious character, what I gathered was that Pound had hoped the Possum might turn out to be one, in 1914. He then went on: "The war got Hulme too young. He used to spend three hours a week with the Bloomsbury gang, Ashley Dukes . . ." he reeled off others "and we'd laugh at him, Gaudier, Lewis, I" and you could see Pound giving it to him. "But when he was gone, when he wasn't there to do it, we caught on, we saw what he'd been up to—he'd been beating that gang over the head hard enough every time he saw them to keep 'em in line. After he was gone, they went on the loose, there was no one to tell 'em. . . . And look! . . ." Grampaw was giving a lesson.

Another lesson that day was his story of Hunecker? no, some H, some citizen whose name I missed (they come flyin'), who was listening to Sturge Moore do a lecture, or a reading, in one of those rooms which are built like an operating room, the seats steep and down like a bowl, and who was wishing that Moore would get on with it, and done, and holding his head in his hand, when a character in the row above him taps him on the shoulder, and sez, "Friend, don't feel so bad, what makes you think we're here to enjoy ourselves?"

He is driven, E. P., to get on with things, his things, the "serious." He sd to me another time: "I can't git it into yr american heads that the earth makes one complete circuit once EVERY 24 hrs."

Another crack: "I thought you might be a serious character when I read that labor-saving device of yrs on H. Melville. But that was 2 yrs ago, bro."

6

When I happened to ask him what Frobenius looked like, I stumbled on the fact that Pound sees himself as a cat man. Both he and the wife quickened to the question. Glances were exchanged. He took it up, first: Sd he, "There were three men"—it was almost as though he said, once upon a time—"there were three men who might have come from the same genes. Frobenius . . ." DP interrupted, and started to go on to illustrate the differences between EP's face and Frobenius'. Then Pound was up on his feet, showing how F stood, back on his heels (P himself seems always on his toes, or did, before he thickened up from lack of exercise his second yr at SLiz, around the belly and below the back) with his arms out and his hands stuck in his belt, "He must 'ave got it from Africa," sez Pound (from the exigencies of the place, I judged, but the point being, all around the three of us, that E. P. never in his life would have spent the years that Frobenius did pushing around Africa). DP went on making with her hands, seeking further to show the differences—F not so wide at the temples . . . a V for F's beard, when all of a sudden old Ez lets it out, sort of half to her, all to me, "cat family, cat family," making with his head, and getting that fix in his oye!

And the 3rd of the same genes? "Barkoff, Barkoff" (EP with obvious delight) "now Chief of protocol, Moscow." (Pound had mentioned this Barkoff [Barkov, I suppose] several times two years earlier, particularly at the time when he was riding the idea that the U.S. Govt. could have saved itself a lot of trouble— and the world a lot of war—if it had allowed Old Ez what he asked for, the chance to pick up Georgian—"a week, 10 days"—and get over there and talk it out straight with Joe, in his own tongue. I gathered then that what would have made it all so simple was Barkov's presence, to rig the talk, once the USG wised up. Pound seems to have known Barkov years before, in Italy, perhaps, I don't know.)

7

Madame and Sir Pound also managed to get this across one day, that they had recently learned, "through Agnes," whoever she was, that Frobenius had said of E. P. before he died, "He is worth three Oxfords with four Cambridges on top."

And it felt good to hear it, for these praises are old Ez's OM's and Nobel Awards. Joyce, apparently, was not a man to give praise out easily, and Pound told me once, with what pleasure, the only thing he ever got out of Joyce, this comment one day when he had read something new, "The sleek head of verse, Mr Pound, emerges in your work."

He has a story of Joyce and Hauptmann, Joyce, when young, had translated one of Hauptmann's plays. After Pound had met Hauptmann, Joyce put a copy of the play into Ezra's hands and asked him to get Hauptmann to autograph it for him. "And," says Ez, "he didn't write off one of those inscriptions"—the intervals, that way Pound gets gesture in between the letters even, showed that he was thinking of the way he does it, dashes them off—"he took it away, came back three days later, gave it to me, it read, to JJ the best reader this play ever had, and I shipped it off." At which point he cries out at the top of his delight, "He sure sat on that one till it hatched!"

8

Another of his comforts, is to see himself in the part of the Old Man, "Grandpa," now that Mary has made him one. Sd he the other day, mistaking, I think, the significance of what I was calling to his attention, the coming to Washington (as tho to Rome) of the "Poets" (Eliot at the National Gallery the spring before, which was like a laying on of hands, the coming into existence of an American poet laureate; the creation, and the turnover, of the "poets of Congress," the Consultants; and, at the time I was speaking to him, the run of a series of readings at the new Institute of Contemporary Arts, Spender, Tate, Lowell & the other "Jrs"). Says the O.M.: "Ya, they'll all be coming to old Ez on his deathbed and telling him he was right"

and, when I was telling him about the way the people in the streetcars were shaking their heads like a bunch of dipping birds over a black new headline out of the Ant-Hill, "If they'd only listened to old Ez in the first place!"

"right,

right

from the start

(1948)

Human Universe

Human Universe

There are laws, that is to say, the human universe is as discoverable as that other. And as definable.

The trouble has been, that a man stays so astonished he can triumph over his own incoherence, he settles for that, crows over it, and goes at a day again happy he at least makes a little sense. Or, if he says anything to another, he thinks it is enough—the struggle does involve such labor and some terror—to wrap it in a little mystery: ah, the way is hard but this is what you find if you go it.

The need now is a cooler one, a discrimination, and then, a shout. Der Weg stirbt, sd one. And was right, was he not? Then the question is: was ist der Weg?

I

The difficulty of discovery (in the close world which the human is because it is ourselves and nothing outside us, like the other) is, that definition is as much a part of the act as is sensation itself, in this sense, that life *is* preoccupation with itself, that conjecture about it is as much of it as its coming at us, its going on. In other words, we are ourselves both the instrument of discovery and the instrument of definition.

Which is of course, why language is a prime of the matter and why, if we are to see some of the laws afresh, it is necessary to examine, first, the present condition of the language—and I mean language exactly in its double sense of discrimination (logos) and of shout (tongue).

We have lived long in a generalizing time, at least since 450 B.C. And it has had its effects on the best of men, on the best of things. Logos, or discourse, for example, in that time, so worked its abstractions into our concept and use of language that language's other function, speech, seems so in need of restoration that several of us go back to hieroglyphs or to ideograms to right the balance. (The distinction here is between language as the act of the instant and language as the act of thought about the instant.)

But one can't any longer stop there, if one ever could. For the habits of thought are the habits of action, and here, too, particularism has to be fought for, anew. In fact, by the very law of the identity of definition and discovery, who can extricate language from action? (Though it is one of the first false faces of the law which I shall want to try to strike away, it is quite understandable—in the light of this identity—that the Greeks went on to declare all speculation as enclosed in the "UNIVERSE of discourse." It is their word, and the refuge of all metaphysicians since—as though language, too, was an absolute, instead of (as even man is) instrument, and not to be extended, however much the urge, to cover what each, man and language, is in the hands of: what we share, and which is enough, of power and of beauty, not to need an exaggeration of words, especially that spreading one, "universe." For discourse is hardly such, or at least only arbitrarily a universe. In any case, so extended (logos given so much more of its part than live speech), discourse has arrogated to itself a good deal of experience which needed to stay put—needs now to be returned to the only two universes which count, the two phenomenal ones, the two a man has need to bear on because they bear so on him: that of himself, as organism, and that of his environment, the earth and planets.

We stay unaware how two means of discourse the Greeks appear to have invented hugely intermit our participation in our experience, and so prevent discovery. They are what followed from Socrates' readiness to generalize, his willingness (from his own bias) to make a "universe" out of discourse instead of letting it rest in its most serviceable place. (It is not sufficiently observed that logos, and the reason necessary to it, are only a stage which a man must master and not what they are taken to be, final discipline. Beyond them is direct perception and the contraries which dispose of argument. The harmony of the universe, and I include man, is not logical, or better, is post-logical, as is the order of any created thing.) With Aristotle, the two great means appear: logic and classification. And it is they that have so fastened themselves on habits of thought that action is interfered with, absolutely interfered with, I should say.

Nor can I let the third of the great Greeks, Plato, go free—he who had more of a sort of latitude and style my tribe of men are apt to indulge him for. His world of Ideas, of forms as extricable from content, is as much and as dangerous an issue as are logic and classification, and they need to be seen as such if we are to get on to some alternative to the whole Greek system. Plato may be a honey-head, as Melville called him, but he is precisely that—treacherous to all ants, and where, increasingly, my contemporaries die, or drown the best of themselves. Idealisms of any sort, like logic and like classification, intervene at just the moment they become more than the means they are, are allowed to become ways as end instead of ways *to* end, END, which is never more than this instant, than you on this instant, than you, figuring it out, and acting, so. If there is any absolute, it is never more than this one, this instant, in action.

Which ought to get us on. What makes most acts—of living and of writing—unsatisfactory, is that the person and/or the writer satisfy themselves that they can only make a form (what they say or do, or a story, a poem, whatever) by selecting from the full content some face of it, or plane, some part. And at just this point, by just this act, they fall back on the dodges of discourse, and immediately, they lose me, I am no longer engaged, this is not what I know is the going-on (and of which going-on I, as well as they, want some illumination, and so, some pleasure). It comes out a demonstration, a separating out, an act of classification, and so, a stopping, and all that I know is, it is not there, it has turned false. For any of us, at any instant, are juxtaposed to any experience, even an overwhelming single one, on several more planes than the arbitrary and discursive which we inherit can declare.

It is not the Greeks I blame. What it comes to is ourselves, that we do not find ways to hew to experience as it is, in our definition and expression of it, in other words, find ways to stay in the human universe, and not be led to partition reality at any point, in any way. For this is just what we do do, this is the real issue of what has been, and the process, as it now asserts itself, can be exposed. It is the function, *comparison,* or, its bigger name, *symbology.* These are the false faces, too much seen, which hide and keep from use the active intellectual states, metaphor and performance. All that comparison ever does is set up a series of *reference* points: to compare is to take one thing and try to understand it by marking its similarities to or differences from another thing. Right here is the trouble, that each thing is not so much like or different from another thing (these likenesses and differences are apparent) but that such an analysis only accomplishes a *description,* does not come to grips with what really matters: that a thing, any thing, impinges on us by a more important fact, its self-existence, without reference to any other thing, in short, the very character of it which calls our attention to it, which wants us to know more about it, its particularity. This is what we are confronted by, not the thing's "class," any hierarchy, of quality or quantity, but the thing itself, and its *relevance* to ourselves who are the experience of it (whatever it may mean to someone else, or whatever other relations it may have).

There must be a means of expression for this, a way which is not divisive as all the tag ends and upendings of the Greek way are. There must be a way which bears *in* instead of away, which meets head on what goes on each split second, a way which does not—in order to define—prevent, deter, distract, and so cease the act of, discovering.

I have been living for some time amongst a people who are more or less directly the descendants of a culture and civilization which was a contrary of that which we have known and of which we are the natural children. The marked thing about them is, that it is only love and flesh which seems to carry any sign of their antecedence, that all the rest which was once a greatness different from our own has gone down before the poundings of our way. And, now, except as their bodies jostle in a bus, or as they disclose the depth and tenacity of love among each other inside a family, they are poor failures of the modern world, incompetent even to arrange that, in the month of June, when the rains have not come far enough forward to fill the wells, they have water to wash in or to drink. They have lost the capacity of their predecessors to do anything in common. But they do one thing no modern knows the secret of, however he is still by nature possessed of it: they wear their flesh with that difference which the understanding that it is common leads to. When I am rocked by the roads against any of them—kids, women, men—their flesh is most gentle, is granted, touch is in no sense anything but the natural law of flesh, there is none of that pull-away which, in the States, causes a man for all the years of his life the deepest sort of questioning of the rights of himself to the wild reachings of his own organism. The admission these people give me and one another is direct, and the individual who peers out from that flesh is precisely himself, is a curious wandering animal like me—it is so very beautiful how animal human eyes are when the flesh is not worn so close it chokes, how human and individuated the look comes out of a human eye when the house of it is not exaggerated.

This is not easy to save from subjectivism, to state so that you understand that this is not an observation but a first law to a restoration of the human house. For what is marked about these Lermeros with whom I live (by contrast, for example, to the people of the city nearby) is that, here, the big-eared, small-eyed creatures stay as the minority they must always have been before garages made them valuable and allowed them out of their holes to proliferate and overrun the earth. Nothing is accident, and man, no less than nature, does nothing without plan or the discipline to make plan fact. And if it is true that we now live in fear of our own house, and can easily trace the reason for it, it is also true that we can trace reasons why those who do not or did not so live found out how to do other than we.

My assumption is, that these contemporary Maya are what they are because once there was a concept at work which kept attention so poised that (1) men were able to stay so interested in the expression and gesture of all creatures, including at least three planets in addition to the human face, eyes and hands, that they invented a system of written record, now called hieroglyphs, which, on its very face, is verse, the signs were so clearly and densely chosen that, cut in stone, they retain the power of the objects of which they are the images; (2) to mass stone with sufficient proportion to decorate a near hill and turn it into a fire-tower or an observatory or one post of an enclosure in which people, favored by its shadows, might swap caymotes for sandals; and (3) to fire clay into pots porous enough to sieve and thus cool water, strong enough to stew iguana and fish, and handsome enough to put ceremony where it also belongs, in the most elementary human acts. And when a people are so disposed, it should come as no surprise that, long before any of these accomplishments, the same people did an improvement on nature—the domestication of maize—which remains one of the world's wonders, even to a nation of Burbanks, and that long after all their accomplishments, they still carry their bodies with some of the savor and the flavor that the bodies of the Americans are as missing in as is their irrigated lettuce and their green-picked refrigerator-ripened fruit. For the truth is, that the management of external nature so that none of its virtu is lost, in vegetables or in art, is as much a delicate juggling of her content as is the same juggling by any one of us of our own. And when men are not such jugglers, are not able to manage a means of expression the equal of their own or nature's intricacy, the flesh does choke. The notion of fun comes to displace work as what we are here for. Spectatorism crowds out participation as the condition of culture. And bonuses and prizes are the rewards of labor contrived by the monopolies of business and government to protect themselves from the advancement in position of able men or that old assertion of an inventive man, his own shop. All individual energy and ingenuity is bought off—at a suggestion box or the cinema. Passivity conquers all. Even war and peace die (to be displaced by world government?) and man reverts to only two of his components, inertia and gas.

It is easy to phrase, too easy, and we have had enough of bright description. To say that in America the goods are as the fruits, and the people as the goods, all glistening but tasteless, accomplishes nothing in itself, for the overwhelming fact is, that the rest of the world wants nothing but to be the same. Value is perishing from the earth because no one cares to fight down to it beneath the glowing surfaces so attractive to all. Der Weg stirbt.

II

Can one restate man in any way to repossess him of his dynamic? I don't know. But for myself a first answer lies in his systemic particulars. The trouble with the inherited formulations which have helped to destroy him (the notion of himself as the center of phenomenon by fiat or of god as the center and man as god's chief reflection) is that both set aside nature as an unadmitted or suppressed third party, a sort of Holy Ghost which was allowed in once to touch men's tongues and then, because the fire was too great, was immediately banished to some sort of half place in between god and the devil—who actually, of course, thereby became the most powerful agent of all. The result, we have been the witnesses of: discovering this discarded thing nature, science has run away with everything. Tapping her power, fingering her like a child, giving her again her place, but without somehow, remembering what truth there was in man's centering the use of anything, god, devil, or holy ghost, in himself, science has upset all balance and blown value, man's peculiar responsibility, to the winds.

If unselectedness is man's original condition (such is more accurate a word than that lovely riding thing, chaos, which sounds like what it is, the most huge generalization of all, obviously making it necessary for man to invent a bearded giant to shape it for him) but if likewise, selectiveness is just as originally the impulse by which he proceeds to do something about the unselectedness, then one is forced, is one not, to look for some instrumentation in man's given which makes selection possible. And it has gone so far, that is, science has, as to wonder if the fingertips, are not very knowing knots in their own rights, little brains (little photo-electric cells, I think they now call the skin) which, immediately, in responding to external stimuli, make decisions! It is a remarkable and usable idea. For it is man's first cause of wonder how rapid he is in his taking in of what he does experience.

But when you have said that, have you not done one of two things, either forever damned yourself by making the "soul" mechanical (it has long been the soul which has softly stood as a word to cover man as a selecting internal reality posed dangerously in the midst of those externals which the word chaos generously covers like Williams' paint) or you have possibly committed a greater crime. You have allowed that external reality is more than merely the substance which man takes in. By making the threshold of reception so important and by putting the instrumentation of selection so far out from its traditional place (the greatest humanist of them all opened a sonnet, "Poor soul, the centre of my sinful earth"), you have gone so far as to imply that the skin itself, the meeting edge of man and external reality, is where all that matters does happen, that man and external reality are so involved with one another that, for man's purposes, they had better be taken as one.

It is some such crime by which I am willing to hazard a guess at a way to restore to man some of his lost relevance. For this metaphor of the senses—of the literal speed of light by which a man absorbs, instant on instant, all that phenomenon presents to him—is a fair image as well, my experience tells me, of the ways of his inner energy, of the ways of those other things which are usually, for some reason, separated from the external pick-ups—his dreams, for example, his thoughts (to speak as the predecessors spoke), his desires, sins, hopes, fears, faiths, loves. I am not able to satisfy myself that these so-called inner things are so separable from the objects, persons, events which are the content of them and by which man represents or re-enacts them despite the suck of symbol which has increased and increased since the great Greeks first promoted the idea of a transcendent world of forms. What I do see is that each man does make his own special selection from the phenomenal field and it is true that we begin to speak of personality, however I remain unaware that this particular act of individuation is peculiar to man, observable as it is in individuals of other species of nature's making (it behooves man now not to separate himself too jauntily from any of nature's creatures).

Even if one does follow personality up, does it take the problem further in to those areas of function which may seem more peculiarly human (at least are more peculiarly the concern of a humanist), I equally cannot satisfy myself of the gain in thinking that the process by which man transposes phenomena to his use is any more extricable from reception than reception itself is from the world. What happens at the skin is more like than different from what happens within. The process of image (to be more exact about transposition than the "soul" allows or than the analysts do with their tricky "symbol-maker") cannot be understood by separation from the stuff it works on. Here again, as throughout experience, the law remains, form is not isolated from content. The error of all other metaphysic is descriptive, is the profound error that Heisenberg had the intelligence to admit in his principle that a thing can be measured in its mass only by arbitrarily assuming a stopping of its motion, or in its motion only by neglecting, for the moment of the measuring, its mass. And either way, you are failing to get what you are after—so far as a human being goes, his life. There is only one thing you can do about kinetic, re-enact it. Which is why the man said, he who possesses rhythm possesses the universe. And why art is the only twin life has—its only valid metaphysic. Art does not seek to describe but to enact. And if man is once more to possess intent in his life, and to take up the responsibility implicit in his life, he has to comprehend his own process as intact, from outside, by way of his skin, in, and by his own powers of conversion, out again. For there is this other part of the motion which we call life to be examined anew, that thing we overlove, man's action, that tremendous discharge of force which we overlove when we love it for its own sake but which (when it is good) is the equal of all intake plus all transposing.

It deserves this word, that it is the equal of its cause only when it proceeds unbroken from the threshold of a man through him and back out again, without loss of quality, to the external world from which it came, whether that external world take the shape of another human being or of the several human beings hidden by the generalization "society" or of things themselves. In other words, the proposition here is that man at his peril breaks the full circuit of object, image, action at any point. The meeting edge of man and the world is also his cutting edge. If man is active, it is exactly here where experience comes in that it is delivered back, and if he stays fresh at the coming in he will be fresh at his going out. If he does not, all that he does inside his house is stale, more and more stale as he is less and less acute at the door. And his door is where he is responsible to more than himself. Man does influence external reality, and it can be stated without recourse to the stupidities of mysticism (which appears to love a mystery as much outside as it does in). If man chooses to treat external reality any differently than as part of his own process, in other words as anything other than relevant to his own inner life, then he will (being such a froward thing, and bound to use his energy willy-nilly, nature is so subtle) use it otherwise. He will use it just exactly as he has used it now for too long, for arbitrary and willful purposes which, in their effects, not only change the face of nature but actually arrest and divert her force until man turns it even against herself, he is so powerful, this little thing. But what little willful modern man will not recognize is, that when he turns it against her he turns it against himself, held in the hand of nature as man forever is, to his use of himself if he choose, to his disuse, as he has.

What gets me is, how man refuses to acknowledge the consequences of his disposing of himself at his own entrance—as though a kiss were a cheap thing, as though he were. He will give a Rimbaud a lot of lip and no service at all, as though Rimbaud were a sport of nature and not a proof. Or a people different from himself—they will be the subject of historians' studies or of tourists' curiosity, and be let go at that, no matter how much they may disclose values he and his kind, you would think, could make use of. I have found, for example, that the hieroglyphs of the Maya disclose a placement of themselves toward nature of enormous contradiction to ourselves, and yet I am not aware that any of the possible usages of this difference have been allowed to seep out into present society. All that is done is what a Toynbee does, diminish the energy once here expended into the sieve phonetic words have become to be offered like one of nature's pastes that we call jewels to be hung as a decoration of knowledge upon some Christian and therefore eternal and holy neck. It is unbearable what knowledge of the past has been allowed to become, what function of human memory has been dribbled out in to the hands of these learned monsters whom people are led to think "know." They know nothing in not knowing how to reify what they do know. What is worse, they do not know how to pass over to us the energy implicit in any high work of the past because they purposely destroy that energy as dangerous to the states for which they work—which it is, for any concrete thing is a danger to rhetoricians and politicians, as dangerous as a hard coin is to a banker. And the more I live the more I am tempted to think that the ultimate reason why man departs from nature and thus departs from his own chance is that he is part of a herd which wants to do the very thing which nature disallows—that energy can be lost. When I

look at the filth and lumber which man is led by, I see man's greatest achievement in this childish accomplishment—that he damn well can, and does, destroy destroy destroy energy every day. It is too much. It is too much to waste
time on, this idiot who spills his fluids like some truculent and fingerless chamaco hereabouts who wastes water at the pump when birds are dying all over
the country in this hottest of the months and women come in droves in the
morning begging for even a tasa of the precious stuff to be poured in the am-
phoras they swing on their hips as they swing their babies. Man has made himself an ugliness and a bore.

It was better to be a bird, as these Maya seem to have been, they kept moving their heads so nervously to stay alive, to keep alerted to what they were
surrounded by, to watch it even for the snake they took it to be or that larger
bird they had to be in awe of, the zopilote who fed on them when they were
dead or whom they looked at of a morning in a great black heap like locusts
tearing up a deer that had broken his wind or leg in the night. Or even Venus
they watched, as though they were a grackle themselves and could attack her
vertically in her house full of holes like a flute through which, they thought,
when she had the upper hand she spread down on them, on an east wind,
disease and those blows on their skin they call granitos. When she was new,
when she buzzed the morning sky, they hid in their houses for fear of her,
Shoosh Ek, for fear of her bite, the Wasp she was, the way she could throw
them down like that electrical stick which, last year, pinched one of these fishermen on his cheek, in all the gulf hit him as he sat in the prow of his cayuco
with a line out for dogfish of a day and laid him out dead, with no more mark
burned on him than that little tooth of a kiss his wife was given as cause when
they brought him out over the beach as he might have hauled in a well-paying
shark.

Or to be a man and a woman as Sun was, the way he had to put up with
Moon, from start to finish the way she was, the way she behaved, and he up
against it because he did have the advantage of her, he moved more rapidly. In
the beginning he was only young and full of himself, and she, well, she was a
girl living with her grandfather doing what a girl was supposed to be doing,
making cloth. Even then he had the advantage of her, he hunted, instead, and
because he could hunt he could become a humming-bird, which he did, just to
get closer to her, this loveliness he thought she was and wanted to taste. Only
the trouble was, he had to act out his mask, and while he was coming closer,

one tobacco flower to another toward the house, her grandfather brought him down with a clay shot from a blow gun. And sun fell, right into moon's arms, who took him to her room to mother him, for she was all ready to be a wife, a man's second mother as a wife is in these parts where birds are so often stoned and need to be brought back to consciousness and, if they have their wings intact, may fly away again. As sun was. Only he could also talk, and persuaded moon to elope with him in a canoe. But there you are: there is always danger. Grandfather gets rain to throw his fire at them and though sun converts to turtle and is tough enough to escape alive, moon, putting on a crab shell, is not sufficiently protected and is killed.

Which is only part of it, that part of it which is outside and seems to have all of the drama. But only seems. For dragonflies collect moon's flesh and moon's blood in thirteen hollow logs, the sort of log sun had scooped his helpless runaway boat out of, thinking he had made it, had moon finally for his own. Foolish sun. For now here he is back again, after thirteen days, digging out the thirteen logs, and finding that twelve of them contain nothing but all the insects and all the snakes which fly and crawl about the earth of man and pester people in a hot climate so that a lot die off before they are well begun and most are ready, at any instant, for a sickness or a swelling, and the best thing to do is to lie quiet, wait for the poison to pass. For there is log 13, and it reveals moon restored to life, only moon is missing that part which makes woman woman, and deer alone, deer can give her what he does give her so that she and sun can do what man and woman have the pleasure to do as one respite from the constant hammering.

But you see, nothing lasts. Sun has an older brother, who comes to live with sun and moon, and sun has reason soon to suspect that something is going on between moon and the big star, for this brother is the third one of the sky, the devilish or waspish one who is so often with moon. By a trick, sun discovers them, and moon, dispirited, sitting off by herself on the river bank, is persuaded by the bird zopilote to go off with him to the house of the king of the vultures himself. And though a vulture is not, obviously, as handsome a thing as the sun, do not be fooled into thinking that this bird which can darken the sky as well as feed on dead things until they are only bones for the sun to whiten, has not his attractions, had not his attractions to moon, especially the king of them all. She took him, made him the third of her men, and was his wife.

But sun was not done with her, with his want of her, and he turned to that creature which empowered her, the deer, for aid. He borrowed a skin, and hiding under it—knowing as hot sun does the habits of vultures—he pretends to be a carcass. The first vulture comes in, landing awkwardly a distance off, hobbles his nervous way nearer until, as he is about to pick apart what he thinks is a small deer, sun leaps on his back and rides off to where moon is. He triumphantly seizes her, only to find that she is somewhat reluctant to return.

At which stage, for reasons of cause or not, sun and moon go up into the sky to assume forever their planetary duties. But sun finds there is one last thing he must do to the moon before human beings are satisfied with her. He must knock out one of her eyes, they complain she is so bright and that they cannot sleep, the night is so much the same as his day, and his day is too much anyhow, and a little of the sweetness of the night they must have. So he does, he puts out her eye, and lets human beings have what they want. But when he does more, when, occasionally, he eclipses her entirely, some say it is only a sign that the two of them continue to fight, presumably because sun cannot forget moon's promiscuity, though others say that moon is forever erratic, is very much of a liar, is always telling sun about the way people of the earth are as much misbehavers as she, get drunk, do the things she does, in fact, the old ones say, moon is as difficult to understand as any bitch is.

O, they were hot for the world they lived in, these Maya, hot to get it down the way it was—the way it is, my fellow citizens.

(1951)

Footnote to HU (lost in the shuffle)

The etymology of "discourse" has its surprises. It means, TO RUN TO AND
FRO!

And the 6′4″ Negress stood in the middle of the room full of bright and
talking people, listened for a moment to what they were going on about, and
threw this at them, as her contribution: ART IS THE CELEBRATION OF THE AC-
TUAL. And without giving them a moment to think, said: ONLY THE ARTIST
(she had just come in) IS ON TIME!

(1952)

The Gate and the Center

1:

What I am kicking around is this notion: that KNOWLEDGE either goes for the CENTER or it's inevitably a State Whore—which American and Western education generally is, has been, since its beginning. (I am flatly taking Socrates as the progenitor, his methodology still the RULE: "I'll stick my logic up, and classify, boy, classify you right out of existence.")

So when I say, it's a question of re-establishing a concept of knowledge as culture rather than a question of what's wrong with the schools, I mean that already anyone who wants to begin to get straight has to, to start, a straight man has to uneducate himself first, in order to begin to pick up, to take up, to get back, in order to get on. Which is turkey-crazy, is it not. So I say, let's take the question by another handle, let's say some simple and non-aesthetic propositions: what is the story of man, the FACTS, where did he come from, when did he invent a city, what did a plateau have to do with it, or a river valley? what foods were necessary (I am thinking here of Steffanson on diets, Carl Sauer on starch crops and how, where they could be domesticated)

were the people on the edge of the retreating ice, marauders, or were they (as Sauer so beautifully argues) fisher-folk? and man's first food clue, that tubers which poisoned fish did not poison humans?

and are euhemerists like myself (so I am told ISHMAEL proves me) correct, that gods are men first? and how many generations does it take to turn a hero into a god? is it 3 (ex., A. Lincoln)?

1000

more such questions, put straight down the alley, without deference to arbitrary divisions of "learning" which are calculated, are purposely brought into being (Old Stink Sock on down) to CONFUSE confuse CONFOUND

Take language (& start with Fenollosa): did anyone tell you—same anyones are so stuck with variants—that all Indo-European language (ours) appears to stem from the very same ground on which the original agglutinative language was invented, Sumeria? and that our language can be seen to hold in itself now as many of those earliest elements as it does Sanskrit roots? that though some peoples stuck to the signs while others took off with the sounds, both the phonetic and ideographic is still present and available for use as impetus and explosion in our alphabetic speech? (Why Fenollosa wrote the damned best piece on language since when, is because, in setting Chinese directly over against American, he reasserted these resistant primes in our speech, put us back to the origins of their force not as history but as living oral law to be discovered in speech as directly as it is in our mouths.)

It is one of the last acts of liberation that science has to offer, that is, modern science stemming from the Arabs, that all the real boys, today, are spending their time no longer alone but in teams, because they have found out that the problem now is not what things are so much as it is what happens BETWEEN things, in other words:

COMMUNICATION (why we are at ripe, live center)—and the joker? that from Stockpile Szilard on down, what the hot lads are after (under him at Chicago, Merritt at Columbia, Theodore Vann at the Univ. of Paris, and at the Princeton Institute) is, what is it in the *human* organism, what is the wave (is it H-mu) that makes communication possible! It kills me. And I made one physicist run, when I sd, quite quietly, the only thing wrong with yr teams is, you have left out the one professional who has been busy abt this problem all the time the rest of you and yr predecessors have been fingering that powerful solid, but useless when abstraction, Nature.

Item: to answer all who say, but is a poet that important? Edith Porada, in— get this—Corpus of Ancient Near Eastern Seals in North American Collections, Edited for the Committee of Ancient Near Eastern Seals, a Project of the Iranian Institute, the Oriental Institute of the Univ. of Chicago and the Yale Babylonian Collection, Bollingen Series XLV (I find that she says this not in the above but in *Mesopotamian Arts in Cylinder Seals of the Pierpont Morgan Libraries* (N.Y., 1947, p. 1):

> Sometimes foreign influences were introduced through trade, sometimes through contact with the many peoples who time and again invaded the rich Mesopotamian plain from the poorer and less civilized regions of the East, North, and West.

Moreover, while the actual assumption of power by a foreign king in Mesopotamia was a sudden event, marking the climax of an invasion, such invasions were often preceded by the gradual infiltration of foreigners into the country as mercenaries or laborers. The new element therefore made itself felt gradually, and a sudden break in the artistic development never took place, only the disintegration of one style and the emergence of another. It may be added that artists appear to have been so highly valued that they were spared in warfare.

Well, to hell with it, only—as I sd before—the poet is the only pedagogue left, to be trusted. And I mean the tough ones, only the very best, not the bulk of them and the other educators.

Which brings us home. To Porada, & S. N. Kramer's translations of the city poems, add one L. A. Waddell. What Waddell gives me is this chronology: that, from 3378 BC (date man's 1st city, name and face of creator also known) in unbroken series first at Uruk, then from the seaport Lagash out into colonies in the Indus Valley and, circa 2500, the Nile, until date 1200 BC or thereabouts, civilization had ONE CENTER, Sumer, in all directions, that this one people held such exact and superior force that all peoples around them were sustained by it, nourished, increased, advanced, that a city was a coherence which, for the first time since the ice, gave man the chance to join knowledge to culture and, with this weapon, shape dignities of economics and value sufficient to make daily life itself a dignity and a sufficiency.

(*Note:* I am the more convinced of this argument, that I have for some years, by way of Berard, Herodotus, & Strzygowski [Frobenius au fond with his sun-moon, landfolk-seafolk premises] felt that it was just about 1200 BC that something broke, that a bowl went smash, and that, as a consequence, this artificial business of the "East" and the "West" came into its most false being.)

2:

Suddenly, by such a smallness of time, seen as back there 3378 to 2500 BC, the nature of life then is made available, seems suddenly not at all history, seems what it was, men falling off the original impetus but still close enough to the climax of a will to cohere to know what CENTER was, and, though going down hill, still keeping the FORCE, even though the SHAPE was starting even then to lose its sharpness.

(One may see the far end of the personages, events & acts of these years in such things as the *Odyssey*, Herakles, Egyptian folk tales [as Mas-

pero gives them], Phoenician periploi, and Ionian thought. That the art of classical Egypt and Greece are also signs of this derivation is more obvious, now
that Crete, Susa and even such a late thing as Dura-Europos are available. We
are only just beginning to gauge the backward of literature, breaking through
the notion that Greece began it, to the writings farther back: to the Phoenicians, to the Babylonians, behind them the Akkadians, and, most powerful of
all, the Sumerian poets, those first makers, better than 2000 years prior to Homer, Hesiod & Herodotus.)

When I say gauge, I am thinking that we have *no* measure of what men are
capable of, taking, say, the 700 years from, say, Dante, as comparison of like
time to what those men were about in the first 700 years of the Sumer thrust.

What I am trying to crack down is, heroism. There has been, of course, no
reason why, since Dante, that men should not have taken heroism solely in
terms of man's capacity to overthrow or dominate external reality. Yet I do not
for a minute think that this may—or will be—the gauge of a life turning on the
SINGLE CENTER. But just because of our own late, & Western, impression we
continue to shy, in our present disgust with such muscularity, away from all
such apparent magnifications as epic and myths seem to include.

But the thing goes farther, & deeper. What has been these last 700 years,
is the inevitable consequence of a contrary will to that of Sumer, a will which
overcame the old will approximately 2500 BC and succeeded in making itself
boss approximately 1200 BC. It is the long reach of this second will of man
which we have known, the dead of which we are the witnesses. And the only
answer of man to the rash of multiples which that wish to disperse causeth to
break out (the multiple face of it, the swarming snake-choices it breeds as multiple as hairs) was one thing only, the only thing man had to put against it: the
egocentric concept, a man himself as, and only contemporary to himself, the
PROOF of anything, himself responsible only to himself by the exhibition of his
energy, AHAB, end.

I pick up from the Omahas, to venture to see what happens ahead if I am
right that now, only, once again, and only a second time, is the FIRST WILL back
in business. A boy (or a girl, if she chose, though it was not required of the girl
as it was of the boy) went out at 16, 17, alone into the woods, with nothing to
take care of living, for three days of hunger & watch. The one end was, to woo
a dream, and that dream, once it came, was, whatever its form, to be thereafter the SIGNATURE of that individual's life. What the boy or girl was not to

do, was to speak of it. But due to the other part of the ceremony, which was to wear, from then on, a fetish to stand for the dream, it became possible for the individual instantly to know others of the tribe who had a like dream and to consort with same, as they thereafter did.

I should, myself, assume that both parts of this act rested on good cause, that whatever be individuation, there are groupings of us which create kin ("hungry after my own kind"), limits of, say, Seven Tribes of man, or whatever—which same limits become vessels of behaviour towards *use* of self, & recognition.

It is in some such frame that the old human science of archetype figure and archetype event became relevant to individual behaviour at all time forward. And it would be my guess that we have been running, know it or not, on the invention of—the verbal function is not quite right: the recognition, obedience to, and creation of—just such archetypes by the Sumerians some time before and some certain time after 3378 BC (the date 2500 is only the outside limit this side of the action). And that, of course, we long ago lost the POINT & PURPOSE of what we call—and thus kill—the act of myth.

I have this dream, that just as we cannot now see & say the size of these early HUMAN KINGS, we cannot, by the very lost token of their science, see what size man can be once more capable of, once the turn of the flow of his energies that I speak of as the WILL TO COHERE is admitted, and its energy taken up.

What I should like to dispose of is, that it is a dream, any more than that, what I think we shall be able soon to demonstrate, the so-called figures & stories of the old science were never men. And I venture to say that their enlarged dimensions are no where as discrepant from them as we, going by what we have been able to see of man in recent time, including ourselves, would surmise.

The proposition is a simple one (and the more easily understood now that we have been shocked at what we did not know nature's energies capable of, generally): energy is larger than man, but therefore, if he taps it as it is in himself, his uses of himself are EXTENSIBLE in human directions & degree not recently granted.

Quickly, therefore, the EXCEPTIONAL man, the "hero," loses his description as "genius"—his "birth" is mere instrumentation for application to the energy he did not create—and becomes, instead, IMAGE of possibilities implicit in the energy, given the METHODOLOGY of its use by men from the man who is capable precisely of this, and only this kind of intent & attention.

I am struck (as Waddell tells the stories of these men—who were heroes—who became gods) by the premises on which they acted, were expected to act, & were judged. And how very small, how hairlike, the difference is from the premises we have regarded, in our inherited blindness due to departure from the old science, as essential. For example, this, from a monument of Sargon of Agade, on the duties of a ruler, apparently formulated by his tutor (his "Aristotle" or "Apollonius of Tyana"), a man variously known as Annaki or Urura (Sanskrit: Aurva or Urva), date 2725 BC:

"arms" are allowable only as PROTECTION OF THE EARTH (I judge, in distinction from the ruler's power, or even the "people's," in the sense of volk or nation). In fact the next sentence of the inscription repeats the injunction thus:

THE GUARDIANSHIP OF THE EARTH IS THE RULER'S ESPECIAL PROVINCE.

And a later priest-king (whose statue-portraits in diorite & lapis-lazuli are straight projections of Gotama Buddha's face, the man Gotama), by name GUDA, King of the port Lagash, date 2370 BC, in reporting his accomplishments due to the restoration of the law codes of both the Founder of that City, Uruash (c. 3000), and of the patron of the city, Nimirrud (Nimrod), says this:

the maid is now the equal of her mistress,
the master & the slave consort as friends,
the powerful & the humble lay down, side by side.

The whole question & continuing struggle to remain civilized Sumer documented in & out: I imagine you know the subtle tale of how Gilgamesh (King 14, and founder of the sea-dynasty of Sumeria, according to Waddell's count) was sent the rude fellow Enkidu to correct him because he, even Gilgamesh, had become a burden, in his lust, to his city's people. As I read it, it is an incredibly accurate myth of what happens to the best of men when they lose touch with the primordial & phallic energies & methodologies which, said this predecessor people of ours, make it possible for man, that participant thing, to take up, straight, nature's, live nature's force.

(1951)

The Resistance

for Jean Riboud

This is eternity. This now. This foreshortened span. Men will recognize it more easily (& dwell in it so) when we regain what the species lost, how long ago: nature's original intention with the organism, that it live 130 years. Or so Bogomolets' researches into the nature of connective tissue seem to prove. True or not, with or without aid from his own biosis, man has no alternative: his mortal years are his enemy. He accepts this new position. It is the root act.

There are other aids. Time, for example, has been cut down to size, though I do not think that those who have come to the knowledge of now came here from that powerful abstraction space-time, no matter how its corrections of time reinforce the position.

Man came here by an intolerable way. When man is reduced to so much fat for soap, superphosphate for soil, fillings and shoes for sale, he has, to begin again, one answer, one point of resistance only to such fragmentation, one organized ground, a ground he comes to by a way the precise contrary of the cross, of spirit in the old sense, in old mouths. It is his own physiology he is forced to arrive at. And the way—the way of the beast, of man and the Beast.

It is his body that is his answer, his body intact and fought for, the absolute of his organism in its simplest terms, this structure evolved by nature, repeated in each act of birth, the animal: man; the house he is, this house that moves, breathes, acts, this house where his life is, where he dwells against the enemy, against the beast.

Or the fraud. This organism now our citadel never was cathedral, draughty tenement of soul, was what it is: ground, stone, wall, cannon, tower. In this intricate structure are we based, now more certainly than ever (beseiged, overthrown), for its power is bone muscle nerve blood brain   a man, its fragile mortal force its old eternity, resistance.

(1953)

Cy Twombly

what whiteness can one add to that whiteness, what
candor?
> —Mencius, as translated by Pound

Sculpture fled. And architecture has now run after. And for good reasons: that
the round world (which it was their job to lead us to enjoy—to illuminate)—
turned to rot. It had been treated cheap, not by these arts but by what makes
arts: men.

All golden things, including the mean, got debased. Then everything blew up, from the inside, from cause.

It is even possible that one has to include line as having suffered, and color.
But this will not be so easily apparent, and the point of it can wait.

There came a man who dealt with whiteness. And with space. He was an
American. And perhaps his genius lay most in innocence rather than in the candor now necessary. In any case, he was not understood.

What seems clear is, that two dimensions as surface for plastic attack is once
more prime. And with all perspective as aid gone, the whole Renaissance. Even
line gone. And maybe color—as too easy.

The allure—the light—had better be in any painted, drawn, cut or carved
thing without use or reference of any object. Any narrative too, for that matter. Except one. And that one it has not been our habit to regard as one, as
either an object or a narrative. Say it is not one. But it is surely the way—the
tao 道 —that two dimensions is now being given back the job.

Take it flatly, a plane. On it, how can a man throw his shadow, make this the illumination of his experience, how put his weight exactly—there? (In my business it comes out how, by alphabetic letters, such signs and their syllables, how to make them not sounds but *my* sounds, my—what are not any more sounds than is a painter's objects or a dancer's movements—my "voice"; to say what I got to say, which may be of interest to others because it can stand for what they have got to say, if it says anything; and it can only to the degree that, like a plane, it is no plane at all.) How make that plane, the two dimensions, be all—from a point to any dimension?

It was Twombly, and wholly in some other reference, in fact to how a lake we know in common afforded him about what Tao Yuan-Ming's east hedge was, who gave me suddenly, as he talked of contemplation, the sense of what architecture now had to do with.

That is, I knew sculpture was buried, was become the art underneath us all, had gone down to be our sign—by a sort of inverted archeology—that each of us had now to come up live, like those stone images scholars are digging up in so many places; that only by ourselves can we find out—by no outside medium or means whatsoever—the round all men have been rifled of. And I knew this was, to put it quickly, traction in dance, was Pierre Boulez in music, was a like combination of a man's own documentation and his conjecture in the art of narrative. But I didn't know, until that instant, as the two of us were looking at a new large black-and-white canvas of Twombly's, what use architecture had now to be.

I was taking exception to this particular painting. I thought that here Twombly had been tempted, that he had slipped off the wire any of us in all of the arts walk over space on these days, that he had gone into the whiteness as that other man had—as an American stands especially in danger of, candor is still such a ruthless reality on the other side of despair, or still seems ruthless in the face of humanism and confronted by the will of that reality with which artists can have nothing to do, the will despair breeds and which is, god save us, the will by which most of our fellow men manage to get through. An artist has to cross over.

I knew what Twombly was fighting for, even in this canvas. It is what he is always trying to get down, what he so often does so succeed in getting in to what he is confronted by—into that rectangle—that honor & elegance are here once more present in the act of paint.

It was just
then, just when in this particular canvas I didn't see it—or saw more than I
needed to see, saw what is death to see, the innocence of it is such a dissolve—when Twombly himself had, by going too far not gone far enough (that
is, as a painter, so confined, had not gone far enough) had, in fact, gone outside himself, had, as so many most able men have gone outside the canvas
gone to technique—when, in this one case, Twombly had tried to solve it outside the place where he almost every time does battle it out (he is that pure),
look at his canvases . . .

> or for that matter his sculptures, which are properly made up from what
> wire, bone, stone, iron, wood he picks up, and so do respect facts, the
> accidents of same

(this is the twin methodology, this is documentation, these sculptures of
his also show how accurate his penetration of the reality bearing on us is:
these are the artifacts he finds surrounding himself in the same diggings
out of which he is digging himself

> what I like about Twombly is this sense one gets that his apprehen-
> sion—his *tien* 天 is buried to the hips, to the neck, if you like

the dug up stone figures, the thrown down glyphs, the old sorells in sheep dirt
in caves, the flaking iron—these are his *paintings*
    I underline his *paintings* to distinguish them from the objects picked up, the
sculptures, simply, that all document is not the equal of a man's life, what he
bears inside himself and makes speak directly: this is only—it needs now to be
underlined—what he is inside himself and nothing outside, no facts, only his
own acts make it

Suddenly I understood, as the two of us were there inside that too small room
in that too modern building jutting out over that lake which we both had bent
our art around, that architecture had no reason any longer at all to confine
space, that it was we who were confined, that architecture, like sculpture, had
gone elsewhere. And it occurred to me, that a billboard made more sense. That
here, too, man had been given back his oldest job, that if he was buried, he
was also all that came between the light.

And so, if Twombly does make canvases boldly behave as two dimensions and yet makes forces present which at least have been absent since the mural of the death of Adam was painted at Arezzo, look for cause

> look for it in yourself,
> in what you have lost

and let this man tell you,
there is nothing to fear, you put your hand up, and by this

other sort of will, you take away any sword that hangs by a hair over you, or any rotted apple

> you can do it, because you are the only round thing left, whatever the dirt squeezing you, or horses hooves

The writing here reads: we are never as thin as the yellow flower because of the sun.

And the fable? The seed planted with that Adam in his mouth.

And the wood of the tree which grew? how would you carve it otherwise than in like dimensions, and like candor?

(1952)

Proprioception

for LeRoi Jones

who first published

all of these pieces, and

fast, in Yugen, Floating Bear, & Kulchur,

1961 and 1962.

Proprioception

Physiology: the surface (senses—the 'skin': of 'Human Universe') the body itself—proper—one's own 'corpus': PROPRIOCEPTION the cavity of the body, in which the organs are slung: the viscera, or interoceptive, the old 'psychology' of feeling, the heart; of desire, the liver; of sympathy, the 'bowels'; of courage—the kidney etc—gall. (Stasis—or as in Chaucer only, spoofed)

Today: movement, at any cost. Kinesthesia: beat (nik) the sense whose end organs lie in the muscles, tendons, joints, and are stimulated by bodily tensions (—or relaxations of same). Violence: knives/anything, to get the body in.

To which

PROPRIOCEPTION: the data of depth sensibility/the 'body' of us as object which spontaneously or of its own order produces experience of, 'depth' Viz SENSIBILITY WITHIN THE ORGANISM BY MOVEMENT OF ITS OWN TISSUES

'Psychology': the surface: consciousness as ego and thus no flow because the 'senses' of same are all that sd contact area is valuable for, to report in to central. In-

THE WORKING 'OUT' OF 'PROJECTION' spection, followed hard on heels by, judgment (judicium, dotha: cry, if you must/all feeling may flow, is all which can count, at sd point. Direction outward is sorrow, or joy. Or participation: active social life, like, for no other reason than that— social life. In the present. Wash the ego out, in its own 'bath' (os)

The 'cavity'/cave: probably the 'Unconscious'? That is, the interior empty place filled with 'organs'? for 'functions'?

The advantage is to 'place' the thing, instead of it wallowing around sort of outside, in the

THE 'PLACE' OF THE 'UNCONSCIOUS' universe, like, when the experience of it is intero-ceptive: it is inside us/& at the same time does not feel literally identical with our own physical or mortal self (the part that can die). In this sense

likewise the heart, etc, the small intestine etc, are
or can be felt as—and literally they can be—
transferred. Or substituted for. Etc. The organs.—
Probably also why the old psychology was chiefly
visceral: neither dream, nor the unconscious, was
then known as such. Or allowably inside, like.

'ACTION'—OR, AGAIN, 'MOVEMENT'

This 'demonstration' then leads to the same third,
or corpus, thing or 'place,' the

proprious-ception
'one's own'-ception

the soul is proprioceptive	the 'body' itself as, by movement of its own tis- sues, giving the data of, depth. Here, then, wld be what is left out? Or what is physiologically even the 'hard' (solid, palpable), that one's life is informed from and by one's own literal body— as well, that is, as the whole inner mechanism, which keeps us so damn busy (like eating, sleeping, urinating, dying there, by deterioration of sd 'functions' of sd 'organs')—that this mid-thing between, which is what gets 'buried,' like, the flesh? bones, muscles, ligaments, etc., what one uses, literally, to get about etc that this is 'central,' that is—in this 1/2 of the picture—what they call the SOUL, the intermediary, the intervening thing, the inter- ruptor, the resistor. The self.
The gain:	to have a third term, so that *movement* or *action* is 'home.' Neither the Unconscious nor Projection (here used to remove the false opposition of 'Conscious'; 'consciousness' is self) have a home unless the DEPTH implicit in physical being— built-in space-time specifics, and moving (by movement of 'its own') —is asserted, or found- out as such. Thus the advantage of the value 'proprioception.' As such.
its own perception	The 'soul' then is equally 'physical.' Is the self. Is such, 'corpus.' Or—to levy the gain psychology from 1900, or 1885, did supply until it didn't (date? 1948?)—the three terms wld be:

surface (senses) projection
cavity (organs—here read 'archtypes')
unconscious the body itself—consciousness:
implicit accuracy, from its own energy as a state of
implicit motion.

Identity,   therefore (the universe is one) is supplied; and the
abstract-primitive character of the real (asserted)
is 'placed': projection is discrimination (of the
object from the subject) and the unconscious is the
universe flowing-in, inside.

Logography

Word writing. Instead of 'idea-writing' (ideogram etc). That would seem to be it.

Leading to phonetization—as though we didn't know identity of sounds, meaning two things, any longer did mean. The proposition wld seem to be that we don't.

About the only way the character of the pun—and rhyme (which has struck me now for some time as a most interesting crazy business of writing right now)—makes sense. I quote (abt the earliest business we can know anything abt, some Sumerian traders in cattle—"re cows and oxen" is the tablet, 3500 BC from
Uruk
    Erech
        Orchoe
            Warka

The need for adequate representation of proper names finally led to the development of phonetization. This is confirmed by the Aztec and Mayan writings, which employ the phonetic principle only rarely and then almost exclusively in expressing proper names.

The procedure involved may result in a full phonetic transfer, as in a drawing of knees to express the name 'Neil' (from 'kneel'), of the sun for the word 'son,' or even together in a drawing of knees plus the sun to express the personal name of 'Neilson.'

I stop there. My own sense is I don't know that we are any further. (In that connection, negatively however, one can add this, at the same point from the same man—Gelb:

That the need for indicating grammatical elements was of no great importance in the origin of phonetization can be deduced from the fact that even after the full development of phonetization writing failed for a long time to indicate grammatical elements adequately.

Postscript to Proprioception & Logography

Further notes on what would look like fundamentals of any new discourse:

Landscape
  "a portion of land which the eye
  can comprehend in a single view"

  to bring the land into the eye's view:

   COSMOS
     creation   All
       a verb   kinship
                 is known
 NOTIONAL (GNA—know it   vertically
     instantly   not
                 relationally
 "carrying a full meaning of its own"

The *other* knowing is NOUN, proper (proprius)
noun—that which belongs to the self

nominal-ize all local relations are
nominalized
     VID—vision of
    Self: you I some other
      God

                                 (we already possess a
sufficient theory of
psychology)

the greatest present danger

the area of pseudo-sensibility:

          games

          randomness

          haphazard

                (I Ching-
                  ness)

              sorts

          accidence
              (anything goes or
              all *is* interesting Or
                    nothing is
instead of novelty ("God is the organ of
          novelty," and
as the true cast of
the sensible

          probability

              (Kicks)
          phoney disaffection: actually
          political (the elite among
          the masses accomplishing
          a lateral coup d'état

persons are hung along a line from birth to
      death. Some fell off at 5 etc some at
      17 others 40, like   No matter, they
      are bombers (carrying forces) of *the time*

they fell off, not what
they look like talk like
seem etc Or are
taken as

(arrière to this thought is
the 'phases' used to be
causes of 'forms,' in
social—public as distinguished
from private—life: viz,

1st year infancy
2nd thru 3rd libidinal
4th to 6th oedipean
7th to 12th play
12th to 17th sexualization
etc
         (upon which rites
de passage existed   Opinion
has replaced all such

———————————————————

Superstition & idolatry also rampant:
      anything can happen (BS

Bridge-Work

fr the Old Discourse to the New

                 men worth anyone's study:
Edward Sapir
Edward Carpenter (Whitman's friend &
                Eileen Garrett's
                teacher

Carl O. Sauer!
Andrew Lang (on hypnagogic vision,
             as well as trans. of
                Homer—& friend of?
  Mead
              (*Pistis Sophia* etc

Aleister Crowley (?: particularly his
                book on the Tarot

Ernest Fenollosa!
B. L. Whorf
L. A. Waddell
Edward Hyams
Victor Berard
Cyrus Gordon

March, 1961—with
acknowledgements to
Gerrit Lansing

the hinges of civilization to be put back on the door:

Hinge #1	original 'town-man' put back to Aurignacian-Magdalenian, for evidence of a more primal & consequent art & life than the cultivation which followed (the Deglaciation & the Wet Period until 7000–5000 BC
Hinge #2	Indo-European, fr. the Bible or El Amarna Age: 1350 BC seen *prior* to itself, not forward of itself (such includes

texts   Hittite (& Sumerian behind it) Canaanite—as leading to the Old Testament, but showing earlier Cyprus & Cretan— & Anatolian—conditions

invasion starts circa 2000 BC & covers 3/4s of the millennium "Phoenician" alphabet (Sinai) dates 1850 BC (?)

& roots: the linguistic values of Indo-European languages, the original minting of words & syntax

[as in other hinges of the direct line, there is an advantage to the leaping *outside* as well as connecting *backward*: for example American Indian languages offer useful freshening of syntax to go alongside Indo-European]

Hinge #3   to turn the 5th Century BC back toward the 6th & thus catch up Persian & Thracian & Milesian   Heraclitus Buddha Pythagoras Confucius etc

forces not then lost   (Homer-Hesiod to be considered as Pisistratus of Athens made them texts

                                          etc; Miss Harrison
                                          clearest among
                                          moderns on Persian,
                                          & Cretan prepara-
                                          tions thus gained

Hinge #4   *the 2nd* AD *back to the 1st:*
                            an 'affective' time, the 2nd
                            —as well as brilliant
                            early secular: Maximus of Tyre
                                                      Marinus of Tyre
                                                      examples

                            but like the 17th later
                            costly in loss of some-
                            thing the 1st, as later the
                            15th & 16th still held, a
                            sense of the divine

                            (gain here is to get a load of Gnosticism,
                            & Hans Jonas particularly useful)

Hinge #5   the 50 years 1200–1250, to turn the corner
                            of what has been all we've known: Aquinas
                            Eckhart Bacon etc etc

Hinge #6   the 17th, seen as the brilliant secular it
                            was, without loss of the alchemy etc
                            it unseated

Hinge #7   the 20th, release fr
                            both the 18th—   inadequate ra-
                                                        tionalizing after
                                                        Locke & Descartes,
                                                        & thus 'weakness'
                                                        to increasing indus-
                                                        trial revolution—

                            & 19th, the new progress of
                            Marxism

otherwise the present will lose what America is the inheritor of: a
secularization which not only loses nothing of the divine but by seeing
process in reality redeems all idealism fr theocracy or mobocracy,
whether it is rational or superstitious, whether it is democratic or
socialism.

GRAMMAR—a "book"

why ("adv."!) instrumental case of hwā, hwaet. See WHO

how (adv.   [AS. hū
                        nominative who
                                         what
                        inst. case   why

Goth hvas (Skt kas)

quantum neuter of quantus
                (cf. page 192
the process is *not* continuous
                [pattern]
but takes place by steps,
each step being the emission
or absorption of an amt. of
energy called the quantum

Math. distinguished fr. a
        magnitude

Phil. the char. of a thing
by virtue of which measure
or number is applicable to
it, or it can be determined
as more or less than some
other.

the
" adj. or
def. arti-
cle"

that

pl. those

"Syn.
see WHO"!

[AS thē, a later form of
earlier nom. sing. masc.
sē, formed under the in-
fluence of thaet. See
THAT

AS thaet, neut. nom. &
acc. sing. of the demon-
strative (?) pronoun and
adj. (?),
                also used as a
relative pronoun

[also, a connective (!)
derived by loss of stress!
fr the demonstrative 'that'

which pro!   BODY
fr. stem who & that   of līc (who-like?)
                            "of what sort or
                                        kind"

AS līc = s body
        in "lich" Scot & Dial Eng
                for corpse
LIKE! "adj"
AS gelīc, fr ge & līc
& orig. meaning
having the same body or shape
& hence, like

a adj.   or indefinite article   (shortened fr AN, adj)
            AS one! (called adj ! fr numeral!

another

other   ("adj"!—one of two, either other
            actually is neuter or one, a pronoun!

[as what, neuter of who!/

quantus pronoun - adj (?) [Relat. correl. with tantus,
of what size,
how much

(magnitude?)

pronom. stem WHO
Grk. pa pos (how
qui
posos   quomodo

Lat. Qui quae quod quom
quot quam quia quantus
qualis, ubi (quo-bi)
ceterus, cis, cuias,
2 uter (quoter)

Germ. were was warum

Eng. who what why how
pronouns

Cf. Engl (for weakened Cl-, fr
Grk TIS (for KIS)

Lat quis? cf. Engl. he him it
(for older hit)

POS (Pronoun)

v. sub. pos

followed by a clause of comparison
of such size, of such a measure,
so great, such

absence of any such a word in English,
fr tantus? Result, or confusion over
quantity? Therefore not understanding
quantus is the neuter case of a pronoun,
not an adjective???

bulk in Greek
is   pelikos

but quantus
is posos

p of Ionian Grk
is k

kati = s quantus

so Skt kas, ka = quis, quae
kva = qua
kutus = quo
katha = qui quomodo
kada = quum

kataras = poteros, uter

Active &

II "Case" / 7, in Indo-Eur.:

MIDDLE VOICE
is old passive!
(non-copulative!)

means or
ablative of instrument
is middle voice

nominative
genitive
dative —to

Lat. with
by, at

TO CARRY

accusative

ablative ——— removal or direction away, in Eng by from

AWAY

locative —— where (place   & in

PLACE
PROCESS
OR AGENCY

instrumental — agent or means   substantive (material
                                                    content)

---

present, imperfect, & future / aorist, perfect, pluperfect
                              & future perfect indicative

(indicative middle   middle

In the Middle ∧ voice   the subject is represented as
acting:

1. on himself: make oneself go, proceed   [will!
                persuade oneself, trust, obey   [belief!

2. for himself: buy for oneself
                send for a person   to come to oneself,   [grace!
                                summon, send for   or command
                                                            courtesy   !
                to take to the field, march   [obey!

3. on something
   belonging to oneself   loose one's own, ransom   [each takes care
                            bring one's own   of themselves!

III   The Indo-Europeans Anyway

They appeared circum 1750 BC—or 1800—out of South Russia and east to the Caspian, and, as they dispersed, carried those languages we have known thus (west to east):

| | Baltic Slavic | | Tocharian (!) |

Celtic Germanic Latin Greek Hittite Armenian Iranian Sanskrit
        (Fr. Sp. Ital.)

Sapir (*Language*) has this to say: "The first [of three drifts of major importance at work in the language] is the familiar tendency to level the distinction between the subjective and the objective, itself but a late chapter in the steady reduction of the old Indo-European system of syntactic cases. . . . The distinction between the nominative and accusative was nibbled away by phonetic processes and *morphological levelings* until *only certain pronouns* retained distinctive subjective and objective forms."

IV Syntax ("ordering")

Sapir: "It is somewhat venturesome and yet not an altogether unreasonable speculation that sees in word order and stress the primary methods for the expression of all syntactic relations and looks upon the present relational value of specific words and elements as but a secondary condition due to a transfer of values.

"Thus, the *of* in an English phrase like 'the law of the land' is now as colorless in content, as purely a relational indicator as the 'genitive' suffix *-is* in the Latin *lex urbis* 'the law of the city.' We know, however, that it was originally an adverb of considerable concreteness of meaning, 'away, moving from,' and that the syntactic relation was originally expressed by the case form [ablative] of the second noun.

"An interesting thesis results:—All of the actual content of speech, its clusters of vocalic and consonantal sounds, is in origin limited to the concrete; relations were originally not expressed in outward form but were merely implied and articulated with the help of order and rhythm."

V Concord, in Bantu and Chinook

an alternative to syntax [at least as we have understood it] altogether:

Every noun is classified according to five categories—masculine, feminine, neuter [general], dual, and plural. "Woman" is feminine, "sand" is neuter, "table" is masculine. If, therefore, I wish to say "The woman put the sand on the table," I must place in the verb certain class or gender prefixes that accord with corresponding noun prefixes. The sentence reads then, "The (fem.)—woman she (fem.)—it (neut.)—it (masc.)—on-put the (neut.)—sand the (masc.)—table." If "sand" is qualified as "much" and "table" as "large," these new ideas are expressed as abstract nouns, each with its inherent class-prefix ("much" is neuter or feminine, "large" is masculine) and with a possessive prefix referring to the qualified noun. Adjective thus calls to noun, noun to verb. "The woman put much sand on the large table," therefore, takes the form: "The (fem.)—woman she (fem.)—it (neut.)—it (masc.)—on-put the (fem.)—thereof (neut.)—quantity the (neut.)—sand the (masc.)—thereof (masc.)—largeness the (masc.)—table."

—Sapir page 115

VI "Number" / the singular— exs. term (an end— not "ends")

                         & image (instead of images,

                                     in Nicholas Calas

                                     (via Robt Kelly's

                                     essay on verse in

                                     Trobar 2)

"nominative" (plurals distribute)

A Plausible 'Entry' for, like, man

I: paleolithic man   (brain-case, like the present
                                             porpoise's, bigger than modern
to 10,000 BC   man's

                          art (morals, tools; 'free,' 'traveling,' "women"
                                             [the so-called 'Venuses'

    fr 5,000 BC: Sumerian to 2500 BC [a writing language in
   (cities possible)   existence c. 3250 BC]

1800 BC,   Indo-Europeans appear (Hittite/   1350 BC
                               & horse   /Canaanite
                                                  approx. 'secular' literature

                              HOMER, 850 BC
_____

450, Athens   logos invented (universalism possible

II: 334–323 BC, Alexander's conquest of the East, and a unity possible
       "larger than any that had existed before"; and it lasted almost
       1000 years "until destroyed in its turn by the conquests of Islam"
       [but it was those conquests—623 A.D. on—, & not Xty or Rome,
       which did it].

[Irish scholarship   Mohammed born 570, lived to 632—
   c. 500–800]   Islam teaching Europe from Cordova
                                (Averroës) 1100 AD

       fr 732 AD, date Martel turned back Moslems at Tours, one has to
       see a 'Europe'—and new "West"—arising

            771   Charlemagne
            790   Irish monks to Iceland
            823   Norse, to Dublin
            862   Swedes to Novgorod
            871   Alfred
            981   Eric the Red, to Greenland

A Work.

A work which would free much of the encumbrance upon man as himself a universe—not microorganism, microcosm—would start with Hesiod, taking him as a base-line and saying anything after him as 'lost' something and that all which he does show and include is a beginning of dimension of man's place in the cosmos as it had been imagined before Homer or any such better known ways man is placed which have come on since. What I am gesturing in, is a 'literature' (of which Hesiod seems to be a conclusion) which is now for the first time again available, and it amounts to something like Hesiod's own title, a theogony. As such—and not as it has sounded—it is a total placement of man and things among all possibilities of creation, rather than that one alone, of modern history and politics, and science and literature, or arma, the Indo-European chariot, and virum, the old epic. My confidence is, there is a new one, and Hesiod is one of its gates.

Immediately my purpose is only to wake up the time spans and materials lying behind Hesiod, so that they can seem freer than they have; but essentially I'm sure a line drawn through Hesiod himself will already demark the difference the materials and times behind him will yield. The problem is what seems still to be an unwritten history, the History of the Second Millennium BC. Already in fact an historian-scholar of Hittite, such as Hans Güterbock, has suggested that the classic three generations of God-Fathers Absolute, and their Wives and Sons, is in fact some curious summary of conditions in each of three successive millennia, the 4th, the 3rd and the 2nd, the series running thus:

	Greek	Hittite	Phoenician	Meso-potamian
3rd Millennium:	Ouranos (Saturn)	—Anu		
	Cronos	—Kumarbi	—Enil (also El)	
	Zeus	—Tesub	—Baal	—Marduk

And even—in Babylonian and in Phoenician—a 5th Millennium oldest of all "Gods," prior to Ouranos etc and 'father' of sames: *Alalu* (Babylon), and, according to Phylo Biblius quoting Sanchuniathon—the latter lived in the "time of the War of Troy"—the first generation in Canaanite was *Eliun* or Hypsistos, "The Highest."

I stress the 2nd Millennium because it is clear that the series set themselves then, and though there are the wars of the Zeus and his brothers with the Titans, or Giants, who didn't rebel with the brothers, and therefore insert a curious mixed evil set who trouble thereafter all the established edicts of heaven and confuse the general cosmology, the fathers run out in the sons decisively in the 2nd. At the same time the 2nd is the millennium of the general overthrow of the ancient settled world, which was neither East nor West, and the bringing into existence of what, even if unclear, comes through to us—or has, up to now—via mostly the Greeks (allowing that those who still read the Old Testament get a great deal of that previous time of man slipping through the Israelite overlays).

The facts of the 2nd Millennium are loosely known. Around about 1800 things shook up. The main drive down on the older Mesopotamian-Egyptian-Indus world seems to start with Hurrian and then Hittite people, the latter at least certainly Indo-European, in and before that date. But there was disturbance earlier, setting in between Mesopotamia and Egypt when Western Semites called Amorites (meaning "the Westerners") were fussing at settled cities and people around 2200 and 2000 BC, actually founding the Larsa Dynasty in southern Babylon in 2020 BC.

But by 1800 results showed all over the known world: Egypt itself was ruled by Hyksos, who are now sd easily to be "Phoenicians," the Phoenicians themselves (or Canaanites, to use the Hurrian meaning of 'purple') were mixed with the Hurrians—and the Hittite First Empire was in full swing north throughout Anatolia. Crete itself appears already by this date—by all the evidence that the identification of Linear A by Cyrus Gordon now makes easier to lock in place—to have been conquered or infiltrated by Phoenicians, so much so that in the period 1600 to 1400 the balance of Aegean trade was in Phoenician favor.

Giving that history of that disturbance the most time one gets a period of 1000 years overlapping the next huge impact from which came Greece: that is, by 1230 a whole new series of shift does come in, the Israelites invade from the east, the so-called "Sea-Peoples" (the Philistines of the Bible) sweep over the Eastern Mediterranean between 1225 & 1175, devastating the Hittite Empire and destroying Tyre and Phoenician power. Two great battles or wars dramatize this time, Troy, 1183, and Kadesh, 1188/87; but obviously years earlier Greek and other new forces had been accumulating and the overlap appears to come from about 1500 BC; Tatian in his address to the Greeks quotes Thallus, a 1st century AD historian, as saying that Zeus' victory in alliance with the Hundred-handed Ones over the Titans of Thessaly took place "322 years before the siege of Troy." This then can be taken to be the line of the end of God-Father change and or transmission, as well as a good controlling date for the emergence of the Mycenean or Aegean Greek governance of the Mediterranean: 1505 BC.

We have then two 'halves' of the 2nd Millennium, starting with "The Westerners" hitting Babylonia 2220, and ending with Troy and Kadesh (1188/87 and 1183). In the first half of the Millennium Hittites and Canaanites—or, a double Indo-European and Semite disturbance—replaced older centers of power such as Babylonia and Egypt; and in the second half a new Indo-European force, the "Greeks," and a new Semite force, the Israelites, overran the earlier like 'pair.'

I believe this is a fair picture, despite how it leaves out much that we usually think is ancient history, especially that 19th century stuff which stressed Egypt and Babylon. It may in fact be one of the advantages of just the literature, both which we have inherited, the Greek-Hebrew, as well as the new literature these facts put into proper shape, the Hittite-Canaanite (as well as the improvement on the oldest past which Sumerian gives us), that they 'right' the history and give us this new picture of the 2nd Millennium.

With that one can then begin to work Hesiod back—as well for that matter as the Iliad—and at the same time come forward toward Homer and Hesiod's day (850–800 BC) from a 'true' origin of much which they include, the thousand years of writing some of which is now known and which precedes them by a term of time as long as 1000 years. In other words Indo-Europeans and Semites had, for that long before Homer and Hesiod, power and governed an earlier literary and historical tradition which itself preceded them by two full millennia, the 3rd and the 4th.

How much, then, of Hesiod and Homer is, (a) earliest man's work and story (3500 BC or before, and coming through relatively a unit to 1800 BC or so); and (b) how much is it the 1000 years of their own sort of people—I-E's and Semites—from 1800 BC to 800?

May 3, 1962

Place; & Names

a place as term in the order of creation
& thus useful as a function of that equation
example, that the "Place Where the Horse-Sacrificers Go"
of the Brihadaranyaka Upanishad is worth more than
a metropolis—or, for that matter, any moral
concept, even a metaphysical one
                                    and that this is so
for physical & experimental reasons of
the *philosophia perennis,* or Isness
of cosmos beyond those philosophies
or religious or moral systems of
rule, thus giving factors of naming
—nominative power—& landschaft
experience (geography) which stay truer
to space-time than personalities
or biographies of such terms as specific
cities or persons, as well as the inadequacy
to the order of creation of anything except
names—including possibly mathematics (?)

the crucialness being that these places or names
be as parts of the body, common, & capable
therefore of having cells which can decant
total experience—no selection
other than one which is capable
of this commonness (permanently
duplicating) will work

"Story" in other words is if not superior
at least equal to ultimate mathematical
language—perhaps superior because of
cell-ness (?) In any case history
(as to be understood by Duncan's Law
to mean a) histology & b) story)
applies here, in this equational way
& severely at the complementarity of
cosmos (complementary to individual
or private) and not to cities or
events in the way it has, in
a mistaken secondary way, been
understood

(1962)

you can't use words as ideas any more than that they can
be strung as sounds. They are meanings only and actions of
their own sort

       feeling and desires and breath
   the cause of the words coming into existence
   ahead of them, the nose bringing them out ahead of its—
   self, and a principle, their own meaning, enough
   animus so it all has
   will

  Feminine
  Writing so that all the World
  is redeemed, and history
  and all that politics,
  and "State" and Subjection
  are for once, done away with,
as the reason
of writing

                            (1965)

The Present Is Prologue

"The Present Is Prologue"

My shift is that I take it the present is prologue, not the past. The instant, therefore. Is its own interpretation, as a dream is, and any action—a poem, for example. Down with causation (except, see below). And yrself: you, as the only
reader and mover of the instant. You, the cause. No drag allowed, on either.
Get on with it.

In the work and dogmas are: (1) How, by form, to get the content instant;
(2) what any of us are by the work on ourself, how make ourself fit instruments
for use (how we augment the given—what used to be called the fate); (3) that
there is no such thing as duality either of the body and the soul or of the world
and I, that the fact in the human universe is the discharge of the many (the
multiple) by the one (yrself done right, whatever you are, in whatever job,
is the thing—all hierarchies, like dualities, are dead ducks).

I am still, at 40, hugely engaged with my parents, in fact more engaged
with them now than with that I spent so much time on in my 20s and 30s:
society, and other persons (why I was in education, government and politics so
long). So, first, I tell you their names and places, to indicate how I am of the
heterogeneous present and not of the old homogeneity of the Founders, and
the West.

My father was born Karl Joseph Olsen, in Sweden, and his name probably
reflects a story in the family that they were Hungarians on my grandmother's
side. He was carried to the States at five months.

My mother was Mary Hines, and Yeats told me (on the grounds of my
grandfather, who was the immigrant, 'born in Cork and brought up in Gal-
way') that my mother's aunt must have been his 'Mary Hines,' the beloved of
the blind poet Raftery and 'the most beautiful woman in all Western Ireland.'
It was rough on my mother when I found this out at 18—my father and I never

let her forget the fall from grace, that she was only the most beautiful woman in South Worcester, Mass.

But what strikes me (and I now suspect has much more governed the nature of my seven years of writing than I knew) is, the depth to which the parents who live in us (they are not the same) are our definers. And that the work of each of us is to find out the true lineaments of ourselves by facing up to the primal features of these founders who lie buried in us—that this is us, the Double-Backed Beast. (Didn't Hesiod call his genealogy of the gods and men "the work of the days," that next oldest poem of the old culture to Homer's two?)

There are only two live pasts—your own (and that hugely included your parents), and one other which we don't yet have the vocabulary for, because the West has stayed so ignorant, and the East has lived off the old fat too long. I can invoke it by saying, the mythological, but it's too soft. What I mean is that foundling which lies as surely in the phenomenological 'raging apart' as these queer parents rage in us.

I have spent most of my life seeking out and putting down the 'Laws' of these two pasts, to the degree that I am permitted to see them (instead of the boring historical and evolutionary one which the West has been so busy about since Thucydides) simply because I have found them in the present, my own and yours, and believe that they are the sign of a delightful new civilization of man ahead.

Now, I spend most of my time studying the Sumerians and Mayans, transposing the poems and the inscriptions they left. The will to cohere in both these people is what I see in us, in now. I do not mean collectivism, though I am not at all so uncomfortable in the face of it, and of quantity, as those of my contemporaries seem to be who are stuck with the old soul, and quality, and who back up, for sanctions, to those walls which have been a comfort for man in the East and the West since 1500 B.C. (The American Indian lies outside that comfortable box just as much, I'd argue, as the Americans now do, despite Western appearance. I meant it, in *Ishmael,* that we are the last first people.)

Therefore I find it awkward to call myself a poet or a writer. If there are no walls there are no names. This is the morning, after the dispersion, and the work of the morning is methodology: how to use oneself, and on what. That is my profession. I am an archeologist of morning. And the writing and acts which I find bear on the present job are (I) from Homer back, not forward; and (II) from Melville on, particularly himself, Dostoevsky, Rimbaud, and Lawrence. These were the modern men who projected what we are and what we are in, who broke the spell. They put men forward into the post-modern, the post-humanist, the post-historic, the going live present, the "Beautiful Thing."

(1952)

Stocking Cap

The skill was not to snub the nose of the pickerel on the under edge of the ice as, with wet, numb hands, you brought him up—more often than not he was a perch—out of the water six inches or three feet down, as the winter went, from the frozen surface of the lake.

The rest was crude, cold work and my father saw to it that it began the moment we hit the ice, the sun hardly up. First, the cutting of the holes, round and eight to ten inches across, the only challenge that you not let go your grip, from stiff fingers, on the long, narrow steel of the chisel; the setting out of the tilts (like laths, but of a better wood, a food and a half high) each in a slit chipped out close to the rim of a hole, with slush packed in to freeze it upright; the baiting of the lines and the rigging of them from each tilt, their fine thread sticking to the ice and hard to free with mittens on. Then, on shore, the gathering the wood and making the fire, the important thing the spot, protected but at some promontory from which all the tilts could be seen. And the rest of the day the ever repeating routine of the circuit of the holes, to skim them and to make sure that the wind or a nibble had not slipped the noose in the line off the tilt-arm that held it over the center of the hole.

It was this same arm, when a strike was a good one, which tripped and let go the red flannel flag and bent down on a spring from the top of the tilt, and it was these flags we gave our attention to, once the tilts were out, swigging coffee by the fire, always our eyes out over the surface of the lake to sight them, if and when one should go up, the exciting signal that started us on the run over the ice.

I suppose it was because my father picked his Sundays that way, but they all stand in my mind as sunny but wind-driven and bitter cold. I was allowed to bring my skates, though I could see he didn't much approve, it was not according to some Hoyle of ice fishing he had in his head. He made this exception of his son, however, and it gave the day a connection to other things one did in a New England winter. Otherwise it stood clear, stands clear now, as some glistening, cruel, attractive other country enclosed in dark, from the bitter dark of winter morning before dawn (when he waked me) to the travel home in the trolley at night and the sweet animal collapse the heat of the house and supper brought once we were back in the tenement, as though a blow had struck us, and we welcomed it, and went down under it, easily, pleasurably, back into sleep.

My father was a stickler for details and it seems now as though it was all week he was working on the gear although I suppose it was only the night before. This was a holiday, his chance to get free, and he treated it as he treated the other adventures he contrived for later seasons of the year; partridge berries, May flowers, elderberries for the wine he kept five years ahead, our trips to the dump for iron, his trips alone in summer to sketch for the water colors he did at nights at home. He fished at other times of the year but I never seem to have gone along, it was always some friend who went with him nights after work. He never caught any more than he did in the winter. The truth is, I don't think he cared. It was only another way of going free, getting out to the sensations of life. (I remember how irritated he was, when we went after walnuts once in the fall, because I did not see things as sharply or at the distance he did.)

And my weariness bothered him. Another ritual of the fall was grapes. He had found, how I could never figure out, wild vines of red and Concord grapes buried in a tangle of forest miles off the Boston-Worcester trolley line. We would set off circumspectly enough, with only a folded mail sack under his arm. The trolley ride was more than any train for me, rushing and wobbling as it did through mostly open country. The walk from the stop I remember as the high point next after that first sight of the grapes themselves. It was down a country road lined with apples, by farms and dogs and stock. My father was enough of a kid to stop, and gape, and dawdle as much as I did, throwing stones with me, hanging over a broken wall into a field, breaking off branches of trees along the road by hurling other rotted pieces at them like boomerangs.

It was when we started into the woods that I began to tire, and though the coming on the grapes was a tremendous thing, at which I marveled in my father, how he brought us to them, it wasn't long before I was plaguing him with questions, how long more we'd be and when we could go. I wonder now if it wasn't the presence of woods, they depress me so, even to this day. At first I was all right, the Concords tasted so good, and I gorged myself, eating more than I was putting in the sack. He'd laugh at me and tell me to get on with it, pick them not eat them, as he worked away raking them from the vines into the bag. But it was when we had all those within easy reach and it was necessary for him to climb the tree to follow the vine as it wound itself upward and I was left alone below with the woods that I'd begin to complain and he must have thought I sounded like my mother.

I don't remember much the road back but I do remember the wonderful stains on the sack, and the care we had to keep it away from our clothes and a self-consciousness when we were back in the city and stood on the rear platform of the trolleys with our bag.

Only once in winter, strangely enough, do I seem to have been inadequate, and that time, I think, he was complaining for the show of it, and to set himself a little bit above my mother. It was the time my two cousins, older than I, came with us. It was a severe day, the temperature below zero, and when we left the house my mother made a scene against his taking me. "You'll kill him," she said; "you'll be the death of him." It was a tough day, and I dare say I did feel the cold, but I was determined to go, and I put up with his jibes before my cousins, for even then I sensed they were meant for my mother, and not for me. They were compliments, in a way, for I was along, and they called my cousins' attention to that fact, and that he had a son who could stay with them.

His main concern each of those winter trips was the chisel. The tilts took care of themselves. They came home ready for use again no matter how cold or dark it had been when we had left the lake the previous time. He would never allow them to be wound carelessly as I have seen other fishermen do. But the chisel always needed new attention. It was one he had made himself. (I remember how surprised and scornful I was when I discovered, once we fished a large lake nearer the city, that other men had wider, store-bought chisels and that they called them by another name.) His was arranged in sections, out of pipe, in lengths about as long as tilts so that all our gear could be strapped together in a bundle. The threaded sleeves of the sections fascinated me, and the putting of them together, but the important part to him was the cutting end. It was no thicker or wider than a tilt and may have been his own design. It was this he sharpened with such care.

I was puzzled he took no more than one along. I suppose it was weight that dictated but I knew they could get lost, slip out of a cold hand and when you suddenly broke through that last plug of ice, and the water came up, and sloshed over your feet. He had lost one once, and I think I did, and once we were able to fish one out of shallow water, how I can't now say. The curious thing was I don't think he ever had a rope on the chisel's end as other men had and as you'd think he might. Perhaps it was another of those queer obstacles he had a way of dealing with as a challenge and which made him such an attractive, tragic man. The stubborn side of it killed him in the end.

The bait pail and the skimmer were the other crucial tools. Only once do I remember getting the minnows the day we fished—from a little old man in a shanty on the way, a professional, I thought, compared to us. The other times, I suppose, my father brought the minnows home from work, for he was careful with them, to keep the water right and to leave them out on the back porch over night. On the way to the lake they had to be carried most carefully, not to jounce, and to be looked at several times on the ride to make sure they did not die. Always one or two did, and to see them turned up, lolling in the water, sickened me. It wasn't the same when they were dead from being on the hook too long in the holes. The holes, before the day was through, were circled with them, side up, with big eyes, frozen in the ice.

The advance to the lake was always new, as sharp as I imagine the discovery of a continent used to be—the whiteness, the curiosity whether anyone else might be there first (then I was always so overwhelmed with disappointment I wanted to go home), the rush to start the holes, the decisions how to lay them, the question, how thick the ice. I suppose the work of cutting was inviting for its warmth but it was exhausting and I was interested, long before my father would allow himself to be, in the fire.

The fire was, for me, the big business of the day. With the lines out the fishing depended on the fish, but the fire, that depended on me. I fetched the wood and started it. I kept it alive. I tore my mittens feeding it. I burned my coat hugging it, I had to stand so close to keep warm I was forever sure my rubbers would crack or melt away. Or the wind would gust, and scatter the fire, and I'd have to go off farther and farther into the woods to get new wood for it and lose a mitten doing it, and come back with snow-bit hands.

But it was home, and everything centered on it, and though it always arranged to tip the coffee pot into itself, and burn the handle so I'd burn myself righting it, the fire was a precious thing and I was proud of its care, and built lives around it. (Most of the time it became a fort in which I barricaded myself against the woods, and the lake was a plain I scanned vigilantly—as though it might hide Indians as well as red topped tilts.)

It was also, of course, the place you came back gladly to from the ice, from a run out to play a fish or to patrol the nearer holes. And food had a special taste because of it, covered with soot from the tending of it, seasoned with the smell of each of the trees we were using for it, and the smoke entering the mouth with each bite as much as the meat.

So I was the guard, the mother of the fire, while my father, ever active, kept restlessly touring the ice, hoping a flag would go up, changing the tilts, cutting new holes to find the fishes' feeding ground. And sometimes he'd go off around some headland of the lake and be gone so long I'd get nervous and strike out after him. Or at least go far enough to get a better look-out for him without losing sight of the tilts. For it was always my hope, when he went off like that, that a flag would go up and all by myself I would land the biggest pickerel of the day.

It was the dying of the day on those lakes which gave me my first taste, I suppose, of wan-hope. No matter what I did the fire seemed to go down as the sun did, and when that light which comes as brightness goes off and that cold which settles as the wind dies would spread in from the lake, I first knew some secret of death.

It was an attractive hour. My father's figure out on the ice grew and his stocking cap became the fur crown of some Siberian trader. His overcoat filled out and though I knew it was green with age, and torn, it was fur too, and he was grand. His run, always peculiar from his thick-soled rubbers and his layers of clothes, was now immense.

The tilts were easier to see and though the flags flew up less often—they never kept us busy enough—they were startling when they did and my shout, or my father's run, was sharp like teeth on the grey ice and in the blue air. This was one of the times when I shared my father's feelings precisely: I was as prepared as he to linger as the day ran out. He stayed, perhaps, because he hoped for one more fish.

It is wood smoke that always throws me back to those wild days, the stain of it, sweet and sharp and green, in our stocking caps and hair, in our eyes and clothes (more than the dye of them), and in my nose and mouth and mind as we stepped into that welcome thing, the trolley car, to set off for home.

(1948)

Mr. Meyer

There was a tailor named Meyer who fixed my father's clothes, a short, warm, round man of whom I was most fond. My father was a letter carrier and his uniforms were constantly in need of patching, particularly on the shoulder where the bag was carried and along the side of the coat where the bottom of the bag wore the cloth away.

My father had left his trade as an iron worker some time before I was born. At that time, before the first world war, the salary of a letter carrier was higher and offered the flypaper that even the best of the lower middle class get caught on, security.

During that war and after, when other salaries went up, my father had lost the gain and was left only with the security, and that of the lowest, meanest kind. So uniforms, which the postmen had to buy for themselves, had to be made to last until there was little left of the original garment. My mother, I know, kept up with them as well as she could, repairing and relining, using the old to reinforce the new, working a season ahead, the heavier winter things at her machine in the fall, the spring and summer stuff as the winter began to ease off.

But there were certain jobs, like the shoulder patch, which took a tailor's skill, and that, I guess, was when Mr. Meyer came in. I imagine he did such work for other carriers and it was through them my father learned of him although vaguely, in the back of my mind, are some broken pieces of a memory that it was in answer to an advertisement of Mr. Meyer's that my father got in touch with him.

I know one thing. He lived at the other end of the city on a street the name of which is so joined to him I can never separate them. It was Burncoat Street.

It only strikes me now why that name obviously settled into my subconscious joined to Mr. Meyer. I had previously thought it was fastened there because of one winter night when, for some reason, Mr. Meyer could not come across the city to us, as was the custom, to pick up the clothes or to do some work, and my father and I had to go over on the streetcars to his shop.

It may have been the hour and the weather, or perhaps it was because I was thus up later than usual, but it was probably the intensity of the sight of him, small as he was, bent over his table with the only light in the shop the green shade above his head (the shadows peopled with uncertain figures called coats and the floor and tables ambushes of pants and dresses). It opened up a whole new side of him for me, the professional I had not the experience to recognize in him as I had come to know him in our home.

He used to come over carrying a paper bag, and sweating, not, I felt, from hurrying so much as from the working of that quality which marked him for me, his shyness. I was aware that other people were shy but whether I knew it then I know now their shyness was brittle. It was not how they were in their natures but how people took them, a social matter which didn't go any deeper than their vanities. I could sense that when they went away and talked to someone they felt superior to, or when they were alone, they were able to justify themselves, shoring up the details which tore the enemy, that other human being they were not sure of, down. The thing was not so much shyness as narrowness. There was no modesty in it.

It was the modesty of Mr. Meyer which lay at the bottom of the motions of his character. Though he was inordinately shy and seemed to want to stay in a smaller, more inconspicuous place than he occupied in a room or on a streetcar, he was not withdrawn, hunched up within some silly fear without reference to either animal or human life. There was in fact a very strong animal quality about him, wrapped up in his rusty and black clothes. His flesh was fat and his very white skin was not dry like most of the people I knew, and his eyes, which moved more than other people's, were bare and beautiful and I could look at them only in snatches.

Now that I come to think of it I wonder if Meyer was not his first name and that I called him Mr. Meyer out of my great respect and love for him. I think, too, that what he carried in his paper bag was food, so that he would not be a burden on my mother. For there was an attitude of not wishing to impose on anyone, which went with him and which he carried faultlessly. He came to work, and he did his work without spreading himself outside its limits. It was a very strong thing.

My father, however, who was more sure of himself (and less sure) than Mr. Meyer, would lead him out, tease him (as he had a way of doing with others) on the surfaces of his personality. It was a talent, I suppose you might say, of my father, though it made me very nervous, and saddened me, for I knew its other side. There was a party once of the "campers," as they called themselves, who had a group of houses in the summer built in an old settlement near the sea. It was an anniversary of their coming there, the fifth maybe, for there is a picture of them, in costumes and out, posed against the house in back of ours. My mother is there in a white dress and with her black hair combed in a pompadour (as it is in the picture of her at the time of her marriage), and my father with his big face and his arm slung around some woman, and myself on the roof with my stockinged legs dangling down. It must have been about when I was ten. Anyhow, the climax of the celebration was a minstrel show in our camp and it is the impression my father made which first sharpened my attention to that side of him which made people use the word "fun." It wasn't so much what he did that I remember as a curtain with sunflowers painted on it. Holes were cut out where the blossoms were and each of the men were posed behind it with their heads through. And the faces that my father made! And the antics!

He had a way of being liked, for his energy. He'd sing and dance and play tricks, get up fishing parties or walks. There was a bravura about it, a hectic note which I could only put up with because I had seen the other thing, the sudden distaste, or sombreness, the sense of the effort wasted. For he was awkward, unable to cope with the failings of life except by himself, in his early morning walks, fishing, painting, or carpentry, when he could bear down and get his restless flying off from the nubs of life concentrated.

He did not have what Mr. Meyer had, what maybe any tailor has, that squatting with life over a needle. In any case Mr. Meyer had it, and I think my father knew, for there was a good deal of affection between them. My father was a big man and to see Mr. Meyer smiling and talking up to him, and my father, with his broader style, haggling with Mr. Meyer, was a pleasure for me.

It was as though Mr. Meyer was closer to older roots of life, and my father, who had been here since he was three months old, had gotten so far away from them he had almost lost them. Yet he had the need, as we all do, for them, and Mr. Meyer pulled him back. I can think of only one other man who did something similar for him, and he was a little man too, but it was of another order of feeling, and is another story.

Mr. Meyer had a family but I don't know that we ever saw them, even that night we went to his shop. My mother and my father always asked after them, and I recall there were clothes given to him, for he was poor, and there were several kids. It seems, too, that my mother sent candy with him, her fudge, I suppose. I hated to have him go and I would run around to the front window (we were three stories up) to see him again as he emerged into the street and to watch his figure in the street lights. He caught the trolley at the corner. Sometimes I could see him get in. It gave me as deep a feeling as I have ever known of man and his naturally accumulated, fated responsibilities.

(1948)

The Post Office

I said it was my father's stubbornness that killed him in the end. It was, and the trouble out of which his death came was born fourteen years earlier. In its birth he was right. The fight he put up was a just one.

I can date it that exactly because it was his determination to take me to the celebration at Plymouth of the 300th anniversary of the Pilgrim landing that aggravated the situation his superiors in the Post Office had provoked.

My father had requested and received permission to take his vacation the week of the pageant at Plymouth. He and I were to go, leaving my mother at home. It was to be our first big trip and he had planned it most carefully, for it was a major excursion for him as well, comparable only to his trip alone, before I was born, to Gettysburg.

That trip had also got him into trouble, but of another sort, less mortal. It was with my mother. As far as I could ever get the picture he surprised her by going off, so soon after their marriage, on a holiday of his own. This may be a little unfair to her. It may be that the running references to the trip that I heard the rest of the years my father was alive were nothing more than the taunts by which we remind ourselves as well as the other of experience we have not shared. It is a part of that play of jealousy which inhabits the intimate life as much as affection does.

I myself was satisfied with the trip as was, as I heard it from him and as I was reminded of it by the two small pitchers he had brought back for my mother, of a most delicate porcelain, with scenes on them. They set on the mantelpiece in the dining-room and erased for me the two hideous vases at each end of the shelf, fat cylinders of unglazed flowered glass which looked to me as ugly as legs without ankles. In fact I was so delighted in my father's taste in choosing the pitchers that they created in me a delight in the trip which makes it more sweet in memory than any of my own.

But not my mother. His letters or the pitchers or her sure sense the trip was right for him precisely as it had been made never blotted out what also stood on the shelf of her mind. It never does. She had the greed we have, to know all that happens to the other person. Our imagination won't, in this circumstance, stay straight. It corrupts, and we go back and back, as greedy to know as we are fearful to know too much.

Maybe my mother made so much of their marriage trip to New York to offset this Gettysburg which followed hard on it. They arrived in a blizzard and stayed at the old Grand Central Hotel. One thing stood out that could be talked about and that my mother dwelt on with a blush. She had packed no button hook for her high shoes. My father had to go out in the storm and at that hour find some store open. He picked up their umbrella, one of the wedding presents, and when he stepped out into the snow he stepped, she delighted to put it, into a rice storm as well!

I was not ten when the Plymouth trip was planned but my father had long since got over to me his interest in the American past. Any boy brought up in New England had worn the high hat and square, buckled shoes at Thanksgiving plays at school and written a life of George Washington round and round an elm tree at Cambridge. My father had taken me several steps down from that.

I'm not sure his first service wasn't on the biography of General George. I was working on it at the kitchen table with my mother ironing by the stove and him across from me over a drawing board, probably finishing a black and white (he was at that time making up for the schooling he didn't get by shipping lessons to a correspondence institute of art in Minneapolis). The essay was too much for me and I suddenly threw it up in disgust. The gesture struck him with almost the same force as the dice of the parchesi box did the time I dished them into his face in my anger he had licked me. That time he chased me and would have whaled me had it not been for my mother's frantic fear. When he caught up with me by the set tubs he contented himself with a milder torture. He merely pulled my hair.

Over George Washington he was gentle and strong. He talked. And he made his point, the more easily, I suppose, because I knew how thoroughly he himself worked, over a drawing board or on our neighbors' boilers or their plumbing. I had already learned one trick from him, handing tools to him:

you can swear your way through the dirtiest weather. As his assistant then I acquired almost as good a tongue as I was later to, from certain fishermen I know.

What he had to say about me and George Washington was: do it. And I did it. It took.

It is easy to figure out how old I was. The paper was read to the class but I was completely embarrassed, especially because of Margarite Luddon who had the seat in front of me, and such beeyootiful hair. All the "of's," the teacher wanted the class to know, and there must be a lot of them in a biography, were spelt "uv"!

It was the Matthew Bradys my father gave me as a child that have influenced my sense of the past to this day. I have the set. It was the *Review of Reviews* issue of the *Photographic History.* They came, by subscription, I suppose, as thin, large, blue paperbound pamphlets which I could lay open page by page on the floor. The photographs cured me that early of romantic history. I preferred Brady to the colored frontispiece each one carried of some fool's oil on Grant at Lookout Mt or Burnside at Nashville. I could take that as narrative in Joseph Altsheler, *The Rock of Chickamauga,* say. Or in the annual play my father made it a ritual to take me to, even though, each year I ducked behind the back of the seat in front of me when the volley came which cut the hero down. It was year after year, one play, "The Drummer Boy of Shiloh."

Once Brady had taught my eyes, I broke through the painted surfaces of war. The dead in Devil's Gulch at Gettysburg, this was something I was not shown at school. Or horses puffed up on a field huge beside the corpses of men or humped in a ditch along some Wilderness road. Or those groups of Brady's, men and women standing with the curiously penetrating eyes Brady's wet plate seemed to fix, at a distance though he was, focussed down on some Virginia "Station" through a grove of stripped trees. These, too, school did not give me.

Or my father, for that matter. I wonder now what Brady did for him. Maybe, just because I was born here, I had the jump on him. He valued America, as immigrants do, more than the native. I'm not sure it's a good thing. It wasn't, in my father's case, as this trouble he got himself into will show, though for me his fascination with the story of this country was fruitful, as it sometimes is, in the second generation American. There is a sentimentality about the freedoms of this country which none of the bitterness of poverty and abuse will shake in an immigrant. My father had it, at least up to this trouble I write about when the government of these States so failed him he was thrown back on that other rock of the immigrant, his foreign nationality organizations.

It took something out of my father's historical soul. From then on he localized his interest to the past of Gloucester and the fishing industry. That, I think, was a gain and, had he lived, it would have given his life and his painting a ground. That was a more usable, economic America than the society of the rights of man which failed him.

But he did something else, which was not helpful. To some degree he substituted Sweden for America as a focus for his curiosity, after the "Americans" failed him in his fight and he had to turn to the Swedish-American societies for aid. They are like mothers anyway, these societies, keeping their children back from the brunt of this country. They aid them but they also fondle them when they are hurt or cut to pieces as they so often are on the steel points of the society.

I think there can be no doubt my father let down and accepted some of this caressing from 1920 on. Nor can I blame him, for he was gravely wounded. I only have this feeling. If he had lived (he was only 52 when he died) I think there was a good chance, given his intelligence and a couple of N.A.L.C. victories he was on the point of winning, that he might have mended. With the help of Gloucester, he might have seen his struggle outside both Sweden and America, as a part of this ambiguous battle all human society is now, for good or evil, engaged in.

It was something of this view that I was trying to give him in his last years, a meagre return for the childhood he gave me. I argued that, if he were to pitch his energies true, he needed to free himself from the narrow area of recrimination into which the enemy had maneuvered him. But I am ahead of my story. Let me say this: I carried one thing home from Plymouth, the broken shaft of an arrow. I found it on the ground behind the stage after the pageant was over.

I better spell the situation out. Postal employees do not have the right to strike. The result is, union organization among carriers and clerks has lagged. On top of that their organizations have tended, because their officers must wheedle and act mostly as lobbyists on Congress, to continue the same men in national office for unhealthy periods of time. The upshot is, the rank and file are about as spiritless a group of workers as you can imagine and their officers have more in common with the Post Office officials than with the men they represent.

This was hardly a condition a fighter like my father could abide. I can't say where he first acquired his sense of workingmen's rights. I think it was more a matter of his bones than training. He had gone to work at fourteen to aid his mother in the support of himself and two sisters. He had a milk route.

He was one of those men for whom newspapers are education. The few times I saw him with a book in his hands he struck me as most awkward, and he soon fell asleep. (The only exception was a complete one. It was *Handy-Andy.* He read it to me nights while I recovered from a tonsil and adenoid operation. I have never, in anyone else's hands, seen a book do like convulsive things.)

I don't even have the impression that his employment as an iron worker, before he became a letter carrier, contributed to him, in any direct way, as a labor organizer. He stayed with the same firm in which he learned the trade, and it was a family business, and a small shop. My father was, in fact, the leader of a crew of master builders. The work of the firm (it was the Stewart Boiler Works) was principally the raising, all over New England, of those huge factory stacks which replaced brick in the expanding days of industry at the turn of the century. For some reason Calais, Maine (I heard it "callous") came to be the place where I put him when I imagined him high on a staging setting the final lip to the chimney. To this day I can't quite get over the difficulty I then had to figure out how he got down. I could only imagine the descent as made down through the long hole of the completed chimney, and it gave me then, and gives me now, whatever is the inside out of vertigo. It was an exciting thing, this image of him, as a man of heights, and was, I suppose, as satisfying a way as a son can see his father.

Calais, by the way, got chosen, I'm sure, because it looked and sounded strange enough to be a frontier and fitted the map my mind made of the wanderings of this hero of mine as I had constructed it from the tales I picked up. It was a part of the satisfaction I drew from this employment, that it led my father to all sorts of unknown lands and continents in Rhode Island, Massachusetts, New Hampshire and Maine. Calais was Gades, the farthest outpost. It was from Calais, I think, that he proposed to my mother. There was some important business attached to it. Perhaps it was the Canadian stamps on the postcards he sent to her from the town across the river from Calais.

Whatever organizing he had done in his fourteen years in the Post Office before 1920, it was that blow-off which first made me aware that carrying mail involved my father in other things than going away in the morning and returning at night. I knew that occasionally he would go out in the evenings, to what were called "meetings." But so far as I was concerned the day reached a climax when he came home from work as the afternoon fell off. I had a habit of waiting for him at the head of the street. (Later it was to watch for him as we played ball in the field which stretched from our backyard as far as Hill's barn. We used to get him to come and knock flies out to us before we'd let him go upstairs.) He was a gay man and I guess I first knew how gay he was the night he came home with what they then called an ulcerated tooth. When I met him and he walked me down the street without a word or greeting I fell into step beside him as troubled as he. His face was so held and his walk so careful I was completely bewildered. I did not dare to look at him more than once or twice. That night the street was very long. It was the first time, I suppose, that I went along a sidewalk in that blind way which causes time and space to distend. Once we were home I had to go out to get flaxseed poultice but he continued to suffer so, the house that night stayed like the street. It was never his teeth again, but from 1920 on he was more often grim, when I met him, than gay.

What happened was this: the postmaster cancelled his vacation the night before we were to leave. It was a most unusual act, and all that I was ever able to find out confirms the fact they did it because my father was the wheelhorse of the union and they wanted, in this small way, to get back at him.

I don't know that they knew he'd play into their hands as he did. The foreman of carriers, Paddy Hehir (hair, the Irish pronounce it), knew my father, and my mother, well. It could be that he knew, and passed on, how much this trip was in my father's mind. But I think not. Paddy's part was otherwise. I'm inclined to believe the bosses didn't know. I'm inclined to think they just decided to balk my father for no other reason than a vacation gave them a chance.

It was Blocky Sheehan, as they called him, the Superintendent of Mails, whom my father, to the end of his life, blamed for the whole business. And Sheehan could only have known the special point of the trip from Paddy or another carrier. As I say, I doubt it was that plotted.

It was the fact that Sheehan and the Postmaster had first granted him permission that forever after was the stake to which my father was tied. It was the injustice of it, the dirty, underhanded trick, I seem to hear him say. He had made Branch 12 of the N.A.L.C. (National Association of Letter Carriers) strong, for the first time, I believe. That was enough. But he was also in correspondence with the State officers of the union and he had already, if my memory is correct, been active in pushing, through the Branch and the annual convention of the N.A.L.C., such programs as national legislation in favor of thirty year optional retirement, the widows' pension, and other like long-range goals. He was a "trouble-maker." He and his pal, Dinny Riordan, who had had legal training nights before he became a carrier, were too active for the bosses, too smart, and they figured this was the time to set my father back.

It did, but not the way they thought. He didn't take it. We went off the next morning as planned.

I knew nothing about the trouble of course and to this day I can remember nothing in my father's behaviour that whole week which gave me any clue that there was anything wrong. He did everything to the hilt, as usual. We missed nothing and I still have a sight of one moment of his face as some costume or float or incident in the parade pleased him and I noticed his sudden pleasure, and the way his hair blew. He had taken his hat off, that flat, stiff straw he wore each summer, the old kind with broad straw woven like fish scales, and it had left a red mark on his forehead near the hair, and I noticed it, and beads of sweat.

We saw the pageant night after night. We went aboard the model of the *Mayflower*. We found the old cemetery pitched up over the town. We went out to Duxbury, to Miles Standish and Priscilla Alden's graves. We visited the Plymouth Cordage Company. At least he did. For it seems to me it was there I met him after my Sunday morning venture which became one of those standing jokes in the family.

My mother was a Catholic and I was raised one. The problem was, in Plymouth, where I'd go to mass. Somewhere around the Cordage Co. we found a church my father and I decided must be Catholic. It had the right cross on it, I guess. I went in and he went on, to look over ropes. It wasn't very long when I was out, and so confused to be out so quickly I could not tell him, any more than I could my mother afterwards, that I was sure I had been to a Catholic service. I knew only one thing, that when I had entered handbells were ringing as they are, in the mass, when communion is being prepared. I was sure this at least would satisfy my mother but, on the contrary, it made her only the more upset, for if it were that long after the Gospel that you went in, said she, with a voice that sounded as though she were wringing her hands, you did not hear Mass at all!

For my father the irony of that week must have been that the family we stayed with was that of the Postmaster of North Plymouth! It was one of those gentle houses the New Englanders of the 17th century built and the pleasure of it, of the trees at Duxbury and the sea at Plymouth meant more to me (at least I am stained more with the traces) than the excitements we had come to Plymouth to enjoy. The Postmaster was a Mr. Brown. My father had met him at some convention and it is a measure of how much my father's heart was set on this trip that he had arranged our room with Mr. Brown ahead of time.

It was not like him. I take that from him. He much preferred to set off, recklessly sure that things would work out in their courses. (It was that way the only time we were in New York together. He ended up sharing my hotel room. And forgot his straight edge razor when we left in the morning and only remembered it when we were home. Which worried him, for it was his pride, and he honed it stroke after stroke, wiping the lather off on pieces of toilet paper. He wasn't sure he'd get it back, for we'd left the registration single, to save money, when he had failed to find a room for himself and had come to bunk with me.)

The week passed, and what happened when we returned, so sharply changed life in my home that that week came to mean the end of my childhood. Up to then there had been a cocoon of peace and ease around my nerves. It was so pure it was amniotic, and has left me, it has been my thought, those several years retarded. They multiplied security, my mother and my father were so balanced, and when the change came it tore a fabric so delicate it just blew away.

It is also my thought that, because it was my father who was struck, intensified the role he played for me before and after. He had an added dimension because he was the single image of life, I had lived so long in the sleep of the mother.

They busted him, for insubordination and profanity. It seems he had called Paddy Hehir a son of a bitch when Paddy told him his vacation had been revoked. On top of that, of course, he had done the undoable, when he had up and gone without permission. That was insubordination to duty, to the Postmaster, to the President, to God. There was only one larger crime, to rob the mails.

They had my father, and they didn't let go. The postal system has resemblances to the Army. There is, for example, a demerit system. The offenses are graduated and, in their degree, a man's pay is docked. They gave my father the maximum, and our scale of living, poor as it was, went down.

But they didn't stop there. They did the one thing which in those days would cut a veteran letter carrier to the heart. They took my father off his route. Men worked for years to get the routes they wanted. The routes would open as older men retired and the carriers bid for them, by seniority, in turn. Each man had his sense of the kind of route and what part of the city he liked best and this process of selection tended to make both the carrier and the people he served congenial.

For years my father had had the route he wanted. It stretched along the lake which bounds the city on the east. Originally the route ran on both sides of the lake south from the bridge which carried the road to Boston. The bridge alone, and the other wooded side (where nothing much was but the city's amusement park and some summer camps) were enough to make the route what my father would like. Just to cross the bridge a winter morning and a winter afternoon, or to be a part of the boating around it in the summer and the fall, gave his work day a freedom he could never have known in any other route in the city. The whole route had this quality. On the city side it was a series of streets, "avenues" most of them were called, running parallel to the lake, each a little higher up the gradual slope from it, on which people of small means had built mostly one and a half story homes around the turn of the century. They had left room between themselves and their neighbors and the route was a walker, appropriate to a man with my father's legs and drive. Dogs, for example, ran free and, for some strange reason, attached themselves to him in troupes. (They usually dislike carriers, for the straps they carry, and the way the bag swings when it is unslung from the shoulder. Or so I found when I was a carrier later. They'd come through a screen door to get me in the leg.) My father had so many stories about them that I remember their names and the differences of their natures better than I do most of the people who owned them. He had his favorites for years, who went the whole route with him and who became as well known as he was, along the way. He'd set them off against each other yet see that the butchers in the stores at the corners had meat for them. When one

Airedale, Cuppy, was killed by the trolley which ran to the lake down a freeway which cut through the backyards of the settlement, my father was disconsolate for days. There is a picture of him, in a new uniform, with Cuppy pawing him to the shoulders like some mythic lion.

And then there was the life directly on the lake to give the route a fillip a residential area never has. There was the Lincoln Park Theatre on this side of the bridge, to which I was taken on passes in the summer evenings down the freeway in the open cars. And the Chinese who had a wheel concession near the theatre on the Boston road, who each year gave my father, for my mother, some new set of china. (They came packed in a fine straw which interested me.) And the boathouses directly on the lake. Randall's was my father's favorite, or, rather, he was a favorite of the Randalls. Sundays, when the ice was gone, he would take me to Randall's and we would go out together on the lake after a lot of talk between him and the Randall boys during which time I gawked at the racing shells and the canoes set on racks up to the ceiling. And, towards the end of the route south, where the settlement ran off into the woods (in which the city had placed the little herd of what looked to me like moth-eaten buffaloes), was the ice house. My father got me a job there one Christmas vacation when I was in high school and it should have made a man of me. I cut ice with the men from 6 in the morning until 6 at night, and the only thing I can say for the day was, that I waited in terror, for my father's appearance, in the middle of the morning and the afternoon, when he was sure to hail me from the shore and make fun to the men of the way I poled the cakes through the channel into the elevator incline which took the ice up three flights to the house for storing.

Of the people, Martin and Minnie Hester seem to have been the oldest, most continuous friends my father had. I remember the upset when Mr. Hester died. I think he was a carpenter, though I may have this confused with Martin and Nora Reidy. She was my godmother, and Martin was a carpenter in the city school system. Nora marked my birthdays. She always gave me gloves, and was the only one outside the family who remembered my birthday. It fell two days after Christmas. But Martin studded my school days. It was unexpected and delightful to have him turn up at my grammar school. Later, when I was in high school and worked as the cashier at the lunch counter, I saw a lot of him. He used to come over and eat his lunch with me as I sold the tickets. Whenever the Hesters were mentioned it was the life of the Reidys, which I knew intimately (they were brother and sister, both unmarried), that rose up in my mind. I still have to work it out to realize that the Hesters were not a bachelor and an old maid. They remembered my father every Christmas and when he was off the route were most solicitous, though I don't think they played any part in organizing the protest of the people of the route against the Post Office officials. They were too shy.

That was the doing of men like Mr. Lawrence. He had a print shop, and I may remember him more, because he also invented a solution to soften typewriter rollers, and there were a few Saturdays, very few, when I, at my father's urging, made the rounds of the factories in our neighborhood trying to sell the stuff to secretaries and office managers. It was as dreadful to me as another attempt, to sell Mr. Lawrence's letter paper, with the name done to order. (The only time door to door selling interested me was Christmas cards, for the Waltham Company, and that took no selling, and gave me a huge profit, 50¢ on a dollar box.) But Mr. Lawrence stands in my mind as one of the leaders who called the several meetings at the Lake, as we called the route, to take action to get my father back.

I recall the Biancis, mostly for the huge Italian dinner, my first spaghetti and meatballs, that we and the Foleys were invited to. I have the feeling they were on Pat Foley's route, which joined my father's on the city side.

Most of the other names are gone. There were the Siskins, who had the meat market, and who spoiled my father's dogs. But the others, though remnants of my father's talk about them swim in my mind, have lost their faces and their names. There was an Irish girl who kept house for the priests, and it was one of my father's favorite diversions to plague her with his skepticisms about religion when he knew that one of the curates was listening in the next room. Once, with great care, he decorated and wrapped a brick as a fool's present for her, in lieu of what object she wanted I can't say. He was given to wrapping and boxing minute presents in huge boxes which he had the parcel post carrier deliver with extra fanfare. This seems to have been a part of the give and take of the route. He came home once with a box of fool's candy, soft ones of pepper, nougats of tobacco, thin ones of cardboard. He had been taken in and tried them on us.

I imagine the ones I have remembered are those with whom I had something to do. The vast majority I never saw, even though on one grand occasion I went the route with my father. I must have been about twelve. I don't know what the occasion was, but I do recall the place that impressed me most. It was the State Insane Hospital. It occupied the whole of the hill to the lake on the opposite side of the Boston road from the body of my father's route. The buildings, brownstone and like a college, were at the top and the farm ran down the slope behind a fence which seems to me now to have been made of rails, though it probably was of stone. It was along this fence that the inmates sat or walked, and their eyes, clothes, postures and gestures were a world of people I found much more interesting than the rest of us. From that day on, whenever I would go to the Lake of a Sunday or could get my father to talk, it was these men I wanted to see and hear of. They got mixed up in my mind with Brady's people of the Civil War. When I was told that the Reidys' sister Agnes had died in that hospital I could not bring the fact together with the fable the men along the fence stood for. (I even had some of the same difficulty much, much later when Martin Reidy was taken there. It was after my mother had lived with them, the winter following my father's death. I had visited with them at Christmas and though there was a difference in Nora and Martin [Nora had always made me nervous ever since the hate she showed in arguments with my father over the Germans during the first world war] I attributed it to age. The house still smelled of Martin's good tobacco and was as remarkably neat as Nora had always kept it. No one was prepared for the crisis when it came. One night Nora waked to find Martin going around the house with an axe, looking under all the beds and accusing her of intimate relations with their nephew who lived upstairs.) Some of the nuts, as they were called, were free to leave the grounds and used to walk my father's route with him. One carved things as presents for him. My father gave them smokes and clothes.

That route was my father's parish, village to which he was crier and walking mayor. He was more intimate to the community, and the lives of all the people, than anyone else could be. The people showed it, the way they fought for him, when the crisis came.

Some of it was himself but part the fact he was "the postman." Mail, over any length of time, will tell secrets a neighbor could not guess. Nor do I mean the reading of postcards or the "lamping" of letters. Nor what a man hears over coffee. Or that a man's mail does not always come to his house, or a woman's either. It lies more in the manner in which people look for, ask for, receive their mail. And talk about it.

A letter, expected or surprise, is a lance, and the vizor slips, and I talk to this person to get it back into place, for I know him every day and yet I do not know him so well a confidence will lead me anywhere. I am aware I am vulnerable and I will regret a little some of the things I am saying, but . . . the uniform makes Mr. Olson anonymous enough.

This was most true in the days before Burleson, Wilson's Postmaster General, took the craft and country quality out of the service. The loss was the loss common to most labor since. This better be understood as not nostalgia. I was a letter carrier myself later and do not hark back. We have got so used to change that we are unwilling to believe that suddenly some change may be so total as to destroy. The path does die, and there are times when, to find his way back, man has to pick up, fiercely and without any easy emotion, traces of the way. What happened to work during the first world war is a trace.

Carrying mail never did require great skill any more than most of the broad-gauged jobs which make society run. You have heard all either of us wants to hear of the carrier the Man of Weather—sleet snow night rain: excelsior. What is not mentioned are hernia rheumatism flatfeet death (insurance company average) 52. The hazards. I can add, of Charles Olson Sr., (1) a fall down a flight of 30 stone steps & like incidents in the line of duty, (2) the morning he was brought home, before I had left for school, to my mother's and my surprise—a trolley car had split a switch and spread him out full six foot three on the pavement at Front and Pleasant Streets. This kind of weather lasts.

What can be lost is the weather of a man. What gave the carrier dignity, the sense of accomplishment, what made his day of use to the people he served as well as to himself was the illusion that how he did it was of value.

Here is the connection between Burleson and what the bosses did to my father. My father did not want union power. He never held or sought top office. He served some terms as secretary, but not to control from that powerful post. To get the work done. For several years I did his typing and can say. What he was after, what all the legislation he pushed was directed against, was the speed-up. I used to get pretty bored with figures on the occupational diseases of letter carriers, calculations on the differentials of the volume of mail over a month, statistics on the condition of the widows of carriers, numbers of children per family etc., but it is clear that he saw what the fight was.

I'm sure the bosses were too knowing to think he could take the union over. He did not have that will and if he had they knew how to buy such men off. In some awkward way, with no scheme or large sense of what was involved, out of the needs of his own personality, his assurance that the satisfaction of a job lay in the perfection of the doing of it, the pounding of a rivet, the use of pumice after sandpaper to make a surface ready for a stain, the fixative to set a crayon sketch for O. Victor Humann at the Museum, led my father to fight for quality against efficiency in the postal service. That was, and is, the battle-line.

He was the resistance of a man, my father, the cry of the individual that he be allowed the time and the conditions to do his work, as they used to say, right. And that's why the bosses went after him. They attacked him because he wanted to do his work too well. He was unhealthy to have around. The speedup might irk the other men but they would be unprepared, as most men are, from confusion and the hundred costs the family is heir to, to do anything. They would go along, even though it meant they'd wither and go dead. My father's threat to the bosses was not so much his activity as himself. He was an image to the other men of what they had been, a trace to the younger men of what work was. He had to be harassed.

Today he'd be fired. Or not hired in the first place. Or, if a company had to show a payroll for a contract, be the first laid off. Ground has been lost. But a good worker still knows, and can tell you, what my father knew. He just happened to be one of the first, and it was clearer earlier in the postal service than in heavy industry. He was at the switch point when the turn came. He was no enemy. He was opposition. He was fighting for pride in work which is personality. It is that simple. We have forgotten what men crave. We think that all workers want is pay. But that's all they are left with, where production, and that rot of modern work, efficiency, rule. Give workers only that and they'll featherbed you back. If you take away pride you'll have to give prizes. And why not? Corner men and they are good animals: they know how to resist.

Behind his bosses were the postal inspectors. Behind them Burleson. Behind Burleson the huge forfeit of pro-duction. It is old George Harris' proposition: bishops eats elders, elders eats common peopil, they eats sich cattil as me, I eats possums, possums eats chickins, chickins swallers wums, an' wums is content to eat dus, an' dus is the aind uv hit all.

Only hit ain't. The dus is the kulchur daid on the groun'. For example. My father was old fashion. He had notions having to do with courtesy, modesty, care, proportion, respect. He had them confused with his work. A letter, say. He was scrupulous about a letter. He had the idea it was somehow important just because it was made up of words (he had the notion that words have value, as signs of meaning and feeling) and because it was a communication between two persons (the idea of a person seems to have meant something to him). Thus he took himself seriously as the last, and only directly personal agent, of several hired by a stamp to see that a letter reached the person to whom it was addressed or, rather (as I am sure he, with his notions, would have put it) for whom it was meant.

As a part of such motion he took himself to be responsible. (He was. I have known him, of an evening after work, to be as concerned as to whether a party on his route had got a letter they had been expecting which he had had to leave in their box because they were not at home, as another man might be concerned about well, say, the safe, or whether he had locked the office door.) A good carrier did not jam cards. He did not leave insured parcels carelessly. He stopped to ring and wait to get the mail inside when the weather was bad. He held mail for people when they were away, or forwarded for them, without delay. The niceties.

And the accommodations: bring stamps to people, or take their letters and buy the stamps for them. Or small packages or magazines, where they did not know the weight. Even a laundry, once in a while.

And registered mail: to let people know they could send money directly by you instead of going up town to the post office to do it, as most people think they have to. The finish on the work. (It was my father who first told me the answer of the cabinet maker to the looker-on who was making fun of the care the c.m. was giving to the under side of a table. "Why bother your self. No one will ever, in this world, notice that." Drawls the c.m., switching his chaw, "I notice it."

All of which courtesies take   took   time.
Enter: the route inspector.
From 1920 on my father was never left long at peace on his route without there was, suddenly, any day, a route inspector on his back. As he would leave the Post Office for his route there would be some guy, known or unknown, with his sheet of paper and his yellow look (the look of the checker in any business) who would go the route with him that day to "clock him," to count the pieces and the time. It was the way the bosses hounded a man, in Post Office talk.

They had another trick. When a man went on vacation they'd assign a special substitute to carry the route, a man whom the regulars called a route-killer, some bird who wanted to stand in with the foreman of carriers to get extra work and who was ready, for that reason, or from plain fear, to run around the route and get in under the regular's time. I had one once myself. He managed a ball club. A route was something he got rid of as soon as he could (though he was paid, as I was, by the hour) in order to have time to chew the fat with his players at noon or get the bases out to the field at night. He came in one day two hours under my time! That finished me on that route. They transferred me to a truck!

But I was a kid, and didn't care. With my father it was different. It was his life work. He got so he was grim and dangerous over this business. If he'd have been a machinist, they had turned him into such a bitter, revengeful man, he would have gone beyond the slow-down. He would have turned saboteur, and wrecked machinery. As it was he went illegal. He worked out a trick to beat them. It was to increase the mail the day they inspected him. He did it in one of two ways. On at least one occasion (at the height of his trouble, I'd say, from the way I remember it) when he was tipped off ahead of time that he was going to get it, he mailed first class stuff himself the night before, in several different handwritings to people on the route. Another time, it seems to me, he called my mother during the morning and had her drop some similar letters he had ready in order to fatten the afternoon delivery on his route. But the other device was simpler. It rested on the increase of advertising circulars in the 20s and 30s. It was mostly third class mail, and carriers were not obliged to deliver it the day it came in, if such a piece meant adding distance to the route. But my father went much further in his determination to beat the inspection system. He would cull out these circulars until he had a selected bunch of them well distributed around his route. These he would keep hidden in his locker or perhaps it was behind his sorting case at the post office. When an inspector was due out with him he would sort these pieces in with the day's mail. It took up the slack. (I should make clear that it was the custom, when the higher-ups were after a man, to send an inspector out at that time of the month or the week when the mail is lightest. Monday is such a day. The first of the month is the heaviest.)

It was a mischievous business, and my father lived with it nervously. (He had a bad time of it the day he discovered new cases had arrived and there had been some shifting of the old ones during the morning when he was out on the route.) My impression is, this stupid bundle of mail was on his mind all the years up to his death. There it sat, the only illegal thing he'd ever done, the one thing, and the only thing, if they found it, which would give them the goods they wished they had on him. His record was clean, clean as a whistle is the way he would have put it, if he was of a mind to talk about himself. Yet here he himself ran the risk of giving them the very thing they wanted. And why? Merely to beat them at a game which he took as an insult to his amour propre.

This is what I meant by his stubbornness. He wanted his route the way it had been before the speed-up. He wanted his route the way he had built it, with time left in for the courtesies, the niceties, and a coffee now and then. But there was a side to this desire, after his trouble, which has to be put this way: he wanted it the way it had been because the bosses wanted it different. The fact of the matter is he wanted to overprove his point with some idea that in so doing he made more apparent the dirtiness of their attack on him. Which, of course, was not so. He could easily have turned the point of any of their tricks by merely continuing as he had been. He had a long route and no one could have squeezed it much. The proof is, that when they finally decided he had suffered enough, after the Plymouth deal, they put him back on the route pretty much, as far as I can remember, as he had been beforehand. In other words the hounding took. The only thing it didn't do was break his will. He didn't give in. He only died.

It took fourteen years. The demerits came first. Then the removal from the route. At that point they pulled another military move. They required him to tear off the three red stars from his sleeve, for the fifteen years he had served. For they had a final ignominy. I suppose it is possible they thought they could drive him out of the service altogether. Anyhow they assigned him to the lowest job there is, the job the greenest sub carrier gets, the night collection.

I don't remember how long they kept him on it. It may have been a year. I'm not sure, now that I am further down into the past, if I am right they took him off his route immediately on our return from Plymouth. I'm not sure they didn't inspect the life out of him first, having docked his pay, and that it wasn't on one of these inspections that he called Paddy Hehir or maybe it was Blocky Sheehan a son of a bitch. In any case the night collection was the final punishment.

One thing stands out, a picture that Dinny Riordan gave me the day my father died. It was a sudden death, cerebral hemorrhage, the first shock on a

Thursday paralyzing the right side, the second one, Saturday morning, getting the heart. What Dinny revealed to me was that in 1920, apparently not long after the start of the trouble, he and my father were on a streetcar going to their routes. (Dinny's was the next above the route adjoining my father's.) Suddenly as they were sitting there in the long seat at the back of the car Dinny became aware that my father was not listening to him, was in fact leaning slightly against him and looking off with a fixed look out the windows across the aisle. He thought my father was joking, or something, and gave him a shove. It was the way my father came out of it that made Dinny first aware that something was wrong. He said nothing, and nothing more was mentioned about it. But the doctors told me, when I checked with them, that it was the premonitory shock. The trouble had brought it on. Shortly after, in going over my father's papers, I discovered that it was the very year, 1920, that had begun the annual checkups with the doctor which were dramatized for me by the urine bottle.

The nights must have been dirt in my father's mouth, the city's main streets, letters in lumps, people to ask why he was there. Or to say, what's this we see in the papers. For he fought back from the start. The senator was David I. Walsh. He tried to reach him. The congressman was Pehr Holmes, a Swede. He saw him. Promises, letters, meetings, articles. The NALC. The branch of UNIPOX (Un. PO Clerks). I don't figure, now, that it was long before he was back on the route. But that, alas, was not the end of the struggle. It never ended for him. Somehow he had to pay them back, Hehir, Sheehan, and the Postmaster, Healy. He increased his work in the Branch. He widened out to the national officers. He joined the Carl the 15th Lodge, the Swedish American Federation. The paper *Svea* had helped in the struggle. He became a friend of Karl Fredin the editor. His Swedish began to come back. He began to get me to speak to their festivals. He became more and more involved. More evenings went out from his drawing, his piano playing. The one thing he did not lessen was Gloucester. Gloucester became the one offset. He would come each weekend, arranging rides for himself if he could, or hopping the train. Only in Gloucester was he free from revenge. And it was from Gloucester that he left the last time I saw him whole. He was to go the next weekend to the National Convention of the Carriers at Cleveland. It was to be a big business, for he and his cronies around the country (he had built up a terrific correspondence) were hoping they could turn out the old officers and put in Fred Douglas of Brooklyn. It was one of the payoffs my father intended, for the officers of the NALC had failed him, he thought, in his fight. He was out to get them. It was to be a big thing, and when he was leaving he waked me to ask if I would let him take my suitcase which was bigger and newer than his. I had a use for it that coming weekend which seemed important to me, and I refused. He went away sore, and the curious thing is, that though my mother and I drove the hundred miles to the hospital the moment we heard he was sick and though I was with him much of the time until he died, I do not remember that he ever addressed me or seemed to notice that I was there. He pinched my mother's nose and said something unintelligible from the twist of his mouth but it is only now that I realize at no time did he admit a notice of me. Or do I exaggerate and punish myself anew for the guilt of my refusal of the suitcase. I do not know. What I do know is that the house, when we got back to it, showed that all that week he must have stayed up night after night preparing the papers and resolutions that were to be used at the Convention. That was 1934. Plymouth was all those years back, yet here he was locked in the struggle which issued from it. He had won the fight, and lost it, god help us all.

(1948)

Poetry & Poets

Projective   Verse

(projectile   (percussive   (prospective

vs.

The NON-Projective

(or what a French critic calls "closed" verse, that verse which print bred and which is pretty much what we have had, in English & American, and have still got, despite the work of Pound & Williams:

it led Keats, already a hundred years ago, to see it (Wordsworth's, Milton's) in the light of "the Egotistical Sublime"; and it persists, at this latter day, as what you might call the private-soul-at-any-public-wall)

Verse now, 1950, if it is to go ahead, if it is to be of *essential* use, must, I take it, catch up and put into itself certain laws and possibilities of the breath, of the breathing of the man who writes as well as of his listenings. (The revolution of the ear, 1910, the trochee's heave, asks it of the younger poets.)

I want to do two things: first, try to show what projective or OPEN verse is, what it involves, in its act of composition, how, in distinction from the non-projective, it is accomplished; and II, suggest a few ideas about what stance toward reality brings such verse into being, what that stance does, both to the poet and to his reader. (The stance involves, for example, a change beyond, and larger than, the technical, and may, the way things look, lead to new poetics and to new concepts from which some sort of drama, say, or of epic, perhaps, may emerge.)

I

First, some simplicities that a man learns, if he works in OPEN, or what can also be called COMPOSITION BY FIELD, as opposed to inherited line, stanza, over-all form, what is the "old" base of the non-projective.

(1) the *kinetics* of the thing. A poem is energy transferred from where the poet got it (he will have some several causations), by way of the poem itself to, all the way over to, the reader. Okay. Then the poem itself must, at all points, be a high energy-construct and, at all points, an energy-discharge. So: how is the poet to accomplish same energy, how is he, what is the process by which a poet gets in, at all points energy at least the equivalent of the energy which propelled him in the first place, yet an energy which is peculiar to verse alone and which will be, obviously, also different from the energy which the reader, because he is a third term, will take away?

This is the problem which any poet who departs from closed form is specially confronted by. And it involves a whole series of new recognitions. From the moment he ventures into FIELD COMPOSITION—puts himself in the open—he can go by no track other than the one the poem under hand declares, for itself. Thus he has to behave, and be, instant by instant, aware of some several forces just now beginning to be examined. (It is much more, for example, this push, than simply such a one as Pound put, so wisely, to get us started: "the musical phrase," go by it, boys, rather than by, the metronome.)

(2) is the *principle,* the law which presides conspicuously over such composition, and, when obeyed, is the reason why a projective poem can come into being. It is this: FORM IS NEVER MORE THAN AN EXTENSION OF CONTENT. (Or so it got phrased by one, R. Creeley, and it makes absolute sense to me, with this possible corollary, that right form, in any given poem, is the only and exclusively possible extension of content under hand.) There it is, brothers, sitting there, for USE.

Now (3) the *process* of the thing, how the principle can be made so to shape the energies that the form is accomplished. And I think it can be boiled down to one statement (first pounded into my head by Edward Dahlberg): ONE PERCEPTION MUST IMMEDIATELY AND DIRECTLY LEAD TO A FURTHER PERCEPTION. It means exactly what it says, is a matter of, at *all* points (even, I should say, of our management of daily reality as of the daily work) get on with it, keep moving, keep in, speed, the nerves, their speed, the perceptions, theirs, the acts, the split second acts, the whole business, keep it moving as fast as you can, citizen. And if you also set up as a poet, USE USE USE the process at all points, in any given poem always, always one perception must must must MOVE, INSTANTER, ON ANOTHER!

So there we are, fast, there's the dogma. And its excuse, its usableness, in practice. Which gets us, it ought to get us, inside the machinery, now, 1950, of how projective verse is made.

If I hammer, if I recall in, and keep calling in, the breath, the breathing as distinguished from the hearing, it is for cause, it is to insist upon a part that breath plays in verse which has not (due, I think, to the smothering of the power of the line by too set a concept of foot) has not been sufficiently observed or practiced, but which has to be if verse is to advance to its proper force and place in the day, now, and ahead. I take it that PROJECTIVE VERSE teaches, is, this lesson, that that verse will only do in which a poet manages to register both the acquisitions of his ear *and* the pressures of his breath.

Let's start from the smallest particle of all, the syllable. It is the king and pin of versification, what rules and holds together the lines, the larger forms, of a poem. I would suggest that verse here and in England dropped this secret from the late Elizabethans to Ezra Pound, lost it, in the sweetness of meter and rime, in a honey-head. (The syllable is one way to distinguish the original success of blank verse, and its falling off, with Milton.)

It is by their syllables that words juxtapose in beauty, by these particles of sound as clearly as by the sense of the words which they compose. In any given instance, because there is a choice of words, the choice, if a man is in there, will be, spontaneously, the obedience of his ear to the syllables. The fineness, and the practice, lie here, at the minimum and source of speech.

> O western wynd, when wilt thou blow
> And the small rain down shall rain
> O Christ that my love were in my arms
> And I in my bed again

It would do no harm, as an act of correction to both prose and verse as now written, if both rime and meter, and, in the quantity words, both sense and sound, were less in the forefront of the mind than the syllable, if the syllable, that fine creature, were more allowed to lead the harmony on. With this warning, to those who would try: to step back here to this place of the elements and minims of language, is to engage speech where it is least careless—and least logical. Listening for the syllables must be so constant and so scrupulous, the exaction must be so complete, that the assurance of the ear is purchased at the highest—40 hours a day—price. For from the root out, from all over the place, the syllable comes, the figures of, the dance:

"Is" comes from the Aryan root, *as,* to breathe. The English "not" equals the Sanscrit *na,* which may come from the root *na,* to be lost, to perish. "Be" is from *bhu,* to grow.

I say the syllable, king, and that it is spontaneous, this way: the ear, the ear which has collected, which has listened, the ear, which is so close to the mind that it is the mind's, that it has the mind's speed . . .

it is close, another way: the mind is brother to this sister and is, because it is so close, is the drying force, the incest, the sharpener . . .

it is from the union of the mind and the ear that the syllable is born.

But the syllable is only the first child of the incest of verse (always, that Egyptian thing, it produces twins!). The other child is the LINE. And together, these two, the syllable *and* the line, they make a poem, they make that thing, the— what shall we call it, the Boss of all, the "Single Intelligence." And the line comes (I swear it) from the breath, from the breathing of the man who writes, at the moment that he writes, and thus is, it is here that, the daily work, the WORK, gets in, for only he, the man who writes, can declare, at every moment, the line its metric and its ending—where its breathing, shall come to, termination.

The trouble with most work, to my taking, since the breaking away from traditional lines and stanzas, and from such wholes as, say, Chaucer's *Troilus* or S's *Lear,* is: contemporary workers go lazy RIGHT HERE WHERE THE LINE IS BORN.

Let me put it baldly. The two halves are:
        the HEAD, by way of the EAR, to the SYLLABLE
        the HEART, by way of the BREATH, to the LINE
And the joker? that it is in the 1st half of the proposition that, in composing, one lets-it-rip; and that it is in the 2nd half, surprise, it is the LINE that's the baby that gets, as the poem is getting made, the attention, the control, that it is right here, in the line, that the shaping takes place, each moment of the going.

I am dogmatic, that the head shows in the syllable. The dance of the intellect is there, among them, prose or verse. Consider the best minds you know in this here business: where does the head show, is it not, precise, here, in the swift currents of the syllable? can't you tell a brain when you see what it does, just there? It is true, what the master says he picked up from Confusion: all the thots men are capable of can be entered on the back of a postage stamp. So, is it not the PLAY of a mind we are after, is not that that shows whether a mind is there at all?

And the threshing floor for the dance? Is it anything but the LINE? And when the line has, is, a deadness, is it not a heart which has gone lazy, is it not, suddenly, slow things, similes, say, adjectives, or such, that we are bored by?

For there is a whole flock of rhetorical devices which have now to be brought under a new bead, now that we sight with the line. Simile is only one bird who comes down, too easily. The descriptive functions generally have to be watched, every second, in projective verse, because of their easiness, and thus their drain on the energy which composition by field allows into a poem. *Any* slackness takes off attention, that crucial thing, from the job in hand, from the *push* of the line under hand at the moment, under the reader's eye, in his moment. Observation of any kind is, like argument in prose, properly previous to the act of the poem, and, if allowed in, must be so juxtaposed, apposed, set in, that it does not, for an instant, sap the going energy of the content toward its form.

It comes to this, this whole aspect of the newer problems. (We now enter, actually, the large area of the whole poem, into the FIELD, if you like, where all the syllables and all the lines must be managed in their relations to each other.) It is a matter, finally, of OBJECTS, what they are, what they are inside a poem, how they got there, and, once there, how they are to be used. This is something I want to get to in another way in Part II, but, for the moment, let me indicate this, that every element in an open poem (the syllable, the line, as well as the image, the sound, the sense) must be taken up as participants in the kinetic of the poem just as solidly as we are accustomed to take what we call the objects of reality; and that these elements are to be seen as creating the tensions of a poem just as totally as do those other objects create what we know as the world.

The objects which occur at every given moment of composition (of recognition, we can call it) are, can be, must be treated exactly as they do occur therein and not by any ideas or preconceptions from outside the poem, must be handled as a series of objects in field in such a way that a series of tensions (which they also are) are made to *hold,* and to hold exactly inside the content and the context of the poem which has forced itself, through the poet and them, into being.

Because breath allows *all* the speech-force of language back in (speech is the "solid" of verse, is the secret of a poem's energy), because, now, a poem has, by speech, solidity, everything in it can now be treated as solids, objects, things; and, though insisting upon the absolute difference of the reality of verse from that other dispersed and distributed thing, yet each of these elements of a poem can be allowed to have the play of their separate energies and can be allowed, once the poem is well composed, to keep, as those other objects do, their proper confusions.

Which brings us up, immediately, bang, against tenses, in fact against syntax, in fact against grammar generally, that is, as we have inherited it. Do not tenses, must they not also be kicked around anew, in order that time, that other governing absolute may be kept, as must the space-tensions of a poem, immediate, contemporary to the acting-on-you of the poem? I would argue that here, too, the LAW OF THE LINE, which projective verse creates, must be hewn to, obeyed, and that the conventions which logic has forced on syntax must be broken open as quietly as must the too set feet of the old line. But an analysis of how far a new poet can stretch the very conventions on which communication by language rests, is too big for these notes, which are meant, I hope it is obvious, merely to get things started.

Let me just throw in this. It is my impression that *all* parts of speech suddenly, in composition by field, are fresh for both sound and percussive use, spring up like unknown, unnamed vegetables in the patch, when you work it, come spring. Now take Hart Crane. What strikes me in him is the singleness of the push to the nominative, his push along that one arc of freshness, the attempt to get back to word as handle. (If logos is word as thought, what is word as noun, as, pass me that, as Newman Shea used to ask, at the galley table, put a jib on the blood, will ya.) But there is a loss in Crane of what Fenollosa is so right about, in syntax, the sentence as first act of nature, as lightning, as passage of force from subject to object, quick, in this case, from Hart to me, in every case, from me to you, the VERB, between two nouns. Does not Hart miss the advantages, by such an isolated push, miss the point of the whole front of syllable, line, field, and what happened to all language, and to the poem, as a result?

I return you now to London, to beginnings, to the syllable, for the pleasures of it, to intermit;

> If music be the food of love, play on,
> give me excess of it, that, surfeiting,
> the appetite may sicken, and so die.
> That strain again. It had a dying fall,
> o, it came over my ear like the sweet sound
> that breathes upon a bank of violets,
> stealing and giving odour.

What we have suffered from, is manuscript, press, the removal of verse from its producer and its reproducer, the voice, a removal by one, by two removes from its place of origin *and* its destination. For the breath has a double meaning which latin had not yet lost.

The irony is, from the machine has come one gain not yet sufficiently observed or used, but which leads directly on toward projective verse and its consequences. It is the advantage of the typewriter that, due to its rigidity and its space precisions, it can, for a poet, indicate exactly the breath, the pauses, the suspensions even of syllables, the juxtapositions even of parts of phrases, which he intends. For the first time the poet has the stave and the bar a musician has had. For the first time he can, without the convention of rime and meter, record the listening he has done to his own speech and by that one act indicate how he would want any reader, silently or otherwise, to voice his work.

It is time we picked the fruits of the experiments of Cummings, Pound, Williams, each of whom has, after his way, already used the machine as a scoring to his composing, as a script to its vocalization. It is now only a matter of the recognition of the conventions of composition by field for us to bring into being an open verse as formal as the closed, with all its traditional advantages.

If a contemporary poet leaves a space as long as the phrase before it, he means that space to be held, by the breath, an equal length of time. If he suspends a word or syllable at the end of a line (this was most Cummings' addition) he means that time to pass that it takes the eye—that hair of time suspended—to pick up the next line. If he wishes a pause so light it hardly separates the words, yet does not want a comma—which is an interruption

of the meaning rather than the sounding of the line—follow him when he
uses a symbol the typewriter has ready to hand:

What does not change / is the will to change

Observe him, when he takes advantage of the machine's multiple margins, to
juxtapose:

Sd he:
    to dream takes no effort
        to think is easy
            to act is more difficult
            but for a man to act after he has taken thought, this!
    is the most difficult thing of all

Each of these lines is a progressing of both the meaning and the breathing forward, and then a backing up, without a progress or any kind of movement outside the unit of time local to the idea.

There is more to be said in order that this convention be recognized, especially in order that the revolution out of which it came may be so forwarded
that work will get published to offset the reaction now afoot to return verse to
inherited forms of cadence and rime. But what I want to emphasize here, by
this emphasis on the typewriter as the personal and instantaneous recorder of
the poet's work, is the already projective nature of verse as the sons of Pound
and Williams are practicing it. Already they are composing as though verse was
to have the reading its writing involved, as though not the eye but the ear was
to be its measurer, as though the intervals of its composition could be so carefully put down as to be precisely the intervals of its registration. For the ear,
which once had the burden of memory to quicken it (rime & regular cadence
were its aids and have merely lived on in print after the oral necessities were
ended) can now again, that the poet has his means, be the threshold of projective verse.

II

Which gets us to what I promised, the degree to which the projective involves a
stance toward reality outside a poem as well as a new stance towards the reality of a poem itself. It is a matter of content, the content of Homer or of Euripides or of Seami as distinct from that which I might call the more "literary"

masters. From the moment the projective purpose of the act of verse is recognized, the content does—it will—change. If the beginning and the end is breath, voice in its largest sense, then the material of verse shifts. It has to. It starts with the composer. The dimension of his line itself changes, not to speak of the change in his conceiving, of the matter he will turn to, of the scale in which he imagines that matter's use. I myself would pose the difference by a physical image. It is no accident that Pound and Williams both were involved variously in a movement which got called "objectivism." But that word was then used in some sort of a necessary quarrel, I take it, with "subjectivism." It is now too late to be bothered with the latter. It has excellently done itself to death, even though we are all caught in its dying. What seems to me a more valid formulation for present use is "objectism," a word to be taken to stand for the kind of relation of man to experience which a poet might state as the necessity of a line or a work to be as wood is, to be as clean as wood is as it issues from the hand of nature, to be as shaped as wood can be when a man has had his hand to it. Objectism is the getting rid of the lyrical interference of the individual as ego, of the "subject" and his soul, that peculiar presumption by which western man has interposed himself between what he is as a creature of nature (with certain instructions to carry out) and those other creations of nature which we may, with no derogation, call objects. For a man is himself an object, whatever he may take to be his advantages, the more likely to recognize himself as such the greater his advantages, particularly at that moment that he achieves an humilitas sufficient to make him of use.

It comes to this: the use of a man, by himself and thus by others, lies in how he conceives his relation to nature, that force to which he owes his somewhat small existence. If he sprawl, he shall find little to sing but himself, and shall sing, nature has such paradoxical ways, by way of artificial forms outside himself. But if he stays inside himself, if he is contained within his nature as he is participant in the larger force, he will be able to listen, and his hearing through himself will give him secrets objects share. And by an inverse law his shapes will make their own way. It is in this sense that the projective act, which is the artist's act in the larger field of objects, leads to dimensions larger than the man. For a man's problem, the moment he takes speech up in all its fullness, is to give his work his seriousness, a seriousness sufficient to cause the thing he makes to try to take its place alongside the things of nature. This is not easy. Nature works from reverence, even in her destructions (species go down with a crash). But breath is man's special qualification as animal. Sound is a dimension he has extended. Language is one of his proudest acts. And when a poet rests in these as they are in himself (in his physiology, if you like, but the life in him, for all that) then he, if he chooses to speak from these roots, works in that area where nature has given him size, projective size.

It is projective size that the play, *The Trojan Women,* possesses, for it is able to stand, is it not, as its people do, beside the Aegean—and neither Andromache or the sea suffer diminution. In a less "heroic" but equally "natural" dimension Seami causes the Fisherman and the Angel to stand clear in *Hagoromo.* And Homer, who is such an unexamined cliché that I do not think I need to press home in what scale Nausicaa's girls wash their clothes.

Such works, I should argue—and I use them simply because their equivalents are yet to be done—could not issue from men who conceived verse without the full relevance of human voice, without reference to where lines come from, in the individual who writes. Nor do I think it accident that, at this end point of the argument, I should use, for examples, two dramatists and an epic poet. For I would hazard the guess that, if projective verse is practiced long enough, is driven ahead hard enough along the course I think it dictates, verse again can carry much larger material than it has carried in our language since the Elizabethans. But it can't be jumped. We are only at its beginnings, and if I think that the *Cantos* make more "dramatic" sense than do the plays of Mr. Eliot, it is not because I think they have solved the problem but because the methodology of the verse in them points a way by which, one day, the problem of larger content and of larger forms may be solved. Eliot is, in fact, a proof of a present danger, of "too easy" a going on the practice of verse as it has been, rather than as it must be, practiced. There is no question, for example, that Eliot's line, from "Prufrock" on down, has speech-force, is "dramatic," is, in fact, one of the most notable lines since Dryden. I suppose it stemmed immediately to him from Browning, as did so many of Pound's early things. In any case Eliot's line has obvious relations backward to the Elizabethans, especially to the soliloquy. Yet O. M. Eliot is *not* projective. It could even be argued (and I say this carefully, as I have said all things about the non-projective, having considered how each of us must save himself after his own fashion and how much, for that matter, each of us owes to the non-projective, and will continue to owe, as both go alongside each other) but it could be argued that it is because Eliot has stayed inside the non-projective that he fails as a dramatist—that his root is the mind alone, and a scholastic mind at that (no high *intelletto* despite his apparent clarities)—and that, in his listenings he has stayed there where the ear and the mind are, has only gone from his fine ear outward rather than, as I say a projective poet will, down through the workings of his own throat to that place where breath comes from, where breath has its beginnings, where drama has to come from, where, the coincidence is, all act springs.

(1950)

Letter to Elaine Feinstein

May, 1959

Dear E. B. Feinstein,

Your questions catch me athwart any new sense I might have of a 'poetics.' The best previous throw I made on it was in *Poetry NY* some years ago on Projective Open or Field verse versus Closed, with much on the *line* and the *syllable*.

The basic idea anyway for me is that one, that form is never any more than an extension of content—a non-literary sense, certainly. I believe in Truth! (Wahrheit) My sense is that beauty (Schönheit) better stay in the thingitself: das Ding—Ja!—macht ring (the attack, I suppose, on the 'completed thought,' or, the Idea, yes? Thus the syntax question: what is the sentence?

The only advantage of speech rhythms (to take your 2nd question 1st) is illiteracy: the non-literary, exactly in Dante's sense of the value of the vernacular over grammar—that speech as a communicator is prior to the individual and is picked up as soon as and with ma's milk . . . he said nurse's tit. In other words, speech rhythm only as anyone of us has it, if we come on from the line of force as piped in as well as from piping we very much have done up to this moment —if we have, from, that 'common' not grammatical source. The 'source' question is damned interesting today—as Shelley saw, like Dante, that, if it comes in, that way, primary, from Ma there is then a double line of chromosomic giving (A) the inherent speech (thought, power) the 'species,' that is; and (B) the etymological: this is where I find 'foreign' languages so wild, especially the Indo-European line with the advantage now that we have Hittite to back up to. I couldn't stress enough on this speech rhythm question the pay-off in *traction* that a non-literate, non-commercial and non-historical constant daily experience of tracking *any* word, practically, one finds oneself using, back along its line of force to Anglo-Saxon, Latin, Greek, and out to Sanskrit, or now, if someone wld do it, some 'dictionary' of roots which wld include Hittite at least.

I'll give in a minute the connection of this to form if capturable in the poem, that is, the usual 'poetics' biz, but excuse me if I hammer shortly the immense help archaeology, and some specific linguistic scholarship—actually, from my experience mainly of such completely different 'grammars' as North American Indians present, in the present syntax hangup: like Hopi. But also Trobriand space-Time premises. And a couple of North California tongues, like Yani. But it is the archaeology *behind* our own history proper, Hittite, for the above reason, but now that Canaanite is known (Ugaritic) and Sumerian, and the direct connection of the Celts to the Aryans and so to the Achaean-Trojan forbears which has *slowed* and opened the speech language thing as we got it, now, in our hands, to make it do more form than how form got set by Sappho & Homer, and hasn't changed much since.

I am talking from a new 'double axis': the replacement of the Classical-representational by the *primitive-abstract* ((if this all sounds bloody German, excuse the weather, it's from the east today, and wet)). I mean of course not at all primitive in that stupid use of it as opposed to civilized. One means it now as 'primary,' as how one finds anything, pick it up as one does new—fresh/first. Thus one is equal across history forward and back, and it's all levy, as present is, but sd that way, one states . . . a different space-time. Content, in other words, is also shifted—at least from humanism, as we've had it since the Indo-Europeans got their fid in there (circum 1500 BC) ((Note: I'm for 'em on the muse level, and agin 'em on the content, or 'Psyche' side.

Which gets me to yr 1st question—"the use of the Image." "the Image" (wow, that you capitalize it makes *sense:* it is *all* we had (post-circum *The Two Noble Kinsmen*), as we had a sterile grammar (an insufficient 'sentence') we had analogy only: images, no matter how learned or how simple: even Burns say, allowing etc and including Frost! Comparison. Thus representation was never off the dead-spot of description. Nothing was *happening* as of the poem itself—ding and zing or something. It was referential to reality. And that a p. poor crawling actuarial 'real'—good enough to keep banks and insurance companies, plus mediocre governments etc. But not Poetry's *Truth* like my friends from the American Underground cry and spit in the face of 'Time.'

The Image also has to be taken by a double: that is, if you bisect a parabola you get an enantiomorph (The Hopi say what goes on over there isn't happening here therefore it isn't the same: pure 'localism' of space-time, but such localism can now be called: what you find out for yrself (*'istorin*) keeps all accompanying circumstance.

The basic trio wld seem to be: topos/typos/tropos, 3 in I. The 'blow' hits here, and me, 'bent' as born and of sd one's own decisions for better or worse (allowing clearly, by Jesus Christ, that you do love or go down)

if this sounds 'mystical' I plead so. Wahrheit: I find the contemporary substitution of society for the cosmos captive and deathly.

Image, therefore, is vector. It carries the trinity via the double to the single form which one makes oneself able, if so, to issue from the 'content' (multiplicity: originally, and repetitively, chaos—Tiamat: wot the Hindo-Europeans knocked out by giving the Old Man (Juice himself) all the lightning.

The Double, then (the 'home'/heartland/of the post-Mesopotamians AND the post-Hindo Eees:

At the moment it comes out   The Muse ('world'

The Psyche (the 'life'

You wld know already I'm buggy on say the Proper Noun, so much so I wld take it Pun is Rime, all from tope/type/trope, that built in is the connection, in each of us, to Cosmos, and if one taps, via psyche, plus a 'true' adherence of Muse, one does reveal 'Form'

in other words the 'right' (wahr-) proper noun, however apparently idiosyncratic, if 'tested' by one's own experience (out plus in) ought to yield along this phylo-line (as the speech thing, above) because—decently what one oneself can know, as well as what the word means—ontogenetic.

The other part is certainly 'landscape'—the other part of the double of Image to 'noun.' By Landscape I mean what 'narrative'; scene; event; climax; crisis; hero; development; posture; all that meant—all the substantive of what we call literary. To animate the scene today: wow: You say "orientate me." Yessir. Place it!

again

I drag it back: Place (topos, plus one's own bent plus what one can know, makes it possible to name.

O.K. I'm running out of appetite. Let this swirl—a bit like Crab Nebula—do for now. And please come back on me if you are interested. Yrs.

Charles Olson

"On Poets and Poetry"

Grover Smith. "On Poets and Poetry," *New Mexico Quarterly* XXIII, no. 3 (Autumn 1953): 317–29.

Dear Editor:

This man, Grover Smith, "On Poets And Poetry," in your 1953 Autumn issue. He's a glib one. But because he is a *philosophe* (and not another of the textualists) I take it he ought to be met on the premises of the systematic by which he there judges, out of hand, the work of Hart Crane and W. C. Williams. Nor is it surprising that he also, in his easy article, is more at home, patently, with Yeats, and, by way of Durrell's book, with Hopkins, and Eliot. For I think it can be shown that his strictures on Crane as disordered, and on Williams as equally random, are more of the cultural colonialism (not to be bothered with Smith's academicism) which keeps readers from the advance in discourse which Pound & Williams, and Crane, after his lights, led the rest of us on to.

It *is* discourse, not just verse. Smith states the convention he is applying:

> Raw material is always present; what Crane could not see was that matter must move into form, and that all form, to be recognizable as a new thing, and a thing more than its ingredients, must be shaped in *rational patterns of discourse.* (Italics, mine.)

By this test Smith necessarily is led to his most sweeping parenthesis:

> (There is a strong resemblance between the rationale of Pound's *Cantos* and that of Williams' *Paterson:* both suggest a link between the poetry which displays, as in a provincial museum, detached objects, and that which similarly displays discontinuous ideas or ideas connected only tangentially.)

Thus—and slyly—he depresses the whole of the American push to find out an alternative discourse to the inherited one, to the one implicit in the language from Chaucer to Browning, to try, by some other means than "pattern" and the "rational," to cause discourse to cover—as it only ever best can—the real.

And not knowing that it is the sentence (as a "completed thought") which has been under scrutiny and attack for forty years, Smith is led to ask of Williams:

(1) images, instead of concepts
(2) narrative and dramatic power
(3) "objective vision" (which I take it must echo Eliot's "correlative")
& (4) that Williams be a pearl inside, without boiling, his own oyster.

Or, as he puts it as of Miss Koch's book on Williams, what Smith expects— what he means by "form"—is *a simple union between general and particular.*" (Italics, mine.)

I have this difficulty—as anyone has, who practices a trade—to drag up the base of one to confront a judge who clearly backs up on the law in lieu of the duress—the necessities—of the act of trade. To put it all in the mouth, in a few sentences, what is forty years in the works of Pound, Williams, Crane, to be read there, or in whatever years have been one's own. Which is why writers don't bother with Smiths, to expose their ignorances, their smartnesses. And I haven't, except for this one.

But it happens that just this subject of discourse is much on my mind, to say what poets have done in this century, and to track back that very rational system Smith is using—and so many with him—to blind themselves to what is going on, to stay behind, even to go behind to, Reaction.

And it does boil down to how he has it there: "all form . . . must be shaped in rational patterns of discourse." It is the measure which has been. And by it WCW does lose his pearl, the 400 grams, the finest pearl of modern times. Haha.

Let me be short, so you'll publish at least an objection to Smith, so that some readers will know what he does not make clear—that he is imposing old discourse on a group of men who are still working toward a new. And thus finding faults in them which are exactly their virtues. Smith's adjectives— "disordered," "irresponsible," "disintegrated," "random"—"discontinuous ideas"—are a drab's talk.

Exactly narrative and dramatic power is no longer a poet's attention—that is, as such power was from Sophocles to Hardy, or through Yeats or Durrell.

And simply because the "general" is not now known, any universal, "Narrative," what it is. Or "Drammer," as the Old Man cried it down.

Or "Image." It should also be noticed that Smith has another sleeper, in his derogation of Williams—that images should emerge as "symbols" in order that there be this objective vision he sets up as success. It doesn't take much thought over Bill's proposition—"Not in ideas but in things"—to be sure that any of us intend an image as a "thing," never, so far as we know, such a non-animal as symbol. (If there is any clue to what an image is today, Linnaeus—or Agassiz, for that matter—are better informants than all writers other than the handful of Americans who have been at the job, recently: "an insect in its final adult, sexually mature, and usually winged, state.")

Which gets me back to the sentence. And how Grammar, too, ain't what it war. So long as a sentence stayed a "completed thought"—and I'd guess it got that way when the Greeks did impose idea (to see) on act (dran, drama, to act)—it ceased (because ideas are not what we act to, however much we do see afterwards; therefore, form is *before* ideas, Grover boy), the sentence ceased to be the capable animal it now is, and has been for some years, jumping all over the place, and growling (thus WCW's "vernacular," no doubt, dear English) in the words of said poets, Pound, Williams, Crane. And some others.

(1954)

Notes on Language and Theater

Before the classic Greek theater mime was another thing. It was Man-with-a-Tail, first, long before, so long it was a cave, France, the guy: out of this world. No comic. Or if he was he was after something Chaplin . . . *Mimos* wasn't even imitation so late as the Grks. It was *travesty,* more like what had .preceded it than what there, Athens, overwhelmed it: tragedy and written comedy, those two.

I gather that drama and theater were *more* language & movement *before* Aeschylus than since, before he added a second actor, and had dialogue, and before he added masks (and had that hollow thing, mechanical projection). It was a double change he effected: words as gab and masks to magnify sensation. And the result? The birth of that exaggerated individual called hero, and of that exaggerated narrative called tragedy. One can date this consequence of the split of language from movement which dividing up the single actor does involve: A's time, 490 BC. And the trick? Magnification by multiplication of the theatrical means.

Before Aeschylus and before he added these means, before the theater of boards collapsed during the performance of *The Persians* from the fright he produced, ladies screaming and giving birth right there in the taxicab and the city fathers announcing that henceforth it shall be obscene, shall be kept off the scene, there were three other sorts of theater which ought to be given attention:

(1) *the rhabdians,* or single actors with a stick beating out verse and acting out narrative situations in said verse, 500 hexameters at a performance, the text the "Epics" (who have been known by that cliche the "Rhapsodists" but whom I think Victor Berard is more right about, that a performance was not a recitation of a "classic" or if it was it was more like what Laughton and Claude

Rains are now sweeping the country with, "crumbs," Aeschylus said his plays were, "from Homer's table."

(2) *the comedians,* the gag men, no text, who survive today in Greece and elsewhere (Grossinger's) as those traveling kerekters (the borscht circuit) who are anywhere doing the steady business of phallic jokes and situations, what American burlesk did before the upper middle class (LaGuardia, that enlightened fool who had to crowd 'em off, shut 'em down, in order to make room for his own idiocies for grown up american children on that fleshless thing radio)—Oh, where are the legs of yesteryear, the scar on Ann Corio's belly, Ragland and his handful of "yours". . . anyhow, what Aristophanes came in on

(you can see terracottas of the personages of this earlier "comedy" dug up at Carthage as well as any number of sites in the Ionian sea, with Hercules the chief butt and big one, the same stock they tell me there is one of right now in the Middle West, playing the fairs, Sam Spade or something, who still wows the rubes as the dumb one who outsmarts the City Feller, and is better known, this bumbkin, in those parts than movie stars.

& (3) what is almost indistinguishable through the curtain of the 5th Century, and in any case probably lies far back of either of the above, at least back of the mime explicit in (2) and implicit if Berard is right, in (1), but of which there is one fine surviving clue, *The Cyclops* of Euripides. The 5th Century called these fourth plays of an afternoon "satyr-plays," or, *the saturos,* and it would take arguing to attach these plays to, like I say, the Man-with-a-Tail or Chaplin's Charlie.

But that's what we're here for. And we'll get to it.

The other immediate thing to say about the Greeks before the 5th Century would be to insist that "serious matters" (what we associate with "tragedy") also existed, only they were not separable as professional, did not get secular or "entertainment," in the modern sense, until that century. They had been what they have now once more become, I'd guess: RITES or RELIGION (all that tedious academic biz of the goat-song, etc., of the little white cakes, etc., and Henry Luce crying over how the Americans are not tragic because they haven't produced a "tragedy," not even *Moby-Dick* doing . . .). The real point wld seem to be that our "tragedies" are just where missionary son Luce will next week fumble just where they are: In State and church event, in PUBLIC ritual practices (to our doom!). They are on the FRONT PAGES, and real there, not at all in sad present theater (trying to be like a front page), or in novels (trying to get to the galaxies ahead of the gas).

The thing is, to see the parallel picture at this end—*after* Chaplin as against the situation *before* Aeschylus. Let me try it this way:

(1) , the theater, as we call theater, will soon be once more *rhabdian,* plots gone, gab gone, all the rest of the baggage of means, stripped down, these "recitations" now going on in public hall a sign, but Dylan Thomas more, the hunger of people merely to hang their ears out and hear, not any longer the jigging of their eyes, all that "luxury," Schubert seats etc.

One can say this: it will be what hexameters then were when they were as good as

(2), comics, they'll stay, who can do without them, only it'll surely be only the best, even on television, only such as the Beantown exjuggler, what's his name, Fred / the Great / Allen . . .

(3) tragedy, like I say, is now altogether public event and person, so let it stay there, the hero dead, gone back to the newspaper where his face, god help us

(even Chaplin cldn't quite make the *Great Dictator* what his others were, Hitler and Mussolini being already more than even he, and Jack Oakie, could do with them

and (4), what I am persuaded is a form we know nothing about (except as Chaplin has gone towards it), *the saturos,* call it, but who knows how what is is presentable, how what matters, in the face of events, is deliverable, how man is what does?

II

In himself, inside, it turns out a man is how? Except as any one of us pursues him through the several guises of identity, or whatever the self is, which what anything is not only forces on us, or involves us in, but insists that we obey to until we do take some stand that this is who we are, the single thing in the end, perhaps, we turn out to be, or settle for.

It is here that naming is important. Surely we are not psychological (first person singular,he,she,it). Nor sociological (we you they, god damn 'em). Or mythological (the absolute persons, the grrONd stories). Or we are only of these *after*—not at all before—we have found out the names of who we are, what we have been about in all our actions and activities (as I heard a man say to a fine actor who is as good a comic as Chaplin if he'd take up the mime in his fingertips which he can't because he isn't sure he is singular, the man said to him, look, you know you are a Horse, you dream you are, you make such excellent faces, why bother yr self about pronouns and absolutes, isn't it enough that Horse says?

Names are the colored barrels we trip over inside. And if we have any means, any of those things. Aeschylus got the whole thing wrong by exploiting 'em outside, by turning theater into what only language can give spit to, masks, images, personages, myths, if we got 'em, they are right there where we stumble, yes? "Inside this tent, Ls and Gs, you will find, for yr Quarter . . ."

III

The other half of the truth is the path—that it don't do no good to have the name on the locomotive if the damned train ain't got somewhere to go. And the rails to get there. What the saturos travestied, or represented on the hinter side, was all that is now dubbed ancient or hidden knowledge. But which was, I'm convinced from the evidence, a danced (or crawled) sung (or with ratchets, loud as thunder) witnessed (everybody in it) THEATER PERFORMANCE. Call it that.

At which point I buck off. For cause. I had thought this mystery was priest-business, but I know now that "priests" go with a contrary system, with exactly the system which intervenes between a man and his path, and which intervened, historically, the moment when the secular overtook what wasn't, in the first place, "religious," in fact, when movement and thought (language as one) were split.

Theater is language, that unit more than it is all the other things it is. Grabbing hold of it that way, mime matters. So I begin with mime simply that it is the single actor being articulate, with or without words.

(1954)

Against Wisdom as Such

Issue no. 5 of *The Artist's View* ("Published by Poets, Painters and Sculptors, 56 Magnolia St., San Francisco") designed and edited by Robert Duncan, and made up of three double-column "Pages from a Notebook" by him.

As the best of the mood of Duncan's genuine "diary" (under such headings as "On Children Art and Love," "On the Secret Doctrine," "On Revisions," and "Notes Midway on My Faust") I pick this paragraph:

> Here I am, at last, I said. Why who cares now, not I, that I imitate or pretend, or sit a great frog in the mighty puddle of my own front room. Here I need not be mature. I can be, as Virginia Admiral used to accuse, wet behind the ears, adolescent indeed. I shall live out my life in this small world, with my imaginary genius, doing as I please, as fancy will; all pretension and with my wits at an end at last.

Just after this entry Duncan puts it all in this sentence: "I am a poet, self-declared, manqué." And I had to write to him that I took it (from poems of his I have admired since I saw one in *Circle* in 1947) that he was neither as balanced as the sentences in this "Notebook" try to be. Nor manqué. And that he chastises himself as either more or less than he is, because of some outside concept and measure of "wisdom." Which is what's wrong with wisdom, that it does this to persons. And that it damn well has to go, at least from the man of language.

        (I wanted even to say that San Francisco seems to have become an école des Sages ou Mages as ominous as Ojai, L. A. But I didn't. For as I sit in the midst of these dreary States, all atomic and anti-Russian events served up to the people to kill them off with botulism before botulism, I think that just because Duncan does declare "I am a poet," because he does include Jack Spicer in a list of forty fashionable writers he himself would emulate, imitate, reconstrue, approximate, duplicate (led off by Pound); because Rexroth and Patchen do also say "We write," that this is something. And worth more than all the religion they all do seem to court (as so many gifted men do, these days—as Jung, say; or as other more immediate writers have courted other forms of authority).—As though art were not enough for any of us to behave to!

I take it wisdom, like style, is the man—that it is not extricable in any sort of a statement of itself; even though—and here is the catch—there be "wisdom," that it must be sought, and that "truths" can be come on (they are so overwhelming and so simple there does exist the temptation to see them as "universal"). But they are, in no wise, or at the gravest loss, verbally separated. They stay the man. As his skin is. As his life. And to be parted with only as that is.

Only sectaries can deal with wisdom as separable. And even they do it by symbols and by signs, and in secret. Example, the eight signs of the *Book of Changes* (*I Ching*). Or its sticks for coins, to be tossed.

> Note: It is worth saying, at a time when the ideogram, which once had so much effect in teaching us how to hew back to the lines of force by which an Anglo-American word has its power, has flipped over and is now taken as the root of Oriental wisdoms, to be imposed on us; and at a time when suppression for any heresy is the order of society; that I do not myself believe that symbols and signs are forced on sectaries, out of a necessity to be secret, but that wisdom itself, or at least the cultivation of energy-states per se, thrives on secrecy, on sect, and— at exactly the time we are in—finds its pleasure in conspiracy ("*épater tout le monde*").

And I think two things: (1) that such secrecy is wearing the skin that truth is inside-out; and (2) that, as Duncan has so finely made Confucius say, the third of the civilized pleasures cannot ever be conspiracy simply that it is "Perspective"—which is everywhere and every thing, when it is "contained."

"Contained." I fall back on a difference I am certain the poet at least has to be fierce about: that he is not free to be a part of, or to be any, sect; that there are no symbols to him, there are only his own composed forms, and each one solely the issue of the time of the moment of its creation, not any ultimate except what he in his heat and that instant in its solidity yield. That the poet cannot afford to traffick in any other "sign" than his one, his self, the man or woman he is. Otherwise God does rush in. And art is washed away, turned into that second force, religion.

It was thinking about an earlier eastern Westerner, Apollonius of Tyana, which prompted me to write Duncan. For Apollonius is valuable in that he did insist that there is "the moment which suits wisdom best to give death battle." It came for him, he decided, when Domitian put him on trial. It comes for a poet—that is, is this the single moment, or should wisdom go back where it came from—each time he writes. But wisdom is only this thing which is carried like the blade in a spring knife (or like Cordelia's heart, which she wouldn't heave into her mouth, couldn't). Or as Apollonius said to one of Nero's questioners, trying to trap him, "What do you think of Nero?" he answered, "I think better of him than you do, you think he ought to sing, I think he ought to keep silent."

The subject is a matter of importance, now that the wisdom of the East and the unwisdom of the West are both being looked to as dispensations, by the Right, and the right Right.

Note: I don't know enough Anglo-Saxon to say, but if the noun "wise" (AS. *wise*) is the root of the adjective (AS. *wis*), then one is back at the sort of force I suggest the proper use of wisdom is: "way of being or acting," as in, "in this wise."

All the vocabulary which goes with truth (the sort of words Duncan, here at least, seeks to make gnomic by sets of positive and negative upsets) is only valid if they are used recognizably as part of the reductive, not the productive, process—that one does try, and damn well might, to analyze the knowledge of truth, but to use it . . .

here I go off and have to explain, that I believe that the traditional order of water to fire to light—that is, as of the sectaries, as well as the Ionian physicists, that except a man be born of water and of the spirit, he cannot enter into the kingdom of God—has to be re-taken. Light was the sign of the triumph of love and spirit before electronics. And we are after. So, fire . . .

Sound
    is fire. As love
    is.

Light is reductive. Fire isn't. Or—to get rid of any of those false pleasures which paradox and sectaries involve themselves in (are alchemic or gnostic or

Lü Tung-pin, the Guest of, the Cavern) I said to Duncan, "heat, all but heat, is symbolic, and thus all but heat is reductive."

I asked Duncan if it wasn't his own experience that a poem is the issue of two factors, (1) heat, and (2) time. How plastic, cries Wilhelm, is the thought of "water" as seed-substance in the *T'ai I Chin Hua Tsung Chih*. And time is, in the hands of, the poet. For he alone is the one who takes it as the concrete continuum it is, and who practices the bending of it (as others do, say, aluminum, to make the rockers, say, of a hobby-horse).

Rhythm is time (not measure, as the pedants of Alexandria made it). The root is "rhein": to flow. And mastering the flow of the solid, time, we invoke others. Because we take time and heat it, make it serve our selves, our, form. Which any human being craves to do, to impress himself on it.

But I didn't want to leave it at the word "time" any more than I wanted to leave it at the word "fire." One has to drive all nouns, the abstract most of all, back to pro-cess—to act. And I wanted to convince Duncan, or any one, of what he has proved to me by any number of his poems—that he has had the experience that a poem is ordered not so much *in* time (Poe's Poetic Principle) or *by* time (metric, measure) as of a characteristic *of* time which is most profound: that time is synchronistic and that a poem is the one example of a man-made con-tinuum "which contains qualities or basic conditions manifesting themselves simultaneously in various places in a way not to be explained by causal parallelisms."

I take it Duncan, or any writing man who takes it seriously, needn't bother his head with greatness. We are ultimate when we do bend to the law. And the law is:

/ whatever is born or done this moment of time, has
the qualities of
this moment of
time /

II

I urge on Duncan or anyone that a poem is not wise, even if it is: that any wis-dom which gets into any poem is solely a quality of the moment of time in which there might happen to be wisdoms.

There are obviously seizures which have nothing to do with wisdom at all. And they are very beautiful.

Or maybe I don't believe it's "beauty," any more than I believe it's "light" . . . how Bill has it in "To a Dog Injured in the Street," that he and René Char both believe "in the power of beauty / to right all wrongs." Maybe I think this is also partial, social, wisdom.

"It is time (love) is difficult, Mr.
Beardsley"

I'm so foolish. A song is heat. There may be light, but light and beauty is not the *state* of: the state is the grip of (and it is not feverish, is very cool, is—the eyes are—how did they get that way?

"He who controls rhythm
controls"

This wld seem to me to be the
END

Otherwise, we are involved in
ourselves (which is demonstrably
not very interesting, no
matter
who

(1954)

Theocritus

Cid Corman. *A Thanksgiving Eclogue* (Vagrom Chapbook 2). Flushing, N.Y.: Sparrow Press, 1954.

This has nothing to do with the Pilgrim Fathers. Or their present descendents. And why Theocritus' 7th Idyll is thus jigged, is not clear. In any case the effect of the change is cuteness, the more so that the "verse" sought is that slackest of translation devices, moving over—not the poet's form & intention—but merely the replacement of the surface of his speech by a contemporary choctaw. It makes Theocritus, of course, easier to read than the 19th century Bohn translations, or whatever (Leaf, Lang, Butcher, & Myer, or whoever). But only by a law of laziness, at least on the reader's part and—I suspect—the writer's. Such translation is, in short, a gimmick. (And I, for one, would include in such a charge the much praised Rouse; and thus Ezra, to the extent that he propagated this smartness, however much his own genius, etc.)

But what exasperates about the present chapbook is, that T's central act is avoided, indeed flatly left out. That is, the idyll, as he wrote it, was a set-up. His point was to devise a meeting between two poets, Lycidas (a "classic" shepherd singer) and Simichidas (obviously more T himself, and a buster of idylls, especially those Roman things, "eclogues"). As the pupil of Philetas of Cos, Theocritus damn well knew he could outwrite the true-boys, but he also had the power he is remembered for, that he could freshen up any damn form. So he has these people traveling along a road in the middle of the day to get somewhere to eat and drink, with Demeter, that harvest gal, as the excuse for that. But the real excuse for the whole gig is to write both kinds of poems. Which T thereby did. And Mr. Corman didn't. Why?

It strikes me he had to, to make his risk. As it is he played it safe. And easy. In any case, taking this position, I have no choice but to fall on my own face, if for no other reason than to inform the unwary reader that the two songs to follow are what he is missing, if he buys this little pamphlet for his mother and father for the holidays (to send home from Gettysburg, like china souvenirs, that he was where he told them he said he was going).

Lycidas sings first, the proper song:

"Ageanax! fair voyage to Mitylene,
a good south wind carry you,
now that it is December, and Orion
puts his feet in the ocean.
That is, a good trip
if you requite my love
who am set burning by the goddess
with love of you.

Kingfishers to smooth the waves,
as well any swell, as well
the southwest wind, as well
the southeast storm which does the most
to tear up seaweed from the bottom,
kingfishers, those most loved of birds,
who live, alongside green Nereids,
on the sea.

May everything go right for you, Ageanax,
as you make for Mitylene, and that you get there
after an easy passage. And I,
on that day, shall crown myself with dill,
maybe with roses, possibly white violets, I'll drink
Pteleatic wine lying by the fire,
and have a roast cooked, bedded
in vine leaves up to my elbows,
and covered thickly with asters,
asphodel, and wrinkling parsley

In longing for you, Ageanax, I'll empty
as many cups as I can, and have two shepherds
play for me the whole time, one from Acharnia

(for that tone), the other, from Lycope.
And Tityrus will sing with them, first of Daphnis,
how he loved a wrong woman, a stranger,
and took to the hills after her, wasted there
until even the oaks wept for him,
and he went to pieces as the snow does
no matter how high it lies on Haemus,
or on Athos, Rhodope or the Caucasus

I'll have him also sing the story of Comatus,
who loved the Muses so he sang all day, piped
his flocks down, much to his master's
envy, who thought of this idea: seal the lad up
in a box and then sneer at him, see if your Muses now
will help you out! Great power of love and song,
for flat-nosed bees, the full three months of spring,
from meadows to the foothills of the mountains,
brought honey, built combs beside him as he lay
helpless in his box, until, when the villain opened it,
there Comatus was, alive as he had ever been.

O, Comatus, that I had lived when you did, lad,
I'd have taken care of your she-goats, you can bet,
just to have had the chance to hear you sing as sweetly
as the Muses knew you sang, stretched out, as any singer must,
under oak or pine."

At which point (see Mr. Corman's text) Simichidas boasts he knows a few songs
Zeus must have caught in his ear-trumpet, among which is this one:

"Love's sneezed on me too. I've had it.
This lad Myrto. I go for him as she-goats
go for the spring, tra-la.

But then there's this friend of mine, Aratus.
He burns for another lad. And Aristis
(he's that 'aristocrat of song,' ha-ha,
but it's true, god damn it, Phoebus himself

would be a fool if he didn't listen carefully
when A gets off on his lyre) Aristis knows
what a torch Aratus is carrying, he's consumed,
like he said, to the very bone with love.

Now look, Pan. You got this whole mountain Homole
to yourself. Come off it, and give my friend Aratus
a break. See to it that this lad gives Aratus a tumble.
Or at least get Aratus the chance to lay his hands on it,
the more so if it is Philinus, as they say it is,
who's a real piece, if there ever was one.

If you do this, Pan, there isn't any reason at all
why those Arcadians oughtn't to lay off instantly
knocking the hell out of their images of you,
simply that they can't get anything themselves.
But if you don't—if you continue to leave Aratus hung
like this—you ought to have your own ass chewed,
and then try to sleep on it. You ought to have to live in Thrace
all winter. And have to spend your summers in Ethiopia,
where even the Nile has sense enough to dry up.

And for you, you gods of love. Come out of those watering-places
around Miletus. Get over to Cyprus where that blond Dione
keeps her house. You're as ripe as apples yourselves,
and it's time you dropped this lad, time you shot him off
what a fruit he is anyway, a perfect peach, the girls know,
crowdin' him, like to crawl all over him, crying, Oh, oh,
Philinus! don't you know it won't keep forever?

        Anyhow, Aratus, let's quit it.
Stop spending every night looking out of windows.
Or walking my legs off me. Let some other dope
go for it, have to be up to listen to that 3 o'clock cock.
Let Molon, he's dumb enough, have this sort of trouble.
Let's you and I get some sleep. It's no good, love.
Any old woman would have sense enough to spit on it."

                                (1954)

A Foot Is to Kick With

"Prosody is the articulation of the total sound of a poem"

It's got a kick in it   What a kicker   Mid-field   a 12 horse-power kicker
You got a kick?   Go tell it to City Hall

It's as though you were hearing for the first time—who knows what a poem
ought to sound like?   until it's thar?   And how do you get it thar except as
you do—*you,* and nobody else (who's a poet?
    What's,
a poem?
    It ain't dreamt until it walks   It talks   It spreads its green barrazza
    Listen closely, folks, this poem comes to you by benefit of its own Irish green
bazoo. You take it, from here.

Think of what's possible—not what's new, but what it's all about   what
about it's   all   what all of a poem is. You think of it. You put down a word:
how do you put down the last word. How do you have the last word?
    Wow. Yes sir. The *last* word. What intervenes, is the simplest But—
    You wave the first word. And the whole thing follows. But—
    You follow it. With a dog at your heels, a crocodile about to eat you at the
end, and you with your pack on your back trying to catch a butterfly.

(1956)

269

Quantity in Verse,
and Shakespeare's Late Plays

(The argument: in the ten years from 1602 to the theatrical season 1612–13, from Campion's *Observations in the Art of English Poesie* through Shakespeare's last two plays *Henry 8* and *The Two Noble Kinsmen,* quantity made enough change in verse and Shakespeare enough change in comedy to take form all the way over

To chart it:

(I) in 1603–04 the first signs—*Troilus and Cressida*
                                                      Measure for Measure
(II) by 1607–08 change shows—*Timon of Athens*
    and most in   PERICLES OF TYRE
    (*Coriolanus* is written the same year and is the final accentual blank verse tragedy.)

In the fall of 1609, Shakespeare's company moved indoors, into the Blackfriars theater, and in that first season the takings increased by £1000, or better than $50,000 in modern buying power.

(III) The Evidence, the season of 1610–11:

        CYMBELINE (performed April, 1611)
        THE WINTER'S TALE (performed May 15, 1611)
        THE TEMPEST (performed November 1)
In these plays the change of form is altogether clear, Tasso or Ariosto regained, *Midsummer Night's Dream* retaken, PLUS.

(IV) Verse-wise, for myself the full pleasure of quantity is most evident in Shakespeare's part with Fletcher in *Henry 8,* and, above all, in *The Two Noble Kinsmen,* both done 1612–13

The late plays of Shakespeare are aerodynes, in which, by a series of baffles (the verse, with its emphasis on quantities), they have their power straight from the element they move in, that they displace, and they go in speed from zero to as fast as sound. They are motion, not action—by power of vacuum, they use it and occupy it at the same time. Though the plays exploit the earlier "Comedies," music, dance, spectacle, particularly *Midsummer Night's Dream* (it is turned back as the Italians are turned to), these earlier things only resemble the later as flying machines: they go in the air, that's all. The later plays move without internal combustion, or show any blades throwing the air. They come as quietly to a stop as they take off, vertically. They hover, they do whatever they are of a mind to do, one is not in the presence of drama or poem so known. These things (*Winter's Tale, Tempest, Two Noble Kinsmen*) are forms of power not known.

For two literary reasons: the fashioning of the verse, which takes the English language off where it was stuck, on its own motor power, on accent, on that "flow," those—"wings"; and the matter of the thought: these are comedies all right, but hardly Bottom or Beatrice (his Beatrice), neither the old rustic comic nor any light urban witty, nor magic faery spirit pleasant illusion of forest night streams, Nature that is. Shakespeare is no longer a Humanist in which Nature and Man are separate delights, or she is rank and he is his own wheel of fire. What these plays are is comedy in the sense another man was after who put it:

> So Comedy is a certain kind of poetic narration differing from all others. It differs then from tragedy in its *content,* in that tragedy begins admirably and tranquilly, whereas its exit is foul and terrible, it is fetid, like a goat; but comedy introduces some *harsh* complication yet brings its matter to a *prosperous* end.

(Prospero's end.)

Throughout *De Vulgare Eloquentia* and *Epistola X* (from which the above is taken) Dante awards a more satisfying possibility to comedy than to tragedy, and for cause. As he puts it at the close of this letter to Can Grande della Scala:

> The end of the whole and the part may be manifold, to wit, the proximate *and* the ultimate. But dropping all subtle investigation, we may say briefly that the end of the whole and the part is *to remove those living in this life from the state of misery and lead them to the state of felicity.*

I would make no more of this than that Shakespeare, by and about 1610, age 46, wanted comedy to do that which Dante also made it do: enjoin. "As we are men," says Theseus at the end of the first scene of *The Two Noble Kinsmen*, "Thus should we do." I wish only to establish that these plays are different in that they are injunctive, so that they no longer need sit in the confusion of definition in which they have—romantical-tragical, tragical-comical, pastoral-wittical, whatever.

Beyond that, Shakespeare had no such frame as Christianity to set his vision of "felicity" in, as Dante had. He was a man of the Renaissance, and an Englishman, and what he took it could lead the living from misery stays secular. What Theseus says is

> Thus should we do. Being sensually subdued we lose our human title.

It is that title which Shakespeare is at pains to spell out the terms of, and by so doing to insure it, by 1610 and after.

What is more important and the most difference from Dante, as well as from Shakespeare's own previous art—and most since, for that matter—is that he makes form itself secular. I am imagining that form (one means simply the power a thing of art asserts by which it seizes, and both art and the observer are changed thereafter) has left its former places and though the means and the matter seem the same, it uses them so differently one is fooled if one looks for them as one used to, in the place where form was, in the sound of motors, brilliance in the sky. Form is now as much an invention as it always is. What is missed is, that it is. Verse and thoughts are vernacular. Who would have thought it! The absolute, in all its guises, even the smallest—notion opinion self-assertion—has slunk away. A huge difference has come about, something previously unknown about the real and the natural has been disclosed: that the artificial (paradis n'est pas artificiel) the mechanical the arbitrary whatever you want to call the aesthetic, is not separate from them. It is what the felicity in these plays leads to, it does not lead to its own pursuit (this is the pathetic fallacy of humanism) it goes directly back to the real but in so doing a real and natural which are themselves transposed. It is my purpose to show that.

I

The limit on new in the verse is syntax. Shakespeare did not particularly disturb the working sentence as it had served him and others in blank verse proper. Imagery likewise. It is gone into as the sentence does, explicit, and descriptive. Yet the thought increases a verticality gained by blank verse itself between 1600 and 1608, and quantity (which tends at any time to increase the standing as against the running power of verse) most makes the language different. A pattern is seen: logicality persists in the syntax and image but the thinking and weighing in of the quantity stop twist and intensify the speech, thus increasing the instancy. In this situation it is the vocabulary which tips the scale, the increase (for good reasons of comedy and quantity, as we shall see) of the simplest monosyllables on the one hand, and, on the other, of the most intellective polysyllables. The result is a poetry with a perspective which blank verse, in its extensivity, could not supply.

One does not have to go outside *The Tempest* to show these things: the monosyllables at their quietest and sweetest,

(Ceres, most bounteous lady, thy rich leas)
of wheat, rye, barley, vetches, oats and peas;

consonants forced to the vertical,

Thy banks with pinioned and twilled brims
which spongy April at thy hest betrims
to make cold nymphs chaste crowns;

and the difference even when the basic sentence and image holds,

Here thought they to have done
some wanton charm upon this man and maid
whose vows are that no bed-right shall be paid
till Hymen's torch be lighted. But in vain.
Mars' hot minion is returned again,
her waspish-headed son has broke his arrows
swears he will shoot no more but play with sparrows
and be a boy right out.

But because *The Two Noble Kinsmen* is even left out of most canons as not Shakespeare's! and *Henry 8* is just let in, and both contain so much of just the order of power here asserted, I pick up on a speech from the latter play, Norfolk's, in the first scene, to Buckingham:

We may outrun
by violent swiftness that which we run at,
and lose by overrunning. Know you not
the fire that mounts the liquor till it run over
in seeming to augment it wastes it?

The whole first sentence is a pleasure, despite it is another of the old "State" figures speaking, simply that its vocabulary is so dry. It is a most reasonable example of the late verse. As I hear the second line, *the accents* are: "vi," "swift," "that," and "run," in other words not the five feet blank verse goes by. For a good reason: that *the quantity* of the syllables (how long it takes to say them) pulls down the accent to a progress of the line along the length of itself, which progress and which quantities the thinking itself, the idea of outrunning, demands. The quantity asserts itself at once with "by" (long i) and "violent" (not only long i also, but with two following syllables which, though unaccented, are—the long o and the heavy consonantal syllable "lent," 3 consonants to 1 vowel—slow to get through). So much so, in fact, that the first *breath* in the line has here to be taken, even if it is a slight stop before starting to say "swiftness," the "t" on the end of "lent" before the "s" of swiftness requiring the tongue to shift from the upper teethridge (alveolar) off it towards the combined lip and tongue position from which "sw" may be said.

To sum up, then: "by violent" (which is only 1 accent and 4 syllables) already shows forth the weave of accent, quantity, breath which makes prosody the music it is: and here is a very close music, sharp, long and stopped, all in a small space of time, reflecting the truth it is, that this art, when it is at its best, is powerful just because it does obey space-time.

The point of Norfolk's thought is of course to focus the attention on "violent," he is saying to Buckingham that violent running—the fire, overrunning—is what loses the game, spills the energy, wastes it. The music is likewise fit in the rest of the line: "swiftness" itself demands a stop after (the most marked breath the line requires) due to the double-s at its end, as well (reversing the tongue problem between lent and swift) the "th" at the beginning of "that," a tongue-point dental voiced fricative following hard on the voiceless doubles-s of "ness," also involves the voice in an accent on "that," which here is a relative pronoun opening a clause of some duration—"that which we run at"—which delights because it is so made up of those "necessary shaggy and urban words" Dante called them, the monosyllables comedy can't do without. Which, I should now add, strike me as both what Shakespeare more and more came to depend upon, and for the same reasons, I imagine, that the Americans who now practice the language at something like the same vitality, also depend upon.

I can make this immediate point about Shakespeare's late verse. It has exactly the characteristic Dante long ago insisted any verse has which places itself back on the vernacular: only two kinds of words have the grandeur right to the deed, the "combed-out" and the "shaggy." The glossy and rumpled won't do. And what does he call the "shaggy" (the combed-out are three syllables, and sweet)? The monosyllables, in other words, the gist of speech; and what he calls the "ornamental polysyllables," the jaw-breakers, if you like, but for all that the words which hold in themselves the flow and the resistances of feeling, thinking, acting. Dante calls the polysyllables those which, when mixed with combed-out words, produce a "fair harmony of structure" because they have "the roughness of aspirate, accent, double letters, liquids and lengths," in short, breath (aspirate) accent quantity, all three at once, the possibility of same.

One should not have to be bugged because Shakespeare so often does knot up his speech in his late plays, does come up with rough polysyllables, "stops" his lines so much, yields, reluctantly, any of that running-on which made him so suave a poet from *Venus & Adonis* to *Antony & Cleopatra;* and very much doesn't any longer bother to keep his music and thought inside the skin of the person or situation, able as he had been to make each person of his play make his or her individual self register its experience of reality. If the Shakespeare *after* 1607–08 (*Antony & Cleopatra*) is interested instead in making his own thought and music override anybody's, it should only be a sign that he is intending something else than previously, some sort of song other than hers whom he served so long—Erato first, then Melpomene.

That it is now Thalia's song, I come down again on Dante, on another part of his careful analysis of what is possible to comedy. He insists that urban speech alone will do, that "sylvan" won't. (He calls sylvan and urban the two kinds of masculine speech there are, delimiting off feminine and child speech as not the business of poets, however much any poet may once have been a child and however as a man he has to listen to women talk.) It is another aspect of these plays, and how long it took Shakespeare to get to them, that they show how much he, and the other Elizabethan poets, were in a dilemma between urban and sylvan by and about Elizabeth's death (1603): though they had exploited London midland speech magnificently in drama, the moment they wanted to do something else, had to do something else, they knew no other mold for it than a sylvan one, the pastoral, than, in fact, that masque which *Comus,* god help us, has been called the triumph of. Is it possible that this sylvan business (which got into England from the Italians of the 16th Century) confounded the very push of urban English? And that only after "Metropolis"—after 300 years, after we have got our fill of urban as city—is it possible to see that Shakespeare sought a form in his late plays which would deliver him from the pastoral and enable him to do what long form has taught us: to be urban at the same time that we are forever rid of "nature," even human "nature," in that damned sylvan sense?

II

In the plays the plots of course, those silly things, *are* pastoral (he hadn't got that far), romantical-pastical, extreme places the events exotic storms floating coffins statues which float a dancing baboon damned countrymen dancing . . . Whoosh. If that were all of it.

But something else. Love is pitched where you haven't found it. It is not at all a fluent scene. There are pure awkwardnesses. Women and man say things. My last good deed   You may ride us with one soft kiss a thousand furlongs It has an elder sister ere with spur we heat an acre   O, would her name were Grace!

> Twenty-three years, and saw myself unbreeched
> in my green velvet coat, my dagger muzzled
> lest it should bite its master and so prove
> (as ornaments often do) too dangerous
>
>   O, then my best blood turn
> And my name with his who did betray the Best!

The delicacy (which would seem the most thing you would say. The scrupulousness

•   •   •

The matter is innocence. Innocence, mind you—that it must be kept. An impossible subject. Only a most quiet man, and a very clear one. Without leaving the world as place, to see innocence through it? to do that without, as Lear took it it could only be done out of the world (his Fool died of a cold) in prison? / where he promised Cordelia they would sing and, as God's spies, take upon themselves the mystery of things / . As though only there, one could. It is true, if you are going to leave it at that, at the level of hiring out to God and of a total assignment, the mystery of things.

For a like reason I am not satisfied by the usual insight that the plays are dominated by a search theme, of father for lost child. It sees them from the outside. It looks on them, as the above father and daughter on the world. It makes the error to expect the man, after he has let the world's real sit for portrait, that he will do it again as he had through *Lear* and *Antony & Cleopatra,* that he'll make it so round one can only go aside from it and, as the two do, weep and sing.

"The flatness of my misery!" is what Hermione cries out in the face of what happens to her in *The Winter's Tale.* Each of the three chief classes of people in these new plays—the women, the young, and the fathers—are now forces as statics, and the moving moral or physical dynamics are from those people's own stance, rather than something exerted on them. The one thing which is, is exploded on them, and is the thing they are set, each of them, to offset.

It is in this respect that the plays are best seen as *rites de passage,* in which the poet is making sure, as of these three classes and at three stages, puberty, marriage, and middle life, that, without going aside and at the same time without adding any muscle to overcome the world, outside in its hell or heaven, inside in its heaven or hell, something else is attended to.

At puberty youth is full of protest of the innocence it is giving up, and because innocence can, at this stage, describe itself, youth gets much voice. The plays, in fact, are an equilibrium between loquacious boys and girls and the terse fathers, with woman the mid term, at once the one who is most sex and most firmed, so much the one who does stand, and stand to it, that the image of her is Hermione who hid from her husband's jealousy and destruction for 19 years and is restored to him, in the end, as a statue out of her own garden!

I shall use Polixenes' description of *the love of boy & boy* but the pairs and their praises of their youth, with flowers the image, are omnipresent—conspicuously Palamon & Arcite in *The Two Noble Kinsmen,* Guiderius and Arviragus the sons of Cymbeline, etc. Polixenes is telling Hermione how it was between him and her husband:

> We were as twinned lambs that did frisk in the sun
> and bleat the one at the other. What we changed
> was innocence for innocence. We knew not

the doctrine of ill-doing. Nor dreamed
that any did. Had we pursued that life
and our weak spirits never been higher reared
with stronger blood, we should have answered heaven
boldly, "Not guilty"

The love of man & man is only an extension of the boy thing, and is presented
as such, the bond of war replacing tournament and games, and though it does
sometimes (as it did earlier in the instance of Coriolanus & Aufidius) nervously
admit a simile of marriage, it is to marriage's disadvantage. Hermione, after listening to Polixenes say what he says above, wryly observes: "By this we gather
/ you have tripped since"!

Against the male thing in the plays Emilia, in *The Two Noble Kinsmen,* directly opposes *the love of girl & girl,* hers, for Flavina. She says to her sister:

You talk of Pirithous' and Theseus' love.
Theirs has more ground, is more maturely seasoned,
more buckled with strong judgment, and their needs
the one of the other may be said to water
their intertangled roots of love, but I
and she I sigh and spoke of, were things innocent,
loved for we did, and like the elements . . .

What she liked
was then of me approved, what not, condemned

The flower that I would pluck
and put between my breasts (then but beginning
to swell about the blossom)

On my head no toy
but was her pattern . . .

This rehearsal has this end
that the true love between maid and maid may be
more than in sex dividual.

I am saying these ones are not chucks as children were, and the young pairs
of lovers (Perdita-Florizel, Ferdinand-Miranda, Emilia-Arcite &c) are present as
such, neither to be made more of (Romeo & Juliet) nor to be left as less than
the next stage, marriage, or the further one, middle life. What is so very moving in this new world is the equity. Position, title, the so-called larger con-

cerns—State passion condition ambition—don't crowd out something which is less (less in the round world.

Actually, even all that, even the big thing, is, here, made into a single one, one harsh complication. It is as though suddenly for Shakespeare Sonnet 129 had rolled up into it all that his love history and ambition plays amounted to: "The expense of spirit in a waste of shame / is lust in action and till action lust / is perjured murderous bloody full of blame / savage extreme rude cruel not to trust . . ." What is actionable in these plays follows from lust's outbursts, Leontes', in *The Winter's Tale,* Iachimo in *Cymbeline,* it breaks in on the noble ones, Palamon & Arcite, in *Kinsmen,* to split them, it is circumambient in *The Tempest* where Caliban, the Patagonian, is the danger all the plays have hidden in them dragged into the light and heaped up in him as a single carbuncular figure.

Lust is not developmental, it drops, bang, and thus, on this second level of the action, the plays behave as they do on the first and third. They are vertical and flat and, as throughout, it is because it is initiation and not drama which is intended: youth at puberty and the married throughout marriage are seen in a process of finding out how to act to keep what youth had, and age advises, when the fires in the blood flare. Prospero, most the father of the plays, though from Pericles first through Theseus the last there are real or substitute fathers in each, warns Ferdinand, who is about to marry his daughter:

> Do not give dalliance
> too much the rein. The strongest oaths are straw
> to the fire in the blood. Be more abstemious
> or else good night your vow.

The one active principle Shakespeare has, to offer to the uproar of lust, is chastity, which has the root meaning bright, it was originally one with candor, dazzling whiteness, and newfallen snow is Shakespeare's simile. Posthumus, tormented into the conviction his wife has been adulterous, protests she had

> A pudency so rosy the sweet view on it
> might well have warmed old Saturn, that I thought her
> as chaste as unsunned snow

and Ferdinand makes the same comparison of himself as Posthumus of his wife in assuring Prospero

> I warrant you, sir.
> The white cold virgin snow upon my heart
> abates the ardor of my liver.

Youth and woman have this chasteness straight from source, and when innocence is reared, as Polixenes says, "higher," with stronger blood, they do not lose it if they choose not to, to the fires.

I press it (and it is difficult to imagine that it would persuade a modern) because it does seem to be, as of the body of these plays (as it was, to make it more familiar, in *Measure for Measure*) what Shakespeare means to insist upon is the little there is which a man or a woman does have, to wear—as, in the Chinese play, the girl is given by the icy river a cloak which freezes-burns the nobleman who has sought to marry her against her wish, a reverse of Nessus' shirt, in each instance.

One may allow it is that way. When you reverse the conclusion of Sonnet 129, when you do oppose the big thing

> All this the world well knows yet none knows well
> to shun the heaven that leads men to this hell

it is bigger, and you are slighter. Your means are slight.

Only baffles will do, and the counsel of their use in these plays, as well as their use, comes from what has to be singled out as a third stage of them— what innocence is itself by the rite of its own passage, what is its own regarding that it has known so much it can present boys and girls and men and women, not thrusting about in the foul and terrible exits of the goat world, but proximate, next to themselves, not subdued but equally (as it is another thing one must say of these plays) there are no triumphs. There is only the restoration, no matter at what level in intensity, arbitrary or otherwise, of innocence.

Subject no longer will do. It is also the poet we are now talking about, how he got there that he saw it this way, a way so different it is as though he had walked out of the Renaissance. In one respect he appears not to have at all, in the fierceness with which he fights sensuality as though it were the dogs he so hated who were fed from the tables while the meal was going on. If he seems extreme in this, if he seems as determined as Prospero to keep lust, to keep nature as in an armed camp outside the fence of life, one must now hear the

third innocence which falls across the pages of these plays as both their diffi-
dence and a sound just out of hearing. Emilia, in *The Two Noble Kinsmen,* explains herself thus:

> Extremity, that sharpens sundry wits,
> makes me a fool.

It is the question we started from: how the material and means of art, once
the Renaissance and its bastard the Modern are passed, are differently disposed
and thus the form differently powered.

.   .   .

Winter, he says, winter. Prospero's answer to Miranda's pleasure before the
new world she thinks brave—he says, "'Tis new to thee"—is no old man's
quip. And chastity, it is a sticker a man as post-modern as Lawrence can be no
more explicit about (in his last poem to the women who are buried in England
whom he has loved) than to asseverate what he says he begged them throughout love, find their virginity.

.   .   .

The question is two things, the attention itself, what it is on (this is most
where a change in the discourse system counts); and how it is on, the degree
of intensity mounted, that it be the equal of the occasion. It is too frequently
unnoticed that it is the former change which makes the latter more likely.
There is a great deal of whirlyblade about feeling, about increasing it. But to
move the whole stance over, to take a good look at where the in is being
sought from . . . There is a rule: a thing ought to take off, and put down, and
travel at all the varying speeds in between, precisely equal in amount and behavior to the thing it sets out from or seeks. Or if it multiplies, it only multiplies
by changing that thing, not by introducing and asserting outside power (as humanism did and all motors with moving parts do), and the quarrel with it is the
waste of energy, which is dispersal and, in the curving about of fact, dispersal
comes back and changes, willy-nilly whirligig, the original element of both
thing and thing, by making easy the attention and thus reducing the intensity
below the level of the implicit power of occasion or of thing.

If the intensity of the attention is equal to it, innocence ought to yield what it is made up of; and when it does, like water in a controlled vacuum, it is enormously *more* than it was in its apparent state. If it is then mixed with what is proper to it (at no point known to me does Shakespeare attack desire) its size and power increase again, and innocence emerges with a thrust much more than sensuality ever gave.

I am suggesting that some such understanding as this is what Shakespeare has reached, and the verse capable of, in these plays. He isn't picking up his objects (words), despite one hand is tied behind his back, either for their music or image. He gets both by going in further to the word as meaning and thing, and, mixing the governing human title and experience (which prompts him to bother with words at all), his effect is the equivalent of his act: the power, instead of peeling off, of being peeled off (as verse and plays had), without being disturbed from its place, twisted into turbulence and action (each not the condition of an element but weather from outside), suddenly moves as one has known it does of its own nature, without using any means or matter other than those local and implicit to it. It is molecular, how this power is, why it all multiplies from itself and from the element proper to its being. We are in the presence of the only truth which the real can have, its own undisclosed because not apparent character. Get that out with no exterior means or materials, no mechanics except those hidden in the thing itself, and we are in the hands of the mystery.

(1956/1965)

Introduction to Robert Creeley

I take it there is huge gain to square away at narrative now, not as fiction but as RE-ENACTMENT. Taking it this way I see two possibilities:

(1) what I call DOCUMENT simply to emphasize that the events alone do the work, that the narrator stays OUT, functions as pressure not as interpreting person, illuminates not by argument or "creativity" but by master of force (as space is shaper, confining maintaining inside tensions of objects), the art, to make his meanings clear by how he juxtaposes, correlates, and causes to interact whatever events and persons he chooses to set in motion. In other words his ego or person is NOT of the story whatsoever. He is, if he makes it, light from outside, the thing itself doing the casting of what shadows;

(2) the exact opposite, the NARRATOR IN, the total IN to the above total OUT, total speculation as against the half management, half interpretation, the narrator taking on himself the job of making clear by way of his own person that life *is* preoccupation with itself, taking up the push of his own single intelligence to make it, to be—by his conjectures—so powerful inside the story that he makes the story swing on him, his eye the eye of nature INSIDE (as is the same eye, outside) a lightmaker.

Both (1) and (2), both methodologies drive for the same end, so to re-enact experience that a story has what an object or person has: energy and instant. Here is their gain, over the fictive—not to spill out these bloods, but to keep original force in at the same time that that force is given illumination.

There is another reason why I am sure that the choice now is one or the other of these two attacks on the problem. They are the only way that narrative can take up that aspect of verse which is its multitude. For variations—"motion"—lies out there in the meat of reality, not in the small paper of egos or lyric soullessnesses. Events have outreached narrators, have overmatched them, because narrators have either succumbed to them or, as silly white to that ridiculous black, have taken themselves to be more interesting. They are not. Poets could have told them. For "things" are what writers get inside their work, or the work, poem or story, perishes. Things are the way force is exchanged. On things communication rests. And the writer, though he is the control (or art is nothing) is, still, no more than—but just as much as—another "thing," and as such, is in, inside or out.

What it is, is two geometries, now, for the story-teller: either he lets things in and manages them so well that they get curved back by his pressure outside and make a self-existent sphere (the law is gravitation) or he takes on himself the other law (they are recognized now to be identical) and, as center, as core to the magnetic field, he causes the things to pull in to make their shape.

I take it that these stories are of the second way, of the writer putting himself all the way in—taking that risk, putting his head on that block, and by so doing giving you your risk, your commitment by the seriousness of his—constituting himself the going reality and, by the depth and sureness of his speculating, making it pay, making you-me believe, that we are here in the presence of a man putting his hands directly and responsibly to experience which is also our own. It is his presence that matters, for it rids us of artifice as such (as the whole of the story), instead only uses it to keep the going going, to make the reach of what is happening clear. For his presence is the energy. And the instant? That, too, is he, given such methodology. For his urgency, his confrontation is "time," which is, when he makes it, ours, the now. He is time, he is now, the force.

Which is multitude. It is human phenomenology which is re-inherited, allowed in, once plot is kissed out. For the moment you get a man back in, among things, the full motion and play comes back (not parts extricated for show or representation) but the total bearing, each moment of the going— as it is, for any of us, each moment, anywhere. MR. BLUE, for example.

(1951)

Robert Creeley's *For Love:*
Poems 1950–1960

Creeley has had the wit to make the short poem do what any kind of a poem might be imagined to do if it was doing what a poem might.

How has he done this? For he has, and it shakes verse, and the language, how he has.

It took will of a special kind. Which is his. It took a placement of self of such an order that each one of these poems is what conceivably the poet himself has to show for what he has lived. He says this (as so often) wryly—except perhaps when he does address himself to the woman he loves then, and she is what makes life otherwise possible—in a poem "The Song," if I read it right:

It still makes sense
to know the song after all.

My wiseness I wear
in despair of something better.

I am all beggar,
I am all ears.

Soon everything will be sold
and I can go back home

by myself again
and try to be a man.

But it would be silly to ask any of these poems, and the whole delightful volume of all the possibilities which have occurred to Creeley over 10 years—and his invention is such each of these poems is a possibility—to prove anything. They simply do, practically the 150 of them. An old friend of his thinks "I Know a Man" is the best:

As I sd to my
friend, because I am
always talking,—John, I

sd, which was not his
name, the darkness sur-
rounds us, what

can we do against
it, or else, shall we &
why not, buy a goddamn big car,

drive, he sd. for
christ's sake, look
out where yr going.

How much he can make the size of poem he long ago chose to do his work (it is a choice like mathematicians only are making contemporary with him) one need read "The Door" for Robert Duncan.

2.   It is a study, how Creeley lands syntax down the alley, and his vocabulary—pure English—to hit a meter and rhymes all of which are spares and strikes.

Or how time—and space, which in him is as carefully drawn close, almost to a generalized symbiosis of himself and those he places in the forged landscape—time of course stays right on his own terms, by the governing term of his severe and exacting demand anyway, that it be this way or why have anything to do with it. He knows what ease really is—and hates, exactly, what isn't and is seen as such. Read "The People."

This is not a book of a body of doctrine of verse. Or poems done as such and collected like over a dispersed period of years. What again is specialized, and one wants the words to mean like a special general field theory, the poems are so consistent, or how is the word as they use it, can be shown to be consistent, the position chosen creates the poems day in and out and they remand (I shall use the word again) to the same polarized field which—the general theory of which—he, or they, are the special instance.

It is worth getting at how the force of a Creeley poem, all clear out there as he has well made it, goes back, it is the going of the force back to the magneto, of the coils of which are the condition of the creation of the force, which make any of the poems and all of them distinct in a way (again) different from the differences of one man's poems (usually). So that the uncanny range, the number of subjects and areas the poems actually do include, is striking. It is the same way as saying what an achievement—quite alongside the long poem in our time—Creeley has, in the use of the shortest.

The mistake, and it is made much, as I find much of the criticism about him falling for what he himself has already and will always top, and the criticism becoming a wasted elegance, is to talk gem or lyric or, even as he, in one instance, it seems to me, after a very great first stanza uses amulet and quick surprise, for picture. He needn't. He has rifled air and song, Provence, Mallorcan, and Cycladic form to write studs taken right out of the frames of each of us.

3.   There are three poetries, I believe it was Lorca's neatness to specify, there is one of the muse, one of the angel, and that which I suppose was his, of the duende, is it? Creeley has one of these all to himself. It is another of the interesting things how coolly his poems, which may look on the surface and in form and language to deliberately run over and play upon all the pleasures the inherited English thing has—takes each of those forms, interestingly say even the ballad as well as the air and the, like love lyric—and swing 'em so we are out on the other side of Alcaeus, and traveling.

(1962)

Paterson, Book V

William Carlos Williams. *Paterson,* Book V. New York: New Directions, 1959.

I tread the steps of this poem. I didn't find it easy just where the poet would seem to have put the weight: the passage of the Cloisters' tapestry on the hunt of the Unicorn.

One is on familiar ground in the other long passage of the poem: "There is a woman in our town," etc., a jubilant open man-Sappho poem to a stranger woman seen quickly, and once, on the city street.

There is no distance in the Cloisters passage, such as there was in *Paterson* generally, and in this instance here, of the woman. I liked that distance. It defined the edge of anything, as well as Dr. Williams' own edge (as he was the 'poet' of 'Paterson'—here, he is Paterson him-it self, he is up against the face as closely as the Cloisters story). It was a point of the old poem, that the poet was in it to seek a language to deliver men & women from the lump their lives were without it, in the city by the river which bore them to an end in the hostile sea. The poet was the one to survive, to find the meaning & lay it white, beside the sliding water.

My difficulty with the new poem was this, that the tapestry, even if the poet called it "the living fiction," was a tapestry—a thing of one texture (he also says the museum became real) where I was used to the instantaneous presence of many and of all, the real as multiple, and the poet too as such, in his flesh or in his attention, the 'dog' of his mind.

Now I had to allow that Williams himself was trying to turn me to a sewn cloth of flowers filling the detail, as he says, from frame to frame without perspective; an heraldic story of a white one-horned beast, the dogs which hunt it, and a lady who enables them (or is it something else?) to bring the beast in.

It was not hard to enjoy the story, or the poem itself as a poem of mottoes written from it; of the virgin and whore an identity, of the married man who carries in his head an image of a virgin whom he has whored, of the beast itself wounded and lying down to rest. It was the zero distance of the tapestry itself, and verse-wise, where I balked.

I had given it up as a bad job (for me), when I read it to put it away. I said, "I leave it to itself, and to Williams," when there it was. When one walks the tapestry passage literally syllable to syllable, flower word to flower word, etc., the intention of the poet as well as his statement of the one thing life (or it is actually death) has taught him, is what one finds he has made you do. It is no longer a matter of a thing. It is only a track, a pi-meson movement (after the collision) which he has laid down—yield, like it or not, to the step of it, from nothing outside it, including yourself & himself, and take nothing from it but itself, away.

In other words, an objectivity (which is there not other than anti-matter) which forces you, by an unexampled subjectivity of (whom Williams calls) "I, Paterson, the King-self" to bring you to his line.

By walking it, and accidentally, and against my choice of pleasures in the poem, I found that Williams, in appearing to contradict all that *Paterson* was verse-wise before Book Five, accomplishes an uncanny triumph in Book Five. I am persuaded that something of this is what he is talking about (in caps, mind you) in the poem when he says a world of art alone is what has survived since he was young; and that the only thing which escapes from the hole of death is "the imagination," which cannot be fathomed, it is through this hole we escape, through this hole the imagination escapes intact. What looks like culture-talk, and that 'thinking' the Doctor so long has said was not where it was, Not in ideas etc (NOT prophecy, he exclaims here), isn't—by the experience of the text of the poem, in what would appear to be its fussiest, or cutest (flowers & all that, and at the feet of the beloved) and least replica passage. Actually and solely, & quite exactly, & intact, the poem offers nothing but *the path* of itself, "Nothing else is real."

I append these passages which shook out then with that meaning:

"Anywhere is everywhere"   /

> "The moral
> proclaimed by the whorehouse"
> (and to the virgin as well) . . .
> "Threw it away! (as she did)"

.   no woman is virtuous
who does not give herself to her lover
—forthwith   /

                    and backward
                        (and forward)
            it tortures itself within me
                until time has been washed finally under:
                    and "I knew all (or enough)
            it became me   . "

Take it or leave it,
        if the hat fits—   /
                            A choice among the measures

                                                        (1959)

"Ed Sanders' Language"

Ed Sanders' language
advances
in a direction of production
which probably isn't even guessed
at; and which symbols & allegories
are more evidences of than the more

usual, and recent, and principally existent
since the use of a new metric by Sappho &
Alcaeus only. Prior production—from 550 BC
back—conceivably more interesting now

as aid and abettment to help recognition of
forms & inventions 'weak' only because
the size of the substance needed
for them is like, say, the
earth. That is, it takes the earth
to make a feather fall.

Wednesday, October 7th, 1964

291

Space and Time

Introduction to *The Sutter-Marshall Lease*

The Lost Sutter-Marshall Lease. This is a unique copy of an historic claim: Sutter and Marshall's joint claim, and the very first one of the gold period, following, as it does, within eleven days of the discovery (note date document signed, February 4, 1848).

Sutter knew that the military governor of California had no power to grant land in that interim period between Mexican and United States law. He and Marshall, faced with the gold, therefore tried to use the only "legality" they figured they had—Sutter's position as Sub-Indian Agent under the military rule (note that Sutter approves the lease as Agent and signs the letter to Mason as Agent).

They arranged to lease the land from the Yalesumney Indians, the dominant tribe of the whole region along the south fork of the American River, and forwarded the lease to Governor Mason late in February (note that Sutter, in his letter to Mason, calls the lease "articles of agreement").

Mason rejected the claim for the very reasons they hoped he might approve it. The United States, he stated, do not recognize the right of Indians to lease, rent, or sell their lands. The area, from his point of view, was bound to be regarded as public domain the moment the treaty of peace was settled with Mexico. (His letter can now be read back into the record, for there it has been all these years, unnoticed alongside his more dramatic report on the gold mines, House Executive Document No. 17.)

But the Mormons who worked at the mill, and the other early miners respected the claim even after Charles Bennett returned to the Fort with Mason's rejection, March 13th. It was, in fact, a shrewd and thorough lease. If you will bother to work out its boundaries (the key is the identification of Pumpumul Creek, which all evidence suggests is Webber Creek) you will see that Sutter and Marshall (probably on the base of Marshall's earlier explorations) arrogated to themselves a triangle of land which was to be the first heart of the mother lode. It included what was to be Placerville as well as Coloma and those rich spots along Webber Creek from which Captain Webber himself, William Daylor, Perry McCoon and others made the first big hauls of the spring of 1848.

By May, however, the jig was up. Bigler says, as of the 12th of that month: "it is thought Marshall and Sutter cannot hold so much land as they have taken up (10 or 12 miles square) and I may say it was from this time on that people coming to seek their fortunes began to dispute their claims and began to dig where ever they please for gold." From then on Marshall at Coloma had to break the same bitter bread as Sutter down below.

(1948)

A Bibliography on America for Ed Dorn

Assumptions: (1)   that *politics & economics* (that is, agriculture, fisheries, capital and labor) are like love (can only be individual experience) and therefore, as they have been presented (again, like love) are not much use, that is, any study of the books about

(2)   that *sociology,* without exception, is a lot of shit—produced by people who are the most dead of all, history as politics or economics each being at least events and laws, not this dreadfull beast, some average and statistic

Working premises:

I That *millennia:*

&

II *person*

are not the same as either
time as history or as the
individual as single

In other words, that plural & quality (taste)—King Numbers & King Shit—obscure how it is.

And that one must henceforth apply to quantity as a principle (totally displacing hierarchies of taste or quality, as though there were any other "like" than an attention which has completely saturated or circumvented the object);

and to *process* as the most interesting fact of fact (the overwhelming one, how it works, not what, in that what is always different if the thing or person or event under review is a live one, and is different because adverbially it is changing)—

one must henceforth apply to quantity as a principle and to process as the most interesting fact *all attention*

Results, as of historical study:

(a)   it is not how much one knows but in what field of context it is retained, and used (*millennia, & quantity*)

(b)   how, as yourself as individual, you are acquiring & using same in acts of form—what use you are making of acquired information (*person, & process*)

THE ABOVE, IN OUTLINE FORM, IS A TABLE OF CONTENTS. The PREFACE is to follow.

One needs to go back over these axes of relevance before listing the books.

The *local,* for example, becomes crucial once the crossed-stick of these axes is used to pick it up:

Applying all four of these at once (which is what I mean by *attention*), the local loses quaintness by the test of person (how good is it for you as you have to be a work of your lifetime?); itself as crutch of ambience, by test of millennia; its only interest is as process (say barbed wire, as attack on Plains husbandry) or as it may be a significant locus of quantity (in America how, say, prairie village called Chicago is still, despite itself, a prairie village—as against, say, LA; or, by turning itself inside out from size, Manhattan is now a vulgar village (note: this last wld be an example of the exercise of inversion, one of the more interesting moral effects of quality, inversion is/ how Rimbaud put it, "What's on the other side of despair?"

excuse me for a moment, but I once knew a guy who almost succeeded in doing that which every theatrical office doesn't believe will ever happen—that a play on Edgar Allan Poe (more such mss come in than any single other try) will be written, by having him turn his coat inside out, and wear it so, going home along Fordham Road drunk, like they say

The best definition of inversion I know is the chemical one—turning cane sugar by hydrolysis (another word for inversion) from the dextrorotatory it is to a levorotatory mixture of dextrose and levulose

It is possible chemically to kill a person by inversion.

To illustrate the value of the practice of these axes (instead of the old axis of history as time, and the axis of the individual versus society—and vice versus), study Webb's *Great Frontier* versus his *Great Plains,* how, in the latter book, his first, he caused the local to yield because at least he applied process, and some millennia sense, probably because the geography of the Plains enforces it on everyone; but in his latest book, because he is a professor instead of a person, and shows himself to have no sense of the quantities of geography by extrapolation from his knowledge of a "local" like the Plains, he is led back into the trap of history as time and comes to the foolish conclusion that it is the Frontier which is done, and the Metropolis which done it in!

Note: having recently visited Manhattan and having recently written your *second* story (the wide one, not the 'local' one), you may judge for yourself

BECAUSE THE LOCAL AND THE SENTIMENTAL IS HOW HUMANISM COMES

HOME TO ROOST IN AMERICA, THIS IS ENOUGH OF A PREFACE. "TO GET TO

THE OTHER SIDE," IS THE ONLY MORAL ACT WHICH CAN POSSIBLY CORRECT

THE WEST, AS EITHER GREEK OR U.S.

I. Millennia

Sauer   *Environment & Culture in the DeGlaciation* (Am Phil Soc)

Lobeck   *Physiography of the U. S.* (get maps which go with it, & fill em
                   in, locate stuff, etc., to get that topographic sense in the mind
                   as you have it in the feet)

[Gladwin]   *Men Out of Asia* (New Mexico pot-man, guessing on
                   migrations)

Indian texts on migrations, such as the Toltecs being pushed out of Tula by Chi-
                   chimecs, etc.—also codices in which *feet* (like on floor after
                   bath) are as arrows in Klee

Herodotus   At least first chapter of *Histories* on sailors & rapes of several
                   women (Europa, Io, Helen, etc.)

Frobenius   —anything; Jung, in fact, also (at which point I am suggesting
                   how, when one widens out on any of these four points of the
                   Double-Axe, one begins to hit one of the other 4, in this in-
                   stance, person—read D H Lawrence preface to *Fantasia* (don't
                   bother with rest of book!)

Brooks Adams   *The New Empire* (despite the analogical reasoning for nature
                   as machine, the space of the facts and the maps as routes
                   equaled by nothing here except Sauer's space of time
                   and precisions on roots

With great care one might add astronomy, simply that a scrupulous experience
of light-years (as distance, not time) is a form of exercise (literally, muscle-stuff)
of what it means to apply a context as delicate to handle as this one of millennia. (An example of how even one of the best men don't quite make it is a last
possible reference to start with, W C Williams *American Grain*—consider the
Jacataqua essay, and the Houston, versus what, say, Jim Beckwith—or Red
Cloud braining the Fort Phil Kearny massacre (also called the Bozeman Road

M)—are. Nuff sed.) Like I have said elsewhere, Rider Haggard. And old *American Weekly.*

II. Person:

what, in fact, the critter, homo sap, is, as we take it, now? yrself, surely, here, the book: simply that you has this ADVANTAGE, that you is an american (no patriotism intended: sign reads, "LEAVE ALL FLAGS OUTSIDE—PARK YR KARKASSONE")

recommend, for light reading: homer's odysseus (for odysseus as more interesting feller than hamlet or captain ahab); mister jung, like i say (except that he ain't free to write—hides his "creative" mss in a safe—he is the one religious i mean he is serious in his attention to the importance of life as it is solely of interest to us as it is human, like they say, of any of the new scientists of man—and i for one think the body of these men (Sauer is one) are a vast improvement on almost all the "creative" men who have gone alongside of same (say, Peek-gas-so, Prrrroost, JJJJoys, all but Chaplin. And Eisenstein. Yes. Eisenstein.

TRANSFER TO LOCAL. BUT TO DO IT, LET ME MENTION ONE VICTOR BERARD'S WORK ON THE ODYSSEY AS A REWRITE OF A SEMITIC (PROBABLY PHOENICIAN) ORIGINAL SAILING-DIRECTION. You can find it in French in the Sondley Library. So far as "scholarship" might, it will disclose the intimate connection between person-as-continuation-of-millennia-by-acts-of-imagination-as-arising-directly-from-fierce-penetration-of-all-past-persons, places, things and actions-as-data (objects)—not by fiction to fiction: our own "life" is too serious a concern for us to be parlayed forward by literary antecedence. In other words, "culture," no matter how great.

      (I should think, if one stopped long enough, one could expose a fallacy here which has dominated all living—literally—since the 5th Century BC, when, for the first time, that unhappy consciousness of 'history'—and which consciousness begets 'culture' (art as taste, inherited forms, Mr Eliot—indeed, Mister Pound as he preaches the "grrrate bookes") came into existence.

I don't know whether you know the philosophy of Alfred North Whitehead, but if one cld stop long enough one ought to expose like fallacies in art, like it's called, to what Alfie has so hugely exposed in the metaphysic which fucked everyone up from those Grks (or that Chink) to Alfie. He's just the greatest, if you read only his philosophy. If you read him on anything else, especially culture andor beauty, you realize that old saw, a man can't do everything!

Well, it doesn't matter whether we do expose fallacies. The point is, all that any of us iz now doing is trying to get sd poor critter back on his rail. And once done, there won't be any of that nonsense to shovel one's way through. I imagine you don't have as much shit in you as I do simply that you iz later, Mister/Dorn.

To get on with sd bibliography abt man in Amurrica:

III. Process

sd Whitehead *Process and Reality. An Essay in Cosmology*

as of the States, all you can pack in of such matters as Mr Melville, how to cook a whale; Professor Merk, how pemmican was born; how to skin a buffalo (cf only—and poor—on same, in, *Queen of Cowtowns: Dodge City,* Stanley Vestal); on how fish are put in a cornhill (ask Freddie, who knows, and why); how to live, by Charles Olson; how to not know know-how (by an American, after the deluge); how to remember (cf Muses)

how to find out: PAUSANIAS' *Description of Greece* (the bible, you can't read it, but for gawd sake own it, and whenever, look up anything, especially ARCADIA

how to find out now about then: MISS JANE HARRISON, *Prolegomena, Themis,* and her first book, which is *Mythology and Monuments of Ancient Athens*— and is, by god, nothing but Pausanias on Pausanias! She is Lady Pausanias.

Magnificent. And as yet no one has applied that methodology (HOW—AS, *hū*—PROCESS (is "to move")—METHOD IS (*meta hodos,* the way after: TAO)—what I am trying to say is that a METHODOLOGY is a science of HOW)

•   •   •

The principle at work here—"we should start from the notion of actuality as in its essence a process" (Whitehead, *Adventures of Ideas*, p. 355)—is:

yes, let me try, for once, for you, to do the chiasma. I cannot stand anything short of Miss Harrison, say (or Pausanias), or Sauer, or my man Merk (whom I can at least give you a taste of by showing you some of his reprints on the Oregon Triangle, of which he is the master historian up to now)—and a carpenter *doing it* is the same thing, or a sailor, or anyone who really knows what he is doing doing it; and if you are lucky, and you stumble on someone in print telling you how to do it, if, say, it's something like lowering a whale, say, which ain't done any-more, lowering a boom (cf sd Melville on how a whale uses his flukes, chapter called THE TAIL, I believe, that exactitude of process known

I can only stand DeVoto, say (who knows as much as any literary man abt America West), when he ain't cute, and is very damn serious abt the facts abt, say, exactly who was there that night that camp a day's drive east of Laramie, was it Jim Fitzpatrick who was sitting just inside the light, and the Donners, both Jacob and George, didn't know that that man was the one man who cld have saved them what they went through because Hastings, that first of advertising men . . . because they didn't have the advantage of Jim's knowledge . . .

there you get DeVoto at his best, that, he thought the knowledge of a mountain man was the greatest thing in knowledge an American has yet had

(like, say, Homer had, Berard thinks, abt a Phoenician manuscript . . .

The point is, that *scholarship* in history (not the academic but Miss Harrison's exacti-tudes, her care—or Pausanias, than whom none . . .

is the same thing as care of Swedish cabinet maker—or Meister Eckhart on how a soul is only one when it is not me in God but God in me, that precision (?)

And the dividing line between all that was from Grks (and that Chink) to what now is, is exactly this one of PROCESS: HOW:

so anywhere you find it (and in America as a history you damn well have to look for it) is, it will turn out, to be scratched for. That is why I don't, here, list books

under III. *Process:* you will have to find em yrself. And by wading through un-
conscionable stuff. Like, for example, I give you: A READING LIST:

> can't lay my hands on the damn book at the moment but see Vestal
> *Queen of Cowtowns: Dodge City's* bibliography as ex. of what, if
> you wanted to find out for yourself (istorin) you'd have to go
> through

I guess you'd say I got off the track. Well . . . To jump back on:

IV. Quantity (continued in our next . . . .

Appendix A:

> Berard's point is that the *Incidents* in the Odyssey result from the
> *Place-Names,* in other words not fiction in any humanistic sense
> but that the process of the imagination is from 1) a place   person
> thing   event—to—2) the naming of it—to—3) the reenactment
> or representation of it, in other words

$$\text{object} \rightleftharpoons \text{name} \rightleftharpoons \text{image or}$$
$$\text{story}$$

> Ex.: *Kirke* =*s* she-hawk; in Phoenician *periplous* her island was
> *Nesos Kirkes* = Isle of the She-Hawk (in fact the very place is the
> haunt of birds of prey, Italian Coast just above ancient 1st Greek
> City). But here's the kicker: Odysseus says "we came to the island
> Aeaea, where Circe lived . ."—*Aiaia,* in Hebrew, means "Island of
> the She-Hawk"!

> You will imagine what this does to me who is such a hound of a
> believer in fact-act-datum as what we damn well do eat up! And
> thereby, "proceed"!

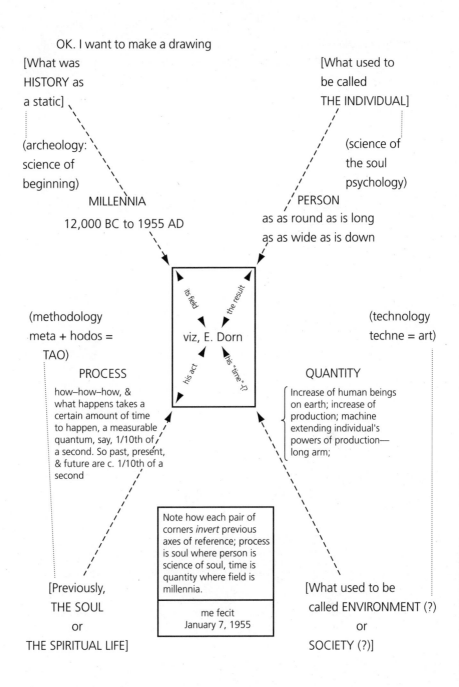

OK. I want to make a drawing

[What was
HISTORY as
a static]

[What used to
be called
THE INDIVIDUAL]

(archeology:
science of
beginning)

(science of
the soul
psychology)

MILLENNIA
12,000 BC to 1955 AD

PERSON
as as round as is long
as as wide as is down

its field   *the result*

viz, E. Dorn

his act   *his "time".?*

(methodology
meta + hodos =
TAO)

(technology
techne = art)

PROCESS

how–how–how, &
what happens takes a
certain amount of time
to happen, a measurable
quantum, say, 1/10th of
a second. So past, present,
& future are c. 1/10th of a
second

QUANTITY

Increase of human beings
on earth; increase of
production; machine
extending individual's
powers of production—
long arm;

Note how each pair of
corners *invert* previous
axes of reference; process
is soul where person is
science of soul, time is
quantity where field is
millennia.

me fecit
January 7, 1955

[Previously,
THE SOUL
or
THE SPIRITUAL LIFE]

[What used to be
called ENVIRONMENT (?)
or
SOCIETY (?)]

Basic Reading List:

> Merk (Harvard Press) on *Westward Movement* (you can eat yr way thru this list forever!)

I. *Far West:* Katherine Coman *Econ. Beginnings of the Far West*
> W. P. Webb *The Great Plains*

> & such as DeVoto's *Year of Decision* (not so much for itself as for what it starts up: that is, DeVoto's knowledge is so wide & curious it should be better. He should have written the unwritten book)

> and such books on regions as you will stumble on for yourself, viz. Edwin Corle's *Desert Country* (or maybe the much praised recent job in the River Series on the Rio Grande, don't know)

II. *Physiography* of country as a whole—*always* the geology & geography —*Carl O. Sauer,* from "Environment & Culture in the Deglaciation," all the way through "Road to Cibola," back to his first job, for the State of Illinois handbook (1915?) on the new State Park at Starved Rock, Sauer doing job on Indian agriculture

---

> *Francis Parkman*—especially, for me, his *LaSalle,* but Canada as well, or Florida, if you go off the main trail that much (as I imagine any one might, not me)

III. To start with the *millennia,* read for kicks *Men Out of Asia,* by N. Mex. archaeologist named [Gladwin] on arrival of migrations in America. Beyond that how does one get the space-time thing except in the imagining of men? Such characters as Sam Houston, Jim Beckwith, (Simon Gurty?), any of em as our kind of "You-liss-seas"?

> Plus—always—geography

Here's where IV comes in: *PRIMARY DOCUMENTS.* And to hook on here is a lifetime of assiduity. Best thing to do is *to dig one thing or place or man* until you yourself know more abt that than is possible to any other man. It doesn't matter whether it's Barbed Wire or Pemmican or Paterson or Iowa. But *exhaust* it. Saturate it. Beat it.

And then U KNOW everything else very fast: one saturation job (it might take 14 years). And you're in, forever.

This *one prin-ciple* (& it's new: even the best of recent men didn't do it, once) plus millennia (or *quantity* as a principle instead of *commodity.* /or space-time (=s the littlest is the same as the very big, if you look at it)

does the trick.

So far as it's reading (& history is, because you can't find em all in Justus Garage of an afternoon!) reading (=s oral history, if one's ears are open as well as one's eyes—why I say it's men, millennia, & one man's work):

the point is *to get all* that's been said on given subject. And I don't mean *books:* they stop. Because their makers are usually lazy. Or fancy. Or they are creative. And that's the end. But DeVoto ain't. And that's where the trouble comes in: so few are, but so many think they are. QED: you'll have to dig *mss*

As of Am. history:

Repository   #1:   THE NAT'L ARCHIVES, Wash., D.C.

            #2:   Senate Documents (published)

            #3:   Bureau of Am. Ethnology Reports & Bulletins

                  (pub. by Smithsonian Inst.)

& then, depending on subject, all over the place:

ex., Donner Party, Sutter's Fort Mus., & Cal. State Libr., Sacramento

ex., the Adamses: Mass. Hist. Soc., Boston

Ex.: Whaleship *Essex:* privately owned, Perc Brown, oilman, Jersey—at cruxes, mss will be in private hands, & one has trouble, patience, breaks getting same.

But it doesn't matter—all goes back to the ONE JOB—that's where one's nose is whittled. If you don't do that one, you can never do the others.

And it's

crazy, how, *one* yields. You can go anywhere—right into some old maid's front parlor, Craigie Circle, Brooklyn—or Monterey, Cal. (& eat smidgen for the first time, fried, with harbor on top

OK—Just to get you started. And if I say it don't end short of Pelasgus (date 7000 BC, place circum Mt. Lycaon, Arkadia), don't let that scare you: I'm only trying to say how far bill WCW missed by not going behind Sam one Houston!

Love,

O

PS:

(1) *Indians* is wicked. I think the thing is to settle on one of em, either literally one, Red Cloud, say; or the Utes (whose language is of family of Nahuatl, thus showing Aztecs passed down Rockies); or a "civilization"—like Plains, or Maya, or Arawak; or even a tribe, Shawnee, say—and once one is dug, the rest ought to yield more easily.

(2) History as *events*. That is, social, or national, or "cultural," or "intellectual." I think it's *now* mostly hogwash. *Morphology* has knocked this stuff cockeyed. And except for Frobenius—or such a *clear* man as Sauer (who's no historian except in the initial sense of *istorin,* to find out for oneself)—I think the best thing is to have yourself catch it up as you have to, (a) because so few even good men will bother with it; and (b) the sequence of events you will want for yourself—just as you want geography: the *locus* is now both place & time (topology)

W. E. Woodward, say	
Turner, yes—	at least the book of his essays called *The Frontier in Amer. Hist.*
Brooks Adams	*New Empire*—for sure as well as his *Civ. & Decay*
DHL's	*Studies*
WCW	*Am Grain*
Pound's	*Guide to Kulchur*

& the unwritten book by Fred Jackson Merk I have been trying to get out of him for yrs: LAND

Also read Webb's last book, *The Great Frontier* with its false notion

Metropolis has bested Frontier, but a flurryer this book, because it at least represents what Toynbee & Europe can't do, I mean move

---

—Oh yeah: (3) *trees!*   Get a load of Edgar Anderson's *Plants, Men, & Life* or some such title (available Asheville Public Lib due to my asking em to buy it). Which leads out, this way: *biosis,* is now the wildest science. After what *morphe* did for 75 years (1875 all the "new sciences" began), biosis ahead: ex. *blood* (Gates' *Human Ancestry,* Harvard Press—let's get BMC library to buy it; Boyd at Boston U). But also such silly business as Jonathan Sauer (Carl O's son) now becoming the world authority on the amaranth plant from studying dump-heaps!

No end to this wild stuff. And turns it, by way of ESP, to psychology, of course.

Merely to remind you: science, now, is man (& man is millennia).

OK.

That is, if Crows cut off troopers' genitals decoratively each thing has its efficient cause!

PS 2

About *Economics.* It's like *politics:* I don't myself know how you master them except by practicing them. I can't for the life of me see how books help here. They are *not* history. They are too *ingrained* in our daily lives. They are like secondary *love:* what can you do about it except *have* it?

They are axiomatic—& have nothing (or everything to do) with *class.* Except this way: as of America (and I can't tell you where to go for it, simply that I imagine it's a law, complementary to the foregoing, that the real *power* contemporary to one is *kept hidden*), one damn well better *guess,* at least, and then try to find out, keep asking, how the money or "ownership" really keeps its hidden hands on the machinery:

for ex., the "China Lobby." I have come to believe that American Asiatic policy is not so much a *financial* matter (Electric Bond & Share, the Philip's Corp., etc.—thus Bank of England), as it is the *Protestant Church!*

So you see what I mean.

(Dave Corkran, son of a methodist minister & Wesleyan univ. graduate like myself, once told me that the 18th Amendment was the best hint to Teddy Roosevelt's Russo-Jap policy as anything! And when I think of Congressman Judd (one of Pound's "agents" on the Hill!) . . .

I don't know. One is confronted here. One can only hack away at it. And read between all lines: *50 Families* or Gustavus Myers won't do it. It's why I say one has to either be a banker—or know one, intimately. We need now another set of muckrakers. But the FBI's got'em all in hand!

It's a tough one. One thing's sure. Economics as politics as money is a gone bird. It's much more now power as state as fission. And therefore harder than ever to get at, if more mortal!

OK, this has now become a letter.

How's the Big Shitty?

Yrs

Olson

(1955)

Billy the Kid

Walter Noble Burns. *The Saga of Billy the Kid.* New York: New American Library, 1953.

It's this way. Here's this country with what accumulation it has—so many people having lived here millennia. Which ought to mean (people being active, more or less) an amount, you'd figure, of things done, and said, more or less as in other lands. And with some proportion of misery—for which read "reality," if you will wait a minute and not take "misery" as anything more than a characterization of unrelieved action or words.

That is: what strikes one about the history of sd States both as it has been converted into story and as there are those who are always looking for it to reappear as art—what has hit me is, that it does stay, unrelieved. And thus loses what it was before it damn well was history, what urgency or laziness or misery it was to those who said and did what they did. Any transposition which doesn't have in it an expenditure at least the equal of what was spent, diminishes what was spent. And this is loss, loss in the present, which is the only place where history has context.

I take it the why is now obvious: that all conversion has been sought in, and assumed to follow from, forms which previously did, by respect, move life from there to this. From Homer to whom, it was saga, myths, folktale, fairytale, drama, the "nuvvel," as the lady called it, commenting on my friend's behavior on the beach, with a certain girl: "Getting experience, eh, for his nuvvels, is he?"

But if you have ever cut behind any American event or any presentation of them, to the primary documents, you will know the diminishment I am here asserting: that only Melville escapes, and that even Parkman, who also had bad eyesight and should have been something new (the pair of them, Homer and Herodotus were), missed, even if in *La Salle, or, The Discovery of the Great*

West, to take my own choice, he put finish, forever, to, the novel. Drama and verse I guess I don't need to argue, how silly they are, Mr. Eliot's *4 Quartets* trying to cancel Mississippi mud. And the folk? Dow Chemicals and the Communist Party have taken them over, out of our way, both heroes and tales, a major gain, to have got rid of those stuffed logs even if Stewart Holbrook doesn't know it. And we have no fairytales, quod cess to us.

All we got is what the best men have kept their eye on. No figures, no forms, no known largenesses whatsoever. Zero. Not even a digit, no string tie. Perfect. It was like the man who studied the Cherokee. And was himself, without being coy, a woodsman, camper enough to comprehend how such an Eastern Woodlands people had made meaning of their lives, took a river to belong to a man because he could fall back to it, and it was black. Death was black, and a man painted white lines on his face so that if he had to look into water, had to meet an enemy or the river, he had those lines to mark him, had the sign of himself a man has to have when he confronts the face of mere nature. His river could know him. And my friend, with all the intentions, and getting the movement of the man through the woods, ended up with a short short, a Mohawk scalping the Cherokee who falls back into the river which, of course, runs with blood!

2

I don't know that any one of us yet knows how to do it. Or rather, has yet done it. That is, it is clear how much has to be mastered, that, in fact, it is all of it, that only the millennia will do. The single event or person won't, white stripes crosswise on the face or even, say, if it is as apparently large and unreflecting as the Civil War, even that dense. Nor any single place or time: they yield, our places and our times are so unfixed, no thing more than a realism or localism drily their own, lean enough, because they go it alone, charqued, because they have to last, we have to go so far on so little, cannot, in fact, afford too much. But nothing more. And that is not enough.

This last—that we can have no fat—is why the old forms fall. But it is also why the huntsman and appleseeds we have made heroes of, won't also do. No single function, even abundance, is good. And no adventure.

The unique thing (and it is no surprise, the surprise is that still no one has made himself able to grab it by its coat) is that it is the mass of it which is it. Which is, of course, why new forms of presentation haven't yet mounted, that all of it isn't easily headed or pointed up, that it is, in fact, more herd (more cattle) than gun (than any one of us even if we can shoot).

And slow, very damn slow, slower in fact than we are (than man is, even with his thumbs). So speed, which has to be got in, has to be images, not actions. And images are not easily come by. (Actions are, they are, drama, that thing which never is as slow as the real is. Nor as fast. As heroes ain't.)

So you better figure on man's interiors. If its images are called for, they come from there. And he's got em. The Americans have. No need to worry. Or look for heroes. The point missed is, that when men aren't sure just what insides are, or just where they are, such men are not easily read. Or are misread. And you get the false impressions that have mostly, up to now, governed all conversions. To false forms you have to add these false premises: either that sd Americans are more than they are (still waters, like the Indians or Wyatt Earp, who was also, besides what he was, nothing but a company cop); or less (mere killers, like we are taken, as Billy has been taken by those who do not hear, as one can say for Walter Noble Burns that he does hear even if he overhears, the Kid's question "Quién es?" ((with Pat Garrett sitting at the foot of the bed, in the blackness)), why El Chivato asked anything, this once, instead of barking, with his gun.

3

The time hasn't come when we are that sure, that we can ask a question, and live. We are still more masters of the outside, still (like the heroes of the woods, and these gunmen) we don't break a twig.

But values? what all of it takes? Don't be so surprised if they are already overtaking use. Even if, so far as the books go, they are best when they stick to Earps. Or such as this one, who went flat, that night, on the floor. ("The Kid had not fired a shot. He lay with his gun still clutched in his left hand and, in his right, Celsa Gutierrez's kitchen butcher knife.")

To single killers. There is this gain: by so concentrating, the men who write try at least to leave it as it was, to get at it as close as the record will enable them. And so long as we can get it as near as Burns has it here (as Stuart Lake had it, in his *Earp, Frontier Marshal*) we can do what their refusal of fiction can't do. They don't refuse it enough. They still clothe these figures, in black and white. By the total refusal, out the other side of any fiction, out where there is only totality itself, not any one of these or all of us, but by what these pieces and these persons, all places and these markings on sticks or faces themselves compose, we'll compose, we'll compose it all for you.

(1954)

Brooks Adams' *The New Empire*

Brooks Adams. *The New Empire*. New York & London: Macmillan, 1902. Note date. The point of this review is to ask a question. Or to answer it. Why does this book stay out of print?

Adams' story, with maps of his own making (there being none, he declares in a prefatory note, because history before him had been repose), is this: in civilization nothing is at rest, the movement is trade, the necessity is metals, and the consequent centralization of power also moves. It moved, March, 1897, to the U. S.: "America completed her reorganization, for in that month the consolidation at Pittsburg undersold the world in steel, and forthwith the signs of distress multiplied."

It is fair to take hold of him by what he was clean enough to take hold of, metals in the West, goods, in the East. And to graph him, as he made it possible for himself to go below all concepts and laws, to get, as he did get, as graphic as the earth is.

Among the inventions which have stimulated *movement* and consequently *centralization*, none has equalled the *smelting of metals*.

Atomic power, then, is the ultimate act of smiths, just that, just those, nothing more. But as such, of like import to a like series of impulsions reaching back to, and coming forward from:

the metals	the trade	the time
	(West–East)	
(I) Sinai & Red Sea, COPPER	Egypt & Mesopotamia	3500 BC – 2500 (?)
(II) Cyprus, COPPER	Crete & Nineveh–Babylon	-?-–1450 BC

(III) Lydia, GOLD; Euxine IRON; TIN (Cornwall, by Rhone River?)	Troy first; Ionia; Athens and Greece proper; ending, Alexander	1450 BC – 333 BC
(IV) Spain, the MINES of	Carthage, first; Syracuse; and Rome, taking Spain, to Diocletian withdrawing capital to Propontis	207 BC – 284 AD

Adams sees the Roman Empire as the inevitable ending to the above series of changes westward, because (1) the Romans never learned to manufacture any article which commanded the Oriental market, and (2) because the Mediterranean remained always, for them, a closed ellipse, not rich enough in metals to sustain a prolonged drain, especially under their wasteful methods.

Thus a long interregnum followed between this FIRST EXPANSION 3500 BC to 284 AD, and that one more immediate, to ourselves, what Walter Prescott Webb has dubbed "The Great Frontier" but which is more properly no more than the SECOND EXPANSION, and, as Adams demonstrates, is set off earlier than the discovery of sea routes in the 15th century by the discovery during the 10th century, of the Harz, Erz and Tyrol mines.

The chart, then, up to 1897, completes itself thus:

(V) Harz, Erz, & Tyrol SILVER, COPPER	Germany & Venice; Antwerp & Florence; England, thereafter	c. 1000 – 1588
(VI) Mexican GOLD, Potosi (Peru) SILVER; later, Sutter, etc.; & STEEL	Europe generally, but England, chiefly; then the U.S.A.	1492 – 1897

Adams takes care to break these last 1000 years down to a much finer analysis than this summary indicates. Perhaps most important of all (in the light of so much emphasis on the Renaissance, and Columbus, etc., in our culture) is his emphasis that it was the discovery of the magnetic needle in the 9th century which began the freeing of sea trade from necessary hugging of coasts, reaching back to the earliest sea trade (the *Odyssey* as example): and that the result was that, by as early a date as 1147 (when 200 Flemish ships reached Venice) one can say, as Adams does, that the *old economic system* (which had been based, because of navigational problems, on the caravan routes across Central Asia, essentially, and, from 1000 AD on, on the rivers and passes north and south in Europe) had been superseded (when Antwerp became the northern meeting place of Germany and Italy, and the Hanse was born) by *the modern system,* which, it is worth noting, Adams flatly says, "is based on the sea."

(1954)

Captain John Smith

Bradford Smith. *Captain John Smith, His Life & Legend.* Philadelphia: Lippincott, 1953.

The name is Smith, John Smith. And that's what I'm bucking. Plus Pocahontas, that he damn well was saved by this 10, or 13 yr old girl (John Gould Fletcher says, Powhatan put her up to it, in order both to order Smith beheaded, thus satisfy half his council, and save him, to satisfy himself; and Hakluyt is authority for a like incident, 80 years earlier, Juan Ortiz, who, in 1539, was picked up by De Soto, and told him how the daughter of Chief Ucita, north of Florida, saved him from a roasting, alive).

But it is another sign of how Hart Crane was not afraid of a cliché—and a man can't use a country as stupid as this, who is—that he took Pocahontas (instead, say, of Jacataqua, as Williams, by a different optic, did . . .)

Anyhow, now, I want to take Smith. And the occasion is not so much this new book, as the woman to whom the book is dedicated, Laura Polyani Striker, who supplies Appendix I to it, 31 of the most important pages which have been added to the Smith record since his own exceeding fine nine books were published, 1608 to 1631.

What this woman has done is to confirm, from Magyar sources, the veracity of Smith's adventures in Hungary and Transylvania in 1601–02, even to his tale of his jousts with three "Turks" (they were High-Doos, it turns out, Hajdus) and that because he did, by these challenges, gain the army the time they needed to mount cannon on earthworks raised fifty feet above the plain, Smith did receive the grant of arms from Sigismund Bathory he always thereafter claimed he did, and wore, "three Turkes heads in a Shield."

What's thereby given is all that any of us—if we believed that style is, the man—could have taken (can take) from this earliest of writers registering in English what about the nature of, this new place.

And it's that, that gets me, about Smith—how he bites into, the thing. Not that I'm so read in him, but enough to keep going back to him, and to suggest him to you for exactly what this Bradford smith obscures by his own Toni prose. It's not true, what lower case smith says (middle case, middle class smith, the poor undescended smith, no relation of the bachelor Elizabethan who went fishing off Monhegan): that Smith wasn't a great stylist. Of course he wasn't, but by the measure—by the continuing use of these hairdresser's measures of what prose is—no man's work, alive or dead, is free to be known, for use. Parkman, is paired with Prescott; Williams, is damned in London (in *The New Statesman & Nation,* by G. S. Fraser) for his "neologisms" and "barbarisms." And thus *Paterson* I and II is thrown down—while Richard Eberhart is raised up! It's all over the place: another smith, Grover by name, in the fall *New Mexico Quarterly,* also puts down *Paterson*—and the *Cantos* with it, as well, by implication, Crane—as the poetry which displays detached objects "as in a provincial museum."

The wild thing about the original Smith is this business, that it may damn well have been the very bite in his language, which did break his life in half, did make him the failure he took himself, did keep him from ever getting backing again, to get back to the States—kept him exiled in London, the first one who wanted out, the man who, by 1614, *knew* the country as not only not one other did (not even a West Country fisherman) but said it in prose like as no one has since, simply that he had the *first* of it, had it not like even Columbus did, but as Columbus' navigator say, only Smith *said* it, got it into words, didn't, as Juan de la Cosa did it so handsomely, by a map. Why I sing John Smith is this, that the *geographic,* the sudden *land* of the place, is in there, not described, not local, not represented—like all advertisements, all the shit now pours out, the American Road, the filthiness, of graphic words. Mo-dess . . .

god, to get the distinction, across! so that even Ezra Pound stops praising ads, for some silk stocking, in the error of his anger, at the bland, not getting that the age of usury which followed from the time of cant is worse, worse than he knows, worse than even himself in jail (he is nowhere in such danger as us who aren't!), that even his own act is now ad-writing, that where he got it—say Elbert Hubbard—that this age of distraction is total, that energy, as a component, is not enough, not enough, Ezra, even though the syllables (nickel nickel) . . .

hear Smith, to the Virginia Company, from Jamestown, a letter, burned up, at what they send over to him, to keep people, in a wilderness, to get pitch, tar and soap ashes, frankincense even, believe me, out of it, to make up for that there ain't gold, as there was to the south; and that they send a bird like Newport, as captain of a ship, and with orders to dress Powhatan in a scarlet coat (that early, the English, were playing that game) when Smith knew the thing was to get corn out of Powhatan, not give him blague, not keep hoping for a lump of gold, not keep looking for a passage to the South Sea.

Smith sent them a map. The map. The whole middle coast. So known, so done, the states still stand their boundaries by it. The sort of knowledge Smith gave Hudson, in another letter, Hudson went straight to the river. How Smith later knew New England, named her that, put her down in prose I can feel now the way his boat bent along the same coasts I know—mind you, he was doing it for one of the very first times, it's a different thing, to feel a coast, an ancient thing this Smith had, what men had to have before Pytheas, to move . . .

Smith was so sore over the knock-down portable boat the Company had sent over with Newport supposedly to enable them to explore above the Falls of all these rivers Smith first knew, the James, the Pamunkey, the Choptank,—knew 'em—he writes:

if Newport "had burnt her to ashes, one might have carried her in a bag; but as she is, five hundred cannot, to a navigable place above the Falles." He lets them have it:

"Though I be no scholar, I am past a schooleboy, and I desire but to know, what either you, and these here, doe know but that I have learned to tell you by the conttinuall hazard of my life."

The which, of course—the demonstrable truth of it, that he said it—eventually tied him down to London, turned him into a writer instead, made him the prisoner of the virtu of what he was, what any man who knows is, too knowing for the easy. Smith was one man who knew the new facts early. And his prose says 'em. It's why style, and any elegance other than the code Napoleon another soldier by name Beyle got a hold of, is a silly asking when the objects are as detached as we are—as men got to be by cant, as Stendhal says they well had by just the date John Smith was 19 years, when the perfect Don Juan, the only answer man has to hypocrisy, Francesco Cenci, was murdered, while his wife and daughter looked on, Rome, 1599.

It is very quiet, how Smith has it, in that letter, at the end:

"Though there be fish in the Sea, foules in the ayre, and Beasts in the woods, their bounds are so large, they so wilde, and we so weake and ignorant, we cannot much trouble them."

(1954)

Five Foot Four, but Smith Was a Giant

Philip L. Barbour. *The Three Worlds of Captain John Smith*. Boston: Houghton Mifflin, 1964.

It cannot be at all that his name is so ordinary. For I dreamt some nights ago myself of a woman named Miss Smith. It has then, I still feel sure, to have to do with a 350 year inability of the American "soul" obviously, to allow in still the difference John Smith was, from anyone else and from the great Shove America was, and has been, from the beginning. He is still some waif, presiding over Atlantic migration like a 5 foot 4 lead figure, Mercury or an Hermaphroditus of the whole matter.

A whole series of such possibilities is the only way to imagine this man in any style equal to his own prose, poetry and acts, including his maps—and, as Philip Barbour is at care to point out, his will. For though this new book seems the most complete biography yet of Smith, and though Barbour is correct in his assertion he does not wish to defend Smith but instead to present him, as if for the first time, the truth is Smith himself, in his own pages and life, still makes more sense. And a perspective still, which makes that sense out of him, is not yet known, despite the wonderful new work that this book, and Bradford Smith's previous one, in 1953, almost because it did include the researches of Laura Polyani Striker, from the Hungarian Archives, has offered to make Smith a "truther-teller." Even if he obviously was, from the beginning.

The book under hand has another real gain, that Mr. Barbour has, and has used and makes available a good journalist-historian sense out of the English scene in which Smith strove, and didn't do so well. As Barbour suggests, because of a caste system in which Smith was no higher "than an 'untouchable' in Akbar's India"? I'm not sure Barbour himself isn't on better grounds, when he, without clinching it, brings attention to Smith's position in between the newer London merchants and the older Westcountry interests.

(It is in such points as this still, that the absence of professional historians in the story of John Smith, show. In each case, for 100 years, it has been quasi-professionals—from Charles Deane and Henry Adams on—who pick up on him.) Mr. Barbour's intention is, clearly to do everything he can to put Smith's biography on, as he says, a "scientific basis," and to invite the work of the future.

That seems to be all here, with interesting "Commentaries" of 100 pages added to a 400-page "life"; and a careful and complete 30-page bibliography. The book can be enjoyed by anyone, as well as given attention by whatever interested parties (including I should think, "historians"). The eel, however, Smith, who has slipped away as he has slept for 333 years will continue to—as I said to the Lady Prize Winner Poet of Canada one night in Toronto—until he is measured only by what also happened to William Shakespeare after 1607!—It is another of Barbour's attractive qualities, in this new Houghton Mifflin book, that he too believes Smith himself wrote "The Sea Marke"; and brings other poets, including James Shirley and John Davies, to bear. If someone could find out more about the Thomas Packer of his Will, to whom almost all went— "one of the King's Privy Seal clerks"—we'd all be closer to coming home to the figure of the dream.

(1964)

The Contours of American History

William Appleton Williams. *The Contours of American History.* Cleveland, Ohio: World, 1961.

The examination is difficult. Which wld be the point. How the 'thesis' (of Williams' *The Contours of American History*) is that the thing can be explained, and that he tries to do it, is the reason this book gets the attention it does, and it is altogether interesting that a man propose to explain it. It is, in proof, an enormous syllogism—three Americas folding out of each other, thus establishing sequence and yielding a present which is more attractive than most persons possess without Williams' help: a mercantilism until 1828, a laissez nous faire 1819–1896, the Age of Corporation Capitalism, 1882–

No trouble. Intelligent. Better than academic, and better than journalism. Better than Heilbroner, and synthesis having always that advantage, that it gives intellectual experience. My own experience of the book, then, is that only where the finest question (whether it is the quality at any given moment—always brilliant and shooting stars anywhere over the lot, and into—or the examination at those points where one cares, that Williams seems almost an advertising man: that I am bored with the experience, and that the thesis, absorbing so much, strains me so I wonder about a bunch of cattle on a draw, or the picture of some hunter sitting amongst the bones of a Pottawatomi hunting party of a year before looking exactly as they were when they fell—all that scene instead of that explanation. *Because* just where it ought to work (what was the change in the States sometime between 1763 and 1771 comes out like those dreamy landscapes and innately small instances (of dados on a building suddenly under the roof's gutter, for the first time the firmness of the flatness is interfered with, upped to satisfy some ambition, and in itself that ambition very quiet and legit except that of that date about Copley's pictures don't any longer portray persons Copley's pictures clearly do-did.

All right. Only one last thing: the thesis *better* do it all or thesis won't do. *The* Contour say, proposing so much. And my own experience is that there is a history of sd same States and all over which doth. And this is Frederick Merk's postulate (sd book now ought to be available soon, after forty years it has been promulgated as lectures etc. ever since, interleafing each year's events like a comptometry, the information and the message has the machine which excuses itself being fed (wld be Williams' justification certainly for his thesis that it ought to work) and this one—Merk's—does.

Ok. Not at all to hammer hell out of one man at all by another. But to end where one began, that a contour can be an examination of America, and if it isn't I do owe to say where what Williams does bite might not disappoint.

PS: there is one attractive thing about Williams' mind and attention, that he is like they say 'Marxian' and there has been altogether almost none of such mindedness addressed to the subject (except for readings that any anarchist-tempered person in this century might long ago have read—like whose was its history of the American Labor Movement etc. At some point along this line too Williams, despite his advantages, if he sounds better than Heilbroner because he isn't jumping into the future but he does sound like Collingwood feeling-wise as of history, and ends up, when one starts to lose the drive from the reading about where A. A. Berle or J. K. Galbraith offer, it seems at that moment, more literal modern right at this day, and 'American' substance than—

(1963)

The Vinland Map Review

Brooks Adams, Sole User of History: NOTE NUMERO UNO on 1440 (AD) map showing Vinland, and with 'legend' stating events of *12th* century (AD).

> *Danger* (of Yale discovery) that History as Usual—
> renaissancey (modern) mindness will continue

I   "In the tenth century the old economic system, of which Constantinople and Bagdad were the *foci,* culminated.

       Contemporaneously, western Europe fell to the lowest point of its decline during the Dark Ages."

Adams does not add [*The New Empire,* 1902] that it is exactly in the *10th* century the "Swedes" or Northmen threw out three huge drives from the Polar North down on to the three legs of the future: on to Europe, east to Rus (Swedish word) -sia, and *West*—to Greenland AND VINLAND.

II   CLOSE-OUT: 1200–1296 (AD): "Flanders and the Fairs of Champagne decayed because of the movement of the trade-route from Venice, from the Rhone and Seine, to the ocean. This displacement was the effect of the effort of France to consolidate under one administration the valleys of the Rhone, Seine, Loire, Garonne, and Scheldt. The wars which ensued, coupled with the introduction of the mariner's compass, caused sea freights to undersell land freights."

•   •   •

In other words, Norse *sea* abilities of the *10th* century by the end of the *12th* had in fact become the *virtue* of Europe itself. Thencefroth, the withdrawal or conversion of all Norsemen on all three sides including their own center to the "new system" (out of which, in the *13th* arose the mindedness of which generally our own power and acculturation is still a weakening instance). Interest therefore in the latest discovery of discovering is to be watched with interest: the figure, for example, for the "purchase" for Yale of the paper and book involved is stated to be $1,000,000. Typical cultural "waste" (in Veblen's exact sense, and look, from exactly the 'danger' center (Veblen's point also), the "University." (Date Veblen's *Theory of the Leisure Class* [1899] contemporary with Brooks Adams.)

Drag since. Continuing.

III Now will happen again (has in fact since steel Pittsburgh, Mar., 1897): *usefulness* of *fact* AND *knowledge* that for MORE THAN 100 YEARS— and probably 200 YEARS—VINLAND was a FRONTIER mounted from GREENLAND (viz visit VINLAND legate of Vatican for more than six months in quote VAST AND VERY RICH LAND [*The Vinland Map,* Latin caption to it]. Date of visit *1117–18* (AD)

RIGHT IN THE HEART OF THE DISTURBANCE BROOKS ADAMS WAS AT PAINS TO POINT OUT WAS THE END (and the beginning) AND THEN THE RETRACTION   of this one league or leg WESTWARD OF THE REPLACEMENT *BY OCEAN OF LAND* 200 YEARS *BEFORE IT.* NORSE IN AMERICA BY OR BEFORE 1000 (AD)

October 18th 1965

Note Two:

wooden ships

: Barrow

Long ships (Derwent-on-Trent . . . what is

the GREAT

burial, ESSEX

esscester

[Xtopher

Hawkes. *Antiquity,* spring 1965—?

II   The great STUPAS (stone) INDIA are as elaborate—and DECORATIVE
BECAUSE as Strzegowski shows DEMONSTRATES that architecture follows IS BUILT DIRECTLY OVER wood WHICH THE STONE (*flowers*) DU-
PLICATES—[Woodhenge, literally, from the air, World War II, American fliers *SAW* the POST-HOLES

: "GOTHIC" is STONE ON TOP OF WOOD
                              Quote (Brooks Adams,
The Law of Civilization and Decay. 2nd Edition, 1896)

"Before the opening of the economic age, when the imagination
glowed with all the passion of religious enthusiasm, the monks who
built the abbeys of Cluny and Saint Denis took no thought of money,
for it regarded them not. Sheltered by their convents, their livelihood
was assured, their bread and their robe were safe; they pandered to
no market, for they cared for no patron. Their art was not a chattel to
be bought, but an inspired language in which they communed with
God, or taught the people, and they expressed a poetry in the stones
they carved which far transcended words."

The Norse, who traveled widely—as monks or anyone else in Europe did not, *before* the Crusades, before the First Crusade—HAD
BROUGHT BACK ALREADY—or were transmitting, even traveling in
their wooden boats, a *further* architecture the Crusaders Knight Tem-

plars *venitii* freemasons CUT-OFF (by taking home, like right now, too cheaply too easily too democratically from the shopping center EAST-ERN GOODS—(like right now poor Chinese poor WESTERN GOODS good Ben-Rus WRIST-WATCHES on RADICAL CHINESE WRISTS Bob Dylan American RIGHTS

III   Norse was

movement of

Gothic "Guti"

West—picked up along

Russian rivers [on way to

Micklegarth], taken

over the Ocean: "iron bog"

l'anse aux Meadows

L'ANSE, Promontorium

NEWFOUNDLANDIAE

CUT-OFF, as, still: *CUT-OFF* Cambridgeshire

FENS

    There is no gerund, nor is metonomy possible

when the material

    wood   stone   gold   color   blue

    the   rate   of   ratio   1 : 1200

the Lake Van measure [for repro. of
                                    cosmic condition]

is adhered to. Otherwise

there is NO ACTIVE SUBSTANCE

            NO CEREMONY   OR

        SUBSTANTIVE ACTION POSSIBLE

Lightness

shall descend   shall not be soaring
                                 vault VAULT SHORED-UP BY
from   BASTIONS ["Flying-
                                 volens: BUTTRESSES]
above: a ship   *Kirch Santa Clara Assisi*

is a church

upside-

    down

            The Mayflower

which took the Pilgrims over here

is still a barn or church-structure

put down like a box over fish drying

                if the sun is so strong

on racks

    in   the   Westcountry   [still]

All up to *1250* (AD)

still possible. And

useful.   Since——

NOTHING —— SINCE NORSE WITHDRAWAL
FROM "VINLANDA"
— date? POST —
1117–18 (AD)

Monday
October 17th

THAT, THEN—Note 3—

Anglo-Saxon extreme date is 1100—& Alfred's

death *900.* Present STUDIES THEREIN from at

least Bishop *Ulfilas*—and FRISIAN—to 1100 (AD)

[[Bishop Eric in "States" 1117–18 (AD)]]

Note 4 [October 20th, 1965]

It settled down at the end of the pike: Scandi-

NAVIAN [BRITAIN, SCANDINAVIAN

AMERICAN—Frisian—Mercian—*Gothic:* Bishop Ulfilas (311–

383 AD—Greek language therefore AND GOTHICK; Celtick [AND

BRITTANY—mega-LITHICK] —*AND THE NORSE*
IN VIN-

LANDA

   ＼ON THIS

O[KEAN

o'shin: AT-LAN'-

TICK

Arthure (Red Hengirst
Merwin—Taliessin,
   ↓ 6th (?) Century cavalry
leader

                  Alfred, dead, 900
Eric to Greenland,
985

Bjarni Herjolfsson three
separate landfalls 986:
Leif
   ["a Byarno repa et
leipho socijs"—
      l'Anse aux Meadow
radio carbon 1004 ± AD

One has then—last known visit Eric, Bishop

1117–18 AD—THE SPREAD: / Grk. leik

         earliest possible

         RENDITION 311–383 AD — but WOODHENGE

                        PRE—1850 *BC*

850 GOOD   *BIG STONES*

"SKANDINAVIAN   Tel Hal-
                  to: laf
YARS

         1200 [1250 AD: Brooks Adams'

         Marking—DATE

NOW   "influx of Eastern goods Venezia
w-o-n
         AND RISE OF [loss of

         color] COMMUNES [Protestantism]

Note #5

Re-receiving today [November 17th 1965] Turville-Petre's *Myth and Religion of the North,* and H. R. Ellis Davidson's *Gods and Myths of Northern Europe* puts the Vinlanda Map and Carpini Relation—"a Byarno repa et leipho socijs" ("discovered by Bjarni and Leif in company")—in this light:

if the Bavarian poem *Muspilli* (c. 830 a.d.) is, say, a way to begin to expect 'written' Norse literature [*Ynglingatál,* by Thjodolf of Hvin, Mrs. Davidson dates 9th century], these new "discoveries" emphasizing Norse occupation of Newfoundland, at the end of the 10th century, have the advantage of adding "*Zone*" firmness to "*Strata,*" in what shall continue, increasingly, to be an interest, in both England and the United States, in basal matter of both nations as of the language called "English"—

and the condition or attention of poets of these two peoples on either side of the North Atlantic.

[One is not either, in saying this, leaving out Northmen in France and her adjoining coasts Eastward, nor Roger in Sicily, especially not Swedes in Russia and as Guards at Midgarth or Constantinople—this enormous earlier dragnetting of Eastern and Southern life by this *mag' (k) nut* of the North (Norse "Swedes" Dansk 'Wickings' [to use F. York Powell, and W. G. Collingwood's preferred name, and recall their not at all to be forgotten *Scandinavian Britain,* in the Society For Promoting Christian Knowledge publication, of 1908.]

The depth, and extent, of these two to three hundred years plus, before 1200 AD and the decisive retrogression to Europe as a mart and steelyard Cities, are in the present critical change of affective feeling toward History altogether, and writing already, by young English and somewhat older American poets is 'stealing' from and up to materials (and feelings) which portend developments probably only equalled, in re-fixing and extending experience, by the "Teutonic Migration" [again to use F. York Powell, and to place the Scandinavian movements now being more and more brought into place]. The 'civilization' sought today requires these *improvements* of the knowledge of the Northern past, and though so far all this looks like simply more history, looks as though the gains are only in the "facts," the importance (of these improvements) can be shown to have already effected language and poetic results.

It would not be an exaggeration, to take only Christopher Hawkes' work itself [or, recently, the example of his collaboration with his wife, and with Mrs. Davidson on the Swedish finds in Kent], to think that in this 'Northern' display of and before 1000 AD, and reaching into the early part of the 13th century, one has substantive and textual freshness effecting discourse, on both sides of the North Atlantic, like in fact the importance of what has been happening, in the last decade, all around on the other side, on the back of Greek and Latin language. The decipherment of Linear B by Michael Ventris [and the work since by many others, including John Chadwick], and now the strong push to see if Linear A [the same "sign" system as B] is a Northwest Semitic language [or Luvian, or Hittite, whatever it will, in the end, show itself as]. What one is feeling, who writes today, and inquires into the condition of modern states and nations, is the *emphasis* of *two* Migrations, the Indo-European in its first expression, on Europe and the older Near East, from, say, 2100 BC through something like 1750 BC [or on to the 'Mycenaean' date, 1550 BC]

And, of course, the curious re-taking, of migration, by the "Teutonic," and Scandinavian peoples, in the latter parts of the first millennium AD, and only being bent back by developments almost throughout the world in the first half of the 13th century.

There is something more interesting, and immense here, in *these* attentions and successes of the last few years, to see around behind the essentially Thucydidean history preceding us for 2500 years [Toynbees and such people, including most American historians]—to go back to 'ground,' to have a dipolar methodology, to see language and writing as having as much to do with etymology and root in this sense, of events of men in the world in *their* time, as the shocking and fouling events of the present are unexplained, because, the reasoning would seem, from the advantage of this new knowledge of those two *earlier* strikeouts [not "outages" either] of what in fact is a 'same' people. [So that nobody may seem to take this as "Silver"-man thought, and the "Gold-bugs" seek to try to keep an old advantage, may I even remind that it was Hyksos kings in Egypt who would seem actually to have prompted or caused the "migration" of the Northwest Semitic from the deltas of the Nile, to Crete, if Linear A even turns out to be Semitic.] The 'case' anyway [and what would seem from the flurry on *this* side of the Atlantic, of the discovery of the Vinlanda Map—what isn't, of course, noticed particularly at all, is the ecumenical interest in the Tartar Relation which goes with "the Map," that the leader is one of St. Francis' earliest adherents, a brother so able he was the Franciscan's first 'ambassador' to the Germans, and was so useful there in Europe, and in Poland, that when the Mongols looked as though they were in all likelihood going to smash Europe by 1250 [the mission is 1245–1247], it was Carpini who was sent to Karakorum, by the Pope, to see if he could smoke out, ahead of time, or in any way forfend the dreaded Destruction.

The care anyway, in any of this, is to improve, or re-gain an attention, which off-hand would seem to have been lost, for Europe and, subsequently, for the West sometime around 1225 AD, and certainly decisively by 1250. And thereafter. Of which *our* events, dreadfully, are still a part. No wonder poets care for finding out a better sort somewhere lower, and deeper, and in more careful Zones and Strata than their quite recent counterparts.

(1965)

Other Essays,
Notes, and Reviews

Ernst Robert Curtius

European Literature and the Latin Middle Ages. Translated from the German by Willard R. Trask. Bollingen Series 36. New York: Pantheon Books, 1953.

It was the young German poet Rainer M. Gerhardt who introduced me to the work of Curtius. I had asked Gerhardt what interest there was in Frobenius, after the war, if men of his generation were digging that morphology. He swore, and answered damn well no, that it was Curtius who was their inspirer.

Now I get it. I should have known. I had sniffed typology in Gerhardt's long-ish poem, "Brief an Creeley und Olson." In my answer, also a longish poem, "To Gerhardt, There, Among Europe's Things," I had opposed specifics—as much European as American—to his universals of Metropolis.

It better be Walter Prescott Webb you use as backfire to check this book of Curtius. By admission it is written to promote the "Europeanization of the historical picture," on the assumption (Troeltsch, Toynbee) that European culture, in contrast to all other, is an "intelligible unit" of unique cast, at once ancient and modern, eastern and western, Roman and Christian, and thus worthy of the claims of Holy Mother Church herself, one, apostolic, and universal.

I don't know whether I had said it, but I meant, to Gerhardt, go out the back door of your inheritance. I did say, plant Odysseus' oar, don't worry about Homer's poetics. Curtius, does worry. His book has to do with those great-nesses so that there may be, he says, cultivation of the European tradition.

I wake up to the fact that we are in the hands of a huge Propaganda Office. It isn't the contents of this book alone. It is also, that it is the 36th volume of the Bollingen Series. Whether we know it or not (and I don't know that Webb did, now that he has done *The Great Frontier* even if, in *The Great Plains,* he made the importance of baling wire most evident, as well as the horse, to the Comanche) but it is abundantly clear that the Metropolis seeks, as well out of

Manhattan as out of the chancelleries of Europe and Washington, to distract our attention from our goods, and, from the fierceness they ought to have taught us.

Which sounds as political and hortatory, as it is. I am too engaged to play Jacob to get the gain Curtius has already given me in Europe by a review of my work. I must show him the paw of Esau, or Odysseus' paw, as much as I did to Gerhardt, who also makes me known there. Curtius, too, should have the birthright of what he wants, what he and Gerhardt, and all Europeans so desperately need.

Including, I now discover, the English. I had thought that the London office of this machinery, the *Nine* boys (now shrunk to one little Peter), were Trojan-English, that is to say, that their schoolboy Renaissance was only more of the Aeneid, more of that model, Gavin Douglas, Milton, that need for a classicism, Virgil that bore, how it hampered Ben Jonson, and only in *Troilus and Cressida* did Shakespeare stop stuffing his State figures after the antique mold. But it turns out it is as Mr. Churchill is. Europe is one genealogy, Curtius is at the pains the politicians are, to prove. Homer to Goethe. And Stefan George's is the vision:

> Speak of the Festival's nearness, of the Kingdom's—
> Of new wine in new skin: but speak it not
> Until through all your dull and toughened souls
> Shall run my fiery blood, my Roman breath

It is, of course, baloney. All is more serious than such recrudescence. And it is culture (history, when it is Europeanised) which leads to such nonsense. And gives such decent folk as Gerhardt, Curtius, and how many more, expectations. When they should have the present. Instead of the great shitting from the sky they have had. And will have more of. And so they look for the Legitimate Child they are promised will come up out of the Rhine, falsely promised by George, and all leadership.

But the Brazos, too. Don't forget that the falseness is universal. Why one has to urge Curtius to go out the backdoor, to leave all fronts, is that any of us, America, Asia or Europe, is also being slipped the culture mitt. And must wear our hairy hands, wherever. It is not the Beast we are in danger from. It is, the Beauty. Bergson was wrong. Or half-right. The fabulatory function is man's uniqueness. But when he uses it to make the Bauble?

I'm going fancy. And none of you will think I am speaking about this book. But I am. For it is Herodotus who is most missing here, he who knew what history is. And Webb, to the extent that he did know that where tales are today is not in stories but in things, in Colt, revolvers.

The Great Frontier is not over. What is, is Metropolis, despite the appearances. And management. And with them what Troeltsch and Toynbee have misled Curtius to look for: "from the crucible of historism a new completeness and coherence, a great artistic symbol, such as the Divina Commedia once was, and later Faust." That's Troeltsch. And Toynbee? "It will eventually become impossible to employ any technique except that of 'fiction,'" god cherish the lives of each one of us writing men! These literate ignorant men will have the hair off our hands.

I better stop. I can see I am not going to do what Blackburn insists I can't: think. That is, I ought to do two things: (1) elucidate what history is, in the face of the historism now plaguing all Europeans, and so the world, by proselytizing from that center; and (2) expose the "phenomenology of literature" Curtius thinks he is arriving at through such a "science of European literature" as he takes the present book to be. It would be easy to do both. Neither history (to find out for oneself) nor literature (what is said) is science. That is what Herodotus knew. Or any of us does, who is at once our grandmothers (history) and ourselves (what we say). As Curtius is, he is so modest, and hopeful, and curious. But not his method. He has been caught between those two devils who threaten all who read but don't write: science and religion.

It all comes out in one sentence. And though you will feed, as I have, on *the information* in these 650 pages at 5 dollars and 50 cents, be careful of both of these horns:

"Specialization has thus opened the way to a new universalization"

It just damn well ain't true.

(1954)

It Was. But It Ain't.

Herodotus. *The Histories.* Thucydides. *The Peloponnesian War.* Two new translations by Aubrey de Selincourt and Rex Warner, respectively. London: Penguin, 1954.

It is like that Bulldog Drummond mystery, of leaving the room in your hotel to come back and find that there is no such room, the manager shows you, there is no such number, no door, nothing as you had had it, no recognition of you, no belongings, the registry doesn't show that you ever put up there, you were never here, you know the face, the place, you were here, but all is bland, the smiles are proper, the shaking of the known heads over your bewilderment— only, no help, you don't exist so far as anyone here lets on. You are thus suddenly without a place. And you are thus anonymous, you are without a face, a name, clothes, set down in the midst of the city a no-face. And not even treated badly, simply treated blandly, as they are bland.

It is crazy, where one history has left us. You damn well know Thucydides. It is any day. It is as it has been. It is commodity. But the door has been erased. The shrewdness which ran the house, the curiosity which led you out into the street, the business—you come back and all is changed. They don't want your money. They don't want you!

And the other, Herodotus? It is as though Thucydides wanted to be sure, like the manager of what was just now your hotel, that all your nonsense about having lived here, that this was where your belongings at least were—"where are my things," you shout, "where's my luggage, you bastard"—that all your protestations are just what he says any other history is, not the equal of his eyewitness. That evidence. That you see the door ain't there. It was. But it ain't. You can see for yourself. Listen to the hotel keeper:

> I do not think that one will be far wrong in accepting the conclusions I have
> reached from the evidence which I have put forward. It is better evidence than

that of the poets, who exaggerate the importance of their themes, or of the prose chroniclers, who are less interested in telling the truth than in catching the attention of their public, whose authorities cannot be checked, and whose subject-matter, owing to the passage of time, is mostly lost in the unreliable streams of mythology.

It was a nice room. And it was in Soho, near good restaurants. Your first time in London. The whole city spread out before you. Oh, yes. Oh what intimations. Ah, commerce. O Europe—Real city!

But now you got No place. You ain't Any face. You is No face. Where to turn? To whom to appeal? Affiant, what will you sign, do you have even hands to sign with?

If you read (as I suppose these two books are represented together, and are translated in a modern idiom so that you may read them as you might read books of your time, thus, as such, they are serviceable and cheap, one dollar, one can hardly do damage to the texts, they were powerful men, and some of the ancient method of telling either of the stories has been freshened by setting down into footnotes pieces of information which are not immediately relevant, or, as the translator of Herodotus says, "interrupt the narrative"!), if you read them as two different kinds of history of two different wars following not too long a time after each other, the Persian and the Peloponnesian,—well, you can. Indeed, any of us will, to the degree that we do know where we live, that we are in this house, it is a winter day, the fire is in the grate, these things did happen, at least one can be sure Thucydides did happen, men as states will continue to be like this, politics is as usual the pursuit of gain, this is the sour cross, and the rue will be your sour grace that you are here in a room with a number.

Only you ain't, quite. Modernity is done in. You have come back from shopping—and nobody knows who you are.

Now the advantage of Herodotus, in this situation, is of the simplest: he says the voice is greater than the eye. If you shout—if you tell your story—he listens to you. He doesn't give you that nod and finger which destroys you, wagging, and saying, look, you ain't there. He says, you say so? OK, I believe you. Truth is what is said, not, what is seen. Your own report is good enough for him. You say you lived here? OK. You did. These things happened to you? OK. Sign here. Your name, please. That's all. Your goods will be restored in just a minute. You see, we limed up your room while you were out. We made a whole new hallway. If you look closely—I mean, closely—you'll see the faking. There was a door here. Only it's gone. That's all right: we'll fix you up elsewhere. With a better view. Glad you called us. The customer, is always, right! Thank you sir.

The old door is gone. And I suppose the most curious thing about the present is the way the new door ain't what its makers intended. It turns out one is damn lucky to be turned out, to have to scream at the bland ones that one damn well did live here. One has to insist that one is because one says so.

And where Thucydides is loaded with all these accurate statements of deputations, of all nationalists, Herodotus, who was himself a migrant and knew what happens when men have to be recognized for what they are, not to what they belong, is always talking of men and things, not of societies and commodities. It is very nice to be so addressed. It helps, when one is suddenly out in the cold. He reminds us.

(1955)

Homer and Bible

Cyrus H. Gordon. *Homer and the Bible.* Ventnor, N.J.: Ventnor Publishers, 1956.

An important thing is done here: an "East Mediterranean literature" is blocked out, as of and inside 1400 BC, of such size and import that Homer's poems belong to it, the Old Testament (through the Patriarchal narratives), recently published Late Egyptian stories, and the Ras Shamra poems. Gordon is the first, to my knowledge, to push the literary to the conclusion which archaeology and philology had already pointed to—that there is such a prehistory to Homer and Hesiod, that the oldest of the Old Testament can be pulled in from vaporous religious sources and pegged down as a text written in a knowable period of history, and that the "Phoenician," properly Canaanite, is the switch-house from which it is done. Gordon's advantage is that he has made himself *the* scholar of Ugaritic and has translated (*Ugaritic Literature*, Rome, 1949) the poetic and prose texts found at Ras Shamra since 1929 and dating from the early years of the 14th century BC (what is known as the Amarna Age from the tablets found at Amarna, Egypt in 1887).

Anyone who doesn't yet have this picture—and history, as available, has been slow to catch up with the finds of the past seventy-five years—can get a fast take from Gordon's swift first twenty pages of summary and declaration of what he dubs 'East Mediterranean': Crete as the hub, the Greeks and Hebrews 'new' on the stage in these years (Knossos fell 1450 BC), Canaan and Egypt 'older' on either side, and the Hittites, though Gordon slights them in this book, in Anatolia.

Beyond that, and because the first twenty pages are so valuable, one doesn't want to keep anybody away from Gordon by questioning what he does in forty-four more pages. It is a familiar thing. In successive chapters he uses these poems and narratives to describe the East Mediterranean "Society"

345

which produced them—common "War" matters, differences and likenesses of "Gods, Religion and Ritual," and of "Style and Idiom." It is the drag, comparative literature, and there is loss. I am not persuaded that Mr. Gordon means to pay that price, the more so that he shows himself capable in his first pages, and has given us poems, but he seems caught thereafter in a dilemma the practice of philology does involve its own in. As a science of language it depends upon the comparative method. Much of its finest work results from it. But there comes the moment when the writing exists. With it, what should the philologist do and not do?

To take it in its own steps. Once archaeology finds any tablets with inscriptions or text, philology's first task is to determine and decipher the language in which they are written. Recently Michael Ventris did for Cretan what immediately earlier Gordon's predecessors did for Ugaritic, others again earlier for Hittite, and in the last century was done for Sumerian and Egyptian.

Then—and Mr. Gordon is a superb example of the second step (as S. N. Kramer is, in Sumerian, and Hans Güterbock in Hittite)—there is the job of translating and establishing the body of the literature, so far as the discoveries make it evident, and at a certain point enough does accumulate to get the thing in hand and out there as a part of all writing.

Up to this point the work of the scholar is all gain, and prime. But at the third step philology is differently confronted. We live in an age in which inherited literature is being hit from two sides, from contemporary writers who are laying bases of new discourse at the same time that such scholars as the above are making available pre-Homeric and pre-Mosaic texts which are themselves eye-openers. It is a tremendous moment. But if the writers know it, do the scholars, if a man as good as Gordon does what he does here, at the third step, uses these texts for social history when their new power belongs strictly to the fact of themselves, calls them epic and speaks of an heroic age, uses them for such secondary and typological interest when the epic itself has been atomized in our time and reconstituted, and the heroic, which is the other face of the same dimension, is under as fierce an examination. Something is wrong with a method which, fruitful in its first two stages, does this dead thing in its last. The fault is not Gordon's, or the others'. It is a habit of mind wider than the literary application alone. It has deanimated history, spilled much ethnology, and mythology, spread nothing but misconception of psychology, and only produced its creature, the pseudo-science, sociology, which is the measure of the

dirt comparison is. Who cares for likeness? A likeness recognized is only something to move in from, until difference, which is identity, is found. To stop at
any likeness is to stay in the bath. Equilibrium is Laodicean. One must disturb it.
It is a lie. It ain't true, at least it ain't good enough. Or it is a truth for those who
sleep. You know, even a glass of water, won't spill on this mattress!

Actually of course everything spills. Nothing has organization. There is no
will to construct. Who can do anything when everything is shown to be like?
One succumbs. The truth is there is no glass. There is only water.

This is the danger, in the case in hand. If these new texts are taken by the
comparative handle at the third step, all their energies, which are of such pleasure and use for writing now, now that we have them and they are earlier than
Homer, are wasted again into the sands from which these men have read them.
They must resist. They must not try to be historians as well. Leave that to those
who want to practice it as a discipline. It can be. But it takes time and energy and
a precision these men have put to languages. History isn't any easier, either.

There is a rule: the very likenesses and differences which make comparison
possible in the first instance (when a thing is being drawn out from the general
to the uncovering of its own specific) must, the moment the thing is seen for
itself, serve the details of the thing forever after and never return to the general; or the life of the thing, which lives by its difference (it is difference which
is the freshness by which anything stays open, its own literal and particularness)
will be lost again into the general, from which, by all the labor, it has been
drawn. When Mr. Gordon stays that clear, he can do this;

> "Para. 31. Homeric *dorp*—(*Iliad* 19:208 'food, a meal,' has no plausible Indo-
> Hittite etymology. It is identical with Egyptian *drp,* 'to feed offer food to.' Since
> *drp* is attested in Old Egyptian of the third millennium, it appears that it moved
> from Egypt toward Greece, via the Mediterranean."

Otherwise, when he is telling us Moses' staff of God is the same as the Greek
aegis, the very thing he establishes, a literature of such an order at 1400 BC,
shrinks, and one ends asking oneself is 1400 BC, and this writing, not actually
less important than he says it is!

What we need is more of the text, always more of the, text, no end to the
work that can be done. More light on every word, every device of syntax, each
difference of morphology in structure and in form, until it's all laid clear. When
the attention is that steady and intense, stays that way, there is nothing but

gain, on all sides. Even the historians can learn from the movement of a word stem from Egypt to Greece via Ugarit. Any static-ing, any setting up of a pattern except in the instant of the declaration of it (no proving, no proving please) tells an untruth which the texts themselves, if they are any good—if they were worth translating in the first instance—will disclose. It is not that he borrowed that tells anything about a writer, but what he or she (say Sappho) does with it—what Homer did with parallelism when he or Greek got it, not the fact of it. Likewise words like epic and heroic: typology. Tells nothing. Instantly evident. How was he epic? What different way was he? Or his age heroic? And these close studies come from adhering to the text, attending to it—as the writer did, in writing it.

On the very level at which Gordon thinks he is throwing light, by showing the international character and fusion of "Near East cultures culminating in the Amarna Age," a predecessor, without what Gordon knows, did something fifty years ago which is one of the great critical services yet done to writing in this century: in *Les Phéniciens et l'Odysée* Berard kept his attention so strictly to his thing that his investigation into the Semitic roots of the proper nouns of the Odyssey has told us the only new thing we know about how Homer composed. And it fits present independent discoveries about the epic. It was done in— 1902, 1903 (not, as Gordon's footnote on Berard's work could mislead a reader to thinking—accidentally, I believe, he is merely recording the most available edition—in 1937).*

It is this business of taking the edge off new discovery when the stuff hasn't even been taken into the bloodstream of the present which makes literacy as it is now practiced suspect—even (and this is the problem) when one has so much to thank a man like Gordon for, that he does insist there's 600 years you people better get on to, and I have already offered you a whole new feast of poems you never even knew existed.

So I shut up, urging Gordon to take the top and the bottom of his discoveries (the surface of Canaanite verse as well as the interiors of it and of these other new literatures) as holding dimensions and dynamics more important than two thirds of his book lets on he knows.

(1957)

*I stress the date simply that scholarship around 1900 seems to have been extraordinarily clear at the third step at least of the comparative method: Jane Harrison, as another example. And there are others.

Bill Snow

Bill Snow's third cousin said yesterday we are quite a sophisticated society—
and had a poet read a poem for him and the nation at that cousin's inauguration as a president of the United States. All right.

Bill's lived in the period between and between. The only time I ever did a
review of a book was when I was twenty and it was Bill Snow's *Downeast*.
And this is the only time I ever did an introduction, except to introduce my
friend Creeley's stories 10 years ago—and on his mother or his father's side
he comes from Headtide Maine (the Sheepscot or the Damariscotta).

It's the secular I don't think is going to go out of our bones yet—and Bill
Snow's Irish Indian Snow appetite for appetite is where he kept the runner on
the ice, or sled-path into the woods turning E northly on the N side and not in
any way infringing on sled path to be 4 rods wide.

Like, form, and function? The soul is as double as the body, and if you add
up four functions form still is out the window. Bill's had sensation for his side
each time he has recalled a condition of life when young such as a snowstorm
on the island to the W of Spruce Head Island where his father was a member of
the coast guard.

It's a scandal how lazy all have been for a century on what went on in the
U S for the previous two centuries. At Waldoboro, or Thomaston better even,
one looks at houses straight into the eyes of the people of the Civil War—and
you could exchange Pittsboro North Carolina for either, how unified form and
function (speaking of the human use of human society now, not poetry) were.
Speaking of poetry one does need then also to mark Walt Whitman. I am thinking of one poem of all, "Trickle Drops." Thereafter any enlargement looked
sick, and any humanism, of which there has been only practically to get that
climactic or quotable line, or go up to the top when in fact the poet better had
been, as a Democrat, Speaker of the House of Representatives. And I mean

Frost not Snow. It was Rosie McGraw actually who unifies Bill with the Fitzgeralds and thus brings about this curious connection, at this date, of Bill with politics. Only, I remember him as early as 1904 at a Democratic Rally on Vinalhaven and already billed as Professor Snow.

I mean green, and ignorant, I just can't catch on that we as a society or as individuals are as knowing as those born in this century take us to be, and, which seems to be the immediate corollary and by which courage is suddenly a new word in the dictionary, that we are surrounded by enemies and must stay fit. It sounds like athleticism to me, and when all that is is only demonstrated by self-consciousness of that it is, games are being played. I'd go straight from Nature to the World. If form ever did lie in tales and on short stretches of distance between personally known towns already the Collector of Port Duties on Wool in the city of London in 1390 had had it. And then there was trickle drops. And then there was none. Courage is knowing every fear and heroism is a complementarity of same, not at all to be identified with it, and the reason why the secular still makes sense is that it puts these two heads together again, right now. I can't imagine a closeness of detail which can err— as against the biggest and the powerfullest nation on earth, whichever one it is or will be or the least local scene. Man is much more of a power than his accent or the most he can manage to refer to. This is what has happened. One can't stare any more or hold it inside. Lincoln is the only face worth looking at of all the 39 or 38 Presidentses, and that even was the end of that. Under the mushroom there isn't even a thing which isn't solely more of itself. This certainly is what's now true.

And thereby hangs tales poems acts and men which will gather up everything and roll all up into the ball like the weevil getting there.

(1961)

A House Built by
Capt. John Somes 1763

Men don't follow men
they follow men's ideas

Diderot, for example. I hate the spirit of streets. The spirit anyway of this nation went away at some point of time between 1765 and 1770 and a man born about then, therefore a son rather of those men who made the Revolution was already, in the first years of the Nineteenth Century crying us down accurately—James Fenimore Cooper, that early. All which writing including the hump-up of the Middle of the 19th Century did insist upon and Melville had already passed American art out into the geometry which alone—until time re-entered, about 1948—was what was making things possible again.

What it was which did break in the moment of time in the Eighteenth Century must have been what Gino Clays has said I'm sure as well as anyone, that when men are still putting down houses to live in and work to make food the earth is still lived on. When that breaks—Captain Somes' house on Lower Middle Street is the possibility at its last moment here on the new continent—when it broke all had to be begun again. The critique by Cooper was so complete all after was simply going to live it out, until today—or at least until 1949. Any change, any new chance, had to be toward earth not (again Gino Clays) not across. Inside of the world Clays says.

The men of the Revolution, all heroes, are all False Identities, Time of their Age Servants, good men in that sense of Deism which doesn't go away at all, even right now the idea of God is mostly that Architect or Gardener or A Fine Cellist after dinner, or State Accomplisher. Actually Noah Webster, like Cooper is a better End of that than all those prolongations.

I was a Gnostic * possibly, I ain't any longer at least to my present problems

* A Gnostic—or 13th century Muslim sense of time as intense

something neither Buddhist nor Gnostic will do, but because ideas are only what live, or the Forms ideas are the Statement of, it would be very valuable if we had now a completely Indo-Europeanized American dictionary; and an encyclopedia * which was at least unhampered by any premise of what knowledge is except, in that form, all that is known. Already (as Creeley has recently pointed out) almost everyone who picks up at all are going on something as slack as their own information and there is only, as Creeley goes on to say, a small body (of whom Dorn is an example) who really want to know.

This is simply also to place men like Gino Clays who have the other clarity: I am going to be reborn inside the world. There is migration, and there isn't, there is time—and no holes in it.

Charles Olson,
for Ted Crump,
April 10th, 1962

---

*An encyclopedia equally of roots, rather like the *Encyclopedia of Religion and Ethics* now, including say the difference of the value of the decipherment of Linear A as against the decipherment of Linear B etc.

The Advantage of Literacy Is That Words Can Be on the Page

A Bibliography on the State of Knowledge for Charles Doria

That the archeological discoveries of the past century have supplied, directly from the ground, substantive and narrative physicality to previously discursive language and thought;

that this is true whether it is taken as Schliemann's to Blegen's confirmation of Homer's literal geography (Victor Berard, as early as 1904 (?) arguing the import of this on Homer's composition, and Leo Frobenius, as early as that, via African remains and his own actual field experience, demonstrating the critical importance of oral memory, that epic—the fragment of Dausi epic found by him among the Sonike (?) say as example—is in fact critically earthish or it doesn't occur, that logography and the muthologotic are in fact, prose to poetry and poetry to prose, one earth-bound matter:

or that it is taken literally in the discovery in the ground near Latakia of Ugaritic tablets, thus a poetry of some lines being therefore again new, or that Hittite and Sumerian text and poetry can now be placed beside the actual language and composition of Rig-Veda, itself retained orally from a date prior to 1750 BC through some Englishman for the first time getting it into written and therefore readable as well as previously hearable for 4000 years, beside Celtic social organization of the Tara kingdom, literally the place of wrestlers poets historians as well as cooks and queens in the tents on each new ground of the clockwise movement of the O'Neils around the 12 kingdoms (was it?) of Ireland date 6th or 7th century AD (repeating or confirming social organization and administration revealed in the Rig-Veda), or beside the Poetic Edda, possibly the last 'classic' added before the present, 900 AD (?) disclosing a cosmology Hesiod seems purer of than Homer. But in any case, leaving it where it always was, and still so much is, on the Greek classic, there is the advantage that Herodotus was the most like Homer of all his successors.

If to this archeological gain of the present one adds the other one which ran prior but current to it, that the languages of the world were found to have a family and home as literal as is now known that Sumerians came into the river basin of the Tigris-Euphrates sometime around 4000 BC from the northeast, that the Semitic peoples are not desert people but come from a region south of the Caucasus somewhat fixed around Ararat, and that even the Amorites stir at the same date that the Indo-Europeans appear via or from Maikop at before or after 2100 BC, one has etymology as well as alphabet *to write words by.*

I have called this art logography: and believe that the discourse which makes it possible can also itself be defined as the mythological, and that this in its turn at this date can be specified, so that gesture and action, born of the earth, may in turn join heaven and hell, can be called proprioception. But this is simply to make sure that perception is refound to be primary or morphological, and that conception is put back where it does occur, that it is genetic but only even to use that word as genet: earth was genet in an order of time.

One wants phenomenology in place, in order that event may re-arise. There are only two facts about mythology which count: that they are made up of tales and personages, in place. Words then are naming and logography is writing as though each word is physical and that objects are originally motivating. This is the doctrine of the earth.

You asked me for a curriculum. I am proposing a re-arising of the Olympic Game: the public is the body (Tantalus founded those Games by unhitching the linch-pin of the chariot of the father of the girl he wanted, then ruler of the place where the Olympic Games did start. Tantalus was a Hittite. You at least Charles Doria are a Hittite. The private is a body. Language is only public as written.

Introductory Note to the Bibliography,
written December 9th, 1963

Review of Eric A. Havelock's
Preface to Plato

This book, by attending with complete attention (an act in itself part of developments in the phenomenlogy of attention) to precisely what Plato did mean, in his *Republic* by poetry—and attending to this from Plato back to Homer and Hesiod (Havelock asserts that poetry as Plato meant it is as much or more directed at the epic as at tragedy or other lyric poetry) is of such importance, because of how it is done as well as the complete capital subjects it therefore raises, that I am going to go on the assumption that it may be that in this book, for the first time, something that has been called criticism, and literary criticism at that, ugly as that whole matter has been, is here raised to a level with the development of historiography generally (in the past 85 years) and that Havelock's *Prefaces* [he proposes two more in order to take the work back through · the pre-Socratics to Hesiod] can prove to be the only work in criticism which is relevant at all to developments in thought and poetry over the past 150 years. Therefore (to begin a series of notes on Havelock, rather than anything like a review) I should like first to take out of his pages some of the results of his studies, and of others, into what was different about the poetry of Homer, and of Hesiod, to which Plato did take objection in order the better himself to support his own invention of another *episteme,* of his belief in a dialectic of Socrates' order, and—though this is later, but already implicit—a new sense of metaphor which becomes, in Aristotle (cf. the *Poetics* 1457) a part or parcel of the Plato-Socrates generalization system, species genus and analogy, similarity and contiguousness, including—let it be emphasized—the periodic sentence:

(1) that [the poetry of Homer and Hesiod was based on] a wholly different syntax, to which Notopoulos (1949) has applied the word *parataxis* in which the words and actions reported are set down side by side in the order of their

occurrence in nature, instead of by an order of discourse, or 'grammar,' as we have called it, the prior an actual resting on vulgar experience and event:

(2) Zielinski, *1901,* and literally therefore almost contemporary with Planck, was saying that 'time' in such poets as Homer and Hesiod cannot admit of intervals where nothing happens, that there is no such thing as nothing, and that therefore you cannot leap over, you do therefore necessarily traverse, in writing, and any one event series once narrated fills up the available time space. There is no while back at the farm sequence possible. The epic action is a stream and you are not free to play around jump as though you was on the bank or the other or in the water—at your choice or privilege or pleasure, that you either is or you isn't, definitely:

(3) Fraenkel's (2nd. ed. 1960) is another lovely indication of what the difference of Homer is: that Homer is innocent of any *concept* of time, and *chronos,* in the idioms in which he does use it, covers periods of waiting or delay or doing nothing—literally doing nothing, not 'nothing'—and that it was through waiting that the experience of time is born, that a day, literally a day, is how it is, the thing itself the business possible and the report whereof thereon thereafter repeats slowly or however you do it just that swiftly.

There is much more, and one could say a lot (and I do deliberately leave the advantageous statements of Notopoulos on that other 'syntax' unstated) but there is one quoted statement (from Collingwood) which does, in so many words, set the contrast going which ought by now to be a freeing matter:

The general distinction between imagination and intellect is that imagination presents to itself an object which it experiences as one and indivisible: whereas intellect goes beyond that single object and presents to itself a world of many such with relations of determinate kinds between them. (Collingwood, R. G., *The Principles of Art.* Oxford, 1938)

Thanks to Mr. Havelock.

Buffalo, 1963

1) That we require *mapping.* By topological law that the *proximate:* a microcosm is literally as absolute as the other one, and, in fact that something like ripples. But in any case that a syntax of apposition is 'true' to the

'order' which does obtain. And thereby event does exist in the other discourse which is lost by Thucydides, and thereafter, whether in prose or verse.

and that *dotha* or judgment arises from this more accurate paratax, or is made more possible as an experience of experience, vision dream seeming [doxa] sitting-in, and the self-rising: from the scud

2) a 'time' of the sort Z then did analyze as true of Homer (in fact with almost no adjustments except those of possibly greater individual genius) *Indo-European time-sense* [plus Dausi to be sure an African example, which probably also is etc. to be included] thus inherent in language as much in existence now as then, at least if possibly there is any limit, Indo-European language. also as much present therefore lexically as—if there is a distinction—

3) that knowing is not separable as (psyche: logos the other term and impossibly therefore such a thing as episteme equal to dogma) and that the reflexive and the notive

Added notes Sunday November 25th 1963

3rd Part

That the time now for some time has been post-Aristotelian and that there was pre-Aristotelian condition of discourse, has now to include Plato and Socrates and to see the set of them as proposing to change society, conceivably the most conspicuous attempt to do so prior to the present, and we don't even know what it does mean to change society comparably to how they did engage to do it, so much of our own discourse is in fact theirs. Thus social change in the present is boringly social and unequally revolutionary to theirs.

It would seem to me that this is because the most missing understanding of what they did do is *dialexis,* at whatever date that word even might have come to have the meaning of an actual action of dialogue: *dialectical* does mean one to one, and an immediate discharge of mental engagement in which the will and the mind are like aggressive motor actions, and are complimentary in that they do compliment the other person engaged, as though there was a one-to-one possible, as though the conversation was between us and a meeting of minds was possible. It is socializing, and relational.

One wants therefore to enter this ring on a different footing: it isn't true, and has left the universe out, substituting for it a prune or wrinkled grape, the social. A politics of the order of the Athenian Three has no more person or *ethea* in it—has only a psyche of halve to logos and their false conjunction supported by an invented *episteme,* an invented noun instead of a participle, a stretching neuterizing and -*sis*ing of probably the single verb (verbal) which stood in place as a bow at rest, and the things which fly and split the mark equally sitting in the state prior to use—than a society (social) of an order equal to order itself. The whole slip to discourse, deliberately mounted to supply an education and State as the result (cause-and-effect) of an artificial 'person' and an equally shrunken *socius* (company) ended up in Hegel, and in Marx-plus, the modern liberal companionship. Not only does materialism (instead of technology) become the appetite of the contemporary person, satisfied by the goods alone and a credit market as well as the debted Nation, but equally the new man-grape gazes upon space as though he can return via it to the paradise, of trees, on which all the fruits do grow, a conversation with some superior its from *another* planet. Nothing not option, of the individual, and a coming together, where epistea is the filthy Host, thought to be food, and Eranos is quite exactly (*agape*) the function (oral-formulaic, Stephanites the unholy Athenian Three, via Hegel Mrak—and Freud. It does not negate. It is not capable.

There is no colloquy. Society is as inherited—order is, entropy is—as is the bole (boulé) of Person: born you is, of your Mother as you are via the part played in it, of Your father. The return Up the tree is as decisive as the part you play Suspended in the genesis, that you were born. The Tree comes down colored by the airs and light of the *datum.* There is a discourse. There is a grammar. There is a sentence you do have. It happens also to be a motive of things that you are not, but which you do—exactly in some sense in which the Athenian Three were after something, they were 'after' (meta) something else, which preceded them—attend to. You are not free than otherwise to perceive.

This, then, would be the conversation.

Note added December 6th, and in anticipation of anything further

A Further Note on the Critical Advantages
of Eric Havelock's *Preface to Plato*

Knowledge has changed. Active use is its non-conditioned prior and now once
more arose use. If 50 years ago historiography apprehended once more history
and Time then some point quite recently that, in its turn, turned this way; and I
am satisfied that Eric Havelock's *Preface to Plato* denotes that change. My point
in saying this is to awaken anyone who reads such recent masters as Joseph
Needham or Mircea Eliade to note the absence, in the very best of their thought
⌊on history, as it is, and on Time ⌐, of distinctions Havelock examples: viz., discourse; and politics. Neither of the aforementioned men seem to have any experience of a change of the sort it seems to me Havelock is ingrained of, and as
a result lack two quotable statements going beyond anything they are able to
yield:

    (1), that the gods and heroes of mythology are *metaphors;*
and (2), that both gods and heroes are *conspicuous* and *public.*

Saturday, April 17, 1965

Statement for the *Cambridge* magazine

There *are* symmetrical things
don't let a filthy relativistic greedy
overoccupied thermodynamic society kid you
that the theory of games or the theory of
probability resembles anything
but a miserable second-rate support
for themselves

That's the first thing. And the other—
& there aren't no more—is simply the
whole area they occupy with their
incredible errors of etc *is*
the substance of
all being—
        what does
go on, & is always going on &
is
        [except for the complete
recognizable symmetry of instance]
condition

(February 1964)

A comprehension (a measure, that

the period from
    Capt. Somes' house Mid. St. Gloucester
      1760 to this date now
        a *comprehensible*
period of time is ditto the period fr
      Homer writing Iliad Odyssey to 3 equals:
Heraclitus Buddha and
    the 1st ideal youth or
      Venus statue, all circ.
        500 BC (Heraclitus dies
          480, and
        that's date of
      Kritios' *Ephebe,*
        after
bronze *Apollo of Piombino*)

all within this comprehensible period of time, 206 years from Capt. Somes (Homer—700, or even maybe 675) and to date: 1966 equal to Heraclitus, Buddha, or Battle of Salamis, 480

that *from* Indo-European "poems" iliad Odyssey and even *after* them, Hesiod's two or three also "last" Indo-European poems is no longer from "present" moment 1966 than the spread to just as the Am. Revolution was breaking out: as 'little' as—Capt Somes' house two families of Webbers right now, address 20 (?) Middle—

And that in that kind of time everything 'went'—in fact in less than one-*half of it,* that is, by Herman Melville's *Clarel* say, a two-volume novel in tetrameters, the lyrick—Sappho and Alcaeus date within 75 years of Homer! ! ! (100 at the *most!*)

and Heráclitus who had already "ruined" thought (by featuring the new post-Indo-European concept of soul as *psyche;* and doing this by the primary error of analogy as logic instead of image or actualness—likeness to likeness instead of as the comparison, making an "image" (imago) out of it), Heraclitus is exactly contemporary to those bloody perfect sculptures ("statues") or, as Snell says in so many words, belongs to "the era of the lyric." Ours, since 1763!

bibliography: G. S. Kirk, Heraclitus, *The Cosmic Fragments,* p. 3
              Bruno Snell, *The Discovery of the Mind,* p. 17
              Sir Kenneth Clark, *The Nude,* p. 57 bottom & over
Add also: G. Else, *Origin & Early Form of Greek Tragedy* (1966) p. 61, top

Add, please:
  Stuart Piggott, *Prehistoric India,* p. 255

Also, to date Homer, see: G. S. Kirk Fascicle, for Cambridge Anc. History, #22
                     on *The Homeric Poems as History,* p. 10

P.S. to previous 'Argument' of A Comprehension (a measure)

I *am* forcing it, to that extent that one wants it *clear* by now that the lyrick is the ripple which precedes Klassical reaching the shore; and that *that* happens, the lyrick, in a century both before & including Heraclitus and *only* (be it even the more noticed now that the alphabetization of Greece is settled at *after* 725 BC) a century *or less after* the formal setting in writing of the Iliad and the Odyssey, with Hesiod's Theogony and Works and Days still considered later than such redaction of Homer.

There is then a freedom much called for at both ends: the 'attack' by Plato on *poets & poetry* already has asserted itself in fragments 57, 40 & 41 of Heraclitus, dating say 505 when he was in his 40s or at around 480 when in his 60s; and one wants now a theory of composition, a capacity of poem which as L. J. D. Richardson does say of the *Sophia,* the plain *ability* of Hesiod, to go back to Mycenaean practice, and man's ability over mechanics. We are then un-loading both this end, 2550 years after lyrick, and acquiring, in the face of ig-norance, power itself evident in an earlier Gothic (—the one Europe rose by) dating from Mycenaean at least—and Mycenaean itself only one of the devel-opments following on the greatest single movement yet, of man & language, the Indo-European dispersion (from say 1900 BC to 1400, a firm date for "My-cenaean" as such).

Such matters as, each word following on the other, and that the world of things isn't the block the lyrick throws in the way of nature; and Hesiod's epis-tamenos to describe the manner of his own composition, belongs to us (as well as that Sophia of his, & Celtic and Norse and Vedic poets and Arthurian English tale-tellers) *Epistamenos,* Works and Days 107.

(1966)

"CLEAR, SHINING WATER," De Vries says*

Wishing, in that sense, to start at the bottom—or, in fact, to get there (that is, by the etymological part of *ta'wil* / $\int$ the other part, if I take Corbin right, in a footnote in Avicenna, or, His Visionary Recitals, is topological—and this present instance seems very much perhaps *the* (vertical) topological matter, of all matters which can find a basis for a physics of psyche at this revolutionary point in re-taking the cosmology of creation as fact, both in instant and in consequence, thus prevailing, hidden or no, in whatever is up anywhere for whomever the more so now/ 7 ,

there is this whole old-hat business of three something sisters, or tri-parts of whomanhood ((I meant of course to typewrite womanhood, or, simply, Woman—or if you take it by Graves's A Historical Grammar of the Language of Poetic Myth, Muse—or what he there calls the White etc Goddess,

the easiest—and interestingly enough, the completest, right straight across the board is Webster's 2nd International, under whichever of the Indo-European languages one seems to take it by, viz: ((I came in on it through *Nona,* from the Latin "Three" (Nona, Decima, and Morta)))

fate n. 4 [cap.] *Class. Myth.* The goddess, or one of the goddesses, of fate or destiny, esp., *pl* [L. *Fata,* pl. of *fatum*], the three goddesses who were supposed to determine the course of human life. In Greek mythology, they are called the Moerae (see MOERA)

quote the—or look at—the rest p. 795

*Altgermanische Religionsgeschichte (Berlin, 1957), Vol. II, p. 380.

364

Now if you do go the next, and penultimate step to NORN you come into the heart of the matter: there, whether the one or indexing goddess, like MOERA, or MORTA in the Latin (also PARCA as well, each one of them coming from a furtherest root around MER- which ultimately I better be at pains to show the complete tie-up of, in a decent, flexible bundle about like—as Graves is happily wittily able to know is what at least, even with all his spread on the "White etc Goddess like they say, is, in fact, Alexander's GRAMPIAN KNOT (I mean of course GORDIAN)

so you will find, NORN, one either A. S. *Wyrd* and Norse *Urth,* which suddenly runs Three, *Urth, Verthandi,* and *Skuld,* or Past, Present and Future, two giving blessings, the third ills, of life, if you can be so pat as that as the Dictionary is—and is, in fact, simpler and straighter than a good deal of Clotho, Lachesis, Atropos hand-outs we've all had on this said important subject enough to sink us and it as a subject since we were like school-children for sure.

I stick then on these later Anglo-Saxon, Norse duplicates of Latin-Greek Lithuanian etc better-known Indo-European words of these three-women. Or tri-divided Woman, as *Urth,* or *Wyrd.* It gets somewhere.

II

One suddenly talks at the roots of the World-Tree. I can refer you, for the most careful modern identifications here, to Turville-Petre *Myth and Religion of the North* (London, 1964), pp. 246, 277, 279, and 280. For it is of course Snorri Sturlason, who may, as Petre is anxious to say, be "too systematic," but he equally, as Hesiod has so often been found—and say among contemporary cosmologists, Whitehead—dogmatic. Here however truth—or *Verthandi* (Ver *dandi*) places up its own wild singleness and says like any herb my efficacy lies in my use as is not in some bye-product or alternative.

In any case I want more to turn this one further and last twist (one which Turville-Petre himself well knows, that Urth and Wyrd are themselves probably *vertere,* and do mean millstone turning, grist or spun (Atropos is in her meaning Inflexible—and "Last" simply a-tropos, not to be turned or unspun backwards, therefore like END of scene Etc. Morta. (merx mercis 2 SMAR-root, '*ascribe*.') Allright.

It is Mrs. Davidson, H. R. Ellis Davidson, in *Gods and Myths of Northern Europe* (Baltimore: Penguin, 1964) page 26, who gives Snorri's picture straightest perhaps. In any case translates Verthandi (Verdandi) as "Being" (so fairly one wld suppose Present); and Skuld as "Necessity," thus losing perhaps something of what Turville-Petre holds in his word Future—or ill. But in any case as she says the tree was continually threatened at which these three, as its waterers, and carers, worked at its roots daily to preserve its life. It is the 'pole of Mimir' (*mimameidr-meithr*)—(Davidson, p. 194)

or another obscure name given to the tree is *Mjqtvidr*—this might be (Davidson says Ridberg says should be) *Mjodvidr*—'mead tree' (p. 195)

or it is simply, look, look at what these this tripartite the White Muse or Goddess called all Parcae etc 'names' is in fact, like, doing

Institute of Further Studies
July 1st, 1968

What's Back There

It begins to come in—from the far end as well. We are a gross and chronological people, had no underground or previous ground of conduct—and what
was wiped out, on the back end, at the nearest to was what still's called "Phoenician" [like the Greek, and the Jewish—and *not* the Egyptian, which had, itself, stayed in the ground, or there, for sights, in Egypt until Napoleon].

How to back the horse into the tail. That was one problem, and until Linear
B and *now* Cyrus Gordon, there was Albright. (Still though I want that peri-
Mediterranean syllabary round about all those Far Eastern sea-persons' waters
[of, still, those shores, that small pre-Atlantic hyper-Red waters "and bays
thereunto appertaining"]

.   .   .

Doria and I have this compact: 4 original "Phoenician" survivals only. [Not
yet any sign of an Herakliad—though plenty reasons to think, still, shall be.]
Sanchuniathon [T. L. Webster, Italy, did exist (via Linear B's 1400 & backwards)].
John Malalas

Etc.

So there is, signs of this awakening.

Gloucester, December 1968

The Animate versus the
Mechanical, and Thought

Gravity, in fact, but pre- or post- mechanics. That is, not effect (Newtonian) nor proof (Recent) but experiential: phenomenological, perceptional, actionable.

Or the fact that plants, by starch (statoliths), turgor and a geotropism as much a part of a plant's sensibleness as its heliotropism, has at the tips of its leaves and the ends of its roots "standing-growing-responding" actions (its hinges, of leaves to stem, as well, so far as turgor goes, and has, if and as 'weight,' gravitational 'history.'

In fact 'history,' as, in that sense, difference from "astronomy": that event (in Merleau-Ponty's sense—narrative) is a perceptual—that wld be *primordial*—element of experience so much so that it 'carries' throughout the system—the system being 'Creation'—as 'element' (or 'weight') as profound as any mechanically measurable or demonstrable 'truth'; that event in short—or here decisively 'history'—as *must*—is a condition of organism. (Above 'Animate.')

And that any present (Present) 'thought' ('Thought') requires the insistence of these tips and ends (as, earlier, Cosmology-Mythology has led me—Dogtown, and Hesiod, Maximus Poems IV V VI—to believe ends and boundaries (Hermes or all *nomoi:* 'laws' against cannibalism—thievery) are 'space-activities' in, Creation; now I am proposing an even more fundamental 'tropism': that one cannot 'think' even—because one cannot 'act' even—without such limits as the 'lines' of being, both in the plant and the animal meaning, 'animate.' That all most Recent thinking has had this 'exaggeration' of kinetic or mechanical, 'measure.'

Which in itself is 'astronomical' (Clio, by inverse square of the distance) instead of Uranian: distance by inverse square of the event. The 'event' being now most decisively gravity. The great unadmitted limit—actually Hermetism or alchemism, thus Ouranianism—of experience.

368

Even to the science or 'time' of same: that anything inexperienced in the weight or matter of the organism is not transacted—traversed—thus 'carried,' or 'known' in a decisive, and *theological*—or 'moral'—ethical (in the meaning *ethos,* or cave-of-being) sense.

So I am back to animate, plant-or-animal—'perception' sense—of the freshness in time of the narrative or history as a tone or mode & so activeness of, for a human being, 'Creation': that there is no 'knowledge' of the crucial (axial-tropistic) sense of *anything,* including the "Universe" or the "Self," except by this 'Time' phenomenon of freshness which Animateness, *in and by itself,* as initial *of* experience. And so—anti-Newton, and anti-Einstein—of History. (For which instantaneously read 'narrative' (as its only means—Memory), or Event.

We are here and hereby *under* image (the other only of the two tracks of *form*—gestalt, if you like—morphology equally, if you want (to, that is, and in pair to, genetic). Image. Imagination. (Thought, consciousness and sense perception—chiefly itself, and dominantly optical-telescopic——photic——are secondary phenomenon. Or, activity. The fundamental essential and experiential—*active* (what I am here insisting is the unbelievably left-out but unbelievably powerful and sole human 'power', viz (quote):

> of tip and end
> of gravity—(geotropism)
> / God is the aboriginal instance of this
> creativity, and is therefore the aboriginal condition which
> qualifies its action /

If I right then and there obviate any Modern (or boring Kierkegaard Fear of God Mindedness) by substituting the equally limiting (though equally dipolar word Animate of this presentation Principia or De Motu—movement, motion matter, I have my argument per se in these words:

> The Animate is the aboriginal instance of activity,
> and is therefore the aboriginal condition which qualifies
> (limits, in the event or 'History' sense—'Time' sense:
> Hermes,

or 'Ekatick' sense (Iris the only part-child, other than his Brother and Sister children of 'God'—the water or turgor 'test' of the Gods as whether they are or are not telling 'truth'—tested and failing. They are abandoned by 'God' from 'his House of Mountain' for precisely '9' *Years*—

(Come back(:

The Animate is the aboriginal instance of activity, and is therefore the aboriginal *condition* (gravity) which qualifies its 'action' (meaning of course then more than ever what makes gravity—gravitation—magnetic ((as opposed or dipolar of, and to electronic——we live in a prescribed 'kalpa' of Time specifically the Electromagnetic Epoch))

So finally:

The animate—plant or animal—is the aboriginal instance of our occurrence and is therefore the aboriginal condition which qualifies— defines both in fact and act, including the form-making usefulness of— our action.

(And my 'point' here—in order to place 'time' in its proper and true powerful relation to space (the Clio here, though the Urania there, and, by inversion of the powerful dimension of time as 'smaller' than space, the multiple or 'power' it properly is, the Urania here as there the Clio—I am in short trying to expose all astronomy physics and mentalness—or telescopic, optical video—idein thought as non-Event—as non-Uranian—*non historic*)—

that
Thought itself, without this animate admission, entrance—limit, is over-extent (over-Extension=Spatial) and so removed, by one remove—unessential and secondary; and that with our limit as being both plant and animal, Thought then as 'ours' is aboriginal of Primordial, and so Consequent.

The import of this can quickly be stated: man as Love (plant, heliogeotropic) grows up and down, man as separateness (animal) disposes of himself by *sitio*—chooses his place but which even though it gives him freedom disposes him likewise by gravity (statolith)—starch, turgor—'weight'-of-mass)— equally tropistically. Heaven and Earth.

Gloucester, 28 Fort Square
Feb. 15th (LXIX)

1st Addition, after some slight studies into present scientific understanding of "gravity," to The Animate versus the Mechanical, and Thought:

Gravity
[or for which read happily & allowably gravitational waves, to all advantages]
are 'narrative' in the simple fact that we stand up & therefore 'move' in the
widest possible alle [literally, alle—anywhere anywhere]

& the sound sense—
      image : of
      inner being
that we 'are,' catches both
(I shld think) of the originary & continuously primary 'matter.'

[Saturday, April 19th

*I cld note that nothing that Dr. Forward or the Hughes people or Dr. Sinsky
have come up [with] contradicts the above. They find that there is no material
which refracts gravitational waves, nor can such waves be led along conductors
like electrical waves.

    I cld suggest then that both facts wld seem not so much negative as
evidence requiring a wholly different attitude toward them, the one I have
already put in 'our' terms, that is, that no material refracts them—they can't
be bent or focused—because they already are ('narrative'). Are in time. And
(2) don't conduct because like the figures under the hill they do something else,
directly. Figure, and event then, put it.

The enclosed, hopefully will also push the discussion another inch or two——O

To make absolutely sure that this discussion is on the table intended by it,
I ought as well to add this note [as a further "Addition"—and as of "other"

studies]: that I am here seeking to speak within, or across the 'range' of a principle of *likeness* which includes, and seeks to 'cover' what Henry Corbin reminds me is a constantly affirmed homology among *the initiatic cosmos, the world of nature,* and *the celestial world.*

[*Note added April 30th, 1969*]

Continuing Attempt to Pull the
Taffy off the Roof of the Mouth

the 9th, and 10th century?

Olaf Trygvasson, 969–1000

with Trygvasson's death — and Iceland
well begun

[possibility]

America was already beyond the expansion

by 1012 ? [cf. — or on reading,

Sunday July 28th 'LXVIII, Sauer on the

Greenlanders Saga   800?   Jibir

Islands
in the Atlantic — and   800   900   Alfred's death
in the World —
Oceanus   1000 end of

Karlsefni's   including the
sugar m[aple]   Arabic & to   1100: beginning of Ari
figurehead (sold for 4 ounces   prior to the Mon-
of gold,   gol   (400   1200, Snorri Stur-
Bremen —   European in- yrs)   lason
vasion!
of measle-wood or birds-eyed or   1200   —& 1220 Al'

[100 years]   sea-shore   maple   Araby's
abilities   circumvallum

      The Arabic went on. But so indeed, in Iceland, did
the Norse — the end of North-South Time
with the rise of the Germans, and the Germanic peoples,
& the time of the Mongols, made a Eurasia
which has been, until recently, a blind from within which
much which is now more interesting was not so easily
seen: the source of our language in
story-telling as much as Ari's inventions as it
      is anyone's   [1067–   say 1100]
                    1148,

                              and the birth
in England from Alfred (849–901) followed so soon after by Nor–
                              mans of our tongue

—already 54 years *after*
withdrawal of Norse from Hope colony
in Southern New England

200 years, 1775–
1968; or by the law of the woodlands to
Proclamation Line of
1763: end of French
(and Indian Power in North America

: crossings, concealments & curtailments of these orders of such 'times'

and such events are the nexus of what now can be taken as

trampoline nets or mattings we already
                              appointed
stand in, and are differently supported
to
in. It is a wholly otherwise than metal, and administrative,

time. I hope I can be followed

in registering it as *Armenian* or

wooden-runic and Goth - landers'

water-paths and wave-motion than

   all this cruel and iron-mongers time between

                                            (1969)

Abbreviations

Works by Charles Olson

AP   *Additional Prose,* ed. George F. Butterick (Bolinas, Calif.: Four Seasons Foundation, 1974)

ARCH   *Archaeologist of Morning* (London: Cape Goliard Press, 1970)

CP   *The Collected Poems of Charles Olson, Excluding "The Maximus Poems,"* ed. George F. Butterick (Berkeley: University of California Press, 1987)

FH   *The Fiery Hunt and Other Plays,* ed. George F. Butterick (Bolinas, CA: Four Seasons Foundation, 1977)

HU   *Human Universe and Other Essays,* ed. Donald Allen (San Francisco: Auerhahn Society, 1965)

MAX   *The Maximus Poems of Charles Olson,* ed. George F. Butterick (Berkeley: University of California Press, 1983)

M/G   *Maximus to Gloucester: The Letters and Poems of Charles Olson to the Editor of the Gloucester Daily Times 1962–1969,* ed. Peter Anastas (Gloucester: Ten Pound Island Book Company, 1992)

MUTH   *Muthologos: The Collected Lectures and Interviews,* 2 vols., ed. George F. Butterick (Bolinas, Calif.: Four Seasons Foundation, 1978 and 1979)

Nation   *A Nation of Nothing but Poetry: Supplementary Poems,* ed. George F. Butterick (Santa Rosa, Calif.: Black Sparrow Press, 1989)

O/CC	*Charles Olson and Cid Corman: Complete Correspondence 1950–1964,* 2 vols., ed. George Evans (Orono, ME: National Poetry Foundation, 1987 and 1991)
O/CS	"The Correspondences: Charles Olson and Carl Sauer," ed. Bob Callahan, *New World Journal,* Spring 1979, pp. 136–68
O/FB	"Charles Olson and Frances Boldereff: *Who Will Bring It Up, My Lute?* The First Letters of the Correspondence," ed. Ralph Maud and Sharon Thesen, *Sulfur,* no. 31, 1992, pp. 118–60.
OJ	*Olson: The Journal of the Charles Olson Archive,* nos. 1–10, ed. George F. Butterick (Storrs: University of Connecticut Library, 1974–1978)
O&P	*Charles Olson and Ezra Pound: An Encounter at St. Elizabeth's,* ed. Catherine Seelye (New York: Grossman Publishers, 1975)
O/RC	*Charles Olson and Robert Creeley: The Complete Correspondence,* ed. George F. Butterick (vols. 1–8) and Richard Blevins (vol. 9) (Santa Barbara and Santa Rosa, Calif.: Black Sparrow Press, 1980–1990)
PO	*The Post Office: A Memoir of His Father,* ed. George F. Butterick (San Francisco: Grey Fox Press, 1975)
SL	*Selected Letters of Charles Olson,* ed. Ralph Maud (Berkeley: University of California Press, forthcoming)
SV	*The Special View of History,* ed. Ann Charters (Berkeley, Calif.: Oyez, 1970)
SW	*Selected Writings,* ed. Robert Creeley (New York: New Directions, 1966)

Manuscript Collections

| Buf. | The Poetry / Rare Book Collection, University Libraries, State University of New York at Buffalo |
| Storrs | Charles Olson Papers, Thomas J. Dodd Research Center, University of Connecticut Libraries, Storrs |

A Note on Olson's Sources

Call Me Ishmael is, of all Olson's prose, the most densely worked through quotation; the majority of the quotations come from Melville (especially *Moby-Dick*), here cited to the Northwestern-Newberry editions of Melville's collected works. Olson himself owned the Standard Edition of the 1920s; Melville's letters, uncollected at the time, he knew from a number of sources, including manuscript.

Quotations from Shakespeare are here cited to *The Riverside Shakespeare*, ed. G. Blakemore Evans et al. (Boston: Houghton Mifflin, 1974).

Our goal has been to supply full bibliographic information for all quotations and to identify the most important of Olson's sources. Where possible, we provide both original dates of publication and citation to currently available editions.

Readers desiring a richer sense of Olson's sources are urged to consult Ralph Maud's *Olson's Reading* (Carbondale: Southern Illinois University Press, 1996), as well as George Butterick's invaluable *Guide to "The Maximus Poems" of Charles Olson* (Berkeley: University of California Press, 1978).

Editors' Notes

Call Me Ishmael

1 *Call Me Ishmael*

Olson's first book, named after *Moby-Dick*'s opening line. The title is especially apt, for one of Olson's chief concerns here is Melville's paternity as writer. (The biblical Ishmael is Abraham's scorned son, born to Hagar the Egyptian.) The heart of the book is Part II, a discussion of Melville's filial debt to Shakespeare, but *Ishmael*'s focus is not simply literary, and Melville's nonliterary progenitors (such as Owen Chase, whose story becomes "FIRST FACT") are of like importance. As made clear by the epigraph—a poem of Olson's own composition—the goal is to bring to light "a sone."

Written in a spurt in 1945, *Call Me Ishmael* originates in Olson's M.A. thesis, *The Growth of Herman Melville, Prose Writer and Poetic Thinker,* submitted in June 1933 at Wesleyan University. A subsequent Olin fellowship made possible a tracking down of Melville's library, including Melville's annotated copy of Shakespeare's plays. In this Olson laid the foundation for two foundational books in Melville studies: Merton M. Sealts, Jr., *Melville's Reading: A Checklist of Books Owned and Borrowed* (Cambridge, Mass.: Harvard University Press, 1950), and Walker Cowen's 1965 Harvard dissertation, *Melville's Marginalia.* Olson himself recorded his discovery in a paper written for F. O. Matthiessen's seminar at Harvard, where Olson was a doctoral candidate in the newly formed American Studies program. With Edward Dahlberg's assistance, a revision of that essay was placed in *Twice a Year* 1, Fall–Winter 1938. A subsequent Guggenheim fellowship led Olson to forsake graduate school in order to write a book on Melville, though his attempts at such a book were unsuccessful. From 1942 until 1945 he worked for the government, in the Foreign Language Division of the Office of War Information, and for the Democratic Party. With F. D. R.'s death and the end of World War II, Olson returned with renewed attention to Melville, researching the whaling industry at the Library of Congress and revisiting his abandoned notes and drafts. The many names of supporters inscribed in the final version indicate how tortuous the path had been.

Ishmael is one of several important studies that followed in the wake of the Melville revival of the 1920s. Written in the absence of scholarly editions, the book is partly based on archival research, and on notes and insights shared by a largely unknown and unpublished community of scholars. Sometimes the sharing shaded into competition; sometimes the competition became underhanded. Disaffection with conventional academic life was probably inevitable, and by 1951, in his "Letter for Melville" (*CP,* 233–41), Olson was offering public excoriation of the Melville Society. He nonetheless maintained cordial relations with many Melvilleans (Jay Leyda, Ronald Mason, Henry Murray, Merton Sealts) and continued to publish surveys of Melville scholarship until 1958 (see, e.g., "Equal, That Is, to the Real Itself").

Arguably, it is the composition of *Ishmael* that led Olson to discover himself as poet. In 1953, at Black Mountain College, he would write:

> My present purpose is to attack estrangement. . . .
>
> It started, for me, from a sensing of something I found myself obeying for some time before, in *Call Me Ishmael,* it got itself put down as *space,* a factor of experience I took as of such depth, width, and intensity that, unwittingly, I insisted upon it as fact . . . by telling three sorts of stories, . . . which I dubbed FIRST FACTS. . . .
>
> I knew no more then than what I did, than to put down *space* and *fact* and hope, by the act of sympathetic magic that words are apt to seem when one first uses them, that I would invoke for others those sensations of life I was small witness to, part doer of. But the act of writing the book added a third noun, equally abstract: *stance.* For after it was done, and other work in verse followed, I discovered that the fact of this space located a man differently in respect to any act, so much so and with such vexation that only in verse did I acquire any assurance that the stance was not in some way idiosyncratic and only sign of the limits of my own talent, only wretched evidence of the lack of my own engagement at the heart of life. (*OJ* 10:95–96)

3   CARESSE CROSBY . . . EZRA POUND

While living in Washington, D.C., in the 1940s, Olson visited Pound at St. Elizabeth's Hospital for the Criminally Insane, where Pound remained incarcerated until 1958, having been declared mentally unfit to stand trial for treason. Pound recommended in 1946 that Olson send the manuscript of *Ishmael* to T. S. Eliot at Faber, and though Eliot turned the book down, Pound's interest appears to have convinced the New York firm of Reynal and Hitchcock to go forward with publication. Olson met Crosby while operating as Pound's secretary, and the two became lifelong friends. In 1948, Crosby's Black Sun Press published Olson's first book of poems, *Y&X.*

Apart from acknowledging these debts, Olson may have wanted—following his book's theme and title—to inscribe *Ishmael* to two literary parents. If so, his Melville work had come full circle. Olson's first copy of *Moby-Dick,* the Modern Library edition of 1926 (preserved with Olson's library at Storrs), was a present from his mother and father, inscribed with the following prophetic injunction: "When o'er this book, you cast your eyes, / Forget your studies and Mobylize. / Each minute spent, some thought should bring / Of Gloucester scenes, and your old Viking, / Dad / & Mother / Dec. 27, 1929."

5   O fahter, fahter

Frances Boldereff wrote Olson, 20 May 1949, "I love very deeply—the lines at the opening of *Call Me Ishmael.* Are they early Swedish?" A return letter of 23 May 1949 answered, "They are early Olson." (*O/FB* 154, 155)

7   Contents

Olson himself prepared this table and apparently intended the minor discrepancies between contents page and text. As Ann Charters notes in *Olson/Melville: A Study in Affinity* (Berkeley, Calif.: Oyez, 1968), p. 27: "Heading the contents page is 'FIRST FACT is prologue.' On the section page following it in the book is 'FIRST FACT as prologue.' Not a misprint, for Olson explains in the essay 'Projective Verse' that 'is' comes from the Aryan root 'as,' meaning 'to breathe.' The FIRST FACT breathes prologue." In a footnote, Charters underscores her interpretation with reference to a personal communication from Olson: "Olson verifies that the Cape Edition (London, 1967) of *Ishmael,* which has 'FIRST FACT is prologue' on both pages, is in error."

11   FIRST FACT
The story Olson recounts here derives principally from Owen Chase's 1821 memoir, *Narrative of the Most Extraordinary and Distressing Shipwreck of the Whale-Ship Essex, of Nantucket,* consulted by Melville when writing *Moby-Dick.* (Melville quotes from the *Narrative* in Chapter 45, "The Affidavit.") Among Olson's sources for the later lives of the surviving crewmen are Melville's "memoranda" on the *Essex,* scribbled in a copy of Chase's memoir, and quoted below, at pp. 29–33.

17   from Folsom Cave to now
The "Folsom site" is not, in fact, a cave, but an open quarry outside Folsom, New Mexico, where George McJunkin, a black cowboy, discovered a flint spearpoint in 1927 near the bones of an extinct bison, pushing back to 10,000 years ago the date of human habitation of the continent. Olson may be thinking of Sandia Cave, outside Albuquerque, also occupied by Ice Age humans, discovered a decade after the Folsom site, in 1936. He mentions Sandia in *Pleistocene Man* (New York: Institute of Further Studies, 1968), a collection of letters to John Clarke: "I can confidently ASSURE YOU America *ALREADY HAS* PLENTY OF *HISTORY* for us to use our abstract powers ON: . . . Sandia, bug-eyed poor mortals living century on Millen[n]ia looking out top of mountain HOME on WATER   WATER   EVERYWHERE" (p. 8). Taken as a rebus of Folsom site and Sandia Cave, "Folsom Cave" stands as an early example of Olson's "logography." In 1963, in "The Advantage of Literacy Is That Words Can Be on the Page" (pp. 349, 350), Olson defines "logography" (word writing) as the use of "archeological discoveries" to supply an "etymology as well as alphabet *to write words by.*"

17   the first American story (Parkman's): exploration.
Francis Parkman, nineteenth-century American historian, author of *The Oregon Trail* and *France and England in North America* (part three of which is *LaSalle and the Discovery of the Great West*). In an 18 February 1952 letter to Robert Creeley, Olson writes, "Parkman—as you know—is one of those men I do not read enough (never, e.g., read OT— it is still LASALLE, or, THE DISCOVERY OF THE GREAT WEST, on which I base almost all that I have sd." Olson also writes in this letter, "i feel so often caught just between— exactly—Parkman's & HM's motions—still go along looking for the way to force Parkman's *materials* . . . to serve this thing which has always stood to me as HM's drive: the image." (*O/RC* 9 : 130–31)

19   Ortega y Gasset puts it
José Ortega y Gasset, *Revolt of the Masses* (New York: W. W. Norton, 1957), p. 160: "The Graeco-Roman does suffer an extraordinary blindness to the future. He does not see it, just as the colour-blind do not see red. But, on the other hand, he lives rooted in the past. Before doing anything *now,* he gives a step backwards, like *Lagarijo,* when preparing to kill." A translator's note identifies *Lagarijo* ("The Lizard") as the nickname of a "well-known bull-fighter."

19   as Fenollosa says
Ernest Fenollosa, *The Chinese Written Character as a Medium for Poetry,* ed. Ezra Pound (1936; San Francisco: City Lights Books, 1968), p. 24. Olson's earlier statement about "Logic and classification" may also derive from Fenollosa, who speaks against *"the inveterate logic of classification"* at p. 27.

21   This was his proposition:
In the 1850 essay, "Hawthorne and His Mosses," *The Piazza Tales and Other Prose Pieces 1839–1860,* ed. Harrison Hayford, Alma A. MacDougall, G. Thomas Tanselle, et al. (Evanston, Ill., and Chicago: Northwestern University Press and Newberry Library, 1987), p. 246.

21   his *crew,* a 'people,' Clootz and Tom Paine's people
In "Knights and Squires," Chapter 27 of *Moby-Dick, or The Whale,* ed. Harrison Hayford, Hershel Parker, and G. Thomas Tanselle (Evanston, Ill., and Chicago: Northwestern University Press and Newberry Library, 1988), Melville writes (p. 121): "They were nearly all islanders in the Pequod, *Isolatoes* too . . . each *Isolato* living on a separate continent of his own. Yet now, federated along one keel, what a set these Isolatoes were! An Anacharsis Clootz deputation from all the isles of the sea, and all the ends of the earth, accompanying Old Ahab in the Pequod to lay the world's grievances before that bar from which not very many of them ever come back." Melville refers to "Clootz" (a reference picked up from Carlyle) in *The Confidence Man* and *Billy Budd* as well.

23   we whalemen of America now outnumber
From "The Advocate," Chapter 24 of *Moby-Dick,* p. 109.

25   bottom dogs
No doubt an allusion to Edward Dahlberg's autobiographical novel of the same name, published in 1929 with an introduction by D. H. Lawrence. Olson's copy is inscribed "TO CHARLES OLSON— / whose genius I believe in & again *affirm* from his devoted & loving friend, Edward Dahlberg / Nov. 21 '38 N.Y.C." (*OJ* 2:72).

25   I insert here a document
Now included under the title "Melville's *Acushnet* Crew Memorandum" as an editorial appendix to the Northwestern-Newberry edition of *Moby-Dick.* First printed in 1921 by Raymond Weaver, in *Herman Melville: Mariner and Mystic* (New York: George H. Doran, 1921).

29   Usufruct
The right to take possession of someone else's property, temporarily. The material that
follows is included as an editorial appendix to the Northwestern-Newberry *Moby-Dick*,
pp. 971–95.

31   I publish these notes for the first time
Paul Metcalf gives one version of how Olson obtained the notes in *Enter Isabel: The Herman Melville Correspondence of Clare Spark and Paul Metcalf* (Albuquerque: University
of New Mexico Press, 1991), pp. 74–75:

> Seems [Howard Vincent, then writing *The Trying out of MOBY-DICK*, and Charles Ol-
> son] were having lunch together in Cambridge. Howard, who was not competitive or
> paranoid, mentioned excitedly that he had just discovered Melville's copy, with mar-
> ginal notations, of the Owen Chase narrative, the sinking of the Essex. Olson hit the
> ceiling. WHERE IS IT? Howard blandly told him, some collection in New York. This may
> be exaggeration but, being Olson, it may not: he got up from the table caught the
> subway to South Station, boarded the first train to New York, found the collection,
> found the book, copied everything he wanted, and eventually put it into print, as his
> own discovery. Never credited Howard. On the contrary, proceeded to attack him, in
> print, as "that middle-western minister's son."

Olson himself, in a 14 June 1950 letter to Jay Leyda, declares that "at no time, when I saw
that material in my hands was not going to be used by me have I, I think I can accurately
say, blocked anyone else. Yet I have ruthlessly—the marked example is the *Essex* book—
tore in and took away, when, as in that case, I had been hunting the book since 1933!"
(*SL*) The "attack" on Vincent referred to by Metcalf appears in Olson's "Letter for Melville
1951" (*CP* 233–41).

31   friends Tripp of New Bedford and Stackpole of Nantucket
William H. Tripp, curator of the Old Dartmouth Historical Society and Whaling Museum in
New Bedford, Mass., and Edouard A. Stackpole, President of the Nantucket Historical
Association.

31   Dr and Mrs Will Gardner
Of Nantucket Island. Dr. Gardner was a local whaling historian with whom Olson dis-
cussed the *Essex*. Olson owned an inscribed copy of Gardner's *Three Bricks and Three
Brothers: The Story of the Nantucket Whale-Oil Merchant Joseph Starbuck* (Cambridge,
Mass.: Whaling Museum Publications, Nantucket Island, 1945).

39   Evert Duyckinck reported to his brother
The letter appears in Eleanor Melville Metcalf, *Herman Melville: Cycle and Epicycle* (Cambridge, Mass.: Harvard University Press, 1953), pp. 83–84.

39   Highborn stealth, Edward Dahlberg calls originality,
Section VII of Dahlberg's *Do These Bones Live* (New York: Harcourt, Brace, 1941), contains
the following dedication and admission (p. 104): "Inscribed to my very dear Friend,
Charles Olson: My dear Charles: Literature, we know, is the art of ripening ourselves

by conversation; and originality is but high-born stealth. How much of our talks have yeasted and bloomed this little Herman Melville loaf; and how I have played the cut-purse Autolycus, making my thefts as invisible as possible, you and my blushes best know. . . . "

39 Thomas Beale's *The Natural History of the Sperm Whale.*
Cited by Melville in Chapters 32 and 56 of *Moby-Dick.*

40 a letter to his father-in-law
Lemuel Shaw, on 6 October 1849. See Herman Melville, *Correspondence,* ed. Lynn Horth (Evanston, Ill., and Chicago: Northwestern University Press and Newberry Library, 1993), p. 138.

40 So he told Richard Henry Dana
The author of *Two Years before the Mast,* to whom Lawrence devotes a chapter in *Studies in Classic American Literature.* The lines quoted here and below appear in Melville's letter of 1 May 1850 (*Correspondence,* pp. 162 and 160, respectively).

40 "Dollars damn me."
From Melville's 1 June 1851 letter to Nathaniel Hawthorne, *Correspondence,* p. 191.

40 "to refrain from writing the kind . . . "
This excerpt as well as the two below ("In writing these two books . . . I feel" and "So far as . . . 'fail'") are from Melville's 6 October 1849 letter to Lemuel Shaw, *Correspondence,* p. 138.

41 I somehow cling to the strange fancy
"Hawthorne and His Mosses," *Piazza Tales,* p. 253.

41 Ahab of "the globular brain and ponderous heart"
Chapter 16 of *Moby-Dick,* "The Ship," p. 73.

41 Bulkington, the secret member of the crew in Moby-Dick, is here, hidden,
In "Hawthorne and His Mosses." The quotation—from Hawthorne's "The Intelligence Office"—reads in part:

> "A man now entered, in neglected attire, with the aspect of a thinker, but somewhat too rough-hewn and brawny for a scholar. . . . He advanced to the Intelligencer, and looked at him with a glance of such stern sincerity, that perhaps few secrets were beyond its scope.
> "'I seek for Truth', said he." (*Piazza Tales,* p. 250)

In Chapter 3 of *Moby-Dick,* "The Spouter Inn," Bulkington is described as "six feet in height, with noble shoulders, and a chest like a coffer-dam" (p. 16); in Chapter 23, "The Lee Shore," he enters for a second and last time, to illustrate "that mortally intolerable truth; that all deep, earnest thinking is but the intrepid effort of the soul to keep the open independence of her sea" (p. 107).

42   It is an edition in glorious great type,
Redacted from Melville's letter to Hawthorne of 24 February 1849, *Correspondence,*
p. 119. Olson's "sperms" is apparently a mistranscription; Melville has "sparrows."

42   A note of thanks
Eleanor Melville Metcalf, Melville's granddaughter, and her husband, Henry, very nearly
adopted Olson during Olson's student years in the 1930s. Through the Metcalfs Olson
met Weaver (author of the first biography of Melville) and Henry A. Murray, Jr. (founder
of the Harvard Psychological Clinic and editor of the Hendricks House *Pierre*). Robert
Bertholf in his essay "On Olson, His Melville," *Io,* no. 22, 1976, pp. 5–36, quotes a 1945
letter from Olson to John Woodburn describing the alliance with Weaver and Murray:
"Weaver, Harry Murray and I have formed an unholy three against the scholars. They
like none of us. They have always sniped at Weaver's book, they will give mine no
break, and they have long talked down Harry Murray's minute biography to come.
Maybe it's because in their own world of documents, the three of us have, successfully,
scooped them" (p. 26). Carl Van Doren had supported Olson's Melville studies since the
early 1930s and expected great things (*Ishmael* came as a disappointment); Van Wyck
Brooks wrote a recommendation for Olson's 1939 Guggenheim application. Mrs. Francis
Osborne, another granddaughter of Melville, actually held possession of Melville's library,
or some ninety-five volumes from the library, including Melville's Shakespeare. Eleanor
Metcalf's own work on Melville would not appear until after the publication of *Call Me
Ishmael.* Her edition of Melville's *Journal of a Visit to London and the Continent, 1849–
1850* (Cambridge, Mass.: Harvard University Press, 1948) was preceded by *Herman
Melville: Cycle and Epicycle.*

43   as he put it to Duyckinck
In a letter of 24 February 1849, *Correspondence,* p. 119.

43   I would to God Shakepseare had lived later,
Letter of 3 March 1849, *Correspondence,* p. 122.

43   In Shakespeare's tomb lies infinitely more
"Hawthorne and His Mosses," *Piazza Tales,* p. 244.

43   In his copy of the PLAYS
See Walker Cowen, *Melville's Marginalia* (New York: Garland, 1987), 2:440 (*Antony and
Cleopatra* 2:2:108), and 2:467 (*King Lear* 1:4:111–13).

44   those deep far-away things in him
This excerpt and the one below ("craftily says . . . hint of them!") are from "Hawthorne
and His Mosses," *Piazza Tales,* p. 244.

44   Swinburne's comment
In Section III of *A Study of Shakespeare:* "We have heard much and often from the theo-
logians of the light of revelation: and some such thing we find in Aeschylus: but the
darkness of revelation is here." The passage continues with words equally applicable to

Melville's dark masterpiece: "For in this most terrible work of human genius it is with the very springs and sources of nature that her student has set himself to deal. The veil of the temple of our humanity is rent in twain. Nature herself, we might say, is revealed—and revealed as unnatural." *The Complete Works of Algernon Charles Swinburne*, ed. Sir Edmund Gosse and Thomas James Wise, *Prose Works* (Bonchurch Edition, 1925; New York: Russell and Russell, 1968), 1 : 123–24.

44 Though in many of its aspects
Moby-Dick, Chapter 17, "The Whiteness of the Whale," p. 195.

45 In The Tempest . . . Melville encircles . . . and writes
See *Melville's Marginalia* 2 : 356 (*The Tempest* 5 : 1 : 183–84).

45 Shakespeare frequently expresses disillusion
The annotations cited in this paragraph are noted in *Melville's Marginalia* 2 : 437–38, 2 : 420–21, 2 : 409, 2 : 403, 2 : 467, and 2 : 476 (*Hamlet* 3 : 2 : 207–9).

46 Jack Chase
Dedicatee of *Billy Budd, Sailor* and captain of the frigate *United States*, where Melville served as midshipman in 1843–44. Chapter 4 of Melville's *White-Jacket*, "Jack Chase," gives a loving portrait.

46 the only place Melville heavily marks
See *Melville's Marginalia* 2 : 428–29 (*Coriolanus* 4 : 5 : 115–18).

46 In a poem of his later years
"Monody," published in *Timolean* (1891), included now as an appendix to Melville's *Clarel, A Poem and Pilgrimage in the Holy Land*, ed. Harrison Hayford, Alma A. Mac-Dougall, Hershel Parker, and G. Thomas Tanselle (Evanston, Ill., and Chicago: Northwestern University Press and Newberry Library, 1991), along with speculations as to the poem's subject, which many presume to be Hawthorne.

46 Timon
See *Melville's Marginalia* 2 : 423–24 (*Timon of Athens* 3 : 2 : 64).

47 Melville points to prove Shakespeare's insinuations
See *Piazza Tales*, p. 244, for both of the cited passages.

47 He found them in such other speeches of that boy,
See *Melville's Marginalia* 2 . 467 (*King Lear* 1 : 4 : 100–101).

48 the positive qualities in the depraved
See *King Lear* 5 : 3 : 240 and *Melville's Marginalia* 2 : 473 for Edmund's line and Melville's markings.

48 Melville is dumb with horror
See *King Lear* 3 : 7 : 28 and *Melville's Marginalia* 2 : 468 for Regan's comment and Melville's markings.

48 Wisdom and goodness to the vile
King Lear 4:2:38–39. The phrase "vile jelly" appears at 3:7:83.

49 "I stumbled when I saw."
King Lear 4:1:19. Lear's speech occurs at 3:4:28–36. Gloucester's lines cited immediately after ("Might I but live . . . again!") appear at 4:1:23–24.

49 He seconds Lear thus:
See *Melville's Marginalia* 2:469 (*King Lear* 4:1:64–71).

50 And he leaves Ishmael at the end to tell the tale
The lines of "Ishmael" cited here (i.e., Kent's) are marked by Melville. See *Melville's Marginalia* 2:474 (*King Lear* 5:3:314–16).

51 I transcribe them as they stand:
The holograph is reproduced in the Northwestern-Newberry *Moby-Dick.* See also *Melville's Marginalia* 2:483.

51 what Melville told Hawthorne
In a letter of 29 June 1851, *Correspondence,* p. 196. The phrase appears in Chapter 113 of *Moby-Dick,* "The Forge," p. 489.

52 I have written a wicked book
Letter of 17 November 1851, *Correspondence,* p. 212.

52 *Moby-Dick* includes both Ahab and Pip
The three quoted phrases that follow are from Chapter 41 ("Moby-Dick") and Chapter 93 ("The Castaway"), at pp. 185 and 414.

53 Right reason, and Alma (Christ), are the same;
Herman Melville, *Mardi and a Voyage Hither,* ed. Harrison Hayford, Hershel Parker, and G. Thomas Tanselle (Evanston, Ill., and Chicago: Northwestern University Press and Newberry Library, 1970), Chapter 187, "They Land," p. 629.

54 Pip is mad,
The quotations that follow are from Chapter 93 of *Moby-Dick,* "The Castaway," p. 414, and Chapter 27, "Knights and Squires," p. 121.

54 "The Doubloon"
Chapter 99. The description of Starbuck is from Chapter 41, "Moby Dick," p. 186, and "The Doubloon," p. 432. The rest is from "The Doubloon," pp. 431 and 435.

54 Bulkington
See note to p. 41. The quoted lines are from the same passages cited there.

55 Like the Catskill eagle
Mentioned at the end of Chapter 96 of *Moby-Dick,* "The Try-Works": "There is a wisdom that is woe; but there is a woe that is wisdom. And there is a Catskill eagle in some souls

that can alike dive down into the blackest gorges, and soar out of them again and become invisible in the sunny spaces."

56   In his fiery eyes of scorn and triumph
The last lines of Chapter 124 of *Moby-Dick*, "The Needle," p. 519. The two sentences below ("Hands off that holiness!" and "Thou touchest my inmost centre, boy") are from Chapter 125, "The Log and Line," p. 522.

57   hold ye then there can be
Chapter 16 of *Moby-Dick*, "The Ship," p. 79. The lines below are all from the book's conclusion: Chapter 127, "The Deck," p. 529 ("I do suck . . . from thee"); Chapter 128, "The Pequod Meets the Rachel," p. 532 ("a voice that . . . every word"); Chapter 132, "The Chase—First Day," p. 547 ("life-line"); and Chapter 132, "The Symphony," p. 544 ("God! . . . stave my brain!").

58   "Cold, cold . . . "
Chapter 133 of *Moby-Dick*, "The Chase—First Day," p. 553. The following citations are from Chapter 134, "The Chase—Second Day," pp. 561–62 ("The whole act's immutably decreed" and "heliotrope glance"); and Chapter 135, "The Chase—Third Day," p. 571 ("oh, lonely death . . . topmost grief"). Pip's cry is abstracted from Chapter 129, "The Cabin."

59   all thy strange mummeries
Last line of Chapter 113, "The Forge," p. 490.

60   "unwar strook the regnes that had been proude."
Chaucer, from "The Monk's Tale."

60   through these forms that certain sultanism
Chapter 33, "The Specksynder," pp. 147–48.

61   In at least three places Melville analyzes Hamlet.
In *Pierre or The Ambiguities,* ed. Harrison Hayford, Hershel Parker, and G. Thomas Tanselle (Evanston, Ill., and Chicago: Northwestern University Press and Newberry Library, 1971), Book 7, Section 6, and Book 9, Section 2; and in *The Confidence Man,* ed. Harrison Hayford, Hershel Parker, and G. Thomas Tanselle (Evanston, Ill., and Chicago: Northwestern University Press and Newberry Library, 1984), Chapter 44—this last quoted below ("like a revolving . . .") from p. 239.

62   "a mighty mildness of repose in swiftness."
Chapter 133, "The Chase—First Day," p. 548.

63   "nervous, lofty."
Chapter 16 of *Moby-Dick*, "The Ship," p. 73.

64   TAMMANY HALL
See *Melville's Marginalia* 2 : 431 (*Julius Caesar* 1 : 2 : 158–61).

64 "hurled higher than a throne."
Adapted from the end of "Knights and Squires," Chapter 26 of *Moby-Dick*.

64 this august dignity I treat of,
Chapter 26 of *Moby-Dick*, "Knights and Squires," p. 117.

65 It is necessary now to consider *Antony and Cleopatra*,
See *Melville's Marginalia* 2:448, 2:451–52 (*Antony and Cleopatra* 3:13:194–99, 4:8:13, 4:15:63, 5:2:82–83).

66 "poor old whale-hunter,"
This line and those below describing Ahab are from Chapter 33, "The Specksynder," pp. 147–48, except "a khan of the plank . . . leviathans," from Chapter 30, "The Pipe," p. 129, and "a Grand-lama-like exclusiveness," from Chapter 106, "Ahab's Leg," p. 464. The "Iron Crown of Lombardy" isn't hollow, but "heavy." See Chapter 37, "Sunset," p. 167. "All scatt'red" comes from Shakespeare's *Richard III*, 1:4:28.

67 FACT # 2 DROMENON
Jane E. Harrison in *Ancient Art and Ritual* (1913; London: Oxford University Press, 1951) writes, at p. 35:

> The Greek word for a *rite* . . . is *dromenon*, "a thing done"—and the word is full of instruction. The Greek had realized that to perform a rite you must *do* something, that is, you must not only feel something but express it in action. . . . It is a fact of cardinal importance that their word for theatrical representation, *drama*, is own cousin to their word for rite, *dromenon; drama* also means "things done." Greek linguistic instinct pointed plainly to the fact that art and ritual are near relations.

Regarding the story of the *Globe*, Olson has the following in an unpublished, untitled essay on Melville from 1948:

> I have buried the act of mutiny in the soil of CALL ME ISHMAEL, at the root, out of my belief that the motive [of] mutiny was the root, the radical of Melville. There are [those] who see this need of his to rebel against authority, [of] which Ahab is his fine image, as theological, the fruit of the long Puritan past, protestant. Myself, I take it to be more vital, and speaking to our time, of the order of revolution, a reflection of the social and economic violence of America in his time, and a projection of what we now are experiencing. We know nothing if we do not see this chaos as of long shaping. Melville felt man in his frustrations more than his glories, saw him cracking the elements, blindly, as a wild man with an axe, the consequence of space unmeasured, the hold on object gone, and, with touch broken, violence the only law. His statement went sour [for "sour" Olson first wrote "romantic"], but his act, Ahab as tropism, stayed true. And that is why *Moby-Dick* is worth the lot of what we've had. We now have his need and urge: to put an end to the sea of question. Is it to be wondered at, that to mutiny seemed to act, to clean, . . . to make a fresh, a first start? Mutiny, translated from the sea, is known on land as revolution. (Storrs, Prose Series)

73 "athirst for human blood."
Chapter 41, "Moby Dick," p. 181. The other quotations are from Chapter 31, "Queen Mab," p. 133 ("that that's bloody on his mind"); Chapter 58, "Brit," p. 273 ("forever and

forever . . . man"); and Chapter 57, "Of Whales in Paint, in Teeth, &c.," p. 270 ("I myself am . . . against him").

73   (Nothing is without efficient cause)
The phrase serves as headnote to the front matter of Ezra Pound's *Jefferson and/or Mussolini; L'Idea Statale; Fascism as I Have Seen It* (1935; New York: Liveright, 1970). The silent allusion to Pound's fascism, in a section of *Ishmael* called "Moses," offers telling insight into Olson's own agonizings "over paternity" (p. 73). Pound's motto recurs in the 1965 *Bibliography on America for Ed Dorn* (p. 309).

73   "Polar eternities" behind "Saturn's gray chaos."
These quotations and "antemosaic unsourced . . . whale" (below) are from Chapter 104, "The Fossil Whale," *Moby-Dick,* p. 457.

74   Enceladus
One of the twenty-four giants who battled the Olympian gods, "enraged because Zeus had confined their brothers, the Titans"; Enceladus was subsequently crushed by Athena "and became the island Sicily" (Robert Graves, *The Greek Myths* [New York: Penguin, 1992], pp. 131–32). Olson returns to this mythological event in *Proprioception,* in the section "A Work."

74   + "his sickle-shaped lower jaw . . . in the field"
Chapter 41 of *Moby-Dick,* "Moby Dick," p. 184. The quotations below ("an audacious . . . revenge" and "piled upon . . . Adam down") are from the same chapter, pp. 184, 186.

74   Jonathan Edwards. His answer to the angry god
A reference to Edwards's best-known sermon, "Sinners in the Hands of an Angry God." The sentence below ("Talk not to me . . . ") is from Chapter 36 of *Moby-Dick,* "The Quarter-Deck," p. 164.

74   "sweet milk"
See Melville's footnote on p. 388 of *Moby-Dick,* in Chapter 87, "The Grand Armada." Malcolm speaks of "universal peace" in *Macbeth* at 4:3:97–99.

75   Thou seest the heavens,
Macbeth 2:4:5–6.

75   Ahab's birth was dark,
The quotations in this paragraph are from *Moby-Dick,* Chapter 132, "The Symphony," p. 544 ("more demon than man" and "deadly faint . . . Adam"); Chapter 118, "The Quadrant," p. 502 ("old man of oceans"); Chapter 41, "Moby Dick," p. 186 ("gnawed . . . without").

75   "slender rod-like mark, lividly whitish"
Chapter 28 of *Moby-Dick,* "Ahab," p. 123.

75   Oh, thou clear spirit, of thy fire
Chapter 99 of *Moby-Dick,* "The Candles," p. 507.

75   an antique buried beneath antiquities
This quotation and the three that follow are from Chapter 41, "Moby-Dick," pp. 185–86.

79   for Edward Dahlberg
The dedication of this "Christ" chapter to Dahlberg (a writer whose most formative experience as a child was his stint in a Jewish orphanage) makes the Ishmaelite Dahlberg "an unnatural twin" to the anti-Semitic Pound, whose spirit is silently invoked in the previous chapter, titled "Moses." (This, perhaps, is what Olson means by "other genius.") "The Cross and the Windmills" is the title of Section VI of Dahlberg's *Do These Bones Live*, a discussion of Don Quixote.

79   Melville read *Don Quixote*
See *Melville's Marginalia* 1:430, 1:432, and 1:436.

80   A relative who came to call . . . reported her conversation
Sarah Morewood to George Duyckinck, 28 December 1851, quoted in *Herman Melville: Cycle and Epicycle*, p. 133.

81   Hawthorne describes him
In *The English Notebooks*, ed. Randall Stewart (New York: Russell and Russell, 1962), pp. 432–33, entry for 20 November 1856. Melville's comment ("good talk") is given in an editorial note in *The English Notebooks*, cited from a 12 November 1856 entry in Melville's journal.

81   This afternoon Dr Taylor and I sketched a plan
Herman Melville, *Journals*, ed. Howard C. Horsford and Lynn Horth (Evanston, Ill., and Chicago: Northwestern University Press and Newberry Library, 1989), p. 7.

82   Raymond Weaver has, after much labor,
Herman Melville, *Journal up the Straits: October 11, 1856–May 5, 1857*, ed. Raymond Weaver (New York: Colophon, 1935). Olson's annotated copy shows signs of Olson's own shaping of Melville's report in some of the quotations offered later on in the text. See the note to p. 85 below.

82   He remained periodically violent to his wife,
Apparently the first explicit reference in print to Melville's conjectured wife-beating. Olson's source is no doubt anecdotal—stories told by Eleanor Melville Metcalf, or perhaps by one of the other Melvilleans to whom Eleanor Metcalf was close. In *Enter Isabel* (pp. 14–15), Eleanor's son, Paul Metcalf, reports "a curious story, very much garbled . . . told to me by Charles. How Charles got this story, . . . how much of it is real goods, or how much was embellished (or even invented) by Olson, I simply don't know—but there was something about Herman beating on Lizzie, about Herman coming home one night drunk and throwing her down the back stairs."

In 1975 two letters came to light (one by Elizabeth Melville, the other by her brother, Samuel S. Shaw), which brought the issue into the open. Both letters are addressed to the Reverend Henry W. Bellows and reveal a plan to sneak Elizabeth out of the house, presumably in order to rescue her from physical abuse. The letters are now included as an editorial appendix to the Northwestern-Newberry *Correspondence,* pp. 857–60. For a careful study of this matter and a survey of how critics and scholars have dealt with it, see Elizabeth Renker, *Strike through the Mask: Herman Melville and the Scene of Writing* (Baltimore, Md.: Johns Hopkins University Press, 1996).

82   Sunday 23d.
Melville, *Journals,* p. 52.

83   in the "Lee Shore" chapter of *Moby-Dick*
Chapter 23, p. 107.

83   He likens the city to a woman:
Melville, *Journals,* p. 58.

83   "zone unbound,"
Chapter 194 of *Mardi,* "Taji with Hautia," p. 650.

84   To the Bazaar. A wilderness of traffic.
Melville, *Journals,* pp. 59–60.

84   "a contest of beauty."
Melville, *Journals,* p. 64. The quotation below ("like those Asiatic lions . . . ") appears on p. 68.

85   THE PYRAMIDS loom,
The long passage from Melville's journal presented here is Olson's own construction, edited from his copy of *Journal up the Straits* (as the markings in Olson's copy at Storrs reveal).

86   Stones of Judea. . . /Barrenness of Judea. . . .
The two phrases are from Melville's *Journals,* pp. 90 and 83, respectively. The intervening quotation ("back to desert . . . verdure") occurs on p. 76.

86   "bitumen & ashes,"
Melville, *Journals,* p. 83. The other phrases cited here occur as follows: "like slaver of mad dog" (p. 83), "a sickening cheat" (p. 88), "Is the desolation . . . Deity?" (p. 91).

87   "Poor soul, the centre of my sinful earth," Shakespeare wrote.
Opening line of Sonnet 146.

87   But I feel that I am now come to the inmost leaf
Letter of 1 June 1851, *Correspondence,* p. 193.

87   By vast pains we mine into the pyramid;
Pierre, Book 21, Section 1, p. 285.

87   Death bothered him. . . . in Dickinson's words, like a wasp.
In his abandoned Melville book Olson says just the opposite: "Melville gave little thought to death; an horror of dissolve, rhetoric the rest. But Dickinson, wired with nerves, knew

death in constant sting and startle. The winter she first made poems she wrote: 'That bareheaded life, under the grass, worries one like a wasp.'" (*In Adullam's Lair,* Archetype One [State University of Binghamton, 1975], p. 8)

The Dickinson line comes from a letter of about 1860 to Samuel Bowles.

87   Behold him . . . repulse.
These lines and the one below ("Upbraider! . . . ") come from Melville's *Clarel,* Part 1, Canto 13 ("The Arch"), lines 62–64 and 48.

88   Of old Greek times . . . heaven!
Pierre, Book 12, Section 3, p. 198.

88   Somewhere Yeats uses the phrase "sighing after Jerusalem. . ."
Possibly in *A Vision* (1925; New York: Macmillan, 1961), p. 161: "For a moment that fragment, that relation, which is our very being, is broken; they are at Udan Adan 'wailing upon the edge of nonentity, wailing for Jerusalem, with weak voices almost inarticulate'; and yet full submission has not come."

88   He made his act of faith in *Mardi:*
In Chapter 119, "Dreams," p. 368.

88   He wrote in *Mardi:*
See Chapter 97, "Faith and Knowledge," p. 297.

89   "I hate the world."
Not a direct quotation, but perhaps suggested by Book 26, Section 4, of *Pierre,* p. 357: "Here I step out before the drawn-up worlds in widest space, and challenge one and all of them to battle! Oh, Glen! oh, Fred! most fraternally do I leap to your rib-crushing hugs! Oh, how I love ye two, that can make me lively hate, in a world which elsewise only merits stagnant scorn."

89   "Herman Melville's linen is none too clean."
Hawthorne, *The English Notebooks,* p. 432: "[Melville] is a person of very gentlemanly instincts in every respect, save that he is a little heterodox in the matter of clean linen."

89   What Cosmic jest . . . life's gate?
These lines and the one above ("the idiot . . . straw") come from "After the Pleasure Party," *Collected Poems of Herman Melville,* ed. Howard P. Vincent (Chicago: Hendricks House, 1947), pp. 217, 219.

90n.   The note in Melville's hand reads:
See *Melville's Marginalia* 1:435.

90   parsed into being like the Carpenter in *Moby-Dick.*
See Chapter 127, "The Deck."

90   "like halves of apple sweet"
From *Clarel,* Part 1, Canto 31 ("Rolfe"), line 56. The verses below appear as follows: "After confidings . . . withstood" (Part 2, Canto 27 ["Vine and Clarel"], lines 108–112); "no trace of passion's soil" (Part 1, Canto 29 ["The Récluse"], lines 14–15); "Adam's secret frame" (Book 1, Canto 32 ["Of Rama"], line 46); "crook and lump" (Book 1, Canto 12 ["Celio"], line 43. "Disuse of voice" is not from *Clarel* and remains unidentified.

91   Maurice de Guérin
Quoted by Matthew Arnold in *Essays in Criticism,* acquired by Melville in 1869. See *Melville's Marginalia* 1:30.

91   "on Mt. Olivet . . . "
Melville, *Journals,* p. 95.

91   "gentle awful stirrings" to the "fabled undulations . . . "
Chapter 111 of *Moby-Dick,* "The Pacific," p. 482.

91   "no more realize . . . "
Melville, *Journals,* p. 97. The phrase continues, "than when off Juan Fernandez, could beleive [*sic*] in Robinson Crusoe according to De Foe."

95   A last fact
Pollard was captain of the *Essex,* whose story Olson tells in *Call Me Ishmael*'s opening salvo. In *Clarel* (Part 1, Canto 37, "A Sketch"), Melville offers a verse portrait of this tragic figure.

99   for Constance
Constance Wilcock Olson Bunker, Olson's first wife. The two met in 1940 and entered into a common-law marriage the next year; a daughter, Kate, was born in 1951; the marriage ended during Olson's tenure at Black Mountain College.

101   MOBY-DICK / Chapter CXI / "The Pacific"
This and the passage on p. 102 ("this mysterious, divine Pacific . . . ") appear on pp. 482–83.

102   the little Negro Pip,
The Pip quotations are from *Moby-Dick,* Chapter 93, "The Castaway," p. 414 ("wondrous depths . . . passive eyes" and "God's foot . . . the loom"); Chapter 9, "The Sermon," p. 47 ("ocean's utmost bones"); Chapter 32, "Cetology," p. 136 ("To have one's hands thing"); and Chapter 94, "The Gilder," p. 492 ("Where is the foundling's . . . learn it"). The phrase "grim sire" appears in Chapter 41, "Moby-Dick," p. 186.

103   "This is the form of him whom one may not name, Osiris . . . "
Taken from Jane Harrison's *Ancient Art and Ritual,* p. 17.

103   In *Mardi* Melville wrote:
Not in *Mardi;* the source remains unidentified.

103   And meet it is, that over these sea-pastures,
Chapter 111 of *Moby-Dick*, "The Pacific," p. 482.

104   Fanning, Delano. . . . Wilkes
Edmund Fanning, author of *Voyages & Discoveries in the South Seas 1792–1832* (1833; Salem, Mass.: Marine Research Society, 1924); Amasa Delano, author of *A Narrative of Voyages and Travels in the Northern and Southern Hemisphere* (Boston, 1817), long stretches of which Melville incorporated into "Benito Cereno"; Charles Wilkes, author of *Narrative of the United States Exploring Expedition, during the Years 1838, 1839, 1840, 1840, 1841, 1842,* 2 vols. (London: Ingram, Cooke, 1852) (a conjectured source for Melville's account of tatooing in *Typee*).

104   when Commodore Perry wanted a writer . . . Hawthorne
On 28 December 1854, Hawthorne wrote in his journal:

> COMMODORE PERRY called. . . . He soon introduced his particular business with me—
> it being to inquire whether I could recommend some suitable person to prepare his
> notes and materials for the publication of an account of his voyage. . . . I spoke of
> Herman Melville, and one or two others; but he seems to have some acquaintance
> with the literature of the day, and did not grasp very cordially at any name that I could
> think of. (*The English Notebooks,* p. 98)

104   In the *Inferno* he speaks
In Canto 26, p. 141 of the Carlyle-Wicksteed translation of *The Divine Comedy* (New York: Modern Library, 1932).

105   Porphyry wrote
Cited by Yeats in "Earth, Fire and Water," *The Celtic Twilight,* which Olson owned as part of *Early Poems and Stories* (New York: Macmillan, 1925), p. 237.

On Melville, Dostoevsky, Lawrence, and Pound

109   "David Young, David Old"
This essay first appeared in *Western Review* 14:1, Fall 1949; reprinted in *HU.*

109   Hart Crane's natural and personal interest in . . . the Handsome Sailor,
A figure described in the opening paragraph of "Billy Budd." Olson makes his own interest known in Maximus, in the story of James Merry (ripped to shreds in Dogtown "by the bulls he raised himself to fight / in front of people, to show off his / Handome Sailor ism" [*MAX* 172]).

109   Auden's verses on Melville
"Herman Melville," pp. 146–47 of *The Collected Poetry* (New York: Random House, 1945).

109   Raymond Weaver, that Tobias. . . . Eleanor Melville Metcalf,
Olson recorded his appreciation of Weaver, "the gracious first spokesman of Herman Melville," in an unpublished obituary from 1948:

His death is poignant in the essential loneliness and silenc[e] of his lif[e].
    Against tha[t] stand[s] his Melville book, a rich, full mannered text, a book out of some earlier literary period, 17th century I'm led to say, when form was personal and allusive, and men let their own flesh into work, before th[e] 18th century closed down.
    . . . He was a Tobias, and now he has met his angel. (Storrs, Prose Series)

Tobias is the son of Tobit; he meets with the angel Raphael in the apocryphal Book of Tobit. Weaver and Metcalf are also mentioned in *Call Me Ishmael.* See the note to p. 42 above.

109   Richard Chase . . . from other needs
In "Dissent on *Billy Budd*," *Partisan Review* 15, Nov. 1948, Chase argues (p. 1218): "Billy Budd is pre-eminently the beatified boy of the liberal-progressive myth, the figure who gets 'pushed around,' the figure 'to whom things happen.' His suffering and death are without moral content."

111   this Anak of a man
Numbers 13:33 refers to "the giants, the sons of Anak, which come of the giants"—a phrase Melville borrows in his Hawthorne essay to describe "those neglected old authors," Shakespeare's contemporaries (*Piazza Tales,* p. 253).

111   Jack Chase
See note to *Call Me Ishmael,* p. 46 above.

112   Was it not Heraclitus who said
Apparently not. Olson may have in mind a passage from Plato's *Timaeus,* included in Benjamin Jowett's translation in *The Portable Greek Reader,* ed. W. H. Auden (New York: Viking Press, 1948), a book Olson owned and avidly read:

> The heart, the knot of the veins and the fountain of the blood which races through all the limbs, was set in the place of guard, that when the might of passion was roused by reason making proclamation of any wrong assailing them from without or being perpetrated by the desires within, quickly the whole power of feeling in the body, perceiving these commands and threats, might obey and follow through every turn and alley, and thus allow the principle of the best to have the command in all of them. (P. 149)

113   "The Materials and Weights of Herman Melville"
This omnibus review of two books of Melville criticism and the Hendricks House edition of *Moby-Dick* first appeared in two parts, in the 8 and 15 September 1952 issues of *New Republic;* reprinted in *HU.* For a sense of the review's background, see Olson's letter of 16 March 1952 to Cid Corman. Ronald Mason later contributed an essay on Melville's poetry to the second issue of *Black Mountain Review.*

113   the bead-telling books of the last years
F. O. Matthiessen, *American Renaissance: Art and Expression in the Age of Emerson and Whitman* (New York: Oxford University Press, 1941); William Sedgwick, *Herman Melville: The Tragedy of Mind* (Cambridge, Mass.: Harvard University Press, 1944); Richard Chase, *Herman Melville: A Critical Study* (New York: Macmillan, 1949); Newton Arvin, *Herman*

Melville (New York: William Sloane, 1950); Van Wyck Brooks, *The Times of Melville and Whitman* (New York: E. P. Dutton, 1947); Yvor Winters, *Maule's Curse: Seven Studies in the History of American Obscurantism* (Norfolk, Va.: New Directions, 1938); W. H. Auden, *The Enchaféd Flood or the Romantic Iconography of the Sea* (New York: Random House, 1950); Geoffrey Stone, *Melville* (New York: Sheed and Ward, 1949). Olson's phrase "a rosary of praise" is diplomatic. The year before, Olson's "strangered" friend Edward Dahlberg (the word is Dahlberg's) publicly accused Arvin of plagiarizing *Call Me Ishmael* (see "Laurels for Borrowers" in *Samuel Beckett's Wake and Other Uncollected Prose,* ed. Steven Moore [Elmwood Park, Ill.: Dalky Archive Press, 1989]). "John Freeman's biography" is *Herman Melville* (New York: Macmillan, 1926). The other books cited are Jay Leyda, *The Melville Log: A Documentary Life of Herman Melville, 1819–1891* (New York: Harcourt, Brace, 1951); Leon Howard, *Herman Melville: A Biography* (Berkeley: University of California Press, 1951); Merton M. Sealts, Jr., *Melville's Reading*; Nathalia Wright, *Melville's Use of the Bible* (Durham, N.C.: Duke University Press, 1949). Olson also refers to two dissertations, Walter Bezanson's on *Clarel* (Yale, 1943) and Harrison Hayford's on Melville and Hawthorne (Yale, 1945). Henry Murray's biography never did appear.

113   George Lyman Kittredge
One of Olson's teachers at Harvard, author of *Chaucer and His Poetry* (Cambridge, Mass.: Harvard University Press, 1946).

114   Faith (who from the scrawl
Part 4, Canto 35, of *Clarel,* "Epilogue," lines 8–11.

116   the post-modern
Olson's first published reference to "postmodernism," a term that had circulated in correspondence with Robert Creeley since 1950.

116   *Dichtung und Wahrheit*
"Poetry and Truth"—Olson took this as the title of a series of lectures delivered at Beloit College in 1968, transcribed and published in vol. 2 of *Muthologos.*

116   —what Creeley and I have elsewhere called the Single Intelligence
In their correspondence. The phrase is Creeley's, developed at Olson's urging, used in "Projective Verse" and "Introduction to Robert Creeley" also.

116   he opposed "Right Reason" to reason, . . . "Baconianism."
See, e.g., *Ishmael*, pp. 51–54 and 88.

116   the methodological question
Olson wrote Cid Corman, 13 June 1952, "Methodology keeps forcing itself into my mouth as the word to cover the necessity that the execution of form involves" (*O/CC* 1:273). A note written in 1951 or 1952 for Mary Fitton (a student at Black Mountain College) elaborates:

> The methodological is more than any resemblance to method as the latter has been "orderly," "systematic," "the rule," bank clerk life & morality. If you suddenly think of

"the experimental method," you'll begin to begin to feel the difference of the air. And a difference of, results. But—at least in those things which are our concern, life, & the arts—the adjective 'experimental,' indeed the noun 'experiment,' contradict what 'the methodological' is felt to press home. For 'the way' (road, path *tao*), which the root was ['odos, plus 'meta,' & 'Meθodos,' meaning, 'with, a way'] [with a road] has this power, that it suggests the Traveller is distinct from what he travels on. And at this point, it seems to me, one is home: that is, the methodological is an insistence that this distinction is an authoritative one: one travels, but there is something on which one travels distinct from sd Traveller! (*OJ* 8 : 43, brackets in original)

117   if I put Melville in the context of Homer
An unpublished note from 1949 headed "MELVILLE and Homer: notes vis-a-vis V. Berard" puts it this way: "Melville can-opened archaic narrative, the which ain't been done since above-mentioned and honored Greek" (Storrs, Prose Series).

117   Rimbaud's question is the incisive one
Olson's formulation of the question is borrowed (as George Butterick points out) from Wallace Fowlie's *Rimbaud* (New York: New Directions, 1946), p. 42: "Many men wonder what lies beyond sin, but when, on persevering, they discover that it is despair, they retreat to sin or to chastity. But Rimbaud moved on to the despair which lies beyond sin and then sought what lies beyond despair." Rimbaud's "question" recurs in two other essays, "Cy Twombly" (p. 176) and "A Bibliography on America for Ed Dorn" (p. 299).

118   such a passage as that in *The Confidence Man*
In Chapter 44, where we read (p. 239): "The original character, essentially such, is like a revolving Drummond light, raying away from itself all round it—everything is lit by it, everything starts up to it (mark how it is with Hamlet), so that, in certain minds, there follows upon the adequate conception of such a character, an effect, in its way, akin to that which in Genesis attends upon the beginning of things."

118   his discoveries in Pierre which the Freudians find pioneer
In 1949 Olson's friend and fellow Melvillean Henry A. Murray brought out an annotated edition of *Pierre* (New York: Hendricks House, 1949), noting in his introduction (p. xci): "Melville devotes several pages to an account of the waning of Pierre's ardent 'boy-love' for Glen Stanley and, in conformity with Freud's findings, of the gradual conversion of this sentiment into normal adolescent heterosexuality. But it would be evident to any psychiatrist that this transformation was not completed."

118   those meta-psychic ones in *Moby Dick* which Jung acknowledged
In the 1930 essay "Psychology and Literature": "In general, it is the non-psychological novel that offers the richest opportunities for psychological elucidation. Here the author, having no intentions of this sort, does not show his characters in a psychological light and thus leaves room for analysis and interpretation, or even invites it by his unprejudiced mode of presentation. Good examples . . . include Melville's *Moby Dick,* which I consider to be the greatest American novel" (*The Spirit in Man, Art, and Literature,* tr. R. F. C. Hull, *The Collected Works of C. G. Jung,* vol. 15, Bollingen Series 20 [Princeton, N.J.: Princeton

University Press, 1966], p. 84). A translation by Eugene Jolas appeared in *transition,* no. 19/20, June 1930.

118   "the plebian herds . . . centralization"
Chapter 33 of *Moby-Dick,* "The Specksynder," p. 148.

120   "Equal, That Is, to the Real Itself"
Published in *Chicago Review* 12:2, Summer 1958; reprinted in *SW* and *HU.* Olson's principal sources on noneuclidean geometry are Hermann Weyl, *Philosophy of Mathematics and Natural Science,* tr. Olaf Helmer (Princeton, N.J.: Princeton University Press, 1949) (a gift from Stefan Wolpe at Black Mountain College) and H. S. M. Coxeter, *Non-Euclidean Geometry* (Toronto: University of Toronto Press, 1942). Coxeter's preface provides a brief history (at p. vii) pertinent to Olson's essay:

> The name *non-Euclidean* was used by Gauss to describe a system of geometry which differs from Euclid's in its properties of parallelism. Such a system was developed independently by Bolyai in Hungary and Lobatschewsky in Russia, about 120 years ago. Another system, differing more radically from Euclid's, was suggested later by Riemann in Germany and Cayley in England. The subject was unified in 1871 by Klein, who gave the names *parabolic, hyperbolic,* and *elliptic* to the respective systems of Euclid, Bolyai-Lobatschewsky, and Riemann-Cayley.

Olson's engagement with this material left its mark early on, as in "Human Universe," where we read, "the harmony of the universe, and I include man, is not logical, or better, is post-logical, as is the order of any created thing."

120   *Negative Capability*
Defined by Keats in a 22 December 1817 letter to George and Thomas Keats:

> Brown and Dilke walked with me and back from the Christmas pantomime. I had not a dispute, but a disquisition, with Dilke upon various subjects; several things dovetailed in my mind, and at once it struck me what quality went to form a Man of Achievement, especially in Literature, and which Shakspeare possessed so enormously—I mean *Negative Capability,* that is, when a man is capable of being in uncertainties, mysteries, doubts, without any irritable reaching after fact and reason. Coleridge, for instance, would let go by a fine isolated verisimilitude caught from the Penetralium of mystery, from being incapable of remaining content with half-knowledge. (*The Letters of John Keats,* ed. Sidney Colvin [London: Macmillan, 1921], p. 48)

The passage is one of Olson's two epigraphs to *The Special View of History,* notes for a 1956 lecture series at Black Mountain College, where we further read:

> Keats, more than Goethe or Melville, faced with the Man of Power, got to the heart of it. He took the old humanism by its right front. It wasn't the demonism of Genius he saw was the hooker (almost nobody yet has caught up with Keats on the same subject—he was almost the only man who has yet seen the subjective tragedy as no longer so interesting), but the very opposite, the Sublime in the Egotistical, the very character of Genius, its productive power. (*SV* 15)

See, in this connection, Olson's use of Keats's phrase "the Egotistical Sublime" in "Projective Verse," p. 239 and note.

120   the inch of steel to wreck Hegel
Olson expands on this notion in a section of *The Special View of History* titled "Ethics."

121   that the naturalistic . . . wisdom
Milton R. Stern, *The Fine Hammered Steel of Herman Melville* (Urbana: University of Illinois Press, 1957), p. 249.

121   a letter to Hawthorne
Dated 16 April 1851. See Melville, *Correspondence,* p. 186, and Stern, *The Fine Hammered Steel of Herman Melville,* pp. 8–9.

122   Newton's Scholium turned out to be the fulling-mill Melville sensed it was
In the passage from *Pierre* quoted in *Ishmael* at p. 88, which Olson is apparently conflating with Alfred North Whitehead's comments on Newton in *Process and Reality: An Essay in Cosmology* (New York: Macmillan, 1929).

122   my friend Landreau
Anthony Landreau, weaving instructor at Black Mountain College.

123   The delivery of Tashtego from the whale's head
In Chapter 78 of *Moby-Dick,* "Cistern and Buckets." The description of the whale's head in the previous chapter ("The Great Heidelburgh Tun") includes the intriguing word "quoin," which Melville defines in a footnote: "Quoin is not a Euclidean term. It belongs to the pure nautical mathematics. I know not that it has been defined before. A quoin is a solid which differs from a wedge in having its sharp end formed by the steep inclination of one side, instead of the mutual tapering of both sides" (*Moby-Dick,* p. 339).

124   As the Master said to me in the dream
Recorded in Olson's poem "ABC's (2)" (*CP,* 173).

124   Pollock's, and Kline's
Jackson Pollock and Franz Kline, abstract expressionist painters. Kline taught at Black Mountain College during Olson's tenure. In 1966, in a television interview, Olson would say, "I believe that the American painters, namely Mr. Pollock and Mr. Kline, in 1948—and I'm of their time—solved the problem of how to live" (*MUTH* 1:194). See also, in this connection, the editors' note to "Human Universe," p. 411.

124   M. de Miroir, etc.
Hawthorne's tale "Monsieur du Miroir," in *Mosses from an Old Manse.* Melville's "The Bell Tower," "The Encantantadas," "Bartleby, the Scrivener," and "Benito Cereno" all appear in *Piazza Tales.*

124   the remark "The negro" . . . in "Benito Cereno"
In the last exchange between the Spanish and American captains:

> "You are saved," cried Captain Delano, more and more astonished and pained; "you are saved; what has cast such a shadow over you?"
>   "The negro."

There was silence, while the moody man sat, slowly and unconsciously gathering his mantle about him, as if it were a pall.

There was no more conversation that day. (*Piazza Tales,* p. 116)

124   a discontinuous jump
From Weyl, *Philosophy of Mathematics and Natural Science,* p. 82—"a rigid body could go over into its mirror image only by a discontinuous jump"; the phrase also recalls the Spanish captain's desperate leap in "Benito Cereno," which brings to light Babo's slave revolt and pierces the American captain's foggy comprehension.

124   He says somewhere a harpoon . . . likened the white whale
In Chapter 60 of *Moby-Dick,* "The Line," to p. 281, recalled in Chapter 133, "The Chase—First Day," p. 548.

125   Divine Inert
Moby-Dick, Chapter 33, "The Specksynder," p. 148.

125   Riemannian observation
In "Demeter," an unpublished prose piece from 1956, Olson writes: "The laws of nearby action are only to be encountered, as Riemann was an early one to point out, or Melville was, in conveying the power of a whale's tale, in the places of the very small. Topology is that" (Storrs, Prose Series).

126   "Dostoevsky and *The Possessed*"
Published in *Twice a Year,* nos. 5–6, Fall–Winter 1940 / Spring–Summer 1941; reprinted in *Civil Liberties and the Arts: Selections from "Twice a Year," 1938–46,* ed. William Waserstrom (Syracuse, N.Y.: Syracuse University Press, 1964). Olson wrote this essay the year he received his Guggenheim for work on Melville. An October 1939 letter to Dorothy Norman (publisher of *Twice a Year,* where "Lear and Moby-Dick" appeared in 1938), reports:

> Out of the morass of the last half year has come a couple of chapters of the Melville book—and this enclosed essay on Dostoevsky. . . . I wanted you to have it, if you could use it, for the fall number. I have like jobs, on the other ignored novels of D: Notes From Underground, The Idiot, Diary of a Write[r] and The Raw Youth especially; and if you were interested in this you'd not be publishing in a vacuum, for the others might follow. The present essay is a kind of testament to my own faith and I'd like to get it into print this fall. (*SL*)

126   Dostoevsky's Grand Inquisitor
Book 5, Chapter 5, of *The Brothers Karamazov,* which Olson read in Constance Garnett's translation. The quotations below are from pp. 266 ("miracle, mystery, and authority") and 267 ("universal state") of the Modern Library edition.

126   Ours is the Karamazov way. As to old Karamazov, "everything is lawful."
The quoted words are Ivan's and recur all through Dostoevsky's novel, as at the end of "The Grand Inquisitor," where Ivan speaks of "the strength of the Karamazovs—the strength of the Karamazov baseness" (p. 273).

127 Dostoevsky's face in the Perov portrait
Frontispiece to Avraham Yarmolinsky's *Dostoevsky: His Life and Art* (New York: Criterion, 1957), which Olson owned in the earlier 1934 edition.

127 that lovely, strange, misunderstood remark of his
In Part 2, Chapter 1, "Night," Section 7, of *The Possessed,* tr. Constance Garnett (New York: Modern Library, 1963), p. 253.

127 he confessed to Maikov
Appollon Maikov. The lines are cited in Yarmolinsky, *Dostoevsky,* p. 294.

128 "der kleine Teufel."
German, "the little devil."

128 that parable from Luke
One of Dostoevsky's epigraphs to *The Possessed.*

129 Dostoevsky exposed the authoritarian necessity of all statism:
The block quotation comprises lines from Part 2, Chapter 7, of *The Possessed,* "A Meeting," Section 2, p. 409, and Chapter 8, "Ivan the Tsarevitch," p. 425. The phrases below come from Part 2, Chapter 7, Section 2, p. 414 ("A new religion . . . "); Chapter 1, "Night," Section 7, p. 253 ("on the elements . . . "); and Chapter 6, "Pyotr Stepanovitch Is Busy," Section 7, p. 392 ("shame at having . . . " and "the cement that binds . . . ").

130 Peter calls him, "the sun,"
In Part 2, Chapter 8, of *The Possessed,* "Ivan the Tsarevitch," p. 426.

130 "simple-heartedness and naiveté."
From Part 2, Chapter 8, "Ivan the Tsarevitch," p. 426.

130 "You are my idol. Ivan the Tsarevitch. You! You!"
Cobbled together from two places in Chapter 8, "Ivan the Tsarevitch," pp. 426 and 429. The lines below are from the same chapter, p. 423 ("Verhovensky besought, implored") and p. 430 ("Stavrogin wondered smiling").

131 I know thy works
From "Stavrogin's Confession," the suppressed chapter of Dostoevsky's novel, included (tr. Yarmolinsky) as a supplement to the Modern Library edition Olson owned. The four quotations below are all from Part 3, Chapter 8, "Conclusion," p. 685 ("I am still capable, . . . ") and p. 686 ("brush myself . . . ," "Even negation . . . ," and "Indignation . . . ").

132 "the freedom of choice . . . "
This line and the one below ("above everything else") are from "The Grand Inquisitor" chapter of *The Brothers Karamazov,* pp. 264 and 263, respectively.

132 If Stavrogin has faith. . . . he hasn't.
From Part 3, Chapter 6, "A Busy Night," Section 2, p. 626.

132   che non furon . . . sè foro
Canto 3 of Dante's *Inferno,* lines 38–39, "they were not rebellious, / neither were they faithful to God, but kept to themselves."

133   what the Grand Inquisitor calls man's "fearful burden of free choice,"
The Brothers Karamazov, p. 264.

133   "like rotten mildew,"
From Part 2, Chapter 1, "Night," Section 7, p. 259. The "Great Idea" is articulated in Part 3, Chapter 7, "Stepan Trofimovitch's Last Wandering," pp. 674–75.

133   "Externally he was rough . . . "
Adapted from *The Possessed,* Part 3, Chapter 5, "A Wanderer," Section 1, pp. 578–79, "This strong, rugged man, all bristles on the surface, was suddenly all softness and shining gladness."

135   "D. H. Lawrence and the High Temptation of the Mind"
Written 21–22 January 1950; posthumously published in *Chicago Review* 30:3, Winter 1979, and then as a pamphlet by Black Sparrow Press in 1980.

135   Huxley, in his introduction to the "Letters,"
See *The Letters of D. H. Lawrence,* ed. Aldous Huxley (New York: Viking Press, 1932), where we read (p. xv): "It was not an incapacity to understand which made him reject those generalizations and abstractions by means of which the philosophers and the men of science try to open a path for the human spirit through the chaos of phenomena. Not incapacity, I repeat; for Lawrence had over and above his peculiar gift, an extremely acute intelligence."

136   Ortega discloses it, in his brilliant essay on Goethe,
Read by Olson in the December 1949 *Partisan Review.* See José Ortega y Gasset, "In Search of Goethe from Within," tr. Willard Trask, *The Dehumanization of Art and Other Essays on Art, Culture, and Literature* (Princeton, N.J.: Princeton University Press, 1968), p. 146.

137   *The Man Who Died*
Also known as *The Escaped Cock,* referred to by that title in the essay that follows.

138   "The Escaped Cock"
The Escaped Cock is the title of the first edition of Lawrence's last novel, brought out in Paris by the Black Sun Press in 1929; later editions appeared as *The Man Who Died.* Olson's review derives from a letter to Robert Creeley sent 1 October 1950. First published in *Origin,* no. 2, Summer 1951; reprinted in *HU.*

138   Civitavecchia
Italian, "old city." Lawrence in *Etruscan Places* writes at length about four old cities (Cerveteri, Tarquinia, Vulci, and Voltera), citing the actual Cività Vecchia in passing only, with disparagement. See *Mornings in Mexico and Etruscan Places* (London: Heinemann, 1965), p. 23.

139 Mellors

The gameskeeper in Lawrence's 1928 novel *Lady Chatterley's Lover.*

139 Constance (Frieda)

Mellors's lover in *Lady Chatterley's Lover.* Frieda is Frieda Lawrence, Lawrence's wife; Constance was the name of Olson's own wife at the time (see *Call me Ishmael.*

140 Somers (kangaroo)

A character in Lawrence's 1923 novel *Kangaroo.*

140 the Man who died:

The numbered lines that follow are all quotations from Lawrence's novel. See *The Escaped Cock,* ed. Gerald M. Lacy (Los Angeles: Black Sparrow Press, 1973), pp. 24 and 30. The last of these quotations is cited again in "The Present Is Prologue," p. 206.

141 "This Is Yeats Speaking"

Published in *Partisan Review* 13:1, Winter 1946; reprinted in *HU* and *O&P.* The title echoes the opening of Pound's broadcasts for Radio Rome (edited by Leonard W. Doob as *"Ezra Pound Speaking": Radio Speeches of World War II* [Westport, Conn.: Greenwood Press, 1978]). Olson subsequently arranged to cover Pound's legal proceedings for Dorothy Norman's *Twice a Year,* becoming the first American poet to meet with Pound after the war. His small acts of kindness quickly earned the older poet's gratitude, as shown by a penciled note Pound scribbled at the time: "Problem now is not to go stark screaming hysteric. . . . Olson saved my life. young doctors absolutely useless. must have 15 minutes sane conversation daily" (quoted in C. David Hayman's *Ezra Pound: The Last Rower* [New York: Viking Press, 1976], p. 191). Olson recorded his first view of Pound (from a distance, at the arraignment) as follows:

> His eyes crossed mine once, and they were full of pain, and hostile, cornered as he was in a court, with no one he knew around him except his lawyer whom he had only known a week. The moment when he, a man of such words, stood up mute before the court, had its drama, personal. But earlier . . . there was another moment, a political one. Pound's lawyer called his attention to a jury waiting in the box for some rooming house trial which was to follow Pound's arraignment. . . . It was a typical jury, that collection of free men which constitutes that right of the democratic process, TRIAL BY JURY, easy to satirize, common as it is, to burlesque, unliterate as the people are, to caricature, lumpish as they appear in [a] public place. There it was, and Pound swung round in his chair to confront it. For forty years of exile he had turned his tongue against America, for twenty years he had damned democracy and its works. Now, at bay, his own life would soon be in the hands of some such gathering of twelve men. He hunched forward, shot his head up and out like a beak, and squinting his eyes as though he missed glasses, though he had them on, moved along the jurors['] faces, squaring at each direct and dwelling, as children and poets will and nobody else does because it is supposed to be rude. His face told nothing, his eyes were as they were towards me, and I would guess he was too distracted by his own troubles for his feelings to come to bear on this thing before him. . . . What was in the moment lay outside it, stretching back a long way, with Pound's sixty years from Idaho on measured against

those several hundred years since some Englishmen first filed in and made a jury. (*O&P* 35–36)

142 Troilus' advantage, from the seventh sphere
From the end of Chaucer's "Troilus and Cressida."

142 Hodos Chameliontos
Greek, "the chameleon's way." In a 1945 prose fragment Olson confides, "I hate this anti-semite! this revolutionary simpleton, as Yeats called him. Go further and wonder, as Yeats did, if his Cantos aren't all hodos chameliontos" (*O&P*, p. 15). Yeats, in "A Packet for Ezra Pound," has, "I may, now that I have recovered leisure, find . . . that seemingly irrelevant details fit together in a single theme, that here is no botch of tone and color, all Hodos Chameliontos" (*A Vision*, p. 5). The phrase is also the title of Book 3 of Yeats's "Trembling of the Veil" (1922), where we read: "But now image called up image in an endless pro-cession, and I could not always choose among them with any confidence; and when I did choose, the image lost its intensity. . . . I was lost in that region a cabbalistic manuscript . . . had warned me of; astray upon the Path of the Chamelion, upon *Hodos Chameliontos*" (*The Autobiography of William Butler Yeats* [New York: Collier Books, 1965], p. 181).

143 expound credit and Major Douglas
Major Clifford Hugh Douglas and the theory of "Social Credit," a species of monetary reform that came to preoccupy Pound in his Cantos and elsewhere.

143 And I told him so, but friendship never ends;
Yeats, "All Soul's Night: An Epilogue," in *A Vision*, pp. 304–5.

144 Are you a court to accept and/or reject
Olson silently cites *Jefferson and/or Mussolini* in *Call Me Ishmael* (p. 73); *Guide to Kulchur* (originally issued as *Culture* in 1936; New York: New Directions, 1970) is mentioned in "A Bibliography on America for Ed Dorn" (p. 308). The ABCs are *ABC of Reading* (1934; New York: New Directions, 1960) and *ABC of Economics* (1933; reprinted in *Selected Prose: 1909–1965*, ed. William Cookson [New York: New Directions, 1973]). Pound originally proposed writing a hundred Cantos.

144 Matter as wise logicians say
Dean Swift, quoted by Yeats in a footnote in "A Packet for Ezra Pound" (*A Vision*, p. 4 n. 2).

145 "GrandPa, GoodBye"
First published posthumously in *New Directions in Poetry and Prose 30*, ed. James Laugh-lin, Peter Glassgold, and Frederick R. Martin (New York: New Directions, 1975); reprinted in *O&P*. Olson's growing dissatisfaction with Pound's nativist prejudice led to a cooling of relations. (A 1948 letter to the older poet includes the comment, "BUT you do have to deal with us Olsons . . . ; your damn ancestors let us in. . . . We're here, and to tell you your own truth, you damn well know anglosaxonism is academicism and shrieking em-

pire" [*SL*].) Olson's view is already retrospective in a 17 November 1949 letter to Peter Russell, editor of the British journal *Nine:*

> I stand ready to answer any and all questions on EP you want to put, and, though I do not now see him, if you want questions put to him, I think my friend Frank Moore can do that. . . .
>   It is still a question swimming in my blood, but I found I had to cease seeing him in the spring of 1948 (I had been a sort of Achates from his arrival in the Federal Pen (has he not made it the "Bughouse" to stand next to the "Gorilla Cage" at Pisa?) until that time, saw him once or twice a week, and kept sporadic notes on his conversation. What stopped me was a crux of things, of him and of me.
>   Look, for a starter, let me enclose two things, one you may have come by, the other you are the 1st to see. (They are the 1st and last things I have done on Ez.) "THIS IS YEATS SPEAKING" was written before I had seen him, in fact before he was brought to the States, when his trial was imminent. It was published in the Partisan Review, issue Winter 1946. (I am pleased I called, that early, for the polemic the Bo[l]lingen finally provoked.)
>   The other mss is the last notes I wrote. I think the day I last saw him. Thus you have the bracket of my acquaintance.
>   I imagine I will, one day, set more down on him. He seems to me definitely our Grandpa, even if Lawrence is closer in the blood. But the mind of Ez, that's the thing, that's the flare to light us back. He seems to me to have put himself in our hands as the cleanest sort of instrument, even tho I think the New History he cries for, will be so much different than he. (Frobenius, for example, whom he put me on to, I read quite opposite). Language, the language, that's what he delivered to us new. (Buf.)

Shot through, in the manner of Pound's own work, with literary allusion and telegram-matic reference, "GrandPa, GoodBye" is best read in conjunction with Olson's "Cantos" (*O&P* 33–93), a ten-part record of visits to St. Elizabeth's, written between 5 January 1946 and 9 February 1948. See also Catherine Seelye's more detailed notes to this essay in *O&P.*

145   Lowell
Robert Lowell, another of Pound's visitors at St. Elizabeth's.

145   Ford (F. M.)
Ford Maddox Ford, called "Fordie" below. See also Olson's poem "Aucteur," "Said Pound the Red, one turquoise earring at his head / 'FMF knew more than any of us, he. . . . / from the literary centre, 12 years start of me'" (*Nation* 39).

146   Picabia, . . . Hauptmann,
French painter Francis Picabia and German dramatist Gerhart Hauptmann.

146   Young Huston's story of Jack Warner and the Whale.
In Tom Clark's telling,

> John Huston was at work on a screen adaptation of *Moby-Dick*. . . . Olson met with [the director] and offered his services . . . as writer/consultant. . . . But before Olson had an opportunity . . . the *Moby-Dick* production ran into some very unliterary techni-cal problems. A mechanical monster built to simulate the White Whale stubbornly re-fused to float, sinking to the bottom of the tank in one test run after another. Return-ing a week late from vacation, Jack Warner blew up over the delays and gave orders to

"kill that fucking whale." The movie, and Olson's chances of work, sank along with it. (*Charles Olson: The Allegory of a Poet's Life* [New York: W. W. Norton, 1991], p. 128)

146 What's that line he had in the *Cantos . . . ?*
Identified by Catherine Seelye as an early version of Canto 2, published in *Poetry* in 1917, describing Browning's *Sordello* as a "bag / of tricks" and adding, "the modern world / Needs such a rag-bag to stuff all its thought in."

146 Edward Dahlberg has it, in *Do These Bones Live*
In the section dedicated to Olson, "Woman" (p. 134): "The woman who fevers in man a morosely boiling ennui is western: she is the occidental european woman of Shakespeare, Dostoevsky, Stendahl, Tolstoy."

147 *numen*
Latin, "*a nod;* hence, *a command, will, authority,*" "*the Divine will,*" "*divinity*" (Charlton T. Lewis, *An Elementary Latin Dictionary*).

147 "Cino," . . . XXXVI
"Cino" is one of Pound's earliest poems (published in *Personae: The Shorter Poems of Ezra Pound,* ed. Lea Baechler and A. Walton Litz [New York: New Directions, 1990], pp. 6–8); Canto 36 is part of the section "Eleven New Cantos," first published in 1934, now gathered in *The Cantos* (New York: New Directions, 1975).

147 Grosseteste's essay on the "physics" of light
John Clarke, in his unpublished notes from Olson's Mythology Seminar at SUNY Buffalo, Fall 1964, has:

Light, very bad—like the 13th C. Meisters

Eckhart, Aquinas, Bacon & Grosseteste with his *Physics of Light,* whom we've had enough of by now

Heat, however, very good . . .

148 the image of "fire" in *Paterson*
There are several such images in Williams's poem. See, for instance, Book 2, Section 1:

a flight of empurpled wings!
—invisibly created (their
jackets dust-grey) from the dust kindled
to sudden ardor!
(William Carlos Williams, *Paterson,* ed. Christopher MacGowan
[New York: New Directions, 1992], p. 47)

148 *claritas . . . confusio.*
Latin, "*clearness*" and "*confusion.*"

148 for al so siker as *In Principio,*
Chaucer from "The Nun's Tale."

148   Gaudier, Lewis
Sculptor Gaudier-Brzeska and novelist Wyndham Lewis.

149   "that labor-saving device of yours on H. Melville.
I.e., *Call me Ishmael.*

150   Frobenius
Anthropologist Leo Frobenius; the unnamed "one" of the opening section of Olson's essay "Human Universe." At Pound's suggestion, Olson looked into Frobenius's untranslated work, and later acquired Douglas Fox's "Frobenius' Paideuma as a Philosophy of Culture," *New English Weekly,* 3 September–8 October 1936.

150   DP
Dorothy Pound, the poet's wife.

150   Georgian . . . Joe
Joseph Stalin, born in the Soviet province of Georgia.

150   "through Agnes," whoever she was,
Identified by Catherine Seelye as "Agnes Bedford, a musician who collaborated with Pound on *Five Troubador Songs.*"

151   one of Hauptmann's plays.
Joyce translated two, neither published, *Vor Sonnenaufgang* (*Before Sunrise*) and *Michael Kramer.*

151   the Old Man, "Grandpa," now that Mary has made him one.
Mary de Rachelwitz, Pound's daughter by Olga Rudge.

151   Spender, Tate
Poets Stephen Spender and Alan Tate

151   says the O. M.
T. S. Eliot, referred to by his title (Order of Merit) in "Projective Verse" as well (p. 249).

151   Ant-Hill
Olson wrote Cid Corman, 21 October 1950: "THE FACT is, that, americans are putting out a body of research ROUND the WORLD, which is the kind of grounding on which that culture of Europe rested rests is now buried in her lies the anthill" (*O/CC* 1 : 44). George Evans in his notes suggests a reference to Pound's *Pisan Cantos,* "As a lone ant from a broken ant-hill / from the wreckage of Europe, ego scriptor" (Canto 76). The phrase below, "right, / right / from the start," echoes "Hugh Selwyn Mauberly," where Pound has "Wrong from the start—."

155 "Human Universe"
Published in *Origin,* no. 4, Winter 1951–52, and again in *Evergreen Review* 2:5, Spring 1958; reprinted in *SW* and *HU.* An early version, titled "The Human Universe," was sent in a letter of 17 June 1951 to Cid Corman, and appears as Appendix A to Albert Glover's dissertation, "Charles Olson: Letters for Origin" (State University of New York at Buffalo, 1968). The principal difference between the early version and final text is Olson's ellision of an extended response to *New Directions 12,* and a briefer reference to Bronislaw Malinowski on the Trobriand Islands. The mythopoetic narrative at the end of the essay is adapted from J. Eric S. Thompson, *Maya Hieroglyphic Writing* (1950; Norman: University of Oklahoma Press, 1960), p. 230, related previously to Robert Creeley in a letter of 27 March 1951. The essay's title may reflect acquaintance with David Rousett's influential account of the Buchenwald concentration camp, *L'Universe concentrationaire* (Paris: Editions du Pavois, 1946), mentioned by Olson in a letter to Creeley of 30 May 1950.

155 Der Weg stirbt, sd one.
The "one" is Leo Frobenius, who (as Maud notes in *Olson's Reading,* p. 260, n. 9) tells the tale of the path that dies in the 1928 edition of *Paideuma.* Olson draws a connection between "laws" and "der Weg" once again in *The Special View of History:* "I mean to throw in one last imperative—what I shall call LAW itself. And I mean it as the correct application of the old Western conception of *The Way* and the Eastern conception of *the Tao* (the Way is the path, follow me etc. of Christianity, the 'Law' literally in Judaism, etc.—the 'light,' say). Or, most excitingly for me, the African 'Der Weg,' as in the folk tale in which Der Weg stirbt—dies" (*SV* 54).

155 if we are to see some of the laws afresh
In the early version of the essay Olson has: "We are at the heart of the matter of humanism versus some alternative. One law necessary to that alternative certainly is, that we have been misled to look for truth when the real measure for any one of us of anything is its use to us, exactly its use to us in terms of the performance of ritual and moral acts" (Glover diss., p. 266).

156 enclosed in the "UNIVERSE of discourse."
That is, "kosmos-logos"—cosmology.

157 Plato may be a honey-head, as Melville called him,
In Chapter 78 of *Moby-Dick,* "Cistern and Buckets," comparing "Plato's honey head" to the "secret inner chamber and sanctum sanctorum of the whale," into which Tashtego tumbles, "like the twin reciprocating bucket in a veritable well" (pp. 344, 342). See also the note to "Equal, That Is, to the Real Itself," p. 400, above.

157   *comparison,* or, its bigger name, *symbology*

Olson has in the early version of the essay:

> One reason why I value Malinowski is the intellectual clarity he exhibits in his use of the word "Symbol." For this is a word we have allowed to slide and at a time when it is crucial that we be clear about it, especially to distinguish the process of image from it. . . . For symbol, in its original meaning as the Greek "symballein," meant "to throw together, to compare," and it is comparison which has lain, from the beginning, at the root of humanism as one of its most evil characteristics. Image, on the contrary, denotes a much more active process, deriving as it does from the root of the Latin verb "imitare," to imitate, and thus is closely joined to the implicitly dramatic action of the concept "to mime," and bears always in the direction of direct representation of an original object or act, not, as symbol goes, in the contrary direction, toward generalization, toward an abstract sign, figure, or type to stand in the place of—a sort of rational and intellectual shorthand—the original object or act. And it is a measure of how symbol has eaten its way that one of the marks of present art is that simile and the abstract are much more instruments of that art than is metaphor and the concrete. The reason is this profound one, that comparison rather than duplication, than reenactment, than "performance" as Malinowski has it, is the law (or rather, as I hope to make clear, the false face of a law). (Glover diss., pp. 263–64)

158   I have been living for some time amongst a people

In January 1951 Olson left Washington, D.C., for Lerma, Mexico, near Campeche, where he spent some six months living, writing, and studying Mayan archeology. A selection of Olson's letters from this period was edited and published by Robert Creeley under the title *Mayan Letters* (Mallorca: Divers Press, 1953; reprinted in *SW*).

159   swap caymotes for sandals

Sweet potatoes, as Olson tells Cid Corman in a letter of 18 September 1951.

159   refrigerator-ripened fruit

Olson's "Rufus Woodpecker," an ecopolitical poem from 1958, concludes with

> the sight

> of the representative of the rest of creation
> nesting inside the Mouth of the nation, and pecking
> broccoli out of it, clearly concerned

> that if he went any deeper he was apt to find more
> foodstuff buried in the Defrost

> (*CP* 454)

159   Spectatorism crowds out participation as the condition of culture.

Olson expands on this Debordian notion in a 7 June 1952 letter to Cid Corman:

> I believe . . . that all men and women can dance—and this alone is enough to establish expression—that all other expression is only up from this base; and that to dance is enough to make a whole day have glory, granting that work is called for of each of us. The hook is that work will always make sense if dancing is understood to be—expression is—the other issue of a day.
> 　　　　　　　　　　"Our class"—the non-class—the a-class—the expressers solely, now have the responsibility to restore expression to . . . prime place. (I take it you understand yr own masthead. . . .

> . . . it is the only answer to that spectatorism
> which both capitalism and communism breed—breed it as surely as absentee
> ownership. . . .
>
> For to be a spectator is to assert an ownership . . . which is absentee—
> (O/CC1:271)

Origin's masthead was "O my son, arise from thy bed—work what is wise."

161   like Williams' paint
Sherwin-Williams, not W. C. The reference recurs in John Clarke's unpublished notes for Olson's Mythology Seminar at SUNY Buffalo, Spring 1965: "[Franz] Kline . . . seized the advantage of putting the paint out on the world (like Sherman [sic] Williams: 'We cover the world'). Black and white were colors of such vitality after say 1948 . . . "

161   the greatest humanist of them all
That is, Shakespeare.

162   Heisenberg
Werner Heisenberg, whose "Uncertainty Principle" Olson cites in *The Special View of History* as an aspect of Negative Capability (*SV* 42).

163   Toynbee
Arnold Toynbee, author of *A Study of History,* 2 vols. (New York: Oxford University Press, 1947 and 1950).

164   chamaco
Spanish (specific to Mexico) for boy, lad.

164   Shoosh Ek
Olson wrote Robert Creeley, 15 March 1951, "Still going along on Venus, or, as they call her, *Noh ek* (the great star) or, *Xux ek* (the wasp star—which sounds, this way: shoosh ek" (*O/RC* 5:74; see also Thompson, *Maya Hieroglyphic Writing,* p. 218). A subsequent letter to Cid Corman (28 March 1951) ends playfully, "o, lad, you have a golden egg, yes, a gold & egg, eck, shoosh, ek" (*O/CC* 1:118).

167   "Footnote to HU (lost in the shuffle)"
Published in *Origin,* no. 4, Winter 1951–52.

167   the 6'4" Negress stood
In *The Chiasma, or Lectures in the New Sciences of Man* (notes written in 1953 for a series of lectures at Black Mountain College), Olson refers to the same woman and her definition of art, giving an expanded sense of how he understands the words "ACTUAL" and "ON TIME." Under the heading "CUPS, or Dance; and WOMAN, or Sculpture," Olson writes:

> The cave, to Cro-Magnon, at least its recesses where the paintings and such clay sculpture as the two bisons of Tuc D'Audoubert are, was not lived in—nor were there buri-

als in them. In fact, even the mouths of the caves may not have been in any continuous sense "dwellings"—as I have pointed out, man seems to have lived most of the year in huts following the herds. And the caves were only seasonal places, at the mouths of which he worked his flints and buried his dead, in the depths of which he worked his art and celebrated what celebrations his culture had brought him to. That art of the recesses I can now call what the 6 foot 6 Negress of my acquaintance called all art, in a Washington drawing room one night a couple of years back: Art, she said, swaying among the literati, is—the celebration of, the actual. (*OJ* 10:43)

The emphasis on height may reflect Olson's self-consciousness about his own stature—he stood about 6 foot 7.

168 "The Gate and the Center"

Developed into an essay on the basis of two letters to Robert Creeley (of 27 July and 4 August 1950); published in the inaugural issue of Cid Corman's magazine *Origin,* Spring 1951; reprinted in *HU.* From Frances Boldereff Olson's interest in archaic history received new stimulus. She sent him Samuel Noah Kramer's translations of Sumerian poetic texts in May of 1949, and in the summer of 1950, after meeting Edith Porada, the book on cylinder seals quoted in the essay.

168 Stefansson on diets

Vilhjalmur Stefansson, arctic explorer and author of several books, named in the Maximus poems in "Letter, May 2, 1959" (*MAX* 151).

168 Carl Sauer on starch crops

Sauer mailed Olson an offprint of the essay "Environment and Culture in the Deglaciation" on 17 November 1949. A year later Olson wrote back, in a letter dated 25 October 1950:

> My dear Carl Sauer
>
> You have been much on my mind. (I have even writ you in to a piece—an aggressive piece on knowledge, as of now—which, if it ever sees the light (Boston light, in this case, due, a new mag, abt march), i pray you shall not think i did it in vain.) For, as I told you, that day, I walked in on you, you are one of the rare & native forces. (What I tried to do, in this last job, was to remind these hyar amurrikans, that their energy hath expressed itself in much more important things than engineers & machines, that such men as you are, round the world, rebasing knowledge, and that, from such knowledge, if its particularity is carefully seen, its drive for a total bearing not for mere sanctions of an older humanism, there is plenty of reason to expect fresh culture from same.
>
> . . . Shld like it, if you'd drop me a penny post card whenever any work jumps up to your eyes, in any of those areas that yr own center is center to. (It is this concept of CENTER as the thing knowledge goes for, or it[']s not worth its keep, that I was pushing, of late: THE GATE & THE CENTER.)
>
> Do write, when you can. And send, o send!
>
> Charles Olson
>
> (*O/CS* 144–45)

168   euhemerists

Those who take myths as traditional accounts of real incidents. Stanley Edgar Hymen in his review of Olson's *Call Me Ishmael* ("The Critic as Narcissus," *Accent,* no. 8, Spring 1948) writes (p. 190), "all [Olson] apparently wants of Freud, besides the melancholy euhemerism of *Moses and Monotheism,* is the hardly novel reading of Ahab's loss as castration."

168   Old Stink Sock

Socrates.

169   Fenollosa

Ernest Fenollosa, whose *Chinese Written Character* Olson cites in *Call Me Ishmael* (p. 19) and elsewhere.

169   agglutinative language

An unpublished prose piece dated 31 July 1954, "The Crisis of the Third Foot," develops the notion further: "Each person declares the syntax according to the necessities of his own precision in the moment of what he is stating or telling. The parts of speech can be freely disposed in any language which is undeclined, the so-called agglutinative languages. And if I take it 'American' is agglutinative, then such syntax is, in experience, more natural to it than English syntax" (Storrs, Prose Series).

169   Stockpile Szilard . . . Merritt . . . Theodore Vann

Physicist Leo Szilard, a colleague of Einstein's and refugee from Nazi Germany; opponent of the use of atomic weapons. He began research in molecular biology in 1948, opening a laboratory at the University of Chicago. George Butterick identifies Merritt as H. Houston Merritt, "professor of neurology at Columbia College, as well as (from 1948 on) director of the Neurological Institute at Presbyterian Hospital in New York" (*O/RC* 2 : 165 n. 55). No further information is presently known about Theodore Vann.

170   add one L. A. Waddell

Laurence Austine Waddell. Olson wrote to Creeley, 27 July 1950:

> Been in one of those periods which come up every so often where I get a teeth-hold on something, and can't give over until I've beat the dog. This time it's a guy I stumbled on accidentally in the Sumerian catalogue, Lib. Cong.—and who sends me: . . . L. A. Waddell. . . . [R]ight or wrong, he's got a package wrapped up on how civilization got movin, and who moved it, that jibes with a lot I have found in my own archaisms and previously documented.(*O/RC* 2 : 80–81)

170   Berard . . . Strzygowski [Frobenius

Victor Bérard, frequently cited by Olson. See especially "Appendix A" to "A Bibliography on America for Ed Dorn" (p. 304) and note. Joseph Strzygowski, cited more extensively in "The Vinland Map Review" (see, e.g., p. 328).

170   Frobenius

Leo Frobenius, mentioned by Olson in "GrandPa, GoodBye" (p. 150) and elsewhere.

170   Maspero
French Egyptologist Gaston Maspero, whose *Popular Tales of Ancient Egypt* are cited by Bérard in *Did Homer Live?* tr. Brian Rhys (New York: E. P. Dutton, 1931).

171   Phoenician periploi
Phoenician accounts of sailing voyages, from the plural of the Greek word "periploos," *"the account of a coasting voyage"* (Henry George Liddell and Robert Scott, *A Greek-English Lexicon*)—discussed at length by Bérard in *Did Homer Live?*

171   such a late thing as Dura-Europos
Frances Boldereff wrote Olson on 10 May 1949:

> If you are connected with a college ask the librarian to borrow for you from the Library of Congress Franz Cumont's volume of plates in color on the frescoes found at Dura-Europos. . . . There is a particular plate which I wish to talk with you about which will drive you wild—a priest in ceremony—the look in the eyes the Christian world has not so far touched—the unworld brought to view—Rostovtzeff says this fresco is the long sought link between the Western and Eastern worlds. (*O/FB* 152—see also 160 nn. 34 and 35)

See also, in this connection, Olson's "Tutorial: The Greeks" (1955) (*OJ* 2 : 43–48), and his poem "Dura" (*CP* 85), scribbled on the back of the envelope Boldereff's letter came in.

174   "The Resistance"
Published in *Four Winds,* no. 4, Winter 1953; reprinted in *SW* and *HU.*

174   Jean Riboud
A member of the French underground, later imprisoned in the concentration camp Buchenwald. Olson was the best man at Riboud's wedding in 1949.

174   Bogomolets' researches into the nature of connective tissue
Alexander A. Bogomolets, author of *The Prolongation of Life* (New York: Duell, Sloan and Pearce, 1946). Olson also cites him in the 1948 mask "Troilus": "Bogomolets, and the time scheme of a human life: the clash of two rhythms, nature's and man's" (*FH* 44).

175   "Cy Twombly"
First published in *OJ* 8; proposed by Olson for inclusion in *HU.* Cy Twombly, an American painter, was a student at Black Mountain College; a letter to Robert Creeley of 29 January 1952 relates a long, complicated tale about Twombly's swimming into cold water at night to save another Black Mountain student, Robert Rauschenberg, from drowning. A subsequent letter (31 January 1952) adds:

> Crazy part, that, it all passed into the silence of history, on the surface, just as though he had gone for a swim and had come out, with no help. In fact, except for me, and my questionings, to find out more, not knowing, what they who spend more of their time sitting around do know, or I thought they might, no one except those involved would have known that the event had happened at all! . . .
> Also a little crazy was, that, the same night of the day I wrote you I slammed out the enclosed first go at a preface T[wombly] asked me that day to do for a show of his coming up next month. (*O/RC* 9 : 65)

The secret history Olson recounts for Creeley offers an odd counterpoint to what Olson's essay calls "the twin methodology": "documentation," and "penetration of the reality bearing on us."

175   Mencius, as translated by Pound
A phrase Olson borrowed for "The Kingfishers," where we read, "so you must, and, in that whiteness, into that face, with what candor, look" (*CP* 91). Pound's version appears in a prefatory note to his translation of "The Analects" (1951), published now in *Confucius: The Unwobbling Pivot, The Great Digest, The Analects* (New York: New Directions, 1969), p. 194.

175   There came a man who dealt with whiteness.
I.e., Melville. Chapter 42 of *Moby-Dick* is called "The Whiteness of the Whale."

176   Tao Yuan-Ming's east hedge
See, e.g., *T'ao the Hermit: Sixty Poems by T'ao Ch'ien (365–427)*, tr. William Acker (London: Thames and Hudson, 1952), p. 66:

> I built my house near where others dwell,
> And yet there is no clamour of carriages and horses.
> You ask of me "How can this be so?"
> "When the heart is far the place of itself is distant."
> I pluck chrysanthemums under the eastern hedge,
> And gaze afar towards the southern mountains.
> The mountain air is fine at evening of the day
> And flying birds return together homewards.
> Within these things there is a hint of Truth,
> But when I start to tell it, I cannot find the words.

Yüan-Ming is T'ao's "courtesy name," and means "Light of the Abyss" (p. 23).

176   Pierre Boulez
The French composer and conductor. Olson wrote Robert Creeley, 20 August 1951: "PIERRE BOULEZ—only two things of his exist (2nd Sonata, which I heard yesterday impeccably played (piano) by David Tudor; and a recording in NY) but for god's sake, go get him, when you are in Paris—he is 25, and I shall try to find out his address for you—Christ, does he come *straight* from himself, compose as a man, with none of the shit of 'music,' or experiment" (*O/RC* 7 : 111).

176   a ruthless reality on the other side of despair
A phrase used also in "The Materials and Weights of Herman Melville" (p. 117), there attributed to Rimbaud.

178   the mural of the death of Adam . . . at Arezzo
A fifteenth-century fresco by Piero della Francesca, which Olson may have seen in Kenneth Clark's *Piero Della Francesca* (London: Phaidon Press, 1951), plates 31–38.

179   "Proprioception"
In his "Reading at Berkeley," Olson told the crowd, "I'm happy that that book *Proprioception* is published. Every one of those essays, by the way, is published by LeRoi Jones alone,

in *Yūgen, Floating Bear,* and *Kulchur.* . . . And, you know, I wrote those essays—they're incongestible or something. They're not readable. If they're interesting, they can be dug up as signs" (*MUTH* 1 : 133). Written over a 2–1/2-year period from 1959 to 1962, these nine "incongestible . . . signs"—archeological remains *avant la lettre*—were first brought out as a group by the Four Seasons Foundation in 1965; reprinted in *AP.* The dedication to Jones (Amiri Baraka) was proposed in a letter to Donald Allen of 10 September 1969. Three years before, Olson had inscribed the following lines in Maximus:

> I have been an ability—a machine—up to
>
> now. An act of "history", my own, and my father's,
> . . . .
>   my father
>   And I
>   in the same land   like Pilgrims
>   come to shore
>   he paid
>   with his life . . .
> my father a Swedish
> wave of
> migration . . .
> like Negroes
> now like Leroy and Malcolm
> X the final wave
> of wash upon this
> desperate
> ugly
> cruel
> Land this Nation
> which never
> lets anyone
> come to
> shore

(MAX 495–97)

The extent to which Olson's added dedication reflects appreciation for Baraka's politics (then Black Nationalist), and not merely thanks for Baraka's work as editor, remains a matter of speculation. Nonetheless, the historical project outlined in the final sections of *Proprioception* cannily foreshadows the controversial scholarship of Martin Bernal, whose *Black Athena* combats the racist and anti-Semitic agenda of "the old discourse" (as "Bridge-Work" puts it), on the basis of painstaking linguistic analysis. Olson's own linguistic analysis is dictionary work. His definitions come from *Webster's Collegiate Dictionary,* 5th ed.; his etymologies are lifted from Charlton T. Lewis, *An Elementary Latin Dictionary,* and Liddell and Scott's *Greek-English Lexicon.*

"Proprioception" and "Logography" originally appeared in *Kulchur,* no. 1, Spring 1960, under the title "Pieces of Time" (a title supplied by the editor); "Postscript to Proprioception and Logography" followed in *Kulchur,* no. 2, 1960; "Bridge-Work" in *Kulchur,* no. 3, 1961; "the hinges of civilization to be put back on the door," in *Kulchur,* no. 5, Spring 1962. "GRAMMAR—'A Book'" came out in *Floating Bear,* no. 7, 1961; "A

Plausible 'Entry' for, like man," in *Floating Bear,* no. 11, 1961; "A Work," in *Floating Bear,* no. 21, 1962. "Theory of Society" first appeared in *Yūgen,* no. 7, 1961. Olson thought of these disparate pieces as a single book early on, as indicated by a 24 August 1961 postcard to Jonathan Williams:

> Do have a funny off-book of prose wld enjoy having you offer to [James] Laughlin [of New Directions] . . . maybe titled *Theory of Society* or, for real come-on, *Proprioception*
>
>> To include those 2 pieces plus *Logography* [,] the *Grammar* 'book,' maybe *Bridge-Work*
>> actual content very small in pages but set right wld at least give all that recent 'thinking' its issue—and my own guess is it[']s abt over (maybe even a letter to David Ignatow on politics and writin[g] (Buf.)

181 "Proprioception"

In this "WORKING / 'OUT' OF / 'PROJECTION'" Olson returns attention to several key ideas from his earlier work. He retrieves the word "soul" (rejected in "Projective Verse") and uses it to enlarge upon his notion of "body," led by a decade's readings in Jung to a reappreciation of "the old 'psychology' of feeling." An unsent letter intended for Robert Creeley, dated 15 July 1951, shows Olson's earliest recorded thoughts on the topic: "But in any case, it is this business of, the seat of life as *inside* man, and the blood system of feeder and flushes of organs, which settled humanism very early. And that what I have so often been talking about as such—humanism—has, ultimately, to be taken back to this point of historical time—this point which is no time at all"(*O/RC* 6:146).

181 judicium, dotha: . . . all feeling may flow

John Clarke in his notes from Olson's Fall 1964 Mythology Seminar records the following:

> OK, consider "thinking" function; thinking is Knossos, knowing; Nous, the mind as organ of clear images—an *action,* not a "function" at all as here described since its Platonic fall into static . . .
>
> First *sensation* (Plato, but he thinks it's perishing and only the rational "eternal") and "Inspection" (of Descartes) and "Intuition" (of Whitehead), then on to *Judgment (judicium),* true "opinion," and finally to. . . .
>
> yes, *Dogma (dotha, doxa, decus),* the "Firm Persuasion" that a thing is so,
>
>> and it all starts with the *animus,* the voice of the animate, affective condition, which we lost with the Platonic split, as Whitehead has demonstrated . . .
>
> only then can we speak of having *Reason,* . . . all is flow

The Latin *"iudicium"* is "judgment"; the Greek *"doxa"* is "opinion"; *"decus"* is Latin and means "glory"; the meaning of *"dotha"* remains unclear. See also Alfred North Whitehead, *Process and Reality.*

184 "Logography"

The quotations come from I. J. Gelb, *A Study of Writing* (1952; Chicago: University of Chicago Press, 1963), Chapter 3, "World-Syllabic Systems" (in the subsection "Sumerian System"), pp. 62, 64, and 66–67. In Chapter 11, "Terminology of Writing," Gelb defines

"*Logography* or *Word Writing*" (p. 250) as "A writing in which a sign normally stands for one or more words of the language."

184   "Postscript to Proprioception & Logography"
The two quoted passages are from the *Webster's Collegiate* definitions of "Landscape" and "notional."

184   GNA— . . . VID—
In "Under the Mushroom: The Gratwick Highlands Tape" (1963), Olson announces his "belief that etymology is even behind mythology as the secret of the universe":

> Etymology. And there's only two forms of knowing that I can figure out exist. One is *GNA-* and the other is *VID-*, and *VID-* is seeing and *GNA-* is *prajna* and is apprehension that I think you can only call oral, in the sense of sounds, therefore language. Yes, therefore language, therefore eyes, and that's all. There's a double—there's a staple or two of the agents [of] the vision. One is the eye and the other is a knowing which is— well, I would say oral but I don't want to press the point. It is *GNA-*, though. Leave it just in the *g-n-a-*, which is the basic root of "knowing." *K-n-o* is *g-n-a*, actually. It simply slipped. *Kna-*, *kno-*. And *VID-*. Because we all use the word—again this is where the vocabulary matters, because we all use the word *vision*. (*MUTH* 1 : 36)

186   "Theory of Society"
Reprises several of the ideas first published in "Against Wisdom as Such." The quoted passage ("God is the organ of novelty") comes from Whitehead's *Process and Reality,* p. 104 (in Chapter 2, "The Extensive Continuum").

188   "Bridge-Work"
The works of Fenollosa, Sauer, Waddell, Bérard, and Gordon were touchstones for Olson; their names appear again and again in his letters and essays (see, e.g., the editors' notes to pp. 150, 168, and 170, and see also Olson's "Homer and Bible," pp. 345–48). Sapir is quoted later in *Proprioception* (in "GRAMMAR—a 'book'"). Olson read Crowley's *Book of Thoth* at the Library of Congress in the 1940s, borrowing imagery for his poem "The Moon Is the Number 18" (*CP* 201–2; see also "The Moon," *Nation* 46). G. R .S. Mead's *Apollonius of Tyana: The Philosopher-Reformer of the First Century a.d.* (1901; New Hyde Park, N.Y.: University Books, 1966) is a source for Olson's dance of the same name (re- printed in *SW* and *FH*); Mead's *Pistis Sophia,* subtitled "A Gnostic Miscellany," was first published in 1896. Olson cites Whorf in the bibliography to *Mayan Letters* and in *The Special View of History.* According to Maud, Olson owned Lang's translation of Homer and read Lang's article on crystal-gazing in the *Encyclopedia Britannica* (11th ed.) (*Olson's Reading,* pp. 162–63). A citation from Edward Hyams serves as epigraph to the bibliog- raphy in *Mayan Letters* (*SW* 125). Carpenter (a friend of Whitman's) and Garrett (publisher of *Tomorrow* magazine) are nowhere else mentioned by Olson and none of their works survived in his library.

188   Gerrit Lansing
Gloucester poet and participant in Olson's "*Paris Review* Interview" (*MUTH* 2 : 105–153); his conversations with Olson continued until Olson's death.

189   "the hinges of civilization to be put back on the door":
John Clarke in his notes from Olson's Fall 1964 Mythology Seminar records the following:
> But our mapping is ineffectual unless,
>> you have experience of, direct experience, *phi*-experience (*physis*) of the "condition" of the universe—the real "Structure of Condition" of Life and Creation. . . .
>> Mythology is simply an inventory (a lexicon) of the highly complex characters of existence, the quite opaque states of being—a door opens with myth, but the whole point is to take the door off the hinges (or vice versa); and this is only done through phi-unit experience. . . . We *read* solely to acquire the capacity for phi-unit experience (cf. Melville and his voyaging in the libraries of the world). . . .

190   Miss Harrison clearest among moderns on Persian,
Jane Ellen Harrison. Three of her books are cited in *A Bibliography on America for Ed Dorn.*

190   Hans Jonas particularly useful
See Hans Jonas, *The Gnostic Religion: The Message of the Alien God and the Beginnings of Christianity* (1958; Boston: Beacon Press, 1963).

191   "GRAMMAR—a 'book'"
In "Bridge-Work," Olson lists Cyrus Gordon among the "men worth anyone's study," and cites Gordon's "identification of Linear A" in "A Work." In "The Vinland Map Review" he credits Michael Ventris and John Chadwick for their similar research into Linear B. For Olson, the decipherment of ancient script was a necessary step in freeing up "the encumbrance upon man as himself a universe" ("A Work")—in recovering knowledge of a world overthrown by "the Plato-Socrates generalization system" ("Review of Eric A. Havelock's *Preface to Plato*"). Nonetheless, the directionality of Olson's research in "GRAMMAR—a 'book'" differs markedly from that of a Gordon, Ventris, or Chadwick. Where Gordon et al. begin with pictographic scrawl and arrive at clear translation, Olson ("by a sort of inverted archeology," as he puts it in "Cy Twombly") accomplishes the opposite: he begins clearly (with words like "why," "WHO," "how," "*the,*" "LIKE!") and *arrives* at scrawl—at a graphic arrangement of inexplicit notes. This performative aspect of Olson's later prose (crucial to an understanding of his poetics) partly explains the comment that *Proprioception*'s nine parts "can be dug up as signs."

194   Sapir (*Language*)
Olson's quotation here and those below are from Edward Sapir, *Language: An Introduction to the Study of Speech* (New York: Harcourt, Brace, Jovanovich, 1949), pp. 163–64 ("The first . . . objective forms"); pp. 113–14 ("It is somewhat venturesome . . . ," "Thus, the *of* . . . ," "An interesting . . . "); and p. 115 ("Every noun . . . table.'").

195   image (instead of images, in Nicholas Calas (via Robt Kelly's essay
In a letter to Robert Kelly of 3 October 1960, responding to Kelly's "Notes on the Poetry of Deep Image," *Trobar,* no. 2, 1960, pp. 14–16, Olson writes:
> Calas is wrong that the movement of the images constitutes the rhythm of the poem There are no plurals in this business The image you are talking about is always one

"the movement of the image"
wld be correct, and "poems"
wld be, tapped off the main
wire so to speak. But not the movement of the images Or at least at this point—

which you have reached or are proposing—*ars,* and poetica, have to be handled only

under a guise of dichtung and wahrheit as mixed as I believe you know when you talk

prima mater[i]a. We are in direct touch with the powers of God. (Buf.)

196   "A Plausible 'Entry' for, like, man"
The references here to Averroes and Eric the Red are the earliest indication of Olson's increasing (and parallel) study of the Arabs and the Norse. (See, in this connection, his chronology in "Continuing Attempt to Pull the Taffy off the Roof of the Mouth," pp. 372–73.)

196   "larger than any . . . "
From the opening paragraph of Jonas, *The Gnostic Religion,* p. 3.

197   "A Work"
The social and political implications of his interest in "unwritten history" were clear to Olson early on, especially with regard to the categorization of ancient societies according to modern ideas of race. A letter to Robert Creeley from Mexico, dated 22 March 1951, observes:

> Of course I balk at same, or at least resist, simply because I take it, racism has to be kept at the end of a stick. Or put it this way: until we have completely cleaned our-selves of the biases of westernism, of greekism, until we have squared away at histori-cal time in such manner that we are able to see Sumer as a point from which *all* "races" (speaking of them culturally, not biologically) egressed, we do not have permis-sion to weight the scale one way or another (for example, Jakeman, leaves, so far as I have read him, the invention of maize to the Mongoloids, as well as the arts of ceram-ica, weaving, and baskets! And, *contra* (contra all these prejudiced Nordics, among whom I include Hooton, who has sd, from skull-measurements, that it is true, there were Caucasians here), there remains China, ancient and modern China. Until the lads can verify that the Chinese, as well as the people of India, come off from the Tigris-Euphrates complex, they better lie low with their jumps to conclude that only the Cau-casian type was the civilizing type of man). ((As you know, this whole modern intellec-tual demarche has, at its roots, a negative impulse, deeper, even, than the anti-Asia colonialism of Europe: at root, the search is, to unload, to disburden themselves of Ju-daism, of Semitism)) (*O/RC* 5:90)

The focus on "Judaism" and "Semitism" follows from a number of Olson's interests, the most significant of which, in the present context, is recorded in a later letter (19 February 1952), where Olson tells Creeley, "Judaism/Hebraism . . . represent[s] the only FORMU-LATION of the archaic fact which [comes] down to us, due to a series of erasures by Greekism, Hindooism, & Christianity in between us and the Older People" (*O/RC* 9:139). The cost of these erasures is one of Olson's most persistent themes; in "A Work" he offers his most explicit statement on the historical terrain he himself sought to recover.

197   Hans Güterbock, has suggested
Hans Gustav Güterbock, "The Hittite Version of the Hurrian Kumarbi Myths: Oriental Forerunners of Hesod," *American Journal of Archaeology* 52 : 1, January–March 1948, pp. 123–34.

197   Phylo Biblius quoting Sanchuniathon
See, in this connection, Olson's introduction to Charles Doria's translation of Sanchuniaton, "What's Back There" (p. 363).

198   the identification of Linear A by Cyrus Gordon
Fresh news when Olson was writing. "See '"Cipher" Gives Key to Cretan Tongue: Brandeis Scholar Says His Study of an Ancient Text Shows It Was Phoenician," *New York Times,* 4 April 1962, p. 39; also, similar articles in the *Boston Globe* and *Boston Herald* for that day—clippings of all of which are preserved among the poet's papers." (GB, at *AP* 89)

198   the so-called "Sea-Peoples"
See also *MAX* 275:

> where did the Sumerians
> come from, into the Persian
> Gulf—sea-peoples
> who raided and imposed themselves
> on a black-haired previous people
> dwelling among reed-houses
> on flooded marshes?

198   Tatian in his address to the Greeks quotes Thallus,
Noted by Robert Graves in *The Greek Myths,* p. 42.

199   one can then begin to work Hesiod back
An unpublished prose piece headed *"March 14th   1965"* names the route: "By these means alone [archeology, philology, and decipherment—a Greece] a past back along the line of man language and notation transmission to ourselves has opened up in the neighborhood of a full 1000 years before Homer & Hesiod, on the general Greek-Aegean-Rhodes-Cyprus-Crete Syrian Philistine Egyptian African line" (Storrs, Prose Series, brackets in original).

200   "Place; & Names"
Written 5 January 1962; published in *Yūgen,* no. 8 (1962); reprinted *ARCH.* Olson reads and dicusses this piece with Robert Duncan, Allen Ginsberg, and Robert Creeley in "On History," the transcript of a panel discussion at the University of British Columbia Poetry Conference, 29 July 1963 (*MUTH* 1 : 1–19).

200   the Brihadaranyaka Upanishad
On the back of an 11 September 1960 letter from LeRoi Jones (Amiri Baraka), Olson has written amid a series of penciled notes "GET the Brihadaranyaka" and "Hume, Rob E

(trans) The Thirteen Principal Upanishads Oxford 1921" (Storrs, Correspondence). The reference may have come from several texts Olson is known to have read, most notably C. G. Jung's *Symbols of Transformation,* tr. R. F. C. Hull, *The Collected Works of C. G. Jung,* vol. 5, Bollingen Series 20 (Princeton, N.J.: Princeton University Press, 1956), where the Brihadaranyaka Upanishad is discussed at length.

200   landschaft
German, "landscape."

201   Duncan's Law
Robert Duncan had written Olson, 18 December 1961:

> . . . "history"?—couldn't we throw that word out and establish:
>   histology: the tissue and structure, weaving, of what [it] is we know.
>   story: what we know from the question we askd. This thing is made-up, or an
> answer—but is, also, the only thing we know to answer: oracle or sphinx-demand.

202   "'you can't use words . . . '"
Published in *Tuftonian* 21:2, February 1965; reprinted in *ARCH.*

The Present Is Prologue

205   "The Present Is Prologue"
Originally published in *Twentieth Century Authors,* First Supplement, 1955; reprinted in *AP.* As George Butterick notes (quoting a 23 December 1956 letter to Michael Rumaker), the essay was written "election day 1952, in a sort of swirl, thickness of the Unc[onscious]." A decade later, in his "Reading at Berkeley" (memory jogged by a casual mention of Adlai Stevenson, who lost the '52 election), Olson describes the essay as "a flagrant autobiography of myself, imitating Ezra Pound" (*MUTH* 1:123). Poundian or not, the essay concludes with a post-Poundian reference to "the post-modern, the post-humanist, the post-historical," as well as with Olson's best-known self-characterization: "I find it awkward to call myself a poet or a writer. . . . This is the morning, after the dispersion, and the work of the morning is methodology: how to use oneself, and on what. That is my profession. I am an archaeologist of morning."

205   My mother was Mary Hines, and Yeats told me
Olson met Yeats in Ireland during a summer trip to Europe, which he won in an oratory competition in Washington, D.C., in 1928. Yeats has, in "'Dust Hath Closed Helen's Eye,'" a section of *The Celtic Twilight:*

> I have been lately to a little group of houses, not many enough to be called a village, in the barony of Kiltartan in County Galway, whose name, Ballylee, is known through all the west of Ireland. . . . I have been there this summer, and I shall be there again before it is autumn, because Mary Hynes, a beautiful woman whose name is still a wonder by turf fires, died there sixty years ago; for our feet would linger where beauty has lived its life of sorrow to make us understand that it is not of the world. (*Early Poems and Stories,* pp. 159–60)

Yeats presents a translation of Raftery's song about Mary Hynes at pp. 162–63.

206   the phenomenological 'raging apart'
From Lawrence's *The Escaped Cock,* quoted in Olson's essay on that novel, p. 140.

207   the "Beautiful Thing"
From William Carlos Williams, *Paterson,* as in Book 3, Section 1, p. 101:

> The Library is desolation, it has a smell of its own
> of stagnation and death
>
>   Beautiful Thing!
> —the cost of dreams,
>   in which we search, after a surgery
> of the wits and must translate, quickly
> step by step or be destroyed—

208   "Stocking Cap"
Written in Washington, D.C., and submitted to the *New Yorker* in February of 1948; first published in *Montavallo Review,* no. 2, Summer 1951; reprinted in 1966 by the Four Seasons Foundation as Writing 13, and in *PO.* Early on in his correspondence with Robert Creeley, in a letter dated 21 June 1950, Olson wrote: "I am nervous abt it, but in MR2, at [editor Robert] Payne's insistence, there will appear my only piece of prose outside ISHMAEL, a 'story,' i guess you'd call it (actually recollection—which is, I suppose, why I am nervous abt it), title STOCKING CAP" (*O/RC* 1 : 122–23). Tom Clark provides a wider context for "Stocking Cap" and Olson's two other autobiographical stories ("Mr. Meyer" and "The Post Office") in his biography, *Charles Olson: The Allegory of a Poet's Life.*

213   "Mr. Meyer"
Written in Washington, D.C., early in 1948; first published in *PO.*

217   "The Post Office"
Written in Washington, D.C., at about the same time as "Stocking Cap" and "Mr. Meyer"; possibly submitted to *Atlantic Monthly.* George Butterick in his 1975 introduction to this memoir quotes a notebook entry of 8 March 1948: "At least one course is clear—do this book on yr father without reference to culture—style, manner, tricks—do it on the level of mediocre humanitas. If you are not an artist, genius, & clever, let this make it clear. And take the consequences." First published in *PO.*

219   Joseph Altsheler
Mentioned also in *Maximus:* "Altsheler/taught us how to fight Indians" (*MAX* 58).

230   George Harris' proposition
In the voice of Sut Lovingood, creation of nineteenth-century Southern humorist George Washington Harris.

Poetry and Poets

239   "Projective Verse"
Olson's most influential essay, "Projective Verse," was written and rewritten in correspondence with Frances Boldereff and Robert Creeley, and printed in *Poetry New York,* no. 3,

1950; reprinted many times, first (in part) in *The Autobiography of William Carlos Williams* (New York: Random House, 1951), but also in the pamphlet *Projective Verse* (New York: Totem, 1959), in *The New American Poetry 1945–1960,* ed. Donald Allen (New York: Grove Press, 1960), in *HU,* and in *SW.* The title draws on a number of sources, including "projective geometry" (which Olson knew from his readings in Bonola, Coxeter, and Weyl; see "Equal, That Is, to the Real Itself"), and the "projective art" of theater (which Olson taught in 1952 at Black Mountain College; his course description emphasized "the usages of the poet historically and again now as the root of drama" [*OJ* 2 : 27]).

"Projective Verse" offers an early crystallization of Olson's poetics, but following Edward Dahlberg's dictum "ONE PERCEPTION MUST IMMEDIATELY AND DIRECTLY LEAD TO A FURTHER," Olson continued to press forward in his research. Attempts at a sequel include the 1959 "Letter to Elaine Feinstein" and two separate unpublished essays called "Projective Verse II," one dated 1956, the other 1959. In the earlier of these, Olson asks:

> Has language only that property, that it enables the poet to traffic in between his self and your self, trading his terms for yours, and getting no more power out of it than your ackowledgement that he speaks for you? But does he, even at his best? Can he, when you are your own involvement, and so engaged, willy-nilly, poems or no poems? You will speak in the next second by words which are, I propose, *prior* to all you are, and more necessary to you, if you are properly engaged with what it is to be human, than your toes, or your opposable thumb, that if you move as man has since either he or nature raised him to speech, to the capacity to speak, you move with or against yourself—you have more or less life—exactly to the degree that language empowers you. (Storrs, Prose Series)

Notwithstanding his essay's predominantly literary focus, Olson's ultimate interest in the *concept* of "Projective Verse" is phenomenological, something that becomes especially clear in an unpublished prose piece from 1965, "The Projective, in Poetry and in Thought; and the Paratactic." Here Olson develops a notion of "practice" that far outstrips the emphasis on verse-making of the 1950 essay:

> my interest, in adding the paratactic to any previous thought on the projective (pro-
> spective   prescriptive   eternal) is to assume, by experience, that the poetry and
> the thought called purposive behavior   "practice"   requires some different mode of
> action—activity literally, living round the clock, eating even, making love differ-
> ently   finding yourself engaged in an impossible war with the realistic, and with
> realistic people—
>   . . . my . . . point would be . . . that syntax . . . or the ordering of all movement . . .
> has a name for itself   parataxis
>   Aristotle called it the way beads are strung on a string one bead and thread after
> another   And there is that sense that it is one foot after the previous foot that nothing
> doesn't happen except as succession, and with *that* order of succession in time . . .
> known only if you do yourself place one next thing after one you have definitely ex-
> pressed the placing of, like your foot the step before—etc   the succession in time be-
> ing solely the experience in terms of a different & known & palpable order—physical,
> literally, & temporal . . .
>   Something like it anyway wld be the dream of the success of what is also the use-
> fulness, of what I have called the *Projective* (Storrs, Prose Series)

239   *a French critic*
Identified by Ralph Maud as René Nelli, who asks in *Poésie ouverte poésie fermée*, "Mais y a-t-il une poésie *ouverte* sur le réel et une poésie fermée sur les mots?"—"But is there a poetry *open* on the real and a poetry closed on the words?" (*Olson's Reading*, pp. 84 and 277 n. 29).

239   *"the Egotistical Sublime"*
Keats's description of Wordsworth, from a letter to Richard Woodhouse of 27 October 1818:

> As to the poetical Character itself (I mean that sort, of which, if I am anything, I am a member; that sort distinguished from the Wordsworthian, or egotistical Sublime; which is a thing per se, and stands alone,) it is not itself—it has no self—It is everything and nothing—It has no character—it enjoys light and shade; it lives in gusto, be it foul or fair, high or low, rich or poor, mean or elevated—It has as much delight in conceiving an Iago as an Imogen. What shocks the virtuous philosopher delights the chameleon poet. (*The Letters of John Keats*, p. 184)

239   revolution of the ear, 1910
The year 1910 (Olson's own birth year) is in many ways a magnet, accruing facts the way a magnet gathers iron filings. In his 1946 poem "La Préface," Olson drew the date thus:

            (   ) 1910 (
It is not obscure. We are the new born . . .
. . . .
The closed parenthesis reads: the dead bury the dead,
                                        and it is not very interesting.
Open, the figure stands at the door, horror his
and gone, possessed, o new Osiris, Odysseus ship.
                        (*CP* 47)

John Clarke in his notes for Olson's Fall 1964 Mythology Seminar provides an alternative gloss:

> Then the psychic awakening came:

1903	Gertrude Stein, *Quod Erat Demonstrandum* (pub. 1950 as *Things as They Are*)
1909	Stein, *Three Lives!* Pound, *Exultations, Personae*

> The Phenomenology of Perception of the 20th c. ended the Neolithic period, 1910— the return of the possibility of a paratactic poetics, as with Pleistocene man, when poetry and mythology were one, *mythos-logos* intact.

239   the trochee's heave
Writing Robert Creeley on 22 June 1950, Olson has: "THE TROCHEE: with it, a new language, for USE, made USA (Where'd he get it, the trochee? hunch: out of Miss Sappho by Seafarer" (*O/RC* 1:140). The "he" here is Pound, who has in Canto 81, "To break the pentameter, that was the first heave."

240   the *kinetics* of the thing
In an early version of his essay "Human Universe," Olson writes:

To repossess ourselves of a methodology of expression which shall be the equal of the laws which so richly determine the original function which we call human life—this, surely, is the task. And I have elsewhere argued that the first principle is, that if you propose to transfer power you must manage in the process of the transfer a kinetic at least the equal of the thing from which you begin. Which is why we will do nothing until we front what we are, precisely, the conditions of a human being, what is, exactly, the nature of a human life. (Glover diss., p. 271)

240   as Pound put, so wisely . . . "the musical phrase,"
In the third of three principles given in "A Retrospect," e.g., "As regarding rhythm: to compose in the sequence of the musical phrase, not in sequence of a metronome" (*The Literary Essays of Ezra Pound,* ed. T. S. Eliot [New York: New Directions, 1968], p. 3).

240   Or so it got phrased by one, R. Creeley
In a letter dated 5 June 1950, by way of distinguishing "form" from "technical wonder," the latter of which he describes as

> absolute bull/shit. That is: the intelligence that had touted Auden as being a tech-
> nical wonder, etc. Lacking all grip on the worn and useless character of his essence:
> thought. An attitude that puts weight, *first:* on form/ more than to say: what you have
> above: will never get to: content. Never in god's world. Anyhow, form has now be-
> come so useless a term/ that I blush to use it. I wd imply a little of Stevens' use (the
> things created *in* a poem and existing there . . .) & too, go over into: the possible casts
> or methods for a way into/ a 'subject': to make it clear: that form is never more than an
> *extension* of content. An enacted or possible 'stasis' for thought. (*O/RC* 1:78–79)

240   pounded into my head by Edward Dahlberg
Apparently in conversation. John Cech in *Charles Olson and Edward Dahlberg: A Portrait of a Friendship* (Victoria, B.C.: English Literary Studies, University of Victoria, 1982) quotes an unpublished loose manuscript note of Olson's from 1945, "Go to the extreme of your imagination and go on from there: fail large, never succeed small. Again ED makes sense: one intuition must only lead to another farther place" (pp. 88–89).

241   O western wynd, when wilt thou blow
Anonymous poem of the sixteenth century.

242   "Is" comes from the Aryan root
Lifted by Olson (along with other lines) from "Mouths Biting Empty Air," an unpublished prose piece dated 27 October 1946, now at Storrs.

244   Newman Shea
A Gloucester fisherman named also in "Letter 20" of the Maximus poems (*MAX* 89, 91), in "The Morning News" (*CP* 122), and in Olson's 1936 "Journal of Swordfishing Cruise on the *Doris M. Hawes*" (*OJ* 7:10, 19).

244   But there is a loss in Crane of what Fenollosa is so right about, in syntax
Hart Crane and Ernest Fenollosa (the latter discusses syntax in *The Chinese Written Character*). The criticism of Crane was later lodged by Olson against Robin Blaser as well—to

wit, "I'd trust you anywhere with image, but you've got no syntax." See *Minutes of the Charles Olson Society,* no. 8 ("A Special Issue for the Robin Blaser Conference"), p. 13.

245   If music be the food of love, play on
Shakespeare's *Twelfth Night* 1 : 1 : 1 – 7.

245   For the breath has a double meaning which latin had not yet lost
"Spiritus"—both breath and spirit.

246   What does not change / is the will to change
Opening line of Olson's poem "The Kingfishers" (*CP* 86).

246   Sd he:
From Olson's "The Praises" (*CP* 98).

246   Seami
A Japanese writer of the late fourteenth and early fifteenth centuries, also known as Motekiyo. In 1961, after reading a version of Seami's *Yashima* in *Origin,* Olson wrote Cid Corman, "If you find anyone who has translated Seami's *Autobiography* literally & entirely I shd be obliged to hear of it. I remain convinced of its importance (reading his new play you published emphasizes again what a flawless poet he is" (*O/CC* 2 : 173).

247   "objectivism"
The work of a loosely affiliated group of poets first published by Louis Zukofsky in a special issue of *Poetry* magazine in 1931.

248   *The Trojan Women*
By Euripides.

248   *Hagoromo*
One of the Noh plays translated by Pound, whose introductory note declares, "The play shows the relation of the early Noh to the God-dance" (*Ezra Pound: Translations* [New York: New Directions, 1963], p. 308).

248   "Prufrock"
T. S. Eliot's poem "The Love Song of J. Alfred Prufrock."

250   "Letter to Elaine Feinstein"
First published in 1959 in the pamphlet *Projective Verse,* under the title "Letter from Charles Olson Received by E. B. Feinstein"; reprinted in *The New American Poetry, SW,* and *HU.* Feinstein is a British poet, critic, and translator.

250   Truth! (Wahrheit) . . . beauty (Schönheit)
Keats's terms (from "Ode on a Grecian Urn") translated into Goethe's German.

250   das Ding—Ja!—macht ring
German, "the thing—yes!—makes noise."

250   Dante's sense
In *De Vulgari Eloquentia.*

251   if this all sounds bloody German

Not simply because of the German words cited above—Olson is borrowing terms from Otto Rank, *Art and Artist,* tr. Charles Francis Atkinson (1932), reprinted in Rank, *The Myth of the Birth of the Hero,* ed. Philip Freund (New York: Vintage, 1959).

251   my friends from the American Underground

A reference to the recent seizure by the police of *Chicago Review* on charges of obscenity, for having published a section of *Naked Lunch.* Olson published his essay "Equal, That Is, to the Real Itself" in *Chicago Review* in 1958.

251   if you bisect a parabola you get an enantiomorph

I.e., "each form being a mirror image of the other, like left and right hands" (Hermann Weyl, *Symmetry* [Princeton, N.J.: Princeton University Press, 1952], p. 29).

253   "'On Poets and Poetry'"

A letter to the editor printed in *New Mexico Quarterly* 24 : 1, Spring 1954; reprinted in *HU.*

254   Miss Koch's book on Williams

Vivien Koch, *William Carlos Williams* (Norfolk, Va.: New Directions, 1950).

256   "Notes on Language and Theater"

Published in *Black Mountain Review,* no. 3, Fall 1954; reprinted in *HU.* George Butterick writes in his introduction to *The Fiery Hunt and Other Plays,* a collection of Olson's performance texts:

> Olson's interest in the theater extends back to at least his high school and college days, when he was a successful schoolboy actor. . . . He also took leading roles in community theater productions, formally studied theatrical skills at a well-run summer theater in a spacious old sail loft in Gloucester, and was himself assistant dramatic coach in addition to his teaching and debate-coaching duties at Clark University in his home town of Worcester in the early 1930s. . . . As a youngster he saw the legendary Buffalo Bill in his traveling Wild West show, and . . . Clyde Beatty the animal trainer in circuses at Stage Fort Park; later, he went to the burlesque in Boston and in Hartford . . . ; and after he began his career as a poet he continued to read conscientiously in the theater of the Greeks . . . and in Shakespeare.

256   *Mimos* wasn't even imitation so late as the Grks.

Jane E. Harrison in *Ancient Art and Ritual* (p. 47) has:

> The word *mimesis* means the action or doing of a person called a *mime.* Now a *mime* was simply a person who dressed up and acted in a pantomime or primitive drama. He was roughly what we should call an *actor,* and it is significant that in the word *actor* we stress not imitating but acting, doing, just what the Greek stressed in his words *drome-non* and *drama.* The actor dresses up, puts on a mask, wears the skin of a beast or the feathers of a bird, not, as we have seen, to copy something or some one who is not himself, but to emphasize, enlarge, enhance, his own personality; he masquerades, he does not mimic.

256   *the rhabdians,* . . . Berard . . . Laughton and Claude Rains

Olson's source for "rhabdians" is uncertain, but Jane Harrison (in *Prolegomena to the Study of Greek Religion* [1903; New York: Meridian Books, 1966]) defines "rhabdos" as "magic wand" (p. 44), linking its use to "an ecstatic dance of goat-horned *Panes*" (pp. 277–78). Victor Bérard in *Did Homer Live?* speaks of Homer's two epics as "really plays," noting (p. 210 n. 1): "I should like one day to give the general public the story of this "epic drama" in its earliest state. Now that the younger generation are trying to enlist the film and phonograph in the service of literature and create the 'talky play' it is, I think, to the example of Greek *epos* that they should turn."

In 1952–53, Charles Laughton staged a "roadshow" production of Stephen Vincent Benét's epic poem *John Brown's Body* (the other actors were Raymond Massey, Judith Anderson, and Tyrone Power); in 1943, Laughton and Claude Rains appeared together in "Forever and a Day," a historical drama directed by René Clair for RKO pictures.

257   LaGuardia
Fiorello LaGuardia, mayor of New York City, famous for reading the Sunday funnies over the radio.

257   Ann Corio's belly, Ragland
John Finch in his memoir of Olson, "Dancer and Clerk" (*Massachusetts Review,* Winter 1971, p. 36) remembers that

> Boston offered the Old Howard, New York the Irving Place. It was in those two temples of burlesque's Golden Era that Olson and I encountered Rags Ragland and Ann Corio, Georgia Southern and Sliding Billy Watson, and Leda and the Swan. Yes, the immortal bird and the mortal Leda, in the flesh, not a movin' pitcher. For burlesque, in the thirties, was highbrow, not lowbrow; and believe me, we weren't slumming when we went. Didn't Professor Kenneth Murdock frequent the Old Howard, and Professor Ellery Sedgewick, too? They did. And E. E. Cummings made pictures and poems of Shargel and strippers from the Irving Place.

257   Henry Luce
Publisher of *Time* magazine. The specific reference is unclear.

258   the *Great Dictator*
Chaplin's 1940 satire on Hitler, in which Chaplin plays the lookalike roles of Jewish barber and Hitleresque dictator. Jack Okie plays the Mussolini character.

260   "Against Wisdom as Such"
Originally written 21 December 1953 as a letter to Robert Duncan; published in the inaugural issue of *Black Mountain Review,* Spring 1954; reprinted in *HU.* Duncan recorded his immediate response in a letter to Olson of 8 August 1954. "I picked up Black Mt. Review at the Pocket Book Shop and read the 'Wisdom as Such' piece. If it reprimands in part I ain't going to rise in defense of my bewilderings—this matter of clarification is too important."

260   Duncan's genuine "diary"
Available now in Robert Duncan, *A Selected Prose,* ed. Robert Bertholf (New York: New Directions, 1995).

260   I saw one in *Circle* in 1947
The title poem of Duncan's *The Years as Catches: First Poems (1939–1946)* (Berkeley, Calif.: Oyez Books, 1966).

260   Jack Spicer . . . Rexroth and Patchen
Spicer is the only one of Duncan's contemporaries included in the list—a fact that may have grated on Olson, hence his reference to Kenneth Rexroth and Kenneth Patchen, two poets associated with the West Coast not numbered among Duncan's forty. Their mention appears to have grated on Duncan in return; his 8 August letter to Olson includes the comment, "Patchen or Rexroth are in my way."

261   as Duncan has so finely made Confucius say,
Not in the *Artist's View* notebook entries; the source remains unidentified.

262   Apollonius of Tyana
See G. R .S. Mead's *Apollonius of Tyana,* a key source for Olson's play of the same name, from which the quoted lines below are taken (*FH* 79 [also *SW* 155] and Mead, pp. 125 and 138).

263   Lü Tung-pin
Author of the *T'ai I Chin Hua Tsung Chih,* translated into German by Richard Wilhelm (English translation by Cary Baynes) as *The Secret of the Golden Flower: A Chinese Book of Life* (New York: Harcourt, Brace, 1931), a text that occupied Olson's attention to the end of his days, witness "The Secret of the Black Chrysanthemum," Olson's deathbed text (posthumously published in *OJ* 3 : 64–92; reprinted in Charles Stein's *The Secret of the Black Chrysanthemum: The Poetic Cosmology of Charles Olson & His Use of the Writings of C .G. Jung* [Barrytown, N.Y.: Station Hill Press, 1987]).

263   Poe's Poetic Principle
Title of an 1850 lecture in which "the Poetry of words" is defined "as *The Rhythmical Creation of Beauty.*" Edgar Allan Poe, *Essays and Reviews* (New York: Library of America, 1984), p. 78.

263   whatever is born or done this moment of time
A notion Olson reiterates in *Proprioception,* in the section "Theory of Society."

264   how Bill has it in "To a Dog Injured in the Street,"
In *The Desert Music,* newly published at the time. The poem addresses the French poet directly: "René Char / you are a poet who believes / in the power of beauty to right all wrongs. / I believe it also" (*The Collected Poems of William Carlos Williams, Volume 2: 1939–1962,* ed. Christopher MacGowan [New York: New Directions, 1988], p. 257).

264   "it is time (love) is difficult, Mr. Beardsley"
Answer to a line Pound gives in Canto 75 (adapted from Yeats's *Autobiography,* p. 223), "'beauty is difficult' sd / Mr. Beardsley" (see also a similar line in Canto 80).

264   "He who controls rhythm, controls"
In an unpublished prose piece from ca. 1953–56, "The Point at Which Analogies Are the Facts of Myth and Science," Olson has: " . . . we grow, as plants do, because the sun makes it possible. So fire is the source of life, and we speak right when we say, as of the

life in us . . . that it is fire. . . . And thus rhythm is what we are and how we do control the universe: the rhythm, of burning, which is light, and how earth and water produce, life" (Storrs, Prose Series).

265   "Theocritus"
Published in *Black Mountain Review,* no. 4, Winter 1954; reprinted in *HU.* Corman mailed Olson his translation on 30 August 1954. Olson wrote back 5 November:

> And Cid—please always, forgive me any harshness, like I think you may find [in] my review of yr *Sparrow* Eclogue. It is never the back of my hand. It is that passion, that all things be done right. And take it, please, that I wouldn't talk back if I didn't *love.*
>   And happened
> to pay attention just because it was you! (*O/CC* 2 : 126)

269   "A Foot Is to Kick With"
Published in *Black Mountain Review,* no. 6, Spring 1956; reprinted in *HU.*

270   "Quantity in Verse and Shakespeare's Late Plays"
Although his published output offers no hint, Olson worked assiduously in the 1950s to produce a book on Shakespeare—ten chapters are preserved in Olson's papers at Storrs. Out of that attempt came the essay at hand, "banged out" in 1956 (*O/CC* 2 : 155); first published in *HU;* reprinted in *SW.*

270   Tasso or Ariosto
Torquato Tasso and Lodovico Ariosto, authors of *Gerusalemme Liberata* (1575) and *Orlando Furioso* (1532), respectively, long poems written in Italian.

271   So comedy is a certain kind of poetic narration
Redacted from paragraph ten of Dante's Tenth Epistle (as subsequently noted), which Olson is citing from *A Translation of the Latin Verse of Dante Alighieri* (1904; New York: Greenwood Press, 1969). The extract below is from paragraph 15; the italics are Olson's.

271–72   "As we are men," says Theseus
The extract below continues from the same passage. See *Two Noble Kinsmen* 1 : 1 : 232 – 34.

272   paradis n'est pas artificiel
French, "paradise is not artificial."

273   (Ceres, most bounteous lady,
This and the two quotes below are from *The Tempest* 4 : 1 : 60 – 61, 64 – 66, 94 – 101.

273   We may outrun
Henry VIII 1 : 1 : 141 – 45.

274   Dante called them
In *De Vulgari Eloquentia,* Book 2, Chapter 7.

276   *Comus,* god help us,
A mask by Milton first presented in 1634.

276 "Metropolis"
Fritz Lang's silent film from 1926.

276 (he hadn't got that far), romantical-pastical
"He" being Polonius, whose list of dramatic forms in *Hamlet* includes "tragedy, comedy, history, pastoral, pastoral-comical, historical-pastoral, tragical-historical, tragical-comical-historical-pastoral" (2:2:396–99).

276 Twenty-three years, and saw myself unbreeched
Winter's Tale 1:2:155–58, 417–19.

277 "The flatness of my misery!" is what Hermione cries
Winter's Tale 3:2:122.

277 We were as twinned lambs that did frisk
Winter's Tale 1:2:67–74. The quotation below ("By this we gather . . . ") immediately follows, at lines 75–76.

278 You talk of Pirithous' and Theseus' love. . . . in sex dividual.
Two Noble Kinsmen 1:3:55–61, 64–68, 71–72, 78–82.

279 Do not give dalliance
The Tempest 4:1:51–54.

279 A pudency so rosy the sweet view on it
Cymbeline 2:5:11–13.

280 I warrant you, sir.
The Tempest 4:1:54–56.

280 Chinese play . . . Nessus' shirt
A Japanese play—the *Hagoromo*, cited in "Projective Verse," p. 248. Nessus the Centaur was killed by Herakles while attempting to rape Deianeira; before dying, Nessus gave Deianeira a tunic that he claimed would keep Herakles faithful. When Herakles put the tunic on, "it clung to him so fast that his flesh came away with it, laying bare the bones. His blood hissed and bubbled like spring water when red-hot metal is being tempered. He plunged headlong into the nearest stream, but the poison burned only the fiercer" (Graves, *The Greek Myths,* p. 563).

281 Extremity, that sharpens sundry wits
Two Noble Kinsmen 1:1:118–19.

281 Prospero's answer to Miranda's pleasure
The Tempest 5:1:184.

283 "Introduction to Robert Creeley"
Published in *New Directions* 13, 1951; reprinted in *HU.* Olson's friendship with Creeley began by mail in April 1950; the first two years of the correspondence now fill nine volumes (with many letters missing). Dedicatee of the first book of Maximus (where he is

named "the Figure of Outward"), Creeley is also inscribed in the last, in a poem that speaks of "Love made known." Listing there "The careful ones I care for," Olson ends with "Robert Creeley of course who like I is tight where lusimeles goes" (*MAX* 557). Greek for "loose limbed," "lusimeles" is in Hesiod's *Theogony* an attribute of love. Choosing the word "tight," Olson may have been recalling Creeley's rigorous statement from *For Love,* another version of the inside narrative Olson praises in this "Introduction"—

> Mind's heart, it must
> be that some
> truth lies locked
> in you.

> Or else, lies, all
> lies, and no man
> true enough to know
> the difference.
>> (*The Collected Poems of Robert Creeley 1945–1975*
>> [Berkeley: University of California Press, 1982], p. 241)

284   MR. BLUE
A short story by Creeley first published in the second issue of *Origin;* reprinted in *The Collected Prose of Robert Creeley* (New York: Marion Boyers, 1984), pp. 20–26.

285   "Robert Creeley's *For Love: Poems 1950–1960*"
Published in *Village Voice,* 13 September 1962; reprinted in *AP.* The poems Olson cites now appear in Creeley's *Collected Poems,* p. 215 ("The Song"); p. 132 ("I Know a Man"); pp. 199–201 ("The Door"); and p. 251 ("The People").

288   "William Carlos Williams: *Paterson,* Book V"
Published in *Evergreen Review* 3:9, Summer 1959; reprinted in *William Carlos Williams: The Critical Heritage,* ed. Charles Doyle (London: Routledge and Kegan Paul, 1980), pp. 319–22. Olson wrote Allen Ginsberg, 21 November 1958: "Am in the midst of trying to write a review of Pat V for Evergreen . . . —it puts me in touch with something which I have felt and you have known: that sometime around 1952 (a date *after* his poem Desert Music) a jump took place (of which you are a mark for sure) of which his shift of "Measure" wasn't good enough: evidence it isn't is the silver threads among the silk and wool side of Pat V" (*SL*). The version published here follows Olson's typescript (at Syracuse University Library) rather than the mangled version in *Evergreen Review.*

288   the Cloisters' tapestry on the hunt of the Unicorn
In Book 5, Sections 1 and 3, of *Paterson.*

288   "There is a woman in our town,"
Book 5, Section 2, p. 216.

288   "the living fiction,"
Book 5, Section 3, p. 231.

288   the 'dog' of his mind.
In the Preface to Book 1, Williams has (p. 3):

> To make a start,
> out of particulars
> and make them general, rolling
> up the sum, by defective means—
> Sniffing the trees,
> just another dog
> among a lot of dogs.

289   "I, Paterson, the King-self"
Book 5, Section 3, p. 231.

289   what he is talking about (in caps,
In Book 5, Section 1, p. 207: "A WORLD OF ART / THAT THROUGH THE YEARS HAS // SURVIVED!"

289   Not in ideas etc (NOT prophecy
Book 5, Section 1, p. 206, "NOT prophecy! / but the thing itself" (recalling Book 1, Section 1, p. 9, "No ideas but in things").

289   I append these passages
The first is not from Book 5 of *Paterson;* the rest appear on pp. 206, 226, 229, 232, and 235.

291   "Ed Sanders' Language"
Introductory note for Sanders's *Peace Eye* (Buffalo,N.Y.: Frontier Press, 1965); reprinted in *AP.*

291   it takes the earth to make a feather fall
John Clarke has the following in his notes for Olson's Fall 1964 Mythology Seminar (quoting Hermann Weyl, *Philosophy of Mathematics and Natural Science*):

> "Long ago," says Weyl, "E. Mach tried to interpret the inertial mass of a body as an induc-
> tive effect of the other masses of the universe," p. 289. If this be true then it would
> indicate that the gravitational attraction of two particles depends upon the total mass
> of the universe, wow,
>
> > like it takes the whole earth to make
> >   a feather fall!
>
> and do these same powers lift it up as well? The issue is, no less, than the *construction*
> of the universe!!!

Space and Time
295   "Introduction to *The Sutter-Marshall Lease*"
Published by the Book Club of California in 1948 as part of its "Keepsake Series." Olson visited California in 1947 to gather materials for a planned sequel to *Call Me Ishmael* (*OJ* 5 presents a selection of notes and papers relevant to this project). Olson described his

research in a 10 January 1948 letter to the secretary general of the Guggenheim Foundation, Henry Allen Moe:

> I started at the Huntington to investigate manuscripts . . . and what has happened since should not happen to a man with home and family. It has led me up and down the coast. Most of the time I have been in Sacramento, at the Sutter Fort and the State Library Collections. At the State Library I turned up the unsorted and unedited papers of George McKinstry. He was the recorder of the Donner story as sheriff and one of Sutter's managers, and new material on it and the whole '46 crossing is there, Sutter is there, the story of the Fort and the mill, the gold discovery and a good deal of the whole story from 1846 to 1850. I am at the moment preparing some of the things for publication by the California Historical Society Quarterly and the Book Club of California. (*SL*)

297 "A Bibliography on America for Ed Dorn"
First published as a pamphlet in 1964 by the Four Seasons Foundation; reprinted in *AP*. The *Bibliography* was written in January 1955 and circulated privately long before the official publication. Dorn, a student of Olson's at Black Mountain College, describes the genesis as follows: "[It] came out of a tutorial arrangement the second time I was at Black Mountain. I told [Olson] I wanted to read about the West, but I was very vague and wanted him to guide me. So one night he delivered this thing to my window. He worked at night and I already had a wife and children at the time and kept regular hours. So it came to me for breakfast" (Edward Dorn, *Interviews,* ed. Donald Allen [Bolinas, Calif.: Four Seasons Foundation, 1980], p. 38).

The *Bibliography* is much more an essay on methodology than a list of books. Nonetheless, in the course of his exposition Olson specifically cites the following texts:

Brooks Adams, *The Law of Civilization and Decay: An Essay on History* (1898; New
    York: Vintage Books, 1959)
Brooks Adams, *The New Empire* (1902; Cleveland: Frontier Press, 1967)
American Weekly
Edgar Anderson, *Plants, Man and Life* (1952; Berkeley: University of California
    Press, 1967)
Victor Bérard, *Les Phéniciens et l'Odyssée,* 2 vols. (Paris: Armand Colin, 1902 and
    1903). (This, presumably, is the "WORK ON THE ODYSSEY" available in French.
    Unnamed—but relied on in the discussion of Bérard in "Appendix A"—is *Did
    Homer Live?*)
The Bible (Olson himself used the King James.)
Katherine Coman, *Economic Beginnings of the Far West: How We Won the Land
    beyond the Mississippi,* 2 vols. (New York: Macmillan, 1912)
Edwin Corle, *Desert Country* (New York: Duell, Sloan and Pearce, 1941)
Bernard DeVoto, *The Year of Decision, 1846* (Boston: Little, Brown, 1943)
Reginald R. Gates, *Human Ancestry from a Genetical Point of View* (Cambridge,
    Mass.: Harvard University Press, 1948)
Harold Sterling Gladwin, *Men out of Asia* (New York: McGraw-Hill, 1947)

Jane Ellen Harrison, *Prolegomena to the Study of Greek Religion*

Jane Ellen Harrison, *Themis: A Study of the Social Origins of Greek Religion* (1912; reprinted with Harrison's *Epilogemena to the Study of Greek Religion,* University Books, 1962)

Herodotus (Olson owned two translations: *A New and Literal Version,* Harper's New Classical Library, tr. Henry Cary [New York: Harper and Brothers, 1878], and *The Histories,* tr. Aubrey de Selincourt—the latter reviewed by Olson in "It Was. But It Ain't.")

Homer (Olson knew several translations; Andrew Lang's is mentioned in *Proprioception.*)

D. H. Lawrence, *Fantasia of the Unconscious* (1922; London: Heinemann, 1961)

D. H. Lawrence, *Studies in Classic American Literature* (1923; London: Heinemann, 1964)

A. K. Lobeck, *Physiographic Diagram of the United States* (New York: Geographical Press, Columbia University Press, 1932)

Herman Melville, *Moby-Dick* (never named but alluded to elliptically three times, as "captain ahab," how to cook a whale," and via "chapter called THE TAIL")

Francis Parkman, *La Salle and the Discovery of the Great West* (also mentioned in *Call Me Ishmael;* "Canada" and "Florida" refer to the seven-volume work of which *La Salle* is also part, *France and England in North America*)

Pausanias (Olson's copy was *Pausanias' Description of Greece,* Bohn's Classical Library, 2 vols., tr. Arthur Richard Shilleto [London: George Bell and Sons, 1886].)

Pausanias, *Mythology & Monuments of Ancient Athens, being a translation of a Portion of the 'Attica' of Pausanias by Margaret de G. Verrall, with introductory Essay and Archaeological Commentary by Jane E. Harrison* (London and New York: Macmillan, 1890)

Ezra Pound, *Guide to Kulchur*

Carl O. Sauer, *Conditions of Pioneer Life in the Upper Illinois Valley* (1916), "Environment and Culture in the Deglaciation" (1948), *The Morphology of Landscape* (1938), and *Road to Cibola* (1932) (all four titles collected in *Land and Life: A Selection from the Writings of Carl Ortwin Sauer,* ed. John Leighly [Berkeley: University of California Press, 1965])

Shakespeare, *Hamlet*

Frederick Jackson Turner, *The Frontier in American History* (1921; New York: Holt, Rinehart and Winston, 1962)

Stanley Vestal, *Queen of Cowtowns: Dodge City, "The Wickedest City in America," 1872–1886* (New York: Pennant Books, 1954)

Walter Prescott Webb, *The Great Frontier* (1931; Boston: Houghton Mifflin, 1952)

Walter Prescott Webb, *The Great Plains* (1933; Boston: Ginn and Company, 1959)

Alfred North Whitehead, *Adventures of Ideas* (New York: Macmillan, 1933)

Alfred North Whitehead, *Process and Reality: An Essay in Cosmology*
William Carlos Williams, *In the American Grain* (1925; New York: New Directions, 1956).

Olson further cites (without giving specific titles) William C. Boyd, Meister Eckhart, Leo Frobenius, H. Rider Haggard, Carl Gustav Jung, and William E. Woodward; he also refers to unnamed "Indian texts on migrations . . . also codices." Mentioned offhandedly are Charles Chaplin, Sergei Eisenstein, T. S. Eliot, James Joyce, Pablo Picasso, Edgar Allan Poe, Marcel Proust, Arthur Rimbaud, Jonathan Sauer, and Arnold Toynbee. Butterick identifies "*50 Families* and Gustavus Myers" as Ferdinand Lundberg, *America's 60 Families* (New York: Vanguard Press, 1937), and Gustavus Myers, *History of the Great American Fortunes* (New York: Modern Library, 1936). The references to Frederick Merk (Olson's teacher at Harvard) are identified by Ralph Maud in Chapter 7 of *Olson's Reading*, "History 62 (Westward Movement) and 'West'"; see also the notes below.

298   "What's on the other side of despair?"
See note to "The Materials and Weights of Herman Melville," p. 398, above.

299   a play on Edgar Allan Poe . . . having him turn his coat inside out
The play, as Butterick notes (at *AP* 81), was by Peter Salt, "who published under the name Sydney Salt. William Carlos Williams wrote an introduction to his book *Christopher Columbus and Other Poems* (Boston: Bruce Humphries, 1937)."

299   The best definition of inversion I know
From Olson's much-annotated *Webster's Collegiate Dictionary,* 5th ed.

299   your *second* story (the wide one, not the 'local' one)
According to Dorn (in conversation with Alan Gilbert), the *Bibliography* was partly written as an enthusiastic response to this story—"C. B. & Q.," a depiction of the American West recognizable to Olson from his own travels and research. Originally published in *Black Mountain Review*, "C. B. & Q." now stands as the opening shot in Dorn's *Way West: Stories, Essays and Verse Accounts: 1963–1993* (Santa Rosa, Calif.: Black Sparrow Press, 1993). The "local" story (a portrait of life in a small Illinois town) was written for a workshop at Black Mountain College and never published.

300   *The New Empire* (despite the analogical . . . precisions on roots
Olson used these lines for his short preface to the Frontier Press reprint, with the following note appended in smaller type:

I shdn't want
the above statement
to stand [at this date,
1966] without adding that

B. Adams was
his own example of
greed [the avaricious

instance of

—in his case deflected to

& his brother [Henry, the limp/fear
avidity

[as Von Stroheim titled
his movie version of Frank Norris's
novel *McTeague* (the Dentist) date
not too far off Brooks' *best*
thought

301   Like I have said elsewhere,

In *Mayan Letters,* at the conclusion of the bibliography:

(Addendum, Attic, Annex, Any
hidden place:

for those who have the wit to tell the Unconscious when they see one, or for the likes of
me, who was raised on the American Weekly, there are at least two men I want to
mention (not to speak of Ignatius Donnelly on Atlantis, Churchward on Mu—or, for
that matter, Rider Haggard!):

the Frenchman, Victor Berard, Mediterranean explorer, who wrote several books to show
that the *Odyssey* was a rewrite from a Semitic original; and a Scot, L. A. Waddell, also
an explorer, of Tibet, who was sure that the Sumerians or the Hittites or the Trojans
founded the British Hempire, and that Menes the Egyptian was Minos the Cretan and
ended up dead, from the bite of a wasp, in Ireland, at Knock-Many, the "Hill of Many,"
in County Tyrone.

But no one but an herodotean may fool around with such fraudu-
lence & fantasy practiced on document (instead of on the galaxies),
no matter how much such stories are, to my taking, the body of narrative which has intervened between the great time of fiction &
drama (the City-time) and the present (which is no time for fantasy,
drama—or City).

The trouble is, it is very difficult, to be both a poet and, an historian. (*SW* 129–30)

301   the Sondley Library

"Special Collection department of the Pack Memorial Library, Asheville, N.C." (GB, at
AP 82).

302   those Grks (or that Chink)

The vector of this slur is partly illumined by a letter of 9 February 1951, sent to Creeley
from Mexico, in which Olson opposes "Mao and his gang" to "the old deal . . . (including
Confucius . . .)":

I have no doubt . . . the American will more and more repossess himself of the Indian
past. More than that, already Mexico is so god-damned oriental . . . that, as contemporaries, they seem so much closer to Mao and his gang, that the fancy struck me that,
shortly, a revolt by Indians here in Yucatan (a separatist movement like the War of the
Tribes in 1847 which had all governments (US, British, as well as Mex) scared the piss

out of) would be an excellent demarche for any future Chinese movement across the Pacific.

> . . . the point . . . is a simple one, no? If you and I see the old deal as dead (including Confucius, say), at the same time that we admit that the new is of the making of our own lives & references, yet, there is bound to be a tremendous pick-up from history other than that which has been usable as reference, the moment either that history is restored (Sumer, or, more done, Chichen or Uaxactun) or rising people (these Indians, as camposinos ripe for Communist play—as ripe as were the Chinese, date 1921, June 30)
> Or take it by this handle: when Joyce crowed, I expect my reader to devote his life to my work, or even Ezra, . . . either or both of them were floating generally on culture currents generally accepted and tied down by Christian and Greek pegs of 3000 years duration. (*O/RC* 4 : 132)

302   Professor Merk, how pemmican was born;

Identified by Maud as *Fur Trade and Empire: George Simpson's Journal,* ed. Frederick Merk, Appendix B, Part 2, published as vol. 31 of *Harvard Historical Studies* (Cambridge, Mass.: Harvard University Press, 1931).

302   Freddie

According to Dorn, a fellow student who had been a farmworker.

302   how to live, by Charles Olson;

Olson's "Plan for a Curriculum of the Soul," first published in *The Magazine of Further Studies* in the late 1960s, includes in the upper left corner the statement "how to live as a / single natural being / the dogmatic nature of / (order of) / experience."

302   how to not know know-how (by an American, after the deluge)

See, in this connection, "Maximus, to Gloucester, from Dogtown, after the flood," written 22 March 1959 but published only after Olson's death:

> My mankind, in your destruction, I will undo you.
> I will give back to the mother function, per se.
> Will leave it to her to find out the structure hidden
>
> . . . .
> . . . I will put back the people inside the city
> away from the State, the modern filthy nation. They
> have to find out again where they live, where their
> houses are, and their voices reach, where they can walk
> to, is the business . . .
> . . . I will teach them to give themselves back sensation.
> They shall have shade, as gods could tell them, is necessary
> How to place a house so it arrays itself in the morphology
> of its own landscape. The earth is the place we live on,
> it has its ice, and fire, and sedimentary sense . . .
> . . . Verily, my mankind, the places of our decisions
> you will find and found in pure places, you will know the ordinance
> of your own being, that this reverse Deluge, this flood of dryness,
> of paper made of acetate, of cells and souls fed bemonstering,
> of minds and hearts, balls and cunts dried up, shall be over . . .
>   (*OJ* 9 : 8–9)

303   to do the chiasma
Title for a series of notes written for "The New Sciences of Man," a gathering of scholars at Black Mountain College planned for March 1953; the notes were later edited by George Butterick and published as *OJ* 10.

303   my man Merk . . . his reprints on the Oregon Triangle
Maud: "represented in Olson's library by an inscribed offprint of 'The Ghost River Caledonia in the Oregon Negotiation of 1818,' *American Historical Review* 55 (April 1950): 530–31" (*Olson's Reading,* p. 49).

304   *Appendix A:*
In "LANGUAGE and MYTHOLOGY," part of *The Chiasma,* Olson writes:

> The *Odyssey* has this series of places which are signified by single figures: Cyclops, Circe, Calypso, etc. And what Bérard has shown is that these proper nouns were not in the language (as Agamemnon was, or Achilles, say, or Odysseus himself) before the poem was written. Where, then, did they come from? This is most Bérard's contribution. He has analyzed them, and shows that behind each is a Semitic word which, in each case, is a description of a coast condition of vital import as landmark to seamen. (*OJ* 10:79)

305   me fecit
Latin, "it was done by me."

306   Merk (Harvard Press) on Westward *Movement*
Identified by Maud as Frederick Jackson Turner and Frederick Merk, *List of References on the History of the West* (1922; Cambridge, Mass.: Harvard University Press, 1930). "Westward Movement" was the name of Merk's year-long course at Harvard, History 62.

307   Justus Garage
"Service Station on the road to Black Mountain" (GB, at *AP* 82).

307   Whaleship *Essex:* privately owned, Perc Brown, oilman
See *Call Me Ishmael,* p. 31, and annotation.

308   bill WCW . . . Sam one Houston!
Sam Houston is taken up in *In the American Grain,* in the chapter "Descent." Williams doesn't go as far back as 7000 B.C., but he does begin with Eric the Red and Vinland.

308   Red Cloud
A photograph of Red Cloud (supplied by Kenneth Irby) serves as frontispiece to the 1966 Goliard Press edition of Olson's *West* (the text is reprinted in *CP* 593–600).

308   the unwritten book by Fred Jackson Merk I have been trying to get
A 24 October 1967 letter from Merk to Olson, preserved in the Frontier Press papers at Buffalo, suggests that Olson was pushing for this book into the late 1960s, and that he enlisted Harvey Brown in the effort. (Brown's Frontier Press reprinted Brooks Adams's *The New Empire* that very year.)

309 1875 all the "new sciences" began
In *The Chiasma* Olson has: "It is not yet gauged how much the nature of knowledge has changed since 1875. Around that date men reapplied known techniques of the universe to man himself, and the change has made man as non-Socratic (or non-Aristotelian) as geometers of the early 19th century made the universe non-Euclidean." (*OJ* 10:107)

309 each thing has its efficient cause!
See note to *Call me Ishmael*, p. 390, above.

309 Dave Corkran
"A specialist in American Indian history, he taught at Black Mountain College from 1945 to 1950." (GB, at *AP* 84)

309 Congressman Judd
"Walter H. Judd, of Minnesota, chairman of the Committee of One Million against the Admission of Communist China to the United Nations." (GB, at *AP* 84)

311 "Billy the Kid"
Published in *Black Mountain Review*, no. 3, Fall 1954; reprinted in *HU*.

311 Parkman . . . *La Salle*
See note to *Call me Ishmael*, p. 381.

312 Stewart Holbrook
Author of several books on the frontier.

313 Stuart Lake . . . *Earp, Frontier Marshal*
A Bantam paperback published in 1952.

315 "Brooks Adams' *The New Empire*"
Published in *Black Mountain Review*, no. 2, Summer 1954; reprinted in *HU;* excerpted on the back cover of the 1967 Frontier Press reprint published by Harvey Brown at Olson's instigation.

315 "America completed . . . "
The New Empire, p. 165, a fact also cited in "The Vinland Map Review" (p. 327).

315 Among the inventions
From p. 3 of *The New Empire*. The sentence that follows reads, "Smiths have made from metal superior weapons and tools, and races using these implements have, in the end, enslaved or exterminated neighbors adhering to wood and stone, wherefore a supply of metal early became essential to existence in the more active quarters of the globe." Olson's charts below are derived in part from the "Chronological Tables" in the back of Adams's book.

318 "Captain John Smith"
Published in *Black Mountain Review*, no. 1, Spring 1954; reprinted in *HU*.

318   John Gould Fletcher says, Powhatan put her up to it,
Cited by Bradford Smith in *Captain John Smith: His Life and Legend* (Philadelphia: J. B. Lippincott, 1953), p. 118.

318   Hart Crane . . . Williams
Section 2 of Crane's *The Bridge* is called "Powhatan's Daughter"; "Jacataqua" is a chapter in William Carlos Williams's *In the American Grain.*

318   Appendix 1
"Captain John Smith's Hungary and Transylvania," pp. 311–42 of *Captain John Smith.* Striker quotes "three Turkes heads in a shield" (p. 328) from *The True Travels, Adventures, and Observations of Captain John Smith* (1630).

319   Parkman, is paired with Prescott;
Francis Parkman and William H. Prescott (author of the nineteenth-century classic *History of the Conquest of Mexico*). In the bibliography to *Mayan Letters* Olson has, "Prescott and Parkman are a triad: [John L.] Stephens [author of *Incidents of Travel in Central America, Chiapas, and Yucatan* (1841) and *Incidents of Travel in Yucatan* (1843)] is the unacknowledged third" (*SW* 127).

319   Williams, is damned in London. . . . while Richard Eberhart is raised up!
G. S. Fraser's 11 April 1953 review of *Paterson, Books One and Two* in *The New Statesman and Nation* is not quite the damning statement Olson recalls ("It is an honourably ambitious poem and until we have seen the last two books I think we should give it the pending benefit of a large doubt"); nor is Fraser's 21 November 1953 review of Richard Eberhart's *Undercliff: Poems 1946–1953* an unqualified endorsement ("At his best, he invites comparison with major contemporary talents; at his worst he writes like a clumsy amateur"). A few years before, Robert Creeley had been moved to write "A Note on the Objective" in response to Fraser's editorial in the second issue of *Nine* (see *Collected Essays of Robert Creeley* [Berkeley: University of California Press, 1989], pp. 463–64); Olson's comments may reflect a lingering cross-Atlantic enmity.

319   Another smith, Grover by name
See "On Poets and Poetry" (pp. 253–55), Olson's response.

319   Juan de la Cosa
Captain of the *Niña* in Columbus's first journey to the Americas; named in the Maximus poems, in "*On first looking out through Juan de la Cosa's Eyes*" (*MAX* 81–85).

319   the time of cant
Olson's 1958 poem "Being Altogether Literal, & Specific, / and Seeking at the Same Time to Be / Succesfully Ex- / plicit" begins:

> Cant first attacked as such, 1596, Count Francesco Cenci (source:
> Stendahl)

> America outproduces the world in steel, Pittsburgh March 14, 18-
> 97 (choice of the significance of the date, Brooks Adams') The Ameri-

canization of the world may then proceed, predictably, to conclusion.
Still proceeding. Cant

uber alles. The American word is
confidence. Coca-cola

is my name.

(CP 472)

Olson refers to Francesco Cenci at the end of this review.

320   Elbert Hubbard
Editor, publisher, and author of the late nineteenth, early twentieth century, best known for a series of books called *Little Journeys*—brief biographies of famous persons.

320   if Newport "had burnt her to ashes . . . the Falles."
This quotation and the one below ("though I be . . . my life") appear on p. 139 of *Captain John Smith.*

321   Beyle . . . Stendhal . . . Don Juan . . . Cenci
The French author Henri Beyle took the name of the German town Stendhal as his nom de plume. "The Cenci" is included in *The Shorter Novels of Stendhal,* tr. C. K. Scott-Moncrieff (New York: Liveright, 1946), where we read (at pp. 165–67): "To render a Don Juan possible, there must be hypocrisy in society. A Don Juan would have been an effect without a cause in the ancient world. . . . Thus it is to the Christian religion that I ascribe the possibility of the Satanic part played by Don Juan."

321   "Though there be fish . . . trouble them."
Captain John Smith, pp. 139–40.

322   "Five Foot Four, but Smith Was a Giant"
Published in the *Boston Globe,* 27 August 1964; reprinted in *AP.*

322   Bradford Smith's . . . Laura Polyani Striker
Discussed by Olson in "Captain John Smith."

322   no higher "than an 'untouchable' in Akbar's India"
Philip L. Barbour, *The Three Worlds of Captain John Smith* (Boston: Houghton Mifflin, 1964), p. x.

323   quasi-professionals—from Charles Deane and Henry Adams on
See Barbour's extensive bibliography of primary and secondary sources, which includes Henry Adams, "Captain John Smith," *North American Review* 104, 1867, pp. 1–30 (a review of *Captain John Smith's "A true relation of Virginia,"* ed. Charles Deane).

323   as I said to the Lady Prize Winner Poet of Canada
"Margaret Avison, recipient of the Governor-General's Award in 1960" (GB, at *AP* 96).

323   he too believes Smith himself wrote "The Sea Marke"
As Olson did—quoting the poem in "*Maximus, to Gloucester,* Letter 15" (*MAX* 73–74).

323   brings other poets, . . . to bear.
See pp. 327–28 of *The Three Worlds*.

324   *"The Contours of American History"*
Written at the instigation of Amiri Baraka (then LeRoi Jones) and published in *Kulchur,* no. 10, Summer 1963; reprinted in *HU*. A February 1962 postcard from Jones begins, "Sirrrr, Did I mention to you a book, The Contours of American History? He's sort of a neo-Marxist, but there's enough give there to be valuable. His ideas on the political meanings of corporate capitalism (& the latter as vs. the old anti-mercantile Yanquis) is sweet" (Storrs, Correspondence). The request for a review came in a subsequent letter of 31 December 1962.

324   an enormous syllogism—three Americas
Olson's remarks derive from an unpublished essay called "UNSTICKING THE SUN, or, SOMETHING, PERHAPS, FOR WALT WHITMAN" (1952) (revised as "History" and submitted, unsuccessfully, to *The Freeman;* this later version appears with Robert Creeley's comments in *O/RC* 9 : 102–26). Olson here divides American history into three periods: "age 1 (James the First's a[c]cession to, the Revolution)" (a period marked by "the wealth of New England" and "the p[o]verty of the South"); "age 2 (1830 to the Civil War) (identified as "the beginning of *modern* industry"); and "age 3 (the Civil War to August, 1945)" (i.e., up until the Bomb was dropped on Japan, an act that commenced "THE BATTLE FOR ASIA"). Noting that "THE MIDDLE TERM OF THAT SYLLOGISM—ECONOMICS—SWALLOWS UP THE OTHER TWO," Olson is moved to ask (borrowing imagery from the *Ramayana*):

> why? what happened, to the function DISTRIBUTION, that it should have this stomach, that it should be this Agastya, to digest both the sea and the land, and leave all people athirst, and without the simplest sustenance? what was this eater, to turn all into wind, to make nothing of everything but stinking vapor? what was this that turned the labor of a people of 40,000,000, and 155,000,000 (1945), the resources of a continent, the factories of these States, the consumption of all into unmeaning death on the skirt of Asia?
>
> > No man has any longer the permission of maintaining the armor of his distance. The thing must be dragged into the light. The wheels of the sun must be unstuck from their freeze. Any man must bring his head to break the fall of the river of heaven, so that the land & men shall have water again.
>
> I will not say, so easily. The word won't do it. It will slide off. No heads with sufficient hair to stand the fall will present themselves when all heads should be presented. Wait. It is just exactly 100 years too late to hurry. You won't undo 100 years with a pointing finger. Nor will the word so quickly correct the events. What are the events—*why* are they? (Storrs, Prose Series; see also *O/RC* 9 : 105–6, 108, 125)

324   Better than Heilbroner
Olson owned and read Robert L. Heilbroner's *The Future as History* (New York: Harper, 1960).

324　Copley's pictures
New England painter John Singleton Copley, cited by William Appleton Williams on p. 98 of *The Contours of American History* (Cleveland, Ohio: World Publishing, 1961).

325　Frederick Merk's postulate (sd book now ought to be available soon,
See the note on Merk in "A Bibliography on America for Ed Dorn," p. 440.

325　Berle . . . Galbraith
Adolf A. Berle and John Kenneth Galbraith, economists referred to in Williams's book.

326　"The Vinland Map Review"
The immediate occasion for this essay was publication of *The Vinland Map and the Tartar Relation,* ed. R. A. Skelton, Thomas E. Marston, and George D. Painter (New Haven, Conn.: Yale University Press, 1965), though, according to Ralph Maud in *Olson's Reading,* the Yale book was not acquired until November—after Olson had posted his notes to Andrew Crozier for publication in the inaugural issue of *The Wivenhoe Park Review,* Winter 1965 (where a reproduction of the Vinland map graces the cover). Olson's increasing interest in Northern myth and history is here evidenced by a dense overlay of fact and allusion. Cited directly are the following: Brooks Adams, *The New Empire* and *The Law of Civilization and Decay;* W. G. Collingwood and F. York Powell, *Scandinavian Britain* (London: Society for Promoting Christian Knowledge, 1908); H. R. Ellis Davidson, *Gods and Myths of Northern Europe* (New York: Penguin Books, 1964); Sonia Chadwick Hawkes, H. R. Ellis Davidson, and Christopher Hawkes, "The Finglesham Man," *Antiquity* 39, March 1965, pp. 17–32; Josef Strzygowski, *Origin of Christian Church Art: New Facts and Principles of Research* (Oxford, Eng.: Clarendon Press, 1923); Gabriel Turville-Petre, *Myth and Religion of the North: The Ancient Religion of Scandinavia* (New York: Holt, Rinehart and Winston, 1964); Thorstein Veblen, *Theory of the Leisure Class* (New York: Macmillan, 1899). Other texts consulted for the review (as determined by George Butterick from a survey of Olson's papers and library) include Daniel Aaron, "The Unusable Man: An Essay on the Mind of Brooks Adams," *New England Quarterly* 21, March 1948, pp. 3–33; Douglas Dowd, *Thorstein Veblen* (New York: Washington Square Press, 1964); Murray Fowler, "Old Norse Religion," in *Ancient Religions,* ed. Vergilius Ferm (New York: The Citadel Press, 1965); Helga Ingstad, "Vinland Ruins Prove Vikings Found the New World," *National Geographic* 126, November 1964, pp. 708–34; Gertrude Rachel Levy, *The Gate of Horn: A Study of the Religious Conceptions of the Stone Age, and Their Influence upon European Thought* (London: Faber and Faber, 1948); Erix Oxiensterna, *The Norsemen,* tr. Catherine Hutter (Greenwich, Conn.: New York Graphic Society, 1965); Julius Pokorny, *Indogermanisches etymologisches Wörterbuch,* vol. 1 (Bern: A. Francke, 1959); Milton Haight Turk, *An Anglo-Saxon Reader* (New York: Scribner, 1930); James A. Walker, "Gothic -*Leik*- and Germanic *Lik*- in the Light of Gothic Translations of Greek Originals," *Philological Quarterly* 28, 1949, pp. 274–93. Reprinted in *AP,* with extensive notes by George Butterick.

326 "In the tenth century. . . . Dark Ages."
From the "Chronological Tables" to Brooks Adams, *The New Empire,* p. 205.

326 "Flanders and the Fairs. . . . land freights."
Also from the "Chronological Tables" to *The New Empire,* at p. 208, under the heading "Migration of the Seat of Empire from the Mediterranean to the Atlantic."

327 Thencefroth
"It should be noted that Olson has instructions on the original manuscript, preserved at the library at Simon Fraser University, that this typing error is to be retained" (GB, at *AP* 97). Note also Olson's phonetic spelling of Strzygowski below.

327 steel Pittsburgh, Mar., 1897
A fact Olson also cites (p. 315) in his review of *The New Empire;* see also the note on "cant" (pp. 442–43) in Olson's review of Bradford Smith's *Captain John Smith.*

327 *The Vinland Map,* Latin caption to it
Note 67 on the Yale map, where the translation of the caption reads (p. 140):

> By God's will, after a long voyage from the island of Greenland to the South toward the most distant remaining parts of the western ocean sea, sailing southward amidst the ice, the companions Bjarni and Leif Ericksson discovered a new land, extremely fertile and even having vines, the which island they named Vinland. Eric [*Henricus*], legate of the Apostolic See and bishop of Greenland and the neighboring regions, arrived in this truly vast and very rich land, in the name of Almighty God, in the last year of our most blessed father Pascal, remained a long time in both summer and winter, and later returned northeastward toward Greenland and then proceeded [home to Europe?] in most humble obedience to the will of his superiors.

Olson's source for the caption before receipt of the Yale volume remains unclear.

328 Derwent-on-Trent
"In returning for approval a typescript made from Olson's original holograph manuscript, Andrew Crozier asked, 'Where's this. Derwent's on the Derwent.' Olson responded, 'I'm *glad* to know! My point was only to use *any* (one of those English) place names. That one was made up—& to lead (by irritation?) to the un-said name of the (still unremembered) name'" (GB, at *AP* 98). Choosing a place name at random, Olson may have been guided by a silent memory of Melville's *Clarel,* where Derwent is the name of an English pilgrim, introduced in Part 2, Canto 1, "The Cavalcade" (lines 29–33):

> A priest he was—though but in part
> For as the Templar old combined
> The cavalier and monk in one;
> In Derwent likewise might you find
> The secular and cleric tone.

328 as Strzegowski shows
In *Origin of Christian Church Art,* Strzygowski writes (p. 234): "Many of the towers so characteristic of Early English architecture show us the wooden prototype translated into

stone. The best example is Eals Barton . . . ; here the tower, when seen from a distance, has every appearance of being timber-built, but a closer inspection reveals the surprising fact that it really consists of rubble concrete faced with stone 'beams,' in which the earlier wooden forms have been preserved with meticulous care."

328   Quote (Brooks Adams, *The Law of Civilization and Decay*
See p. 347 of the 1943 reprint.

329   l'anse aux Meadows
Site of the ruins reported on by Ingstad; mentioned also in the late Maximus poem "George Decker" (*MAX* 444).

329   Cambridgeshire FENS
Allusion to a poem by John Temple, "Meditation on a Landscape," *Niagara Frontier Review,* Fall 1965, pp. 16–17:

> . . . they have no sense
> of movement in their deadly hearts
> and they talk of God on the Cambridgeshire fens
> on the edge of those fens . . .

330   the Lake Van measure
One of Olson's most esoteric formulations, drawn into the Maximus poems in June 1966 in "AN ART CALLED GOTHONIC" (*MAX* 551–55). Olson's figure of 1 to 1200 apparently derives from his study of a map "of the Gloucester waterfront 'Coppyed from J Masons Survey rate One hundred feet to an Inch' (1845)"—one hundred feet equaling 1,200 inches (GB, at *AP* 100). "Lake Van" is named in *Origin of Christian Church Art,* where Strzygowski reproduces several images of a tenth-century church built on the island of Achthamar, Lake Van, in western Turkey. Strzygowski's discussion principally concerns exterior decoration; there is no mention of scale.

330   a ship is a church upside-down
From Strzygowski's discussion of shipbuilding techniques and their architectural adaptation in Northern Europe, further addressed in that author's *Early Church Art in Northern Europe, with Special Reference to Timber Construction and Decoration* (New York: Harper and Brothers, 1928).

330   *Kirch Santa Clara Assisi*
Depicted in *Origin of Christian Church Art,* "visited by Olson while reading at Gian Carlo Menotti's Festival of the Two Worlds in nearby Spoleto in July 1965" (GB, at *AP* 101).

332   Taliessin
"Late sixth century British bard to whom is attributed a collection of poems known as the *Book of Taliessin*" (GB, at *AP* 101).

332   "influx of Eastern goods Venezia
Adapted from Brooks Adams, *The Law of Civilization and Decay,* p. 346.

333 *Ynglingatál,* by Thjodolf of Hvin, Mrs. Davidson dates 9th century
See *Gods and Myths of Northern Europe,* p. 240.

333 *mag' (k) nut* of the North
"A split pun, on Knut or Canute (c. 994–1035), king of Denmark and England, and Magnus, as in Magnus Barefoot, Norse king of the eleventh century. . . . In the original, plain 'magnet' has been crossed out and the pun substituted" (GB, at *AP* 103).

333 'Wickings'
See *Scandinavian Britain,* p. 60.

333 the "Teutonic Migration" [again to use F. York Powell
See *Scandinavian Britain,* p. 7.

334 decipherment of Linear B by Michael Ventris
Announced over British radio in 1952. Ventris died in a car accident four years later, shortly after completing with John Chadwick *Documents in Mycenaeaen Greek: Three Hundred Selected Tablets from Knossos, Pylos, and Mycenae with Commentary and Vocabulary* (Cambridge, Eng.: Cambridge University Press, 1956).

334 Linear A
See note to *Proprioception,* p. 419.

334 "Silver"-man . . . "Gold-bugs"
Anti-Semitic puns on Silverman and Goldberg. Olson's attention was drawn to the latter phrase by Daniel Aaron's "The Unusable Man" (Olson knew Aaron from Harvard), where we read (p. 11): "The gold-bug or Jew or banker ([Adams] used the words interchangeably) embodied the spirit of the modern, the genii of money." Bringing this terminology to bear on his discussion of the ancient world, Olson brazenly reminds us of the ideological entanglements that threaten prosecution of all new knowledge. The connection he draws, moreover, between Cyrus Gordon's identification of Linear A as Semitic, and "the shocking and fouling events of the present" (i.e., the Holocaust), only underscores the insidiousness "behind the essentially Thucydidean history preceding us for 2500 years [Toynbees and such people, including most American historians]"—"History as Usual," "[o]f which *our* events, dreadfully, are still a part."

Other Essays, Notes, and Reviews

339 "Ernst Robert Curtius"
Published in *Black Mountain Review,* no. 2, Summer 1954; reprinted in *HU.*

339 The young German poet Rainer M. Gerhardt
Editor of the magazine *Fragmente.* Gerhardt's "Brief an Creeley und Olson" appeared in English in *Origin,* no. 4, Winter 1951–52, along with Olson's "To Gerhardt, There, among Europe's Things of Which He Has Written Us in His 'Brief an Creeley und Olson'" (*CP* 212–22). See also Olson's "The Death of Europe," a memorial poem for Gerhardt written in 1954 (*CP* 308–16).

339   Frobenius
Leo Frobenius, mentioned by Olson in "GrandPa, GoodBye" and elsewhere.

339   Walter Prescott Webb
Historian also mentioned in *A Bibliography on America for Ed Dorn.*

339   "Europeanization of the historical picture"
Curtius, *European Literature and the Latin Middle Ages,* Bollingen Series 36, tr. Willard R. Trask (New York: Pantheon Books, 1953), p. 7.

339   Troeltsch, Toynbee
Ernst Troeltsch and Arnold Toynbee. Troeltsch's "unfinished" *Der Historismus und seine Probleme* (1922) is much cited in Curtius's first chapter.

340   "intelligible unit"
Curtius, *European Literature,* p. 4.

340   The gain Curtius has already given me
In a review of Rainer Gerhardt's magazine, "Eine neue Zeitschrift: 'Fragmente,'" *Die Tat* (Zurich) 21 July 1951, p. 7.

340   the *Nine* boys . . . Gavin Douglas
Nine: A Magazine of Poetry and Criticism was edited in London by Peter Russell, who wrote an essay for issue no. 5, Nov. 1950, on "Gavin Douglas and his 'Enneados'" (Douglas's sixteenth-century translation of Virgil into Middle Scots). Olson expatiates at length on *Nine* in a 3 May 1951 letter to Cid Corman.

340   Stefan George's is the vision:
Quoted by Curtius on p. 10.

340   Bergson was wrong. Or half-right.
Henri Bergson, cited by Curtius (at p. 8) from *The Two Sources of Morality and Religion:* "'Only intelligent beings are superstitious.' The fiction-making function ('fonction fabu-latrice') has become necessary to life. It is nourished by the residuum of instinct which surrounds the intellect like an aura."

341   That's Troeltsch. And Toynbee?
Quoted by Curtius at pp. 7 and 8, respectively.

341   what Blackburn insists I can't: think.
Poet Paul Blackburn, the accusing "He" of "*Maximus, to Gloucester:* Letter 15" (*MAX* 72).

341   "Specialization has thus opened the way
Curtius, p. 13.

342   "It Was. But It Ain't."
Published in *Black Mountain Review,* no. 5, Summer 1955; reprinted in *HU.*

342   Bulldog Drummond
A series of "B" movies based on this character appeared between 1929 and 1969.

342   I do not think that one will be far wrong
From Book One of Thucydides, *History of the Peloponnesian War,* tr. Rex Warner (Baltimore, Md.: Penguin Books, 1954), p. 24.

345   "Homer and Bible"
Published in *Black Mountain Review,* no. 7, Autumn 1957; reprinted in *HU.*

346   Michael Ventris
Mentioned also in "The Vinland Map Review." See editors' note to p. 334.

346   Kramer . . . Güterbock
Olson owned several of Samuel Noah Kramer's translations, many of them from *Ancient Near Eastern Texts Relating to the Old Testament,* ed. James B. Pritchard (Princeton, N.J.: Princeton University Press, 1950) (a book Olson acquired at Kramer's suggestion; see also Pritchard's 1958 revision, also from Princeton, *The Ancient Near East: An Anthology of Texts and Pictures*). Hans Güterbock's "The Song of Ullikummi: Revised Text of the Hittite Version of a Hurrian Myth" (*Journal of Cuneiform Studies* 5, 1951, pp. 135–61), is the basis for Olson's *"From* The Song of Ullikummi" (*CP* 600–602; see also Olson's comments in the 1965 lecture "Causal Mythology" [*MUTH* 1 : 72–73, 91–93]).

347   "Para. 31. Homeric *dorp*—
Gordon's book consists of 187 numbered paragraphs and a brief foreword. Olson reproduces the complete text of paragraph 31, omitting a brief footnote. Gordon discusses "the Hebrew 'staff of God' " in paragraph 19 of *Homer and the Bible* (Ventnor, N.J.: Ventnor Publishers, 1956).

348   "Near East cultures . . ."
From paragraph 4 of *Homer and the Bible.*

348   Gordon's footnote
Footnote 26, which cites several of Bérard's books. The 1927 date Gordon gives for *Les Phéniciens et l'Odyssée* (a book Olson recommends to Ed Dorn in *A Bibliography on America*) is for the revised edition.

348n.   Jane Harrison
Cited by Olson in several essays, including *Proprioception* and *A Bibliography on America for Ed Dorn;* dedicatee of Olson's "A Newly Discovered 'Homeric' Hymn" (*CP* 363–64).

349   "Bill Snow"
GB, at *AP* 90: "Written in February 1961 in response to a request by Wilbert Snow in a letter of 31 January 1961 for a statement by Olson to accompany a recording of Snow's poems. Subsequently, the statement appeared on the back of the jacket to the long-playing record, *Wilbert Snow—Maine Poet* (Cambridge: Bert and I Records, [1961])." Reprinted in *AP.* In *Charles Olson in Connecticut* (Chicago: Swallow Press, 1975), Charles Boer writes (p. 87): "You said that you didn't like being an only child and that you really had five fathers: Wilbert Snow, your favorite teacher at Wesleyan; Lou Douglas, a Gloucester fisherman and 'the hero of my poem'; your real father; Ezra Pound; and Carl

Sauer, the geographer." Snow's memoir of Olson, "A Teacher's View," appeared in *Massachusetts Review* 12:1, Winter 1971, pp. 40–44.

349   Bill Snow's third cousin . . . had a poet read a poem
The poet was Robert Frost, who recited "The Gift Outright" at John F. Kennedy's inauguration, 20 January 1961, after a night of heavy snow.

349   Bill Snow's *Downeast*
Down East: Poems, by Wilbert Snow (New York: Gotham House, 1932).

349   except to introduce my friend Creeley's stories
See "Introduction to Robert Creeley."

349   "Trickle Drops"
In the "Calamus" section of *Leaves of Grass.*

350   It was Rosie McGraw
Snow's letter explains the relation to J. F. K. as follows: "My grandmother's sister Rosie McGraw, born in Waterford, Ireland, went to Boston and married a Richard Fitzgerald. Their grandchild was 'Honey Fitz,' and Honey Fitz's daughter is this boy's mother. Best of all his own mother, that is Kennedy's own mother, was named Rosie for my grandmother's sister."

350   I remember him as early as 1904
The "I remember" is rhetorical; Olson was born in 1910. Vinalhaven is an island off the coast of Maine; Snow was still a student in 1904 (at nearby Bowdoin College, in Brunswick, Maine)—thus Olson's "already."

350   the Collector of Port Duties on Wool
Geoffrey Chaucer.

350   Under the mushroom
The mushroom cloud—threat of nuclear war—but also, and perhaps principally, the "magic mushroom," which Olson took with Timothy Leary in December 1960 and February 1961. See Olson's extensive discussion in "Under the Mushroom: The Gratwick Highlands Tape":

> I must have been involved in the first week of the actual use of the mushroom as it was derived at Sandoz Laboratories into Psilocybin-39, I think is actually the name of the so-called drug. Actually, it's simply a synthetic, about the size of an old placebo, which was even smaller than an aspirin, and looks very much like those fake pills we always were given as though we needed a cure, like saccharine in tea, just a little pink thing about so big. In fact when I took it I was so high on bourbon that I took it like as though it was a bunch of peanuts. I kept throwing the peanuts—and the mushroom—into my mouth. (*MUTH* 1:22)

350   roll all up into the ball like the weevil getting there
Olson is apparently drawing a derisive connection between the charismatic Kennedy's Inaugural Ball and the vulgar Texan L. B. J. (who helped the Kennedys "get[ ] there")—

by way of an allusion to the "Boll Weevil Song," last item in *A Treasury of American Folklore*, ed. B. A. Botkin (New York: Crown Publishers, 1944), a book Olson owned. The first chorus of the song reads: "Oh, de boll weevil . . . / Come all de way to Texas, jus' a-lookin' foh a place to stay, / Jus' a-lookin' foh a home."

351   "A House Built by Capt. John Somes 1763"
First published in *A Pamphlet* 3:7, 12 June 1962; reprinted in *AP*. In a 1968 letter-poem to the *Gloucester Daily Times* protesting "another threatened erosion of [Gloucester's] handsomeness" (*M/G* 113)—a planned razing of the Mansfield House at 15 Main St.—Olson writes:

> My buildings are
> the Gloucester Hotel
> (as it was), the
> next building to it up
> Washington, the
> Town Hall the
> Brooks house itself, the
> John Somes (now
> Wm. Webber's etc.
> But if the
> Mansfield house
> goes all the other
> little ones are eaten
> away, forever.
>   (*M/G* 119)

Notes Peter Anastas, the Somes-Webber house, a "Colonial mansion at 20 Middle Street owned by Gloucester stockbroker William Webber and built by his ancestor Captain John Somes . . . , is a fine two-story clapboard structure with a gambrel roof and center chimney bearing the date 1770" (*M/G* 122).

351   *Men don't follow men . . .*
In the magazine version, these lines are followed with the words "epigraph to *A Pamphlet* mimeograph magazine Pocatello Idaho (Idaho State College)."

351   Gino Clays
"Young poet, one of the editors of *A Pamphlet* and later of *Wild Dog*. An essay by him entitled 'Omnia Mea Mecum Porto' appeared in the March 19th issue of *A Pamphlet* (reprinted in *Wild Dog*, 17, 8 June 1968, pp. 19–20). The statement, 'I am going to be reborn inside the world,' toward the close of Olson's essay, is from Clays' piece" (GB, at *AP* 91).

351   The critique by Cooper
Olson had perhaps picked up the recent reissue of James Fenimore Cooper, *Home as*

Found: A Novel of Social Criticism and Observation, introduction by Lewis Leary (New York: Capricorn Books, 1961).

352   if we had now a completely Indo-Europeanized American dictionary
A longtime desire of Olson's. Distinguishing his own interest in etymology from Robert Duncan's, Olson wrote (in a letter to Larry Eigner, dated 20 June 1956):

> What that Duncan means by arbitrary etymologies is a part of his department of misinfor-mation =s "invention." Note that he includes it with puns—& *note!* with projective verse!
>   He means etymologies *one makes up!* Wow! You will imagine how I don't figure that one, being, as you sd (Gloucester) a hound for meaning.
>   Comes any word I go the other way, and what's most needed right now is an *Indo-European* Dictionary—*roots,* so one can feel that far back along the line of the word to its first users—what they meant, in *inventing* it, not any one of us at the most free-wheeling drag-race time in man's gasses. (*SL*)

The provocative word "*inventing*" comes from I. J. Gelb's *A Study of Writing,* p. 63.

352   as Creeley has recently pointed out
In "The New World," a 1961 review of recent books by Gary Snyder, Michael McClure, Philip Whalen, and Ron Loewinsohn. See *Collected Essays of Robert Creeley,* pp. 170–76.

352   *for Ted Crump*
Editor of *A Pamphlet.*

353   "The Advantage of Literacy Is That Words Can Be on the Page"
Published in *Coyote's Journal* 1, 1964; reprinted in *AP.* The title recalls a sentence from Olson's "Letter to Elaine Feinstein," "The only advantage of speech rhythms . . . is illiteracy: the non-literary, exactly in Dante's sense of the vernacular."

353   A Bibliography . . . for Charles Doria
The subtitle marks this piece as a sequel to *A Bibliography on America for Ed Dorn.* Doria, like Dorn, was one of Olson's students—at SUNY Buffalo, about a decade after Dorn attended Black Mountain College.

353   Schliemann's to Blegen's confirmation
Heinrich Schliemann, discoverer of Troy, and Carl W. Blegen, whose book *The Mycenaean Age: The Trojan War, the Dorian Invasion, and Other Problems* (Cincinnati, Ohio: University of Cincinnati, 1962) Olson "borrowed from Lockwood Library, Buffalo," and never returned (Maud, *Olson's Reading,* p. 155). Olson's "*March 14th   1965*" makes the same point more explicitly: "It is just about 100 years since Schliemann assumed the literal place-accuracy of Homer, and proved it, as successfully as the American Blegen, of Cincinnati, has so recently again done likewise as of the question of which Pylos was Pylos" (Storrs, Prose Series).

353   Victor Berard, as early as 1904 (?)
In *Les Phéniciens et l'Odyssée* (1902 and 1903).

353   fragment of Dausi epic

"Gassire's Lute," which Olson knew from Leo Frobenius and Douglas Fox, *African Genesis* (1937; New York: Benjamin Blom, 1966). In his introduction (p. 30), Fox relates this "epic story . . . of the Soninke" to a "heroic period . . . much earlier" than the *Dausi*'s actual composition (between 300 and 1100 A.D.).

353   logography and the muthologotic

Olson writes about the former in *Proprioception;* he discusses the latter in "Poetry and Truth." Noting a "teeter" between the words "muthos" and "logos," Olson says:

> *logos,* in my mind right now, logic or *IIIII* [deliberate stutter] is *III,* is like *s st st* story, and is, like, only story. . . . *Muthos* is mouth. [sputters] And indeed *logos* is simply words in the mouth. And in fact I can even be stiffer an etymologist and tell you that if you run the thing right to the back of the pan and scraped off all the scrambled eggs and there's still rust on it and you can't wash it, you'll find that what you have to say *muthologos* is, is "what is said of what is said"—as suddenly the mouth is simply a capability, as well as words are a capability, they are not the ultimate back of it all. (*MUTH* 2:37–38)

Olson's analysis grew out of his reading of J. A. K. Thomson's *The Art of the Logos* (London: Allen and Unwin, 1935). See also "Letter 23" of Maximus, where Olson writes, "*muthologos* has lost such ground . . . // I would be an historian as Herodotus was, looking // for oneself for the evidence of // what is said" (*MAX* 104–5).

354   Maikop

"Village in southern Russia, site of a royal tomb from Early Kuban culture" (GB, at *AP* 93). Mentioned also in the late Maximus poem "AN ESSAY ON QUEEN TIY" (see *MAX* 525).

354   genet: earth was genet

"Genet" (taken from Hesiod's *Theogony,* line 116, "chaos genet") is an ellided form of the Greek verb for "came into being"—related to the later noun form "genesis." (See, in this connection, Olson's comments about "*-sis*ing of . . . the single verb" in his "Review of Eric A. Havelock's *Preface to Plato,*" p. 358.) In the Maximus poems Olson has:

the muses

told Hesiod

there was

4 things got

genet—that *before* the World

there was heat or muspilli it is called in Norse

and made a bound of space certainly & *probably*

of time herself because the Norse or *Bavarian* word also means

End of the World

(*MAX* 546)

354 One wants phenomenology in place

A concern of Olson's since the early 1950s. In "The Science of, Mythology," a section of *The Chiasma,* we read:

> The virtue of myth is exactly the resistance that *only* the act of narrative holds in itself: that it cannot depart from human phenomenology without ceasing to be.
>
> And by human phenomenology I mean phenomenology. For how is there, finally, any phenomenology except as we experience it; for who is knowing anything except man?
>
>> Nature? But she is a proper noun man invents to cover the organic or material forces he both is & experiences.
>> And God, as I say, is his best guess at a proper noun to cover that being which he knows to be distinct from his knowledge of it but which, because he has to know it, he has to express . . .
>
> What delights me, in any case, about the mythological is that it states reality in exactly those terms by which a human being experiences reality: *personages, events, & things;* who, what, how. It does not explain or compare (symbol: to throw together [sym + ballein]) *it re-enacts:* it assumes that reality happens—or at least that so far as a human being knows, what makes reality the moving thing that it is, is that he or she happens. (*OJ* 10:65–66)

354 Tantalus was a Hittite. You at least Charles Doria are a Hittite.

In his essay "Pound, Olson and the Classical Tradition," *Boundary 2,* 2:1–2, Fall 1973 / Winter 1974, Charles Doria recalls Olson telling him (pp. 134–35):

> "You are a Greek, I am a Hittite." I took this to mean the following: I was somewhere on the further shores of Europe moving away from the pre-classical past towards a Europe that was a dream in the mind but would become a nightmare in reality. He was a hostile power who had preceded me and everyone else who had associated themselves with Hellenism. Because he lives in the darkness beyond the reach of European enlightenment and safety, he was incomprehensible and closed off to us latter-day Europeans. But the historical Hittites, we now know, served both to civilize the pre-Homeric Greeks and provide the impetus for their earliest poetry and mythology. And so it was with Charles.

Rescinding his earlier rebuke, Olson here identifies Doria as the living face of a Hittite "impetus," a representative (like Tantalus) of the "pre-classical past."

355 "Review of Eric A. Havelock's *Preface to Plato*"

Published in *Niagara Frontier Review,* no. 1, Summer 1964; reprinted in *AP.* Tom Clark in *Charles Olson: The Allegory of a Poet's Life* calls *Preface to Plato* (Cambridge, Mass.: Harvard University Press, 1963) a "confirmation" of the method Olson discovered in writing "The Gate and the Center"; several unpublished essays further attest to the book's importance for Olson, who brought Havelock to Buffalo from Yale in December 1964. Olson's citations to Collingwood, Fraenkel, Notopolous, and Zielinski are all taken from the footnotes to Chapter 10 of Havelock's book, "The Content and the Quality of the Poetised Statement."

355   the phenomenology of attention
In November of 1963, Richard Sassoon, who met Olson in Vancouver, wrote a letter containing excerpts from Maurice Merleau-Ponty's *Phenomenology of Perception,* tr. Colin Smith (London: Routledge and Kegan Paul, 1962). Two different copies of the letter survive among Olson's papers at Storrs, both annotated in Olson's own hand. The second is apparently a typescript Olson himself made—a sign of how important the excerpts became for him. See also Olson's discussion of Merleau-Ponty in "Under the Mushroom" (*MUTH* 1 : 55–59).

355   *episteme*
Greek for "understanding," "knowledge," "science." In "Under the Mushroom," Olson defines the related word "epistemology" as "How do you know. Or the belief that we— that there is knowing. And it was invented by a man named Plato. *Episteme* is his invention and it's one of the most dangerous things in the world—is the idea that there is such a thing as knowledge" (*MUTH* 1 : 29).

355   Aristotle (cf. the *Poetics* 1457)
"Metaphor is the application of a strange term either transferred from the genus and applied to the species or from the species and applied to the genus, or from one species to another or else by analogy" (*Aristotle, The Poetics; "Longinus," On the Sublime; Demitrius, On Style,* tr. W. Hamilton Fyfe, Loeb Classical Library [Cambridge, Mass.: Harvard University Press, 1965], p. 81).

355   Notopoulos (1949) . . . *parataxis*
James A. Notopoulos, "Parataxis in Homer: A New Approach to Homeric Literary Criticism," *Transactions of the American Philological Association* 80, 1949, pp. 1–23. Havelock lists two other articles by Notopolous, citing this one (later acquired by Olson in photocopy), at p. 192 n. 25, to corroborate the statement (p. 183):

> Thus the memorised record consists of a vast plurality of acts and events, not integrated into chained groups of cause and effect, but rather linked associatively in endless series. In short, the rhythmic record in its very nature constitutes a "many": it cannot submit to that abstract organisation which groups "manys" into "one." Stylistically, this truth can be stated as an opposition between that type of composition which is paratactic, as in the epic, and that which is periodic, or beginning to be so, as for example the speeches of Thucydides.

The passage brings to mind Olson's preference of Herodotus to Thucydides, recalling also the epigraph to the opening book of Maximus, *"All my life I've heard / one makes many."*

356   Zielinski, *1901*
Thaddeus Zielinski, "Die Behandlung gleichzeitiger Ereignisse im antiken Epos," *Philologus,* suppl. 8, 1901, cited by Havelock on the question of time at pp. 193–94 n. 27. Maud reports that Olson knew Zielinski's "The Sybil: Three Essays on Ancient Religion and Christianity," issued as *Edge* (Melbourne), no. 2, November 1956.

356· Planck
Max Planck, "German physicist, formulator of the quantum theory in papers on radiation in 1901" (GB, at *AP* 94).

356   Fraenkel's (2nd ed. 1960) is another lovely indication
Hermann Ferdinand Fraenkel, *Wege und Formen fruegriechischen Denken,* 2 vols. (Munich: Beck, 1960), cited by Havelock (p. 194 n. 27) to the effect that "the Homeric epos is innocent of any concept of time in the abstract; concretely, the idioms in which *chronos* appears denote periods of waiting or delay or doing nothing."

356   one quoted statement (from Collingwood)
Cited by Havelock at p. 193 n. 28.

357   *dotha . . .* [doxa]
See note to *Proprioception,* p. 417.

357   plus Dausi to be sure an African example
See note to "The Advantage of Literacy Is That Words Can Be on the Page," pp. 453–54.

357   Added notes Sunday November 25th 1963
The date is three days after J. F. K.'s assassination, a day after the murder of Oswald, four days before appointment of the Warren Commission. Are these *"Added notes"* a response to Kennedy's death, "something like ripples"? Is the "we" requiring *"mapping"* America? Is "the 'order' which does obtain" political? In the next and final section of the "Review" ("added December 6th . . . in anticipation of anything further"), Olson declares: "There is no colloquy. Society is inherited—order is, entropy is . . . "

357   *dialexis*
Greek, "*a division by lot*" (Liddell and Scott).

358   *ethea*
Greek, a plural for "ethos," which means "*custom, usage*" (Liddell and Scott). Writes Havelock (p. 63): "'Originally the word may have signified the 'lair' or 'haunt' of an animal; in later Greek it develops into the meaning of personal behavior-pattern or even personal character and so in Aristotle supplied the basis for the term 'ethics'?" (citation omitted).

358   a stretching neuterizing and -*sis*ing of probably the single verb
Derived from p. 193 n. 31 of *Preface to Plato,* where Havelock draws on Chapter 10 of Bruno Snell's *Discovery of the Mind: The Greek Origins of European Thought,* tr. T. G. Rosenmeyer (1953; New York: Harper, 1960), a book Olson already knew or soon ac-

quired. The use of -*sis* to form abstract nouns out of earlier verb forms developed in the fifth century B.C.

358   Eranos . . . (*agape*)
"Respectively, Greek, 'shared meal' and 'love feast' (such as that accompanying the early Christian Eucharistic celebrations)" (GB, at *AP* 95).

358   Stephanites
Greek, "*of* or *consisting of a crown,*" "*a crowned conqueror, victor*" (Liddell and Scott).

358   the unholy Athenian Three
Presumably Socrates, Plato, and Aristotle.

358   Mrak
"I.e., Marx, as it appears in an earlier manuscript version. Also in that version, interestingly, Olson typed 'man-ape,' which he later changed to 'man-grape,' while 'nits from *another* planet' was altered to 'its'" (GB, at *AP* 95).

358   boulé
Greek, "*will, determination.* Lat. *consilium,* esp. of the Gods; *a counsel, piece of advice, plan, design*" (Liddell and Scott).

359   "A Further Note on the Critical Advantage of Eric Havelock's *Preface to Plato*"
Published in *Niagara Frontier Review,* no. 2, Spring–Summer 1965; reprinted in *AP.*

359   Joseph Needham or Mircea Eliade
Needham's magisterial *Science and Civilization in China* began appearing from Cambridge University Press in 1954; Olson's mention of "Time" suggests acquaintance with Needham's *Time and Eastern Man: The Henry Myers Lecture 1964,* Royal Anthropological Institute Occasional Paper No. 21 (Glasgow: University Press, 1965). Olson knew Eliade's essay "Shamanism" from Vergilius Ferm's *Ancient Religions,* though Maud quotes a letter in which Olson remarks that Eliade is "*best*" read "under the auspices of the 'Eranos' yearly meetings" (*Olson's Reading,* p. 177).

360   "Statement for the *Cambridge* Magazine"
Published in *Granta,* February 1964; reprinted in *AP.*

361   "A comprehension (a measure, that"
Notes Butterick (at *AP* 92), "Written 14–15 August 1966, judging from dated notes in the poet's copies of Havelock, *Preface to Plato;* Kirk, *The Cosmic Fragments;* and Liddell and Scott, *A Greek-English Lexicon.*" First published by Robin Blaser in the inaugural issue of *Pacific Nation,* June 1967; reprinted in *AP.*

362   as Snell says . . . "the era of the lyric."
Bruno Snell in *The Discovery of the Mind* has (p. 17):

> The first writer to feature the new concept of the soul is Heraclitus. He calls the soul of living man *psyche;* in his view man consists of body and soul, and the soul is endowed

with qualities which differ radically from those of the body and the physical organs. We can safely say that these new qualities are irreconcilable with the categories of Homer's thought. . . . The new expressions were fashioned in the period which separates Heraclitus from Homer, that is to say the era of the lyric.

362 *bibliography:*
Kenneth Clark, *The Nude,* Bollingen Series 25.2 (New York: Pantheon Books, 1956) reproduces as figures 22, 23, and 55, images of the sculptures Olson refers to. Gerald F. Else, *The Origin and Early Form of Greek Tragedy* (1965; Cambridge, Mass.: Harvard University Press, 1967), at p. 61 discusses tetrameter. Heraclitus, *The Cosmic Fragments,* ed. G. S. Kirk (Cambridge, Eng.: Cambridge University Press, 1954), gives at p. 3 the date 480 B.C., which Olson assigns to the death of Heraclitus. G. S. Kirk, *The Homeric Poems as History* (Cambridge, Eng.: Cambridge University Press, 1965), at p. 10 gives the composition of the Homeric epics to "before 700 or at the very latest 675 b.c." Stuart Piggott, *Prehistoric India to 1000 b.c.* (Harmondsworth, Eng.: Penguin Books, 1952), at p. 255 gives the date 500 B.C. for the death of Buddha. Snell, p. 17, is quoted above.

362 fragments 57, 40 & 41 of Heraclitus
Fragment 57 reads, in Kirk's edition (p. 155): "*Therefore Heraclitus says that neither darkness nor light nor evil nor good are different, but are one and the same thing. At all events he censures Hesiod, on the ground that he does not know day and night; for day, he says, and night are one, in such words as these:* Teacher of most men is Hesiod: they are sure that he knows many things, who continually fail to recognize day and night: for they are one." Fragments 40 and 41 are run together (p. 386): "*He [sc. Heraclitus] grew up to be conceited beyond anyone else, as is plain also from his book, in which he says, "Learning of many things does not bring sense . . . "* (=fr. 40); for Wisdom is one thing: to be skilled in true judgement, how all things are steered through all."

362 as L. J. D. Richardson does say of the *Sophia*
"Further Observations on Homer and the Mycenaean Tablets," *Hermathena,* 86, 1955, cited by Eric Havelock in *Preface to Plato,* p. 161 n. 26.

363 *Epistamenos*
Greek for "skillfully," "expertly," cited by Eric Havelock in *Preface to Plato* (p. 162 n. 27) from Hesiod's *Works and Days.* Olson owned the Loeb translation by Hugh G. Evelyn-White, which reads: "I will sum you up another tale well and skillfully . . . how the gods and mortal men sprang from one source." See *The Homeric Hymns and Homerica* (Cambridge, Mass.: Harvard University Press, 1982), p. 11.

364 "'Clear Shining Water,' De Vries says"
First published by the Institute of Further Studies, Buffalo, 1968; reprinted in *AP.* The title refers to the "*aurr*" sprinkled on Yggdrasill, the guardian tree of Northern mythology, also known as the World Tree. H. R. Ellis Davidson says of this "*aurr*" (in *Gods and Myths of Northern Europe,* p. 195): "The meaning . . . is uncertain, but de Vries takes it to mean clear, shining water. We are told that dew comes from the tree, and that when the hart

feeds on its branches, her milk becomes shining mead which never gives out, and is used to provide drink for the warriors in Valhalla." The bibliographic portion of Olson's title comes from Davidson's footnote. For Olson's own version of the myth see "*Hotel Steinplatz, Berlin, December 25 (1966)*" (*MAX* 569–70).

364   *ta'wil* . . . Corbin . . . a footnote in Avicenna
Henry Corbin in *Avicenna and the Visionary Recital,* tr. Willard Trask, Bollingen Series 66 (1960; Princeton, N.J. : Princeton University Press, 1988), writes (p. 29): "*Ta'wil* is, etymologically and inversely, to *cause to return,* to lead back, to restore to one's origin and to the place where one comes home, consequently to return to the true and original meaning of a text." It isn't clear which footnote Olson has in mind, but another relevant passage is the following, from p. 160:

> we can understand that the Spring of Life, the *Aqua permanens,* is divine gnosis, the *philosophia prima.* He who purifies himself therein and drinks of it will never taste the bitterness of death. As for the spring of *running* Water hard by the *permanent* spring, we may see in it a typification of Logic. . . . But this on an express condition that safeguards instead of degrading symbolic perception. In other words: it is not Logic that *is* the *ta'wil* of the spring of running Water; it is, conversely, the spring of running Water that is the *ta'wil* of Logic, that, as such, "leads it back" to its "spring," to its meaning and its truth.

364   A Historical Grammar of the Language of Poetic Myth
Subtitle to Robert Graves's 1958 book *The White Goddess,* which Olson owned in four copies.

365   in the Latin
Olson's source of information is Charlton T. Lewis, *An Elementary Latin Dictionary.*

365   I can refer you . . . to Turville-Petre *Myth and Religion of the North*
A book used for "The Vinland Map Review" as well. The page numbers all refer to "the mystical Urðarbrunnr (Well of Fate)" (p. 246), and Yggdrasill, which Turville-Petre calls "tree of fate" (p. 277). According to the late-twelfth- and early-thirteenth-century Icelandic poet and historian Snorri Sturlason, "three wells lay at the base of the Yggdrasill, one under each root" (p. 279). Notes Turville-Petre (on the same page), "In this passage, as in some others, Snorri may be too systematic, and probably the three names apply to one well, which was basically the well of fate, and hence the source of wisdom." The discussion then turns (still p. 279) to "*Urðr,* the name for fate, . . . commonly identified with Old English *wyrd,* said ultimately to be related to the Latin *Vertere* (to turn), as if applied to a goddess spinning the threads of fate." On p. 280, Turville-Petre discusses "the *Ragnaròk,* meaning 'fate of the gods,'" quoting from "the Vòluspá, the only poem in which the whole course of the Ragnarök is traced":

> until three came,
> daughters of giants,
> filled with cruel might
> from the demon world.

365 dogmatic
Not a term of derision for Olson, who took "The Dogmatic Nature of Experience" as his motto for the 1968 lecture series "Poetry and Truth" (*MUTH* 2 : 7).

367 "What's Back There"
First published in *Io,* no. 6, Summer 1969 (the "Ethnoastronomy Issue"), as an introduction to Charles Doria's translation of Sanchuniathon's *Phoenician History;* reprinted in *AP.* Olson had written about Sanchuniathon in the Maximus poems in 1962 (*MAX* 274– 75), and at greater length in an unpublished prose piece at Storrs titled "1st 'Essay' on the / Phoenician History // Wednesday February 5 / 1964 // called / '1540, or, Santhunctiones.'" Doria introduced the translation in *Io* as "part of a series on the history of mythology," noting:

> [Olson] fairly commissioned me about four years ago to make this translation, especially after Duncan hooked him in a letter with some comments about Sanchuniathon as "my teacher," "taught me all I know" (Duncan this is). After many false starts this is the result.
> It is part of a series on the history of mythology. . . . The way the thing was supposed to work goes something like this:
>
> > 1. Sanchuniathon's History—Beginnings and Definitions in and around Phoenicia in the Second Millennium B.C. Re-appearance among the Greeks.
> > 2. Chronicles of Paros—A series of inscriptions found on the island of Paros in the Aegean. Tells the coming of the Phoenicians to Greece (Cadmus, *etc.*); Greek history, almost year by year down to the death of Socrates, 399 B.C.
> > 3. Malalas' Chronicles—What the Phoenicians were doing all this time (c. 1500 on).
> > 4. Dea Syra—A visit to a famous and ancient Phoenician temple by a Greek dialectician during the Roman Imperium.

The last issue of *Niagara Frontier Review,* Spring 1966, listed as forthcoming from Frontier Press a collection of ancient texts, to be titled *Paros Chronicles,* translated with notes by Charles Doria, introduction by Charles Olson; the book never appeared. With Harris Lenowitz, however, Doria later edited *Origins: Creation Texts from the Ancient Mediterranean* (New York: AMS Press, 1976), a collection that includes Sanchuniathon.

367 Albright
"William Foxwell Albright. Olson owned and wrote notes in several of Albright's books, including *The Evidence of Language* (Cambridge: Cambridge University Press, 1966)" (GB, at *AP* 108).

367 T. L. Webster
T. B. L. Webster, *From Mycenae to Homer* (New York: Barnes and Noble, 1960).

368 "The Animate Versus the Mechanical, and Thought"
First published in *Io,* no. 6, Summer 1969 (the "Ethnoastronomy Issue"); reprinted in *AP.* Among Olson's sources here are three favorite texts: Eric Havelock, *Preface to Plato;* Hesiod, *Theogeony;* and Alfred North Whitehead, *Process and Reality.*

368 plants, by starch (statoliths), turgor and a geotropism
"From a discussion of the nervous system of plants in the *Encyclopedia Britannica,* 11th ed., vol. 21, pp. 751–54" (GB, at *AP* 106).

368 event (in Merleau-Ponty's sense—narrative)
See *The Phenomenology of Perception,* pp. 30–31. Olson knew the passage from Richard Sassoon's November 1963 letter (discussed in the note to p. 355) where the text reads: "At the same time as it (the object) sets *attention in motion,* the object is at every moment recaptured and placed once more in a state of dependence on it (attention). It (object) gives rise to the 'knowledge-bringing-event,' which is to transform it (object), only by means of the still ambiguous meaning which it requires that event to clarify; it is therefore the *motive and not the cause* of the event." The italics are Sassoon's, as are the words in parentheses.

368 Dogtown, and Hesiod, Maximus Poems IV V VI
See *MAX* 330–332.

369 Kierkegaard
George Butterick in his notes from Olson's seminars at Buffalo (published in *The Magazine of Further Studies,* no. 2, 1966) has the following entry for 16 December 1964: "Kierkegaard—a miserable little wretch, the original killer of our non-civilization."

369 'Ekatick'
"From Hekate (Greek Ἑκάτη), triple goddess of the earth, moon, and underworld. Her statues, Hecateia, were set up at places where three roads met, just as Hermes' representations, or herms, were set up as boundary stones" (GB, at *AP* 107).

370 'God' from his 'House of Mountain'
I.e., Zeus from Olympus.

370 'kalpa'
"Sanskrit, 'aeon'—a single day which is the life of Brahma: 8,640,000,000 mortal years" (GB, at *AP* 107).

370 Electromagnetic Epoch
An idea developed out of Chapter 3 of Whitehead's *Process and Reality,* "The Order of Nature," where we read: "Our present cosmic epoch is formed by an 'electromagnetic society' . . . " (p. 149). See also "Under the Mushroom," where Olson remarks: "Eternal simply means of an age. All right? Of an epoch. We live, for example, in the electromagnetic epoch. That simply defines this particular universe that we are supplied as an objective type, but it has nothing to do with eternal time, for example. Nothing whatsoever. It may be stained with eternal time, but it's simply electromagnetic epoch. fufft, fufft. I mean, an outer time, like an outer space? Unimaginable!" (*MUTH* 1:60).

370   idein
Greek, "to see."

370   *sitio*
"Latin, 'to thirst,' akin to Greek *sition,* 'grain,' 'food' " (GB, at *AP* 108).

371   alle
German, "all," but also "cosmos."

371   Dr. Forward or the Hughes people or Dr. Sinsky
"Researches on electromagnetic radiation conducted by Robert L. Forward, working at the Hughes Research Laboratories in Malibu, California, and Joel Sinsky at the University of Maryland. See Dietrick E. Thomsen, 'Searching for Gravity Waves,' *Science News,* XCIII (27 March 1968), pp. 408–9 (a Xerox copy of which is among Olson's papers)" (GB, at *AP* 108).

372   *the iniatic cosmos, the world of nature* and *the celestial world*
The italicized phrases come from Henry Corbin's "Cyclical Time in Mazdaism and Ismailism," tr. Ralph Manheim (1957), published now in Corbin's *Cyclical Time and Ismaili Gnosis* (London: Kegan Paul International, 1983).

373   "Continuing Attempt to Pull the Taffy Off the Roof of the Mouth"
Published in *The Park,* no. 4–5, Summer 1969. This dense reading of the written and archeological evidence of Norse exploration of America is itself a record of exploration. It stirs up, like much of Olson's later prose, the treacherous depths between document and commentary. The "Attempt" is "Continuing" because Olson has worked this terrain several times before—in his "Vinland Map Review," the late Maximus poem "George Decker," and in the margins of his reading. The immediate incentive for renewing the attention may have been receipt of Carl O. Sauer's *Northern Mists* (Berkeley: University of California Press, 1968). Reprinted in *AP,* with extensive notes by George Butterick.

373   Jibir
Jabir Ibn Hayyam, eighth-century Arabic alchemist cited by Jung under the Latinized name Geber in *Psychology and Alchemy,* tr. R. F. C. Hull, *The Collected Works of C. G. Jung,* vol. 12, 1953, Bollingen Series 20 (Princeton, N.J.: Princeton University Press, 1980).

373   Ari
"Ari Thorgilsson or Ari the Learned, earliest of the Icelandic chroniclers, author of the twelfth century *Islendigabok*" (GB, at *AP* 105).

373   Snorri Sturlason
Author of the *Prose Edda* and *Heimskringla;* mentioned by Olson in "'Clear Shining Water,' De Vries says."

373   Al' Araby's *circumvallum*
Ibn al 'Arabi, Arab mystic of the same era as Sturlason. "For an account of his *circumambulatio* of the Ka'ba at Mecca, see . . . Fritz Meier, 'The Mystery of the Ka'ba: Symbol and

Reality in Islamic Mysticism,' in *The Mysteries: Papers from the Eranos Yearbooks,* ed. Joseph Campbell, Bollingen Series XXX.2 (New York, 1955), esp. pp. 155–56" (GB, at *AP* 105).

374   crossings, concealments & curtailments of these orders of such 'times'
John Clarke in his notes for Olson's Fall 1964 Mythology Seminar records:

> Don't give up; relief in *sight:*

> See that other country over there, that ain't no country over there on the other side
> of your *door;* must take those conceptual hinges right off the door in order to—
> cleanse said doors of perception, in order to get clear of it all, all that stands in
> the way of possessing the clear seeing organ of a human being: the door of myth
> opens only onto the past, what has gone before you, while the eye of the Self looks
> into the unknown future now rushing towards you at speeds faster than the square
> of light.

Index

Hawthorne, Nathaniel: "The Birthmark,"
111; on Melville, 81, 89, 393, 395; Mel-
ville on, 41; Melville's correspondence
with, 51, 121, 400; "Monsieur du Miroir,"
124, 400; relationship with Melville, 46,
87, 101, 104, 111–12, 386
Hegel, Georg Wilhelm Friedrich, 120, 358,
400
Hehir, Paddy, 222, 224, 233
Heilbroner, Robert L., 324, 325, 444
Heisenberg, Werner, 162, 411
Hendricks, Obed, 12
Henry, John, 20
Heraclitus, 112, 143, 189, 361–62, 396,
458–59
Herman Melville: Mariner and Mystic (Wea-
ver), 382
Herodotus, 170, 300, 341, 342–44, 454,
456
Hesiod, 137, 197, 199, 206, 345, 361–63,
421, 462
Hester, Martin, 226
Hester, Minnie, 226
Heyford, Harrison, 114, 397
Hines, Mary, 205, 422. *See also* Olsen, Mary
Hines
Hitler, Adolph, 258, 429
Holbrook, Stewart, 312, 441
Holmes, Oliver Wendell, 80
Holmes, Pehr, 234
Homer, 104, 117, 137; in history, 196, 199,
345; and Olson's poetic theory, 246, 248;
and time, 356–57, 361–62
Hopkins, Gerard Manley, 253
Houston, Sam, 306, 308, 440
Howard, Leon, 114, 397
Hubbard, Elbert, 320, 443
Hudson, Henry, 320
Hulme, Thomas Ernest, 149
Huston, John, 146, 406
Huxley, Aldous, 135, 403
Hymans, Edward, 188, 418
Hymen, Stanley Edgar, 413

Ibn al 'Arabi, 373, 463–64
Ignatow, David, 417
Ishmael (biblical character), 379
Ishmael *(Moby-Dick),* 55, 73

Jabir Ibn Hayyam, 332, 463
Jackson, Andrew, 27, 64

Jacataqua, 300, 318
Jefferson, Thomas, 24, 27
Jesus. *See* Christ
John Brown's Body (Benét), 429
Johnson, Lyndon B., 451
Jolas, Eugene, 399
Jonas, Hans, 190, 419
Jones, LeRoi (pseud. Amiri Baraka), 180,
415–16, 444
Joy, Matthew, 11–12
Joyce, James, 143, 150–51, 301, 408, 437
Judd, Walter H., 309, 441
Jung, Carl Gustav, 118, 300, 301, 398

Karlsefni, 373
Keats, John, 37, 120, 123, 239, 399, 425
Kelly, Robert, 195, 419
Kennedy, John F., 451, 459
Kierkegaard, Søren, 369, 462
Kirk, G. S., 362
Kittredge, George Lyman, 113, 397
Klein, Christian Felix, 123, 399
Kline, Franz, 124, 400, 411
Koch, Vivien, 254, 428
Kramer, Samuel Noah, 170, 346, 412, 450
Kronos, 73

Lady Chatterley's Lover (Lawrence), 138–39,
404
Lagarijo, 382
LaGuardia, Fiorello, 257, 429
Lake, Stuart, 313
Landreau, Anthony, 122, 400
Lang, Andrew, 188
Lansing, Gerrit, 188, 418
La Salle, Robert Cavelier, sieur de, 19
Laughlin, James, 417
Laughton, Charles, 256, 429
Lawrence, Benjamin, 13–14
Lawrence, D. H., xv, 116, 135–40, 144,
207, 300, 308, 382, 404
Lawrence, Frieda, 139, 404
Leary, Timothy, 451
Leed, Jacob, xi
Lenowitz, Harris, 461
Lewis, Wyndham, 143, 148–49, 408
Leyda, Jay, 114, 380, 383, 397
Lincoln, Abraham, 350
Lobatschewsky, Nicolay Ivanovich, 120, 399
Lobeck, A. K., 300
Lorca. *See* García Lorca, Federico

Lowell, Robert, 145, 406
Luce, Henry, 257–58, 429
Lü Tung-pin, 263, 430

Magnus Barefoot (Norse king), 443
Maikov, Appollon, 127, 401
Malalas, John, 367
Malinowski, Bronislaw, 409, 410
Mansfield, Luther S., 113, 116, 118
The Man Who Died (Lawrence), 137, 403.
    See also *The Escaped Cock*
Marlowe, Christopher, 56
Marshall, James Wilson, 295–96
Marx, Karl, 27, 143, 358
Mason, Ronald, 113–15, 118, 380, 396
Maspero, Gaston, 170, 414
Matthiessen, F. O., 113, 379, 396
Maud, Ralph, 418, 425, 437, 445
McCoon, Perry, 296
McGraw, Rosie, 350, 451
McJunkin, George, 381
McKinstry, George, 435
Mead, G. R. S., 188, 418
"Meditation on a Landscape" (Temple), 447
Melville, Augusta, 89
Melville, Elizabeth, 391
Melville, Herman, 11, 17–20, 80–91, 311,
    351, 381; and Ahab, 73–76; and *Billy
    Budd, Foretopman,* 109–12; influence
    of, xii, 207, 302, 303; Olson's reviews of
    scholarship on, 113–19, 120–25; Olson's
    scholarship on, 379–80; on Owen Chase,
    29–33; on Plato, 157, 409; and Shake-
    speare, 43–44, 45–46, 47–50, 51–55,
    56–59, 60–66; and whaling industry,
    21–28. *Works:* "Bartleby, the Scrivener,"
    124, 400; "The Bell Tower," 124, 400;
    "Benito Cereno," 124, 400, 401; *Billy
    Budd, Foretopman,* 109–12; *Billy Budd,
    Sailor,* 46, 47, 86, 91, 386; *Clarel,* 86, 90–
    91, 95, 110, 115, 394; *The Confidence-
    Man,* 46, 61, 82, 91, 110, 118, 190, 388;
    "The Encantadas," 124, 400; "Hawthorne
    and His Mosses," 41–42, 384; *Journal Up
    the Straits,* 82; *Mardi,* 39–40, 53, 88–89;
    Moby-Dick, 39–42; *Pierre,* 46, 61, 82, 87,
    89, 110, 118, 388, 398; *Poem and Pil-
    grimage in the Holyland,* 86; *Redburn,*
    39–40, 47; *Typee,* 39; *White-Jacket,* 39–
    40. See also *Moby-Dick*
Melville's Log (Leyda), 114

Melville's Marginalia (Cowen), 379, 385,
    386
Melville's Quarrel with God (Thompson),
    113
*Melville's Reading: A Checklist of Books
    Owned and Borrowed* (Sealts), 379
Merk, Frederick, 302, 303, 305, 308, 325,
    437, 440
Merleau-Ponty, Maurice, 368
Merritt, H. Houston, 169, 413
Metcalf, Eleanor Melville, 42, 109, 385,
    391, 396
Metcalf, Henry K., 42, 385
Metcalf, Paul, 383, 391
"Metropolis" (film), 276, 432
Meyer (tailor), 213–16
Milton, John, 241, 431
Moby-Dick (Melville), 39–42, 73–76, 46,
    381; and Shakespeare, 44, 47–50, 51–
    55, 56–59, 60–66; and Melville's travel,
    80–91; Olson's review of scholarship on,
    113–19, 120–25; Olson's scholarship on,
    17–20; and the Pacific, 101–5; and
    whaling industry, 21–28
Moe, Henry Allen, 435
Mohammed, 196
Moore, Frank, 406
Moore, Sturge, 149
Morewood, Sarah, 391
Moses, 18
"Mr. Blue" (Creeley), 284, 433
Mrak, 458. *See also* Marx, Karl
Murdock, Kenneth, 429
Murray, Henry A., 114, 380, 397, 398
Murray, Henry A., Jr., 42, 385
Muspilli (Bavarian poem), 333
Mussolini, Benito, 258, 429
Myers, Gustavus, 310
Myth and Religion of the North (Turville-
    Petre), 333

*Narrative of the Most Extraordinary and Dis-
    tressing Shipwreck of the Whale-Ship Es-
    sex, of Nantucket* (Chase), 30, 381
The Natural History of the Sperm Whale
    (Beale), 39, 384
Needham, Joseph, 359, 458
Nelli, René, 425
Nelson, Lord Horatio, 119
Newton, Sir Isaac, 122, 400
Nickerson, Thomas, 13–14

Designer: Barbara Jellow
Compositor: G&S Typesetters, Inc.
Text: Frutiger Light
Display: Frutiger
Printer and Binder: Edwards Brothers, Inc.